STUDY TEXT

Professional Certificate in Marketing

Marketing Environment

May 2004 edition

- Fully updated for examinations in December 2004 and June 2005
- New material on key examinable topics
- Updated exam tips and case examples
- Material supporting Assignment route

BPP Professional Education
May 2004

First edition 2002
Third edition May 2004

ISBN 07517 1586 7 (Previous edition 07517 1217 5)

British Library Cataloguing-in-Publication Data
A catalogue record for this book
is available from the British Library

Published by

BPP Professional Education
Aldine House, Aldine Place
London W12 8AW

www.bpp.com

Printed in Great Britain by
W M Print
45-47 Frederick Street
Walsall
West Midlands WS2 9NE

We are grateful to the Chartered Institute of Marketing for permission to reproduce in this text the syllabus, tutor's guidance notes, personal development plan and past examination questions. We are also grateful to Karen Beamish of Stone Consulting for preparing the assignment-based learning material.

■ Introduction ■ Structure and process ■ Presentation of the Assignment ■ Time management for Assignments ■ Tips for writing Assignments ■ Report writing ■ Resources to support the Assignment Route ■ Reflective statement ■ Unit summary

Part A: The organisation and its environment

Part B: The micro environment

Part C: The macro environment

Part D: Environmental information systems

BPP))))
PROFESSIONAL EDUCATION

How to use this Study Text

Aims of this Study Text

To provide you with the knowledge and understanding, skills and applied techniques required for passing the exam

The Study Text has been written around the CIM Professional Certificate in Marketing Syllabus, which is reproduced below.

- It is **comprehensive**. We do not omit sections of the syllabus as the examiner is liable to examine any angle of any part of the syllabus – and you do not want to be left high and dry.

- It is **on-target**. We do not include any material which is not examinable. You can rely on the BPP Study Text as the stand-alone source for the exam.

To allow you to study in the way that best suits your learning style and the time you have available, by following your personal Study Plan (see below)

You may be studying at home on your own, or you may be attending a full-time course. You may like to (and have time to) read every word, or you may prefer to (or only have time to) skim-read and devote the remainder of your time to question practice. Wherever you fall in the spectrum, you will find the BPP Study Text meets your needs in designing and following your personal Study Plan.

To tie in with the other components of the BPP Effective Study Package to ensure you have the best possible chance of passing the exam

Recommended period of use	Elements of BPP Effective Study Package
3–12 months before exam	**Study Text** Acquisition of knowledge, understanding, skills and applied techniques
1–6 months before exam	**Practice & Revision Kit** There are numerous examination questions to try, graded by topic area, along with realistic suggested solutions prepared by marketing professionals in the light of the Examiner's Reports. The September 2004 edition will include the December 2003 and June 2004 papers.
1–6 months before exam	**Passcards** Handy, pocketsized revision notes you can take anywhere and used to refresh the essential knowledge you need.

Settling down to study

By this stage in your career you may be a very experienced learner and taker of exams. But have you ever thought about *how* you learn? Let's have a quick look at the key elements required for effective learning. You can then identify your learning style and go on to design your own approach to how you are going to study this book – your personal Study Plan.

Key element of learning	Using the BPP Study Text
Motivation	You can rely on the comprehensiveness and technical quality of BPP. You've chosen the right Study Text – so you're in pole position to pass your exam!
Clear objectives and standards	Do you want to be a prizewinner or simply achieve a moderate pass? Decide.
Feedback	Follow through the examples in this text and do the Action Programme and the Quick Quizzes. Evaluate your efforts critically – how are you doing?
Study Plan	You need to be honest about your progress to yourself – do not be over-confident, but don't be negative either. Make your Study Plan (see below) and try to stick to it. Focus on the short-term objectives – completing two chapters a night, say – but beware of losing sight of your study objectives.
Practice	Use the Quick Quizzes and Chapter Roundups to refresh your memory regularly after you have completed your initial study of each chapter.

These introductory pages let you see exactly what you are up against. However you study, you should:

- **Read through the syllabus and teaching guide**. This will help you to identify areas you have already covered, perhaps at a lower level of detail, and areas that are totally new to you

- **Study the examination paper section**, where we show you the format of the exam (how many and what kind of questions etc).

Key study steps

The following steps are, in our experience, the ideal way to study for professional exams. You can of course adapt it for your particular learning style (see below).

Tackle the chapters in the order you find them in the Study Text. Taking into account your individual learning style, follow these key study steps for each chapter.

Key study steps	Activity
Step 1 *Chapter Topic List*	Study the list. Each numbered topic denotes a **numbered section** in the chapter.
Step 2 *Setting the Scene*	Read it through. It is designed to show you **why the topics in the chapter need to be studied** – how they lead on from previous topics, and how they lead into subsequent ones.
Step 3 *Explanations*	Proceed **methodically** through the chapter, reading each section thoroughly and making sure you understand.
Step 4 *Key Concepts*	**Key concepts** can often earn you **easy marks** if you state them clearly and correctly in an appropriate exam.
Step 5 *Exam Tips*	These give you a good idea of how the examiner tends to examine certain topics – pinpointing **easy marks** and highlighting **pitfalls**.
Step 6 *Note Taking*	Take **brief notes** if you wish, avoiding the temptation to copy out too much.
Step 7 *Marketing at Work*	Study each one, and try if you can to add flesh to them from your **own experience** – they are designed to show how the topics you are studying come alive (and often come unstuck) in the **real world**.
Step 8 *Action Programme*	Make a very good attempt at each one in each chapter. These are designed to put your **knowledge into practice** in much the same way as you will be required to do in the exam. Check the answer at the end of the chapter in the **Action Programme review**, and make sure you understand the reasons why yours may be different.
Step 9 *Chapter Roundup*	Check through it very carefully, to make sure you have grasped the **major points** it is highlighting
Step 10 *Quick Quiz*	When you are happy that you have covered the chapter, use the **Quick Quiz** to check your recall of the topics covered. The answers are in the paragraphs in the chapter that we refer you to.

BPP
PROFESSIONAL EDUCATION

Developing your personal Study Plan

Preparing a Study Plan (and sticking closely to it) is one of the key elements in learning success.

First you need to be aware of your style of learning. There are four typical learning styles. Consider yourself in the light of the following descriptions. and work out which you fit most closely. You can then plan to follow the key study steps in the sequence suggested.

Learning styles	Characteristics	Sequence of key study steps in the BPP Study Text
Theorist	Seeks to understand principles before applying them in practice	1, 2, 3, 7, 4, 5, 8, 9, 10 (6 continuous)
Reflector	Seeks to observe phenomena, thinks about them and then chooses to act	
Activist	Prefers to deal with practical, active problems; does not have much patience with theory	1, 2, 8 (read through), 7, 4, 5, 9, 3, 8 (full attempt), 10 (6 continuous)
Pragmatist	Prefers to study only if a direct link to practical problems can be seen; not interested in theory for its own sake	8 (read through), 2, 4, 5, 7, 9, 1, 3, 8 (full attempt), 10 (6 continuous)

Next you should complete the following checklist.

Am I motivated? (a) ☐

Do I have an objective and a standard that I want to achieve? (b) ☐

Am I a theorist, a reflector, an activist or a pragmatist? (c) ☐

How much time do I have available per week, given: (d) ☐

- The standard I have set myself
- The time I need to set aside later for work on the Practice and Revision Kit
- The other exam(s) I am sitting, and (of course)
- Practical matters such as work, travel, exercise, sleep and social life?

Now:

- Take the time you have available per week for this Study Text (d), and multiply it by the number of weeks available to give (e). (e) ☐
- Divide (e) by the number of chapters to give (f) (f) ☐
- Set about studying each chapter in the time represented by (f), following the key study steps in the order suggested by your particular learning style.

This is your personal **Study Plan**.

Short of time?

Whatever your objectives, standards or style, you may find you simply do not have the time available to follow all the key study steps for each chapter, however you adapt them for your particular learning style. If this is the case, follow the Skim Study technique below (the icons in the Study Text will help you to do this).

Skim Study technique

Study the chapters in the order you find them in the Study Text. For each chapter, follow the key study steps 1–2, and then skim-read through step 3. Jump to step 9, and then go back to steps 4–5. Follow through step 7, and prepare outline Answers to the Action Programme (step 8). Try the Quick Quiz (step 10), following up any items you can't answer. You should probably still follow step 6 (note-taking).

Moving on...

However you study, when you are ready to embark on the practice and revision phase of the BPP Effective Study Package, you should still refer back to this Study Text:

- As a source of **reference** (you should find the list of Key Concepts and the index particularly helpful for this)

- As a **refresher** (the Chapter Roundups and Quick Quizzes help you here)

Key Concepts

In order to help you transfer your learning to the real world, we use this feature to introduce you to some of the technical terms, abbreviations and 'buzzwords' used by marketing professionals. (These also appear in list form at the back of the text.)

Marketing at Work

The syllabus specifically requires students to develop an awareness of what marketers are actually doing 'out there': what new initiatives are being attempted; what is working and what is not; how different organisations tackle the same tasks. We encourage you to collect cuttings of ads, examples of promotions, articles on marketing campaigns (for example in *Campaign, PR Week, Marketing Week* and other relevant journals and newspaper Media sections). We also encourage you whenever possible (and when professional discretion allows) to swap stories of successes, failures and house styles with other students and practitioners. Our 'Marketing at Work' section will help – but it should only be a prompter to the kind of insatiable curiosity about other people's efforts that makes a good marketing professional.

Action Programme

Marketing Environment may be assessed through workplace tasks, skills audits and/or an integrated Case Study approach. You must get used to attempting a wide variety of marketing tasks and analysing your performance according to relevant criteria. Our Action Programme exercises take you step by step through this active learning process.

Specimen paper

We have included the CIM Specimen Paper, with suggested answers, at the back of the Study Text.

A note on pronouns

On occasions in this Study Text, 'he' is used for 'he or she', 'him' for 'him or her' and so on. Whilst we try to avoid this practice it is sometimes necessary for reasons of style. No prejudice or stereotyping according to sex is intended or assumed.

Syllabus and guidance notes

Aim

The *Marketing Environment* module equips participants to explain the nature of the marketing environment and its relevance for organisations and marketing practice. It provides knowledge of marketing information and its use in organisations, particularly in its application in the strategy and marketing planning processes. It aims to provide participants with a working knowledge of organisations and the various influences of their wider environments.

Participants will not be expected to have any prior qualifications or experience in a marketing role.

Related statements of practice

This syllabus has been based on the statements of marketing practice, a set of practical statements defining what tasks marketers perform at various stages of their marketing career.

Ab.1   Collect information

Ab.2   Interpret and present information

Bb.1   Contribute information and ideas to the strategy process

Bb.2   Contribute to the production of marketing plans and budgets

Learning outcomes

Participants will be able to:

- Distinguish between the types of organisation within the public, private and voluntary sectors, and understand their objectives and the influences upon them.

- Explain the main elements of an organisation's marketing environment and discuss the significance of current and future environmental challenges.

- Describe the interactions between the main elements of the marketing environment.

- Assess the potential impact on an organisation of key trends in the social, technical, economic, environmental, political, legal and ethical environments.

- Demonstrate an understanding of an organisation's micro-environment.

- Explain the process for collecting information about the marketing environment from relevant primary and secondary sources.

- Compare and contrast various techniques for collecting information about the marketing environment.

Knowledge and skill requirements

Element 1: The nature of the organisation and the impact of its environment (15%)

1.1	Demonstrate a broad appreciation of the internal environment.
1.2	Explain the classification of private, public and voluntary organisations, their legal status and operational characteristics.
1.3	Assess comparative strengths and weaknesses of small/medium and large/global sized organisations.
1.4	State the meaning and importance of an organisation's mission and explain the nature and significance of the objectives pursued.
1.5	Identify the internal and external influences on the formulation of objectives and specify the key drivers for organisational change.
1.6	Explain the nature of open systems and the interface between organisations and their marketing environment.
1.7	Represent the organisation as an open system responding to changing environmental conditions.
1.8	Demonstrate the dynamic and complex nature of environmental change and its importance to the development of marketing strategy and planning.
1.9	Appreciate the potential significance of emerging environmental challenges to effective marketing in the present and the future.

Element 2: The micro-environment (20%)

2.1	Describe the external and internal stakeholders that constitute the micro-environment within which organisations operate and their importance to the marketing process.
2.2	Explain the nature of the interactions between the organisation and its various stakeholders.
2.3	Demonstrate an awareness of key internal and external sources of information on the micro-environment.
2.4	Explain the significance of the range of pressure groups interested in the organisation and their potential impacts.
2.5	Specify the role of marketing in managing these pressure groups.
2.6	Explain the importance of monitoring competitors and industries and how the organisation assesses the strategic and marketing implications.
2.7	Examine the impact of competition policies on the organisation and its marketing environment

Element 3: The macro-environment (50%)

3.1	Appreciate the importance of the macro-environment to the marketing process.
3.2	Awareness of key sources of information on the macro-environment.
3.3	Explain the social, demographic and cultural environments and, in general terms, their influence on and implications for marketing.
3.4	Explain the economic and international environments and, in general terms, their influence on and implications for marketing.
3.5	Explain the political and legislative environments and, in general terms, their influence on and implications for marketing.
3.6	Explain the natural environment and, in general terms, its influence on and implications for marketing.
3.7	Explain the importance of the technical and information environments and their actual and potential impacts on organisations, employment, marketing and communications.
3.8	Assess the potential significance of environmental challenges to marketing in the future: e.g. globalisation; single currency; information communication technology; and environmental decline.

Element 4: Environmental information systems (15%)

4.1	Explain why information is important to organisations.
4.2	Explain the concept of a marketing information system and its key role in effective marketing decision-making.
4.3	Explain the importance of marketing research and the information benefits it can provide.
4.4	Identify key sources of internal and external information.
4.5	Utilise, interpret and present secondary and primary data in identifying environmental trends and estimating current demand.
4.6	Explain the techniques available for forecasting future demand and coping with the challenge of environmental change.
4.7	Explain the importance of information systems and the continuing impact of new technologies.

Related key skills for marketers

There is only so much that a syllabus can include. The syllabus itself is designed to cover the knowledge and skills highlighted by research as core to professional marketers in organisations. However, marketing is performed in an organisational context so there are other broader business and organisational skills that marketing professionals should also posses. The 'key skills for marketers' are therefore an essential part of armoury of the 'complete marketer' in today's organisations. They have been identified from research carried out in organisations where marketers are working.

'Key skills for marketers' are areas of knowledge and competency common to business professionals. They fall outside the CIM's syllabus, providing underpinning knowledge and skills. As such they will be treated as systemic to all marketing activities, rather than subjects treated independently in their turn. While it is not intended that the key skills are formally taught as part of programmes, it is expected that tutors will encourage participants to demonstrate the application of relevant key skills through activities, assignments and discussions during learning.

Using ICT and the Internet

- Planning and using different sources to search for and select information; explore, develop and exchange information and derive new information; and present information including text, numbers and images.

Using financial information and metrics

- Planning and interpreting information from different sources; carrying out calculations; and presenting and justifying findings.

Presenting information

- Contributing to discussions; making a presentation; reading and synthesising information and writing different types of document.

Improving own learning and performance

- Agreeing targets and planning how these will be met; using plans to meet targets; and reviewing progress.

Working with others

- Planning work and agreeing objectives, responsibilities and working arrangements; seeking to establish and maintain cooperative working relationships; and reviewing work and agreeing ways of future collaborative work.

Problem solving

- Exploring problems, comparing different ways of solving them and selecting options; planning and implementing options; and applying agreed methods for checking problems have been solved.

- Applying business law; identifying, applying and checking compliance with relevant law when undertaking marketing activities.

Assessment

CIM will normally offer two forms of assessment for this module from which centres or participants may choose: written examination or continuous assessment (the Assignment Route). CIM may also recognise, or make joint awards for, modules at an equivalent level undertaken with other professional marketing bodies and educational institutions.

The Exam Paper

Format of the paper

Part A

	Marks
Compulsory question relating to an article or case study	40

Part B

Three questions from a choice of six relating to the case study (20 marks each)	60
	100

The new syllabus Specimen Paper is reproduced, with BPP's suggested answers, at the back of this Study Text.

Analysis of past papers

Specimen paper

Part A

1   Extract from a book about the environment
     (a)   Explain terms
     (b)   Private sector objectives
     (c)   Control
     (d)   Stakeholder groups

Part B

2   Monitoring environment
3   Social or lifestyle trends
4   Government economic objectives and indicators

December 2003

Part A

1   Macdonalds
     (a)   Research methods and information sources
     (b)   Environmental analysis
     (c)   Legal environment
     (d)   Cultural preference

Part B

2   Dynamic and complex changes, impact on marketing strategy and planning
3   Customer and employee stakeholders
4   Impact on natural environment of political developments and technological breakthroughs

5   Marketing in public sector: marketing research, marketing information system, Delphi technique
6   Developments in technology, competitor environment, suppliers, government intervention
7   Macro and micro environment of a voluntary organisation

June 2003

Part A

1   Report for a travel agency on the global cruise market
     (a)   Forecasting methods
     (b)   Social and demographic trends
     (c)   Two alternative scenarios
     (d)   Evaluation of pressure group concerns

Part B

2   Voluntary sector objectives, stakeholders and culture
3   Pressure groups
4   ICT and competitive advantage in the car industry
5   The business cycle
6   The international environment
7   Marketing information system

December 2002

Part A

1   Enron
     (a)   Explanation of terms
     (b)   Lobbying
     (c)   Online trading
     (d)   Strengths and weaknesses of larger organisations

Part B

2   Open systems; Porter's five force analysis
3   Public sector v private sector marketing environment
4   Natural, international and cultural environments
5   Economic growth
6   Teleconferencing, deregulation green taxes, tariff cuts
7   Expansion of a business

Guide to Assignment Route: Marketing Environment

Introduction

At the time of writing, more than eighty CIM Approved Study Centres offer the Assignment Route option as an alternative to examinations. This change in direction and flexibility in assessment was driven by industry, students and tutors alike, all of whom wanted a test of practical skills as well as a knowledge-based approach to learning.

At Stage 1, all modules are available via the Assignment Route. The Assignment Route is however optional and examinations are still available, depending on your chosen Study Centre.

All of the Stage 1 subject areas lend themselves to assignment-based learning, due to their practical nature. The Assignments that you will undertake provide you with an opportunity to be **creative in approach and in presentation**. They enable you to give a true demonstration of your marketing ability in a way that perhaps might not be possible in a traditional examination.

The Assignment Route offers you considerable scope to produce work that provides existing and future **employers** with **evidence** of your **ability**. It provides a **portfolio** of evidence demonstrating your abilities and your willingness to develop continually your knowledge and skills. It will also, ultimately, help you to frame your continuing professional development in the future.

Whatever type of organisation you are from, large or small, you will find substantial benefit in this approach to learning. In some cases, students have made their own organisation central to their Assignment and have produced work to support their organisation's activities, resulting in subsequent recognition and promotion and so a success story for this approach.

Thus, using your own organisation can be beneficial, especially if your employer sponsors you. However, it is equally valid to use a different organisation, as long as you are familiar enough with it to base your Assignments on it. This is particularly appropriate if you are between jobs, taking time out, returning to employment, or studying at university or college.

To take the Assignment Route option, you are required to register with a CIM Accredited Study Centre (ie a college, university, or distance learning provider). **Currently you cannot take the Assignment Route option as an independent learner**. If in doubt, you should contact the CIM Education Division (the Awarding Body) who will provide you with a list of local Accredited Centres offering the Assignment Route.

Aims and objectives of this Guide

- To understand the scope and structure of the Assignment Route
- To consider the benefits of learning through the Assignment Route
- To help you to prepare your Assignments
- To consider the range of communication options available to you
- To examine the purpose and benefits of reflective practice
- To assist with time management within the assessment process

This guide aims to help you in presenting your Assignment professionally, both in terms of presentation skills and overall content. In many of the Assignments, marks are awarded for presentation and coherence. It might therefore be helpful to consider how best to present your Assignment. Here you should consider issues of detail, protocol and the range of communications that could be called upon within the Assignment.

Structure and process

The **Assignments** that you will undertake during your studies are set **by CIM centrally** and not by the study centre. This standardised approach to assessment enables external organisations to interpret the results on a consistent basis. All Assignments are validated to ensure a structured, consistent approach.

Each module at Stage 1 has one Assignment, with four separate elements within it. This is broken down as follows.

■　　　The **Core Section** is compulsory and is worth 40% of the total marks

■　　　The **Elective Section** has four options, from which you must complete **two**. Each of these options is worth 25% of the total marks. In some Study Centres, the option will be chosen for you. This is done in order to maximise resources and support provided to students.

■　　　The **Reflective Statement** is compulsory. It is worth 10% of the total marks. It should reflect what you feel about your learning experience during the module, how that learning has helped you in your career, and how you expect it to help you in the future.

Each Assignment enables you to demonstrate your ability to research, analyse and solve problems in a range of different situations. You will be expected to approach your assignment work from a professional marketer's perspective, addressing the assignment brief directly, and undertaking the tasks required. Each Assignment will relate directly to the syllabus module and will be applied against the content of the syllabus.

All of the Assignments clearly indicate the links with the syllabus and the assignment weighting (ie the contribution each Assignment makes to your overall marks).

Once your Assignments have been completed, they will be marked by your accredited centre and then **moderated** by a CIM External Moderator. When all the Assignments have been marked, they are sent to the CIM for further moderation. After this, all marks are forwarded to you by CIM (not your centre) in the form of an examination result. Your **centre** will be able to you provide you with some written feedback on overall performance, but **will not** provide you with a detailed mark breakdown.

Presentation of the Assignment

You should always make two copies of your Assignment, keeping a soft copy on disc. Sometimes Assignments go missing, or second copies are required by CIM.

■　　　Each Assignment should be clearly marked up with your name, your study centre, your CIM Student registration number and, at the end of the Assignment, a word count. The Assignment should be prepared using word processing software such as Microsoft Word.

■　　　The Assignment presentation format should meet the requirements of the Assignment brief directly: reports and presentations are the most called-for communication formats. You **must** ensure that your Assignment does not appear to be an extended essay. If it does, you will lose marks.

■　　　The word limit will be included in the Assignment brief. Word limits are specified by CIM and must be adhered to.

■　　　**Appendices** should clearly link to the Assignment and can be attached as supporting documentation at the end of the report. Failure to reference them by number (eg 'Appendix 1') within the report and on the Appendix itself will lose you marks. Only use an Appendix if it adds value to the Assignment. The Appendix is not a 'waste bin' for all the materials you have come across in your research, or a way of making your Assignment seem heavier and more impressive!

Time management for Assignments

One of the biggest challenges we all face from day to day is that of managing time. When studying, that challenge is especially difficult, requiring a balance between work, home, family, social life and study life. It is therefore of pivotal importance to your own success for you to plan wisely the limited amount of time you have available.

Step 1: Find out how much time you have

Ensure that you know how long your module lasts, and the final deadline (eg 10 weeks, 12 weeks, 14 weeks). If you are studying a module from September to December, you will probably have only 10 to 12 weeks in which to complete your Assignments. This means that you will be preparing Assignment work continuously throughout the course.

Step 2: Plan your time

Work backwards from the submission date and schedule your work around the possible time lines. Clearly if you have only 10 to 12 weeks available to complete three Assignments, you will need to allocate a block of hours in the final stages of the module to ensure that all of your Assignments are in on time. This will be critical as all Assignments must be sent to CIM by a specific date.

Late submissions will not be accepted: no extensions will be allowed. Students who do not submit will have to re-enter for the next period and undertake an alternative Assignment.

Step 3: Set priorities

Set priorities on a daily and weekly basis (not just for study, but for other aspects of your life too). This mode of study needs commitment, and some sacrifices in the short term. When your achievements are recognised by colleagues, peers, friends and family, it will hopefully all feel worthwhile.

Step 4: Analyse activities and allocate time to them

Consider the **range** of activities that you will need to undertake to complete the Assignment and the **time** each might take. Remember that there may be a delay between asking for information and receiving it.

Activities:

- Preparing terms of reference for the Assignment, to cover the following. (This should be achieved in one page.)

1	A short title
2	A brief outline of the Assignment purpose and outcome
3	Methodology – what methods do you intend to use to carry out the required tasks?
4	Indication of any difficulties that have arisen in the Assignment
5	Time schedule
6	Confidentiality – if the Assignment includes confidential information, ensure that this is clearly indicated on the Assignment
7	Literature and desk research undertaken

- A literature search encompassing necessary background reading and underpinning information that might support your Assignment

- Writing letters and memos to request information, either internally or externally

- Designing questionnaires

- Undertaking surveys

- Analysis of data from questionnaires

- Secondary data search

- Preparation of first draft report

Build in time to spare, to deal with the unexpected. This may reduce the pressure that you face in meeting deadlines. Do not fall into the trap of leaving all of your work to the last minute. If you miss out important information or fail to reflect upon your work adequately or successfully you will be penalised. Time management (discussed further below) is important, whatever the duration of the course.

Tips for writing Assignments

Everybody has a personal style when it comes to writing. Whatever your approach, ensure that your Assignment meets the **requirements of the brief** and so is comprehensible and coherent.

Think of preparing an Assignment as like preparing for an examination. Ultimately, the work you are undertaking results in an examination grade. Successful achievement of all four modules in a level results in a qualification.

There are a number of positive steps that will help you make the best of your Assignment presentation in order to maximise the marks available.

Step 1 – Work to the brief

Identify exactly what the Assignment asks you to do.

- If it asks you to be a Marketing Manager, then immediately assume that role.

- If it asks you to prepare a report, then present a report – not an essay or a letter.

- If 2,500 words are asked for, then keep to that limit. Any significant variation from the limit needs to be agreed with your tutor.

Identify if the report should be **formal or informal**, to whom it should be **addressed**, its **overall purpose** and its **potential use** and outcome. Being clear on these points will help ensure that your Assignment meets fully the requirements of the brief and addresses the key issues included within it.

Step 2 – Address the tasks

It is important that you address **each** of the tasks within the Assignment. **Many students fail to do this**, overlooking one of the tasks or indeed part of the tasks.

Assignments may have two, three or more tasks. You should establish quite early on, which of the tasks:

- Requires you to collect information
- Provides you with the framework of the Assignment, ie the communication method

Possible tasks will include the following.

- *Compare and contrast.* Take two different organisations, compare them side by side and consider the differences.

- *Carry out primary or secondary research.* Collect information to support your Assignment and your subsequent decisions.

- *Prepare a plan.* Some Assignments will ask you to prepare a plan for an event or for a marketing activity. If so, use a step-by-step approach, a rationale and a timeline, making sure it is measurable and achievable. Make sure your actions are specific and clearly explained. (Make sure your plan is SMART.)

- *Analyse a situation.* This will require you to collect information, to consider its content and present an overall understanding of the actual situation. This might involve looking at internal and external factors and at how the current situation evolved.

- *Make recommendations.* The more advanced you are in your studies, the more likely it is that you will be required to make recommendations. Firstly **consider and evaluate your options** and then make justifiable **recommendations** based on them.

- *Justify decisions.* You may be required to justify your decision or recommendations. This will require you to explain fully how you have arrived at the decision and to give reasons why this is the right way forward, supported by relevant information. In other words, you should not make decisions in a vacuum: as a marketer your decisions should always be informed by context.

- *Prepare a presentation.* This speaks for itself. If you are required to prepare a presentation, ensure that you do so, preparing clearly defined PowerPoint or overhead slides that are not too crowded and that clearly express the points you are required to make.

- *Evaluate performance.* It is very likely that you will be asked to evaluate a campaign, a plan or even an event. You will need to consider its strengths and weaknesses, why it succeeded or failed, the issues that have affected it, what can you learn from it and, importantly, how can you improve performance or sustain it in the future.

All of these points are likely requests included within a task. Ensure that you identify them clearly and address them as required.

Step 3 – Information search

Many students fail to realise the importance of collecting information to **support** and **underpin** their assignment work. However, it is vital that you demonstrate to your centre and to the CIM your ability to **establish information needs**, obtain **relevant information** and **utilise it sensibly** in order to arrive at appropriate decisions.

You should establish the nature of the information required and follow up on possible sources, the time involved in obtaining the information, and any gaps in the information.

Consider these factors very carefully. The CIM are very keen that students are **seen** to collect information, to **expand** their minds and to consider the **breadth** and **depth** of the situation. In your *Personal Development Portfolio*, you have the opportunity to complete a **Resource Log**, to illustrate how you have expanded your knowledge to aid your personal development. You can record your additional reading and research in that log, and you can show how it has helped you with your portfolio and Assignment work.

Step 4 – Develop an Assignment plan

Your Assignment needs to address the brief and present the facts as required by the tasks. The only way you can successfully achieve this is by **planning the structure** of your Assignment in advance.

We looked earlier at the issues of identifying your tasks and of working backwards from your deadline in order to manage your time successfully. The structure and coherence of your Assignment needs also to be planned.

In planning the Assignment, plan to include **all the relevant information as requested**. You should also plan for the use of models, diagrams and appendices where necessary.

Your plan should cover:

- Introduction
- Content
- Main body of the Assignment
- Summary
- Conclusions and recommendations where appropriate

Step 5 – Prepare draft Assignment

It is good practice always to produce a **first draft** of a report. This provides an opportunity to check that you have followed the aims and objectives, the Assignment brief and the tasks related to the actual Assignment. A draft document provides you with scope for improvements and enables you to check for accuracy, spelling, punctuation and use of English.

Step 6 – Prepare final document

There are a number of components that should always be in place at the beginning of the Assignment documentation, including **labelling** of the Assignment, **word counts**, **appendices** numbering and presentation method. Ensure that you **adhere to the guidelines presented**, or alternatively those suggested by your Study Centre.

Report writing

Students often ask 'What do they mean by a report?' or 'What should the report format include?'

There are a number of approaches to reports, formal or informal. Some report formats are company specific and designed for internal use, rather than external reporting.

For the Assignment Route, you should stay with traditional formats.

Below is a suggested layout of a Management Report Document that might assist you when presenting your Assignments.

- **Title page** – includes the title of the report, the author of the report and the receiver of the report

- **Acknowledgements** – this should highlight any help, support, or external information received and any significant help from individuals or organisations

- **Contents page** – providing a clearly structured pathway of the contents of the report – page by page

- **Executive Summary** – a brief insight into purpose, nature and outcome of the report, in order that the outcome of the report can be quickly established

- **Main body of the report divided into sections,** which are clearly labelled. Suggested labelling would be on a numbered basis eg:

  - 1.0   Introduction
  - 1.1   Situation Analysis
  - 1.1.1 External Analysis
  - 1.1.2 Internal Analysis

- **Conclusions** – draw the report to a conclusion, highlighting key points of importance, that will impact upon any recommendations that might be made

- **Recommendations** – clearly outline potential options and then recommendations. Where appropriate justify recommendations in order to substantiate your decision

- **Appendices** – ensure that you only use appendices that add value to the report. Ensure that they are numbered and referenced on a numbered basis within the text. If you are not going to reference it within the text, then it should not be there

- **Bibliography** – whilst in a business environment a bibliography might not be necessary, for an assignment-based report it is vital. It provides an indication of the level of research, reading and collecting of relevant information that has taken place in order to fulfil the requirements of the assignment task. Where possible, and where relevant, you could provide academic references within the text, which should of course then provide the basis of your bibliography. References should be listed alphabetically and in the following sequence

  - Author's name and edition of the text
  - Date of publication
  - Title and sub-title (where relevant)
  - Edition 1st, 2nd etc
  - Place of publication
  - Publisher
  - Series and individual volume number where appropriate

Resources to support the Assignment Route

This guidance presents a range of questions and issues that you should consider, based upon the assignment themes. The detail to support the questions can be found within your BPP Study Text and the 'Core Reading' recommended by CIM.

Additionally you will find useful support information within the CIM websites www.cim.co.uk and www.cimvirtualinstitute.com, where you can access a wide range of marketing information and case studies. You can also build your own workspace within the website so that you can quickly and easily access information specific to your professional study requirements. Other websites you might find useful for some of your assignment work include www.wnim.com – (What's New in Marketing) and also www.connectedinmarketing.com – another CIM website.

Other websites, in addition to those listed on page (xvi) include:

www.open.gov.uk	– *UK government information*
www.adassoc.org.uk	– *Advertising Association*
www.marketresearch.org.uk	– *Marketing Research Society*
www.mintel.com	– *Research Reports*
www.dma.org.uk	– *Direct Marketing Association*
www.theidm.co.uk	– *Institute of Direct Marketing*
www.hm-treasury.gov.uk	– *Government expenditure and policy*
www.bankofengland.co.uk	– *Bank of England*
www.moneyworld.co.uk	– *Investment News*
www.eiu.com	– *Economic Intelligence Unit*
www.europa.eu.int	– *Euro statistics*
www.un.org	– *United Nations Statistics*
www.dti.gov.uk	– *Department of Trade and Industry*
www.tradepartners.gov.uk	– *International economic/cultural situation*

Reflective Statement

The final part of your Assignment will ask you to prepare a 500-word reflective statement. You will be required to reflect upon your **activities** and your **personal development** in the selected areas for the duration of your course. This is an underestimated part of the Assignment, and one which many students fail to address effectively. It is this part of the Assignment that brings all of your work together.

There are a number of **key components** that you should always include.

- Where did you start off at the very beginning of this course? What were your particular strengths, weaknesses and knowledge gaps within *Marketing Environment*?

- What activities have you been involved in to achieve completion of your Assignments?

- What did you do well?

- What could you have done better, and why?

- Do you feel that you have improved throughout the module?

- What value has this learning process added to your overall learning experience?

- Do you feel that the work undertaken will benefit you in your future personal development and organisational development?

- How will you continue to develop this area in the future? How do you anticipate you might use it?

One of the key considerations must be the future. Many people see reflection as a process of thinking about something that has happened in the past. We can also reflect on how this will help us in the future.

You may find that as a result of this learning process your **career aspirations** have completely changed. You may find that you have become more confident and ambitious, and that through consolidating your learning in this way you have considerably more to offer. If this is the case do not be afraid to say so, and demonstrate how the whole learning process has influenced you and how it will drive you forward.

Earlier in this guide you were provided with a range of skills in relation to approaches to Assignments, research and report formation. With the above information and the approaches described you should be able to produce a professional Assignment. Refer back to the earlier part on how to present Assignments and research, if necessary.

Where appropriate, provide relevant **examples** so that you can show your tutor and CIM what your organisation does. This will help to back you up in your evaluation and justifications.

Unit summary: Marketing Environment

You may be feeling that this is going to be hard work! Well, you would be right in thinking this. However, as we suggested earlier, it is likely to be one of the most beneficial learning processes you will embark upon, as you take your CIM qualifications.

The process of development prepares you to be a marketing professional in the future. It provides you with practical experience and opportunities to apply theory in a practical situation. You will demonstrate to your existing or future employer that you have the ability to learn, develop, grow, progress and contribute significantly to the marketing activity within the organisation.

You have been provided with a range of hints and tips on presentation of Assignments, and on the development of approaches to your Core and Optional Assignments.

The Assignment Route, like an exam, is a serious business, and you should consider the level of ongoing commitment that this process requires. The more you put in, the more you are likely to get out. It will not be enough to leave all of your work until the end of the course: this would destroy the ethos and benefit of the Assignment. Use it as a continuous development tool for the duration of the course. A structured approach to the learning process will maximise its benefits to you.

You must ensure that you read the Assignment carefully when it arrives, and address it directly. The CIM qualifications are professional qualifications and therefore, to be successful, you must take a professional approach to your work. We have aimed here to show you the level of detail you should enter into in order to produce an effective and professional piece of work.

Part A

The organisation and its environment

Introduction to organisations

Chapter Topic List	
1	Setting the scene
2	Organisations and their internal environment
3	Different types of organisation
4	Public sector organisations
5	Non-commercial organisations
6	Business organisations
7	Comparing different types of organisation

Learning Outcome

☑ Distinguish between the different types of organisation within the public, private and voluntary sectors and understand their objectives and the influences upon them

Syllabus References

☑ Demonstrate a broad appreciation of the internal environment

☑ Explain the classification of private, public and voluntary organisations, their legal status and operational characteristics

☑ Assess comparative strengths and weaknesses of small/medium and large/global sized organisations.

Key Concepts Introduced

- Organisation
- Formal organisation
- Marketing
- Public sector organisation
- Sole tradership
- Partnerships
- Limited company
- Economies of scale

BPP
PROFESSIONAL EDUCATION

1 Setting the scene

1.1 This chapter is an overall introduction to the Study Text. We discuss the concept of the organisation and the similarities and differences between different types of organisation.

1.2 We start by showing what all organisations have in common and why there is a need for organisations. We introduce systems theory early on as it demonstrates how organisations differ from, but also relate to, the outside environment.

1.3 We then go on to discuss different types of organisation. You need to understand the differences between different types of organisation, particularly between **profit-making** and **non-profit-making** organisations and also the significance of the legal differences between organisations. The organisation structure will have a very significant impact upon marketing, since it affects the way organisations buy and supply goods.

Exam Tip

The syllabus stresses the importance of communicating the concepts and implications of the marketing environment in a variety of relevant formats. Formats that may be requested in the exam include slides, notes for a talk, a checklist and a report. You must ensure if you are asked for a particular format, you follow it; the examiner will not be impressed by an unstructured essay with long paragraphs if bullet point summaries (lists of several short points) have been requested.

2 Organisations and their internal environment

Key Concept

An **organisation** is a social arrangement for the controlled performance of collective goals.

Examples of organisations
A multinational company making and selling cars
An accountancy firm
A charity
A local authority
A trade union
An army
A political party

2.1 These organisations seem, on the surface, to be very different. They do different things and draw their resources from different sources. However, in contrast to other groups of people, such as the family, organisations have much in common.

They are social systems which:

- Are **preoccupied** with **performance**, and adherence to or improvement of standards
- Contain **formal control systems**
- Feature **separation** of tasks
- Require an **ordered environment** (although this may not exist)
- Have a **variety of objectives and goals,** which the organisation exists to achieve

Why organisations exist

ORGANISATIONS

Overcome limitations

Provide companionship

Increase production

Accumulate knowledge

Save time

Objectives

2.2 The relationship of individual and organisational objectives is very important.

(a) An organisation consists of people who **inter-react** with each other.

(b) The way in which people inter-react is **designed** and **ordered** by the **organisation** structure to achieve joint (organisational) objectives. Each individual has his own view of what these organisational objectives are.

(c) Each person in the organisation has his own **personal objectives**.

(d) Organisational objectives must be **compatible** with the **personal objectives** of the individuals concerned if they are to be well-integrated members of the organisation.

Management's role

2.3 Management should:

- Recognise individuals' personal objectives
- Integrate individuals' objectives with those of the organisation
- Recognise individuals' different views of what the organisation's objectives are
- Integrate the different views of the organisation's objectives
- Use human and material resources to achieve objectives most efficiently

Formal and informal organisations

Key Concept

A **formal organisation** is a social unit deliberately constructed to seek specific goals.

[handwritten annotation: formal part — organisation is social unit deliberately together to seek specific goals]

2.4 Examples of an informal organisation are managers who regularly go together for lunch in a local cafeteria or a clique of workmates.

FORMAL AND INFORMAL ORGANISATIONS	
Formal	**Informal**
■ Formal constitution	■ Spontaneous
■ Planned division of responsibility	■ Loose structure
■ Procedures for personnel changes	■ Difficult to determine membership
■ Defined communication channels	■ Flexibility
■ Controlled by centres of power	■ No apparent controls

2.5 Within every formal organisation there exists a complex informal organisation. The formal organisation is a prescribed structure of relationships and ideas; informal organisation, in practice, modifies this formal structure.

2.6 The informal organisation of a company is so important that a newcomer has to 'learn the ropes' before he can settle effectively into his job, and he must also become accepted by his fellow workers.

2.7 The informal organisation of a company, given an acceptable social atmosphere:

(a) **Improves communications** by means of a 'bush telegraph' system

(b) Helps co-ordinate various individuals or departments and establishes unwritten methods for getting a job done. They may be more flexible and adaptable to required changes than the formal ways of doing things.

Authority, responsibility and power in organisations

2.8 Formal organisations need structures of authority and responsibility.

(a) **Authority**

Authority is the right to do something. In an organisation, it refers to the scope and amount of discretion given to a person to make decisions, by virtue of the position he or she holds in the organisation.

(b) **Responsibility**

Responsibility is the liability of a person to be called to account for exercising his authority, actions and results. It is a formal obligation to do something.

(c) **Accountability**

Accountability is the duty of an individual to report to his superior how he has fulfilled his responsibilities.

(d) **Delegation**

Delegation is the process whereby a superior gives a subordinate the authority and responsibility to carry out a given aspect of the superior's own task. Delegation shapes the hierarchical structure of the formal organisation, where authority and responsibility are passed down the chain of command and accountability passes back up.

2.9 Organisational design or structure implies a framework or mechanism with **certain specific functions**.

(a) **Linking**

The organisation links individuals in an established network of relationships so that authority, responsibility and communications can be controlled.

(b) **Grouping**

The organisation groups together the **tasks required** to fulfil the objectives of the organisation, and allocate them to suitable individuals or groups.

(c) **Authority**

Each individual or group is given the **authority** required to perform the allocated functions. The organisation controls behaviour and resources in the interests of the organisation as a whole.

(d) **Co-ordination**

The **objectives** and **activities** of separate units should be brought together, so that overall aims are achieved without gaps or overlaps in the flow of work required.

(e) **Facilitation**

Managers should **facilitate the flow of work**, information and other resources required, through planning, control and other systems.

2.10 Many factors influence the structural design of the organisation.

(a) **Size**

As an organisation grows, its structure becomes more complex; specialisation and subdivision are required. The process of controlling and co-ordinating performance, and communication between individuals, also grows more difficult.

(b) **Task**

Task, the nature of the organisation's work. The division of work shapes structure into functions and individual tasks, and determines how these tasks relate to each other. Depending on the nature of the work, this can be done in a number of ways. The nature of the market/customer base will dictate the grouping of tasks into functions, or sales territories, or customer groups.

(c) **Workforce**

The skills and abilities of the labour force will determine how work is structured and the degree of **autonomy** or **supervision** required. Staff aspirations and expectations may also influence job design, and the amount of delegation that is possible and necessary to retain quality labour.

(d) **Business environment**

Political, economic, social and technological factors present constraints and opportunities.

(e) **Socio-technological systems**

The socio-technical systems approach emphasises the **technology** (organisation of tasks) and **socio-psychological factors** as key determinants of effective design.

(f) **Age**

Age will be the time the organisation has had to develop and grow or decline. Age will also influence whether it is very set in its ways or experimenting with new ways of doing things and making decisions.

(g) **Management style**

There are many different aspects of management. These include how willing management is to delegate; how skilled managers are in organisation and communication; whether teamwork is favoured; whether customer orientation dictates outward focused, flexible structures.

(h) **History**

The structure of a family business, or one with a strong founder, depends on the personality and preferences of those founders and later key players.

The role of marketing

Key Concept

Marketing is the management process responsible for identifying, anticipating and satisfying customer requirements profitably. (CIM)

2.11 Clearly the **customer** is at the centre of the definition. Marketing activity will depend on the requirements of **customers** and the **structure of markets**. It will take account of the longer-term factors affecting the customer base (such as population changes) or the market (such as technological factors).

2.12 However, as we shall see in Chapter 2, the marketer may be working for an organisation that is not primarily focused on the customer.

3 Different types of organisation

WAYS OF CLASSIFYING ORGANISATIONS	
Ownership	Private and public sector
Control	Shareholders, managers and trustees
Activity	Retailers, manufacturers, hospitals
Legal structure	Partnership or limited company
Commercial or non-commercial objectives	Companies, non-profit making organisations, charities
Accountability	Shareholders, government
Sources of finance	Borrowing, the state, investments

Marketing at Work

An advertising campaign for the restaurant chain TGI Fridays contrasted the excitement of TGIs compared with a more sedate environment.

Different types of food are offered, the waiting staff are younger, and the bar staff perform juggling acts when making cocktails.

3.1 Marketers need to be able to understand the effects of different types of organisation on **marketing operations**. Consider the following ways in which organisation structure can affect marketing.

(a) **Buyers**

Organisations are **buyers** of goods and services. A large multi-national is likely to buy in a very different way from a small sole trader. The large multi-national firm may have a substantial purchasing department, systems for assessing supplier reliability and a complex planning process. A small sole trader is unlikely to have such things.

(b) **Sellers**

Organisations are **suppliers** of goods and services. They need to respond to changes in consumer demand. The size, structure and resources of an organisation influence how quickly (if at all!) it is able to respond to marketing opportunities.

Marketing at Work

Fruit drinks such as Snapple began to compete with other soft drinks such as Coca-Cola, which faced a loss in market share as a result of this change in consumer tastes.

Coca-Cola revamped its marketing, and also introduced the *Fruitopia* brand to compete with the rival fruit drinks.

4 Public sector organisations Specimen paper, 12/03

[handwritten notes scrawled across top: Public sector organisations are two types hospitals, post office etc and non commercial structure like courts]

Key Concept

A **public sector organisation** is an organisation controlled directly and/or indirectly and/or funded by central and/or local government.

[handwritten note: Publico sector organisation is an organisation funded controlled in some way by the government (or controlled)]

4.1 In most economies, ownership of organisations is vested either in the government or in private individuals and institutions. Governments make laws, and so provide the environment for activity in the private sector.

4.2 Some public sector organisations are supposed to have a commercial objective, others are not.

[handwritten note: The POST OFFICE is a public sector org.]

(a) Publicly-owned postal services will probably exist to **make a profit** out of mail services.

(b) The armed forces will not be profit-making organisations. *[handwritten note: ARMY is not FOR PROFIT]*

(c) Government departments provide services

4.3 The distinguishing characteristics of the non-profit orientated public sector are as follows.

(a) The public sector can **command resources**.

(b) Ideas of **fairness** underpin service provision (for example, everybody should have the right to an education).

(c) The public sector is based on the idea of **equal rights**. Each individual should have the right of protection from invasion, and should be equal under the law.

[handwritten note: Public sector organisations get their sources from the tax payer or from the government]

4.4 Public sector organisations tend to have different **sources of revenue** to private sector organisations.

(a) Their revenue does not come from the sale of goods and services, but is **raised** directly from the **taxpayer**. It is then allocated towards socially desirable objectives.

(b) Revenue may be provided by **other public sector bodies**. Local authorities, for example, may derive some revenue from central government, some from local taxation.

(c) In the public sector, demand for services **cannot be rationed by charging a high price** (thereby restricting the number of people able to pay). Instead, the resources to provide services are restricted, and these restricted resources determine the volume of services provided. *[handwritten note: FOR example Hospitals]*

4.5 Distinctions between the public and private sectors are becoming increasingly blurred. In particular, the marketing environment of each is becoming similar, as public services are exposed to greater competition.

Advantages and disadvantages of public sector organisations

4.6

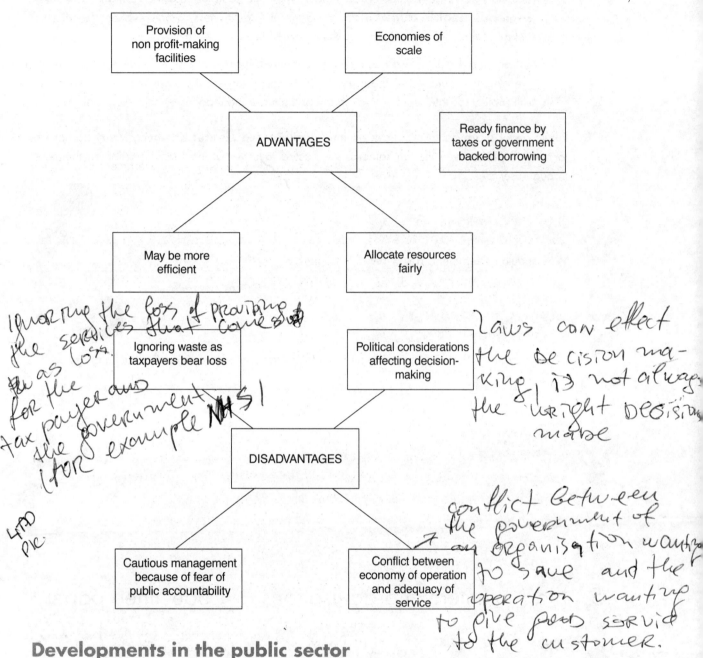

Handwritten annotations:

Ignoring the loss of providing the services that comes out as loss for the tax payer and the government for example NHS

4PD plc

Laws can effect the decision making is not always the wright decision mabe

conflict between the government of an organisation wants to save and the operation wanting to give good service to the customer.

Developments in the public sector

4.7 Public sector bodies are ultimately accountable to the electorate. Four trends in the UK public sector are worthy of note.

(a) More public sector activities will be carried out away from the direct control of central government. Policy is determined by central government, but will be implemented by autonomous **executive agencies**, although such agencies are increasingly assuming a policy forming role also.

(b) Public bodies are more likely to become purchasers rather than providers of services. An obvious example is refuse collection. At one time directly managed by local authorities, this service is now often performed by private sector businesses on fixed-term contracts marked under **compulsory competitive tendering**.

(c) **Market-type structures** were introduced to public sector bodies by the 1979-1997 Conservative government in the UK. In the National Health Service internal market, hospitals have to compete for funds. Their immediate customers might have been **regional health authorities**, or general practitioners, who purchase services on behalf of the ultimate consumer of them, the patient.

(d) Full scale **privatisation** has been implemented in some industries. Public utilities such as the electricity and water industries have been privatised. These industries, however, are still subject to state regulation as many of them are monopolies or near-monopolies.

4.8 Public sector organisations all have an important **service element** to them. Many do not exist to make a profit, even though some are expected to cover at least a proportion of their costs through user fees.

Action Programme 1

Why should governments get involved in commercial activities?

Action Programme 2

In what areas of their activities will public sector organisations use marketing techniques?

Exam Tip

Question 5 in December 2003 covered similarities and differences between the marketing objectives in the public and private sectors.

5 Non-commercial organisations   Specimen paper, 12/03

this are organisations like Hospital not for profit but the are not public organisations like [hospitals schools]

5.1 Some organisations do not exist to make a profit, but nor are they public services.

5.2 Some organisations make surpluses of revenue over expenditure resulting from activities such as running bars and dining rooms, insurance and sickness benefits, holiday clubs and savings clubs. The division and application of the surpluses depends on the organisation and its aims and objectives.

They include professional organisations for which you need membership

EXAMPLES OF NON-COMMERCIAL ORGANISATIONS	
Trade unions	Organisations of workers in trades or industries, protecting common interests, particularly pay and conditions
Employers' associations	Represent and promote business interests of their membership

City charities

EXAMPLES OF NON-COMMERCIAL ORGANISATIONS	
Motoring organisations	Provide services, particularly help with breakdowns
Professional associations	Membership requirements include passing exams and fulfilling ethical standards. May exercise control over professional practices and members' behaviour. Performance measured by prestige, value of qualifications
Charities	Have well-defined goals eg relieving poverty or suffering. Raise money by donations, charity shops and so on. Measure success by promoting beneficiaries' interests, raising public awareness and raising money

Strengths and limitations of non-commercial organisations

5.3 These vary widely but certain general features often occur.

[handwritten: This are well known unknown organisations which people can trust]

[handwritten: voluntary sector]

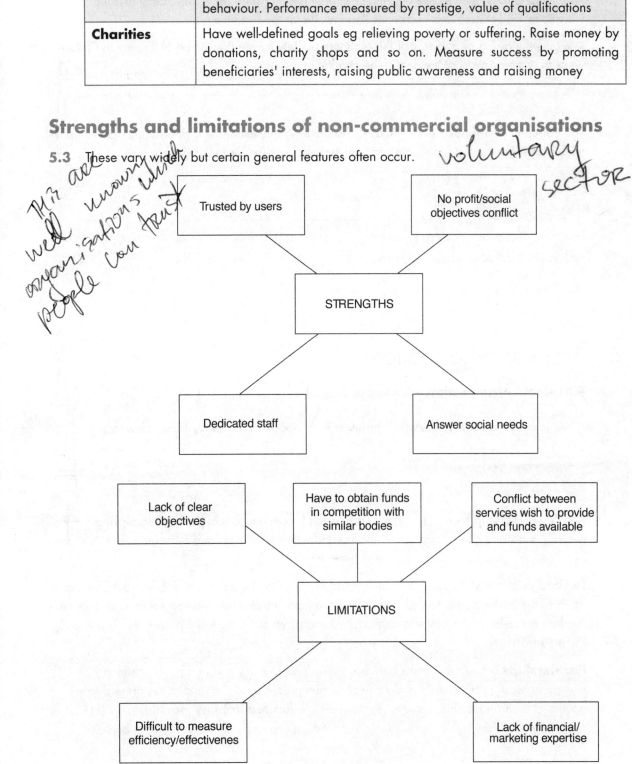

Trusted by users

No profit/social objectives conflict

STRENGTHS

Dedicated staff

Answer social needs

Lack of clear objectives

Have to obtain funds in competition with similar bodies

Conflict between services wish to provide and funds available

LIMITATIONS

Difficult to measure efficiency/effectivenes

Lack of financial/ marketing expertise

Action Programme 3

The Tutor's Guidance Notes for this unit have highlighted the need for you to read a variety of publications including Internet sources. We shall as a result have a number of action programmes throughout this text which require research on the Internet.

As a start, look up the website of a major charity and consider how that charity is using its website to market itself to a person visiting the site for the first time.

We give the results of a review of the National Society for the Prevention of Cruelty to Children's website in the answers at the end of the chapter.

5.4 The non-commercial stakeholders, those who have an interest in the organisation's activities, will include members and donors. We consider stakeholders further in Chapter 5.

Exam Tip

Don't neglect non-commercial or voluntary organisations, as regular questions were set on them in old syllabus papers.

6 Business organisations

6.1 A **business organisation** exists to make a profit.

6.2 A key issue is the degree to which a business is a separate legal entity from its owners.

Key Concepts

A **sole tradership** is a business owned and run by one individual perhaps employing one or two assistants and controlling their work. The individual's business and personal affairs are, for legal and tax purposes, identical.

Limited company status, on the other hand, means that the business's debts and the personal debts of the business's owners (shareholders) are legally separate. The shareholders cannot be sued for the debts of the business unless they have given some personal guarantee. This is called **limited liability**.

Partnerships are arrangements between individuals to carry on business in common with a view to profit. A partnership however involves obligations to others, and so a partnership will be governed by a partnership agreement. Unless it is a **limited liability partnership (LLP)**, partners will be fully liable for debts and liabilities, for example if the partnership is sued.

6.3 Sole tradership and partnerships are concentrated in the small business sector. Most businesses of any size are limited companies. Some small businesses are limited companies, too, but often the owner must give a personal guarantee to the bank for loans to the business.

Sole traders

6.4 A sole trader owns and runs a business, contributes the capital to start the enterprise, runs it with or without employees, and earns the profits or stands the loss of the venture.

EXAMPLES OF SOLE TRADERS	
Retail	Local newsagents
Service industries	Plumbers
Manufacturing and craft industries	Tailoring

6.5 Advantages of being a sole trader

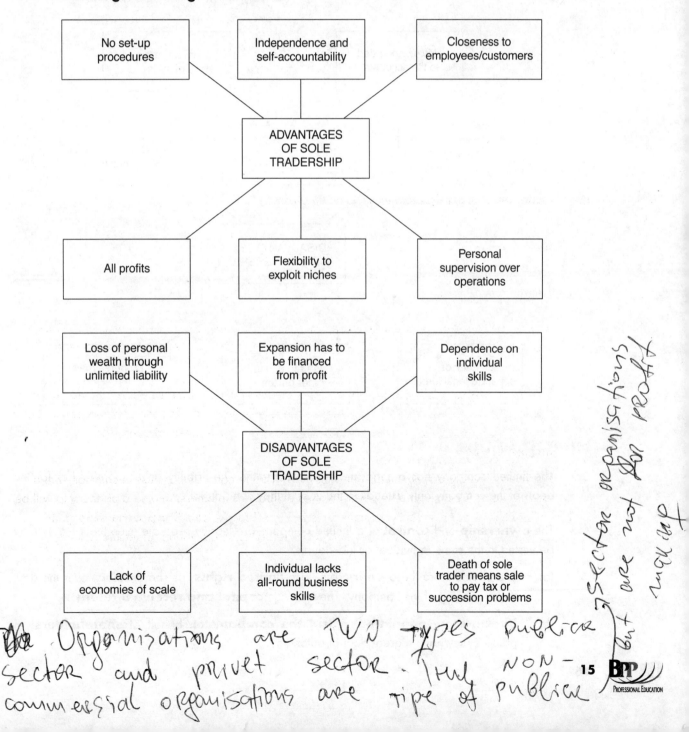

Partnerships — *Legal Medical etc's*

6.6 A partnership is an arrangement between two or more individuals to carry on a business on an agreed basis. Partnerships are found in similar fields to those operated by sole traders, where there are two or more joint owners, and in many professions. Many accountancy firms operate as Limited liability Partnerships (LLPs).

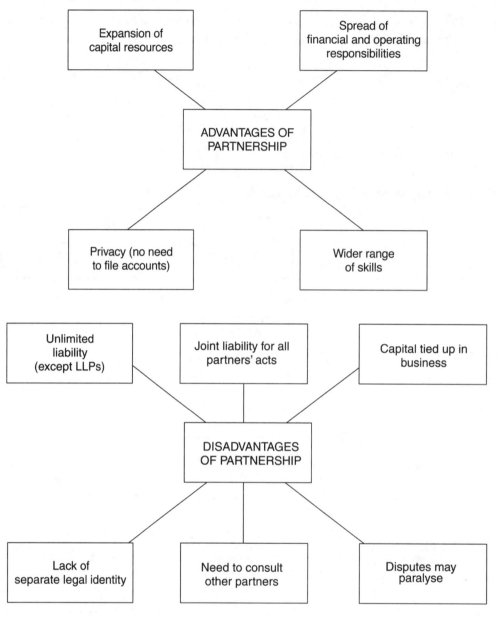

Limited companies

6.7 The limited company has a separate legal personality. The liability of its shareholders for the debts of the company only extends to the capital they contributed.

6.8 The **ownership** and **control** of a limited company are legally separate even though they may be vested in the same individual or individuals.

(a) Shareholders are the **owners**, but have **limited rights**, as shareholders, over the day-to-day running of the company. They provide **capital and receive a return**.

(b) **Directors** are **appointed** to **run the company** on behalf of **shareholders**. In practice they have a great deal of autonomy.

are the private or business sector organisation of the sole Trader / off-licence

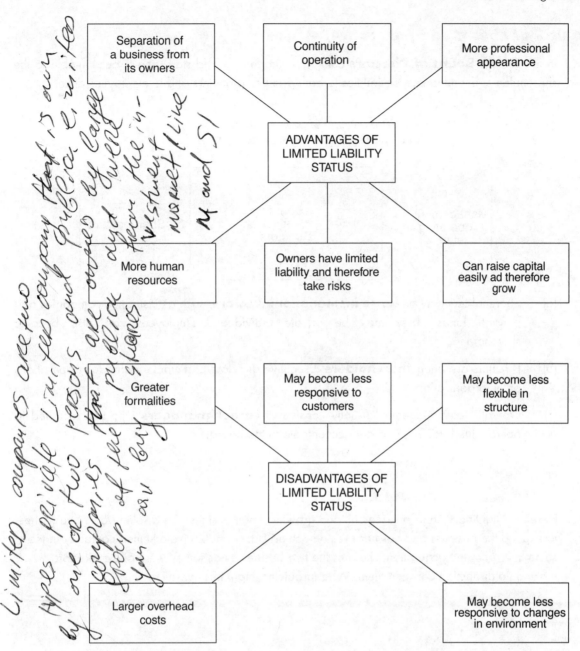

6.9 In the UK, limited companies come in two types: private limited companies (eg X Limited) and public limited companies (eg X plc). They differ as follows.

(a) **Ownership**

Most **private** companies are owned by only a **small number** of **shareholders**. Public companies generally are owned by a wider proportion of the investing public.

(b) **Finance**

A **private company's share capital** will normally be provided by the founder or promoter, business associates of the founder or employer or venture capitalists.

A public company's share capital, in addition, can be raised from the **public directly**, or through institutional investors, using recognised markets.

6.10 Many companies start in a small way, often as family businesses which operate as private companies, then grow to the point where they can invite the public to subscribe for shares. The new capital thus made available enables the firm to expand its activities and achieve the advantages of large scale operation.

Control of limited companies

6.11 In the UK, the **Board of Directors** controls management and staff, and is accountable to the shareholders, but it has responsibilities to both groups, to owners and to employees alike.

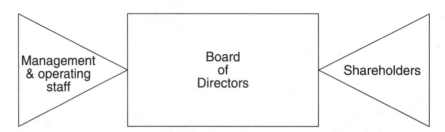

The division of power in limited companies (not always an equal one)

(a) Shareholders may be **large institutional investors**, such as insurance companies and pension funds. They may be private individuals. Employees can also become shareholders.

(b) Directors are often **shareholders**. Executive directors participate in the daily operations of the organisation.

(c) Operational management usually consists of **career managers** who are recruited to operate the business, and are accountable to the board.

Action Programme 4

Florence Nightingale runs a successful and growing small business, as a sole trader. She wishes to expand the business and has her eyes on Scutari Ltd, a small private limited company in the same line. After the acquisition, she runs the two businesses as if they were one operation making no distinction between them. What problems might this cause?

Franchises

6.12 In franchising, the owner of the name of a product or a retail group (the **franchisor**) sells the right to distribute the product or operate under the store name to a **franchisee**. The **franchisee** has independence to sell the product or run the shop as a separate venture. The Body Shop is an example of a franchise operation.

executive directors are those how tame actions in the day by day Business

Business activities

6.13 Business organisations can also be classified by type of activity.

EXAMPLES OF BUSINESS ACTIVITIES	
Manufacturing	Acquisition of raw materials and by use of labour and technology turning them into products
Extractive/raw materials	Extraction and refining of raw materials
Energy	Conversion of one resource (coal) into another (electricity)
Retailing/ distribution	Delivering goods to the end consumer
Services	See below

6.14 The relative importance of these activities in the UK is indicated below. (The figures below include the non-profit making public sector.)

	United Kingdom Number of employees	
	1995 '000	1987 '000
Agriculture	313	321
Construction	838	1,009
Manufacturing	3,942	5,152
Other production	239	508
Services	16,576	14,594
	21,908	21,584

6.15 **Service industries**

Services are distinguished from products.

(a) **Services are intangible**

A service cannot be seen, touched or displayed. Money transmission is a service which customers pay for and which is performed by banks, but the customer does not have anything material to show as a result.

(b) **Services are inseparable**.

In general, services cannot be stored since the production and consumption of a service cannot be separated. For example, when you have dental treatment, the service is consumed as it is produced.

(c) **Services are heterogeneous**.

The quality of the service product is highly dependent on the quality of the person providing it (eg the actors in a play).

6.16 Examples of services:

- Retailing and distribution
- Transport and communications
- Banking and finance
- Public administration and defence (including the army)
- Business services
- Public services, such as education and medicine

7 Comparing different types of organisation 12/02

7.1 We shall now draw together the different types of organisation and compare them on the basis of certain criteria.

Ease of formation

7.2 How do you set up an organisation, especially a business organisation?

Sole tradership

7.3 It might appear easy to set up a sole tradership. After all, a sole trader is not operating under limited liability, and so does not have to endure the legal procedures and expense of setting up a limited company.

7.4 That said, a sole trader cannot avoid bureaucratic irritation and legal regulations. At some stage attention has to be paid to matters such as taxation, health and safety and planning permission.

7.5 None of these requirements are unique to sole traderships but they do indicate that being a sole trader is no guarantee of avoiding bureaucratic procedures.

Partnerships

7.6 Partnerships in theory are just as easy to form as sole traders. However, the partners are **bound** by the terms of the partnership agreement, and there may be restrictions on changing it. A partnership does not necessarily end with the departure of one of the partners, as new partners can be brought in.

Limited companies

7.7 As limited liability status confers significant legal benefits, there is greater regula[formation and status of limited companies than over partnerships and sole traders.

set up

7.8 There are two ways of acquiring limited company status.

(a) Two or more individuals and/or companies agree to set up a company. Appropriate documents are drawn up and the company is registered.

(b) Companies may be purchased **'off the shelf'** in which all the work of setting up the company has been done, although the documents that define the company have to be altered.

Non-commercial bodies

7.9 Most **public sector bodies** are established by legislation, or by delegated authority given to a minister.

7.10 Laws will govern the formation of **trade unions**. To be effective in a work context, a trade union has to be recognised as such by the employer.

7.11 Charities will also be subject to special rules governing their incorporation.

Raising finance

Sole traderships

7.12 Raising finance

- The sole trader's own savings
- The sole trader's family and friends, or any other interested parties
- The bank (overdraft or loan finance)
- The profits of the business

7.13 A sole trader's business and personal affairs are legally the same. A lender, though interested primarily in the affairs of the business, has the benefit that the trader's domestic assets provide additional security.

7.14 Overdraft finance can be withdrawn at any time by the bank. Too many businesses use it for **long-term investment**, whereas overdraft finance is only really suitable for short-term fluctuations.

7.15 A loan is more secure, from the bank's point of view. It enables the unincorporated business to predict the likely repayments. However, these do not alter according to the conditions of trade.

Partnerships

7.16 Similar considerations arise for **partnerships**. New partners are g[contribute additional capital to the partnership when they join. The other m[for a partnership is the revenues and profits of the business itself. Otherwise bank finance.

Limited companies

7.17 **Limited companies** restrict the liability of the shareholders to the amount they initially invested in the company. For this reason, companies are able to raise money through **issuing shares**.

7.18 A share signifies that the owner of the share has an interest, as owner, in the company. It is a form of property which can be transferred to another person, subject to any restrictions imposed by the constitution of the company.

7.19 Share capital can be raised in different ways.

- Privately
- Publicly, by offering the shares for sale on the stock market

7.20 There are restrictions regarding the offer of shares for sale to the public. There must be a **prospectus**, which is subject to detailed rules as to what it contains.

Public sector bodies

7.21 Public sector institutions can command resources raised through general taxation. Some also charge for services. The government does not raise taxes specifically for investment or current spending: they are collected into a **consolidated fund**. The total of government spending therefore contains both short-term and long-term items. Resources are limited by the government's overall financing requirement.

Charities

7.22 Charities raise funds through a variety of methods including:

- Donations
- Legacies
- Membership fees
- Grants
- Fundraising activities
- Commercial operations such as shops
- Loans

7.23 One definition of a not-for-profit organisation is that it seeks to cover its costs; profits are only made as a means to an end such as providing a service, or accomplishing some socially or morally worthy objective.

Size

7.24 Many of the consequences of differences in size between organisations are bound up with the concept of economies of scale.

Economies of scale

12/02

Key Concept

Economies of scale are factors which cause average cost to decline in the long run as output of a firm increases.

[handwritten: cost of producing goes down as new way of producing more cheaply are found. or better ✓ machines are founs and introduces to the market]

Internal economies of scale

Technical economies

7.25 Technical economies arise in the production process.

7.26 Large undertakings can make use of **larger and more specialised machinery**. If smaller undertakings tried to use similar machinery, the costs would be excessive because the machines would become obsolete before their physical life ends (ie their economic life would be shorter than their physical life). Obsolescence is caused by falling demand for the product made on the machine, or by the development of newer and better machines.

7.27 **Indivisibility of operations** is also important.

(a) Some operations must be carried out at the same cost, regardless of whether the business is small or large; these are fixed costs and **average fixed costs always decline as production increases**.

(b) Similarly, other operations' costs vary a little, but not proportionately, with size (ie they are 'semi-fixed' costs).

(c) Some operations are not worth considering below a certain level of output (eg expensive advertising campaigns).

Commercial or marketing economies

7.28 **Buying economies** may be available, reducing the cost of material purchases through bulk purchase discounts. *[handwritten: Buying in bulk reduces price and calls economies of scale]*

7.29 **Stockholding** becomes more efficient. The most economic quantities of inventory to hold increase with the scale of operations, but at a lower proportionate rate of increase.

[handwritten: the bigger the company they can receive discount through a suplier as their own loyal customer for a long time]

Financial economies

7.30 Large firms may find it easier to obtain loan finance at attractive rates of interest. It is also feasible for them to sell shares to the public via a stock exchange.

Action Programme 5

The above list is not exhaustive. Can you add to it?

BPP PROFESSIONAL EDUCATION

External economies of scale

7.31 External economies of scale occur as an **industry** grows in size. Here are two examples.

(a) **A large skilled labour force is created** and educational services can be geared towards training new entrants.

(b) **Specialised ancillary industries will develop** to provide components, transport finished goods, trade in by-products, provide special services and so on. For instance, law firms may be set up to specialise in the affairs of the industry.

The effect of size

7.32 The extent to which both internal and external economies of scale can be achieved will vary from industry to industry, depending on the conditions in that industry. In other words, big-sized firms are better suited to some industries than others.

(a) **Internal economies of scale**

These are potentially more significant than external economies to a supplier of a product or service for which there is a large consumer market. A firm in such an industry may have to grow to a certain size in order to benefit fully from potential economies of scale, and thereby be cost-competitive and capable of making profits and surviving.

(b) **External economies of scale**

These are potentially significant to smaller firms who specialise in the ancillary services to a larger industry. For example, the development of a large world-wide industry in drilling for oil and natural gas off-shore has led to the creation of many new specialist supplier firms, making drilling rigs, and various types of equipment. Thus, a specialist firm may benefit more from the market demand created by a large customer industry than from its own internal economies of scale.

Diseconomies of scale

7.33 Economic theory predicts that there will be **diseconomies of scale** in the long-run costs of a firm, once the firm gets beyond an ideal size. The main reasons for possible diseconomies of scale are human and behavioural problems of managing a large firm. In a large firm employing many people, with many levels in the hierarchy of management, there may be a number of undesirable effects.

- Communicating information and instructions may become difficult.

- Chains of command may become excessively long.

- Morale and motivation amongst staff may deteriorate.

- Senior management may have difficulty in assimilating all the information they need in sufficient detail to make good quality decisions.

7.34 There will not usually be **technical** factors producing diseconomies of scale. The technology of higher volume equipment, on the contrary, is more likely to create further economies of scale.

7.35 The implication of diseconomies of scale is that companies should achieve a certain size to benefit fully from scale economies, but should not become too big, when cost controls might slacken and organisational inefficiency is likely to develop.

Economies of scale in marketing

7.36 Economies and diseconomies of scale also apply in relation to the marketing function. You may be tempted to assume that larger companies enjoy all the advantages. They can employ a specialist marketing department with expert knowledge and can afford large advertising and promotions budgets.

7.37 However, small businesses have many potential marketing advantages over public limited companies. The following are particularly important advantages.

(a) **Overheads**

Overhead costs may be **lower** as a result of having no headquarters staff overheads, among other costs. These cost savings can be passed on to customers, giving a big advantage in price sensitive markets. This effect is noticeable in the market for small building work.

(b) **Flexibility**

Because there is **less bureaucracy** in a small company, it can **respond more quickly** to changes in the marketing environment. It can therefore exploit market niches before their larger competitors move in.

(c) **Development**

The relative lack of bureaucracy can also facilitate the **development** of **innovative products**, of which a larger company may not have had the courage to pursue.

(d) **Closeness to customers**

Small business owners are generally **closer** to their **customers** and may have better knowledge of the marketing environment than decision makers in large organisations whose knowledge comes through lengthy research processes.

(e) **Personal service**

Small businesses can often claim to offer a **personal service** where each customer is known by name. In some markets this can be a big advantage.

Exam Tip

The strengths and weaknesses of different types of business organisation are a very important topic for this exam.

Chapter Roundup

- An **organisation** is a 'social arrangement for the controlled performance of collective goals'. Organisations achieve results through the division of labour and co-operative efforts, which individuals cannot achieve alone.

- Organisations have **goals**. **Business organisations**' primary goal is to provide a return on money invested. This they do by selling goods and services. Many **public sector organisations** have the primary goals of providing a service. A secondary goal is the efficiency and effectiveness with which resources are used.

- The boundaries between public and private sectors are altering with **privatisation** and the introduction of **market-based measures**.

- Non-commercial organisations include trade unions, employers' organisations, professional associations, clubs and **charities.**

- Business organisations can be analysed by **size, legal form** and **activity**.

- **Sole traderships** and **partnerships** tend to be small. They have the advantage of privacy and flexibility, but the disadvantages of vulnerability and unlimited liability, except in the case of **limited liability partnerships (LLPs)**.

- **Limited companies** separate, in theory, ownership from control. The main difference between **private** limited companies and **public** limited companies is that the latter can offer their shares to the general public.

Quick Quiz

1 *Fill in the blank*

   An ...organisation... is a social arrangement for the controlled performance of collective goals.

2 Give three reasons why organisations exist.

3 Which of the following are essential elements of formal organisations?

   A   Authority
   B   Flexibility
   C   Responsibility
   D   Fluid membership

4 Suggest five ways of classifying organisations.

5 Which of the following is not a characteristic of the non-profit making public sector?

   A   Command of resources
   B   Fairness
   C   No financial targets
   D   Equal profits

6   A sole trader benefits from economies of scale.

    True   ☐

    False   ☐

7   What is the arrangement called where a retail group sells the right to operate under the store name?

8   Which of the following would be possible sources of finance for a sole trader?

    A   Savings
    B   Money from friends
    C   Bank loan
    D   Profits

Action Programme Review

1   Governments have become involved in commerce and taken over companies or industries for a number of reasons including the nature of the business (public utilities such as water), the need to preserve jobs (for example, nationalisation of motor firms), national security (for example, aspects of the defence industry) or technological sensitivity (for example, nuclear power). In the last twenty years however many governments have privatised state–run enterprises.

2   Public sector organisations run some activities, for example theatres or swimming pools, that exist to make a return. These need to be marketed to potential customers. They will also need marketing skills to cope with competition, for example compulsory competitive tendering or competition with the commercial sector for potential employees.

    However marketing techniques can also be used in public sector activities that are purely non-profit making. Public sector authorities will need to identify the targets for whom services are being provided, and recognise their needs and desires. These needs and desires will need to be considered in the light of available resources, and the provision of services planned carefully.

    The potential recipients will need to be informed not only that the services are being provided, but also the benefits that they offer. The service provider should not assume that the services will automatically be taken up; if they aren't, it will be a waste of resources providing them. For the same reason the services will have to be delivered effectively to the beneficiaries, otherwise they may stop using them.

    Marketing techniques will also be vital in dealing with others involved in the provision of services. For example public sector organisations may co-operate with charities in seeking to provide services.

3   At the time of review, significant features of the NSPCC's website were:

    (a)   A welcome page focused on the NSPCC's 'Cruelty to children must stop. FULL STOP. Campaign'.

    (b)   A separate Kidszone focused on child users. This area:

        (i)   Again highlights the Full Stop Campaign

        (ii)   Provides links into other campaigns

BPP
PROFESSIONAL EDUCATION

(iii) Provided advice for children who are bullied and tips for children to keep themselves safe

(iv) Has various non-serious features including pop star interviews and a promise of 'lots more fun and surprises' on future visits

(c) A home page that:

(i) Provides links into the Full stop campaign and other campaigns

(ii) Provides a rolling summary of what's new

(iii) Gives links into fundraising and volunteering and how you can help. There is also a section devoted to what media stars are doing for the NSPCC

4   This is quite a tricky question, which Florence had better sort out, for her sake and for that of her customers. For example, if suppliers have contracts with Scutari Ltd, the contract is with the company, and Florence is not legally liable for the debts. If their contracts are with Florence, then they are dealing with her personally. Florence has to make a choice. She can:

(a) Run her entire business as a sole trader, in which case Scutari Ltd's assets must be transferred to her

(b) Run her entire business as a limited company, in which case she would contribute the assets of her business as capital to the company

(c) Ensure that the two business are legally distinct in their assets, liabilities, income and expenditure

5   (a) Large firms attract better quality employees if the employees see better career prospects than in a small firm.

(b) Specialisation of labour applies to management, and there are thus managerial economies; the cost per unit of management will fall as output rises.

(c) Marketing economies are available, because a firm can make more effective use of advertising, specialist salesmen, and specialised channels of distribution.

(d) Large companies are able to devote more resources to research and development (R & D). In an industry where R & D is essential for survival, large companies are more likely to prosper.

(e) Large companies find raising finance easier and can often do so more cheaply. Quoted public limited companies have access to the Stock Exchange for new share issues. They are also able to borrow money more readily.

Answers to Quick Quiz

1   An organisation

2   Three of

- Overcoming problems
- Providing companionship
- Increasing production
- Accumulating knowledge
- Saving time

3   A   Authority

     B   Responsibility

4   Any five of:

- Ownership
- Control
- Activity
- Legal structure
- Objectives
- Accountability
- Sources of finance

5   C   Targets may be set even if the body does not exist to make a profit

6   False. Economies of scale benefit large organisations.

7   A franchise

8   All of them

Now try illustrative questions 1 and 2 at the end of the Study Text

Organisations as systems

2

Chapter Topic List
1   Setting the scene
2   Mission and vision
3   Commercial goals and objectives
4   The systems approach to organisations
5   The contingency approach to organisations
6   Marketing and other functions

Learning Outcomes

☑   Recognise organisations as systems

☑   Understand the meaning and importance of an organisation's mission

☑   Perceive different organisational objectives and drivers for change

☑   Recognise the links between marketing and other functions

☑   Understand the system and contingency approaches to managing organisations

Syllabus References

☑   State the meaning and importance of an organisation's mission and explain the nature and significance of the objectives pursued

☑   Identify the internal and external influences on the formulation of objectives and specify the key drivers for organisational change

☑   Explain the nature of open systems and the interface between organisations and their marketing environment

BPP PROFESSIONAL EDUCATION

☑ Represent the organisation as an open system responding to changing environmental conditions

Key Concepts Introduced

- Mission
- Objectives
- Strategic Business Unit
- System
- Closed system
- Open system

- Stakeholders
- Internal stakeholders
- Connected stakeholders
- External stakeholders
- Business process re-engineering

1 Setting the scene

1.1 In this chapter we consider the mission and objectives an organisation has, and also the different approaches to managing systems.

1.2 We first focus on the organisations' **mission**. The mission of an organisation consists of not just its purpose but also its values, its strategy and its policies.

1.3 Within its mission an organisation may have a number of **objectives**. We focus on these in section 3, describing the various ways in which objectives can be classified, we give examples of the objectives that are important for many organisations.

1.4 We then discuss how organisations view themselves and view their relationships with their environment. This will determine how organisations react to their environment, and in particular respond to changes in their environment. We consider in detail the **systems** and **contingency approaches**.

1.5 Lastly in this chapter we discuss briefly the role of **marketing** within an organisation, and in particular how marketing relates to other departments within the organisation.

2 Mission and vision   6/03

> ### Key Concept
>
> **Mission** is an organisation's rationale for existing at all and/or its long-term strategic direction and/or its values; its basic function in terms of the products and services the organisation produces for its clients.

2.1 Mission and vision give shape and direction to the behaviour and decisions of the organisation and people within it.

(a) **Mission** 'describes the organisation's basic function in society, in terms of the products and services it produces for its clients' (Mintzberg).

(b) **Vision** is 'what we are aiming for'.

[handwritten: The vision is what we want to achieve in future and where we want to be]

Marketing at Work

'The Co-op'

The Co-operative movement is a good example of the role of mission. The Co-operative Wholesale Society and Co-operative Retail Society are business organisations, but their mission is not simply profit.

Rather, being owned by their suppliers/customers rather than external shareholders, they have always, since the foundation, had a wider social concern.

The Co-op has been criticised by some analysts on the grounds that it is insufficiently profitable, certainly in comparison with supermarket chains such as Tescos.

The Co-op has explicit social objectives. In some cases it will retain stores which, although too small to be as profitable as a large supermarket, provide an important social function in the communities which host them.

Of course, the Co-op's performance as a retailer can be improved, but judging it on the conventional basis of profitability ignores its social objectives.

2.2 In *A Sense of Mission*, Andrew Campbell, Marion Devine and David Young note two alternative ways of looking at mission.

(a) 'The strategy school .... views mission primarily as a **strategic tool**, an intellectual discipline which defines the business's commercial rationale and target market ....'

(b) On the other hand, a mission would be defined as the '**cultural glue** that enables an organisation to function as a collective unity'. In this case, it is a set of **values** rather than a description of ultimate commercial goals.

ELEMENTS OF MISSION	
Purpose	Why the organisation exists ■ Creation of wealth ■ Satisfaction of stakeholder needs ■ Reaching higher goal
Strategy	Provision of commercial logic, defining business and competitive advantages and priorities
Values	Beliefs of people working in the organisation, relating to its culture
Policies and behaviour standards	Exist to convert strategy into everyday performance, eg politeness to customers, speed of answering phone calls

For there to be a strong sense of mission, the elements above must be mutually re-inforcing. Strategy and values unite in policies and standards of behaviour.

[handwritten marginal notes: The mission consist of four element. The purpose of existing / how is the company / The strategy / Purpose - what the company wants to be / Value - what the employee believed in relating to it culture / The policies exist to convert strategy into every day performance]

2.4 Some people are sceptical about mission because it is emotional and not a wholly objective concept. However:

(a) **Values** and **feelings** are **integral elements** of **consumers' buying decisions**, as evidenced by advertising, branding and market research. Therefore, a company's decision-making processes further up the line.

(b) Most studies into organisation behaviour show that employees are **motivated** by **more than money**. A sense of mission and values can help to motivate employees. In some jobs, a sense of vocation and professionalism is bound up with the organisation's mission (eg a hospital). *Live e.g. Met Police sense of value and feeling play major Role in moti-mating people*

(c) Many organisations take the **cultural aspect** of mission seriously.

2.5 Mission fuels success for the following reasons.

(a) **Loyalty and commitment**

Employees who feel a sense of mission will be willing to satifice their own interests for the good of the whole. The company, however, has to reciprocate this loyalty.

(b) **Guidance for behaviour**

A sense of mission helps create a work environment where there is a sense of common purpose. In matters of **ethical conflict**, divergencies between organisational values and personal values are hard to resolve if a person's values differ from the organisation's.

2.6 Remember that strong values can be dangerous.

■ They can **filter out uncomfortable environmental information**
■ They can **delay necessary decision-making**

Vision

2.7 A vision gives a general sense of direction to the company, even if there is not too much attention to detail. A vision should be clear. The vision of Apple Computers, in the early days of the PC industry was to 'democratise the computer'. (Hinterhuber and Popp)

2.8 A **vision** is a view of the future state of the organisation or its industry. A **vision statement** may sum it up. For example, the managing director of a personal computer firm might have the 'vision' of 'A computer in every firm'.

MISSION AND VISION	
Mission	**Vision**
Here and now	Future
Motivate	Fails to motivate if too vague
Continual	Renewed if achieved
Realities	Unrealistic?
Relevant	Potentially out-of-date

Mission statements

2.9 Mission statements are formal documents, which might be reproduced in a number of places (eg at the front of an organisation's annual report, on publicity material, in the chairman's office, in communal work areas etc). There is no standard format.

2.10 Most mission statements will include the following.

MISSION STATEMENTS	
Identity of persons for whom the organisation exists	Shareholders
	Customers
	Staff and other employees
Nature of the firm's business	Product it makes or services it provides
	Markets it produces for
Ways of competing	Reliance on quality, innovation, low prices
	Commitment to customer care
	Policy on acquisition versus organic growth
	Geographical spread of its operations
Principles of business	Commitment to suppliers and staff
	Social policy eg non-discrimination or ecology
	Commitments to customers

2.11 Here is an example of a proposed mission and values statement fulfilling all these functions. How good do you think it is?

ROYAL MAIL: MISSION AND VALUES

Royal Mail Business Mission

As Royal Mail our mission is to be recognised as the best organisation in the world distributing text and packages. We shall achieve this by:

■ Excelling our Collection, Processing, Distribution and Delivery arrangements

■ Establishing a partnership with our customers to understand, agree and meet their changing requirements

■ Operating profitably by efficient services which our customers consider to be value for money

■ Creating a work environment which recognises and rewards the commitment of all employees to customer satisfaction

■ Recognising our responsibilities as part of the social, industrial and commercial life of the country

■ Being forward looking and innovative

Royal Mail Business Values

We each care about:

■ Our customers and their requirements for:

– Reliability
– Value for money
– Accessibility
– Courtesy
– Integrity
– Security
– Prompt and timely response

■ All our fellow employees and their needs for:

– Respect
– Training and development
– Involvement
– Recognition and reward

■ The way we do our job and the way it affects our customers both inside and outside the Business

■ Our role in the life of the Community

■ We are proud to be part of Royal Mail

2.12 According to Guy Kawasaki (*Selling the Dream*, 1991) good mission statements exhibit three qualities.

(a) **Brevity**

Brief and simple mission statements are **easy to understand** and remember - they are also evidence of clear thinking. For example, the Girl Scouts' mission statement is 'To help a girl reach her highest potential'. It is short, simple, easy to understand and easy to remember.

(b) **Flexibility**

Flexible mission statements can last a long time. For example, 'ensuring an adequate supply of water' is inflexible and confining; it may not survive the next dry season. By contrast, the Macintosh Division's mission statement was: 'To improve the creativity and productivity of people'. It was flexible enough to accommodate a computer and peripheral products such as laser printers, software, books and training.

(c) **Distinctiveness**

Distinctive mission statements **differentiate** your cause from other organisations with similar missions.

2.13 Ideally a strong mission statement is a powerful tool to help enable an organisation to change to become more **market-orientated.** Mission should define the **products or services** a business offers and therefore its competitive position. It should also define the **competencies** by which the business hopes to prosper, and therefore its **method of competing**.

Marketing at Work

Evaluate the following mission statements against Kawasaki's three criteria.

Glaxo 'is an integrated research-based group of companies whose corporate purpose is to create, discover, develop, manufacture and market throughout the world, safe, effective medicines of the highest quality which will bring benefit to patients through improved longevity and quality of life, and to society through economic value.'

IBM (UK): 'We shall increase the pace of change. Market-driven quality is our aim. It means listening and responding more sensitively to our customers. It means eliminating defects and errors, speeding up all our processes, measuring everything we do against a common standard, and it means involving employees totally in our aims'.

Matsushita: 'The duty of the manufacturer is to serve the foundation of man's happiness by making man's life affluent with an inexpensive and inexhaustible supply of life's necessities.'

Komatsu: 'Encircle Caterpillar.' (*Note*. Caterpillar is a competitor)

Apple Computer: 'Our goal has always been to create the world's friendliest, most understandable, most useable computers - computers that empower the individual ... Our mission is to transform the way people do things by focusing on their experience with our computers. We believe the innovation and creativity of a person's work depends directly on the quality of his or her total experience, not just on the speed of a microprocessor.'

PROBLEMS WITH MISSION	
Problem	**Comment**
Ignored in practice	The inherent danger of mission is that it will not be implemented.
Public relations	Sometimes, of course, mission is merely for public consumption, not for internal decision making.
'Post hoc'	Mission does not drive the organisation, but what the organisation actually does is assumed to be a mission.
Too general	'Best', 'quality', 'major': is just a wish list.

2.14 Certain goals which organisations pursue may undermine mission, because mission becomes subordinate to them. These include the following.

Goal	**Comment**
Survival	Individuals benefit from the organisation's existence (as their employer, for their social life), irrespective of what the organisation actually does. There is a strong incentive for an organisation to survive simply because it keeps its managers in work.
Efficiency	This is the greatest benefit for a given cost. However, an organisation can be efficient (doing things well) as opposed to being effective (doing the right things).
Control	Organisations try 'to exercise some control over their own environments'.
Growth, sometimes	Managers benefit directly from growth, in terms of salaries and status. 'Growth is the natural goal of the manager' as it reduces vulnerability to the environment and other organisations.

2.15 These goals are inter-related: growth can bring efficiency. Of course, growth often does benefit shareholders and fulfils the mission, but not always.

Enforcing mission

2.16 Mission can be enforced in the following ways.

(a) **Formal imposition**

Powerful persons or groups with power can impose their idea of the mission on others.

(b) **Shared values**

A professional organisation (eg a hospital) might pursue mission as part of the professional ethics of the organisation's members.

(c) **Value system and culture**

The organisation with a strong ideology (eg a religious sect) has a strong sense of mission.

3 Commercial goals and objectives   Specimen paper

Key Concept

Objectives are normally quantified statements of what the organisation actually intends to achieve over a period of time.

3.1 Objectives are important for the following reasons.

(a) Objectives **direct the activities** of the organisation towards the fulfilment of the organisation's mission, in theory if not always in practice.

(b) In business organisations, a paramount consideration is **profitability**. The mission of a business, whether this is stated or not, must be to carry on its activities at a profit.

(c) Objectives can also be used as standards **for measuring the performance** of the organisation and departments in it.

Corporate and unit objectives

3.2 **Corporate objectives** concern the firm as **a whole**, for example:

- Profitability
- Market share
- Growth
- Cash flow
- Return on capital employed
- Risk
- Customer satisfaction
- Quality
- Industrial relations
- Added value
- Earnings per share

3.3 Similar objectives can be developed for each **Strategic Business Unit (SBU)**.

Key Concept

A **Strategic Business Unit** is a part of the company that for all intents and purposes has its own distinct products, markets and assets.

[handwritten: yeah]
[handwritten: SBTUB]
[handwritten: The Strategic Business Unit is a part of the company that for all its purposes uses its own markets products]

3.4 **Unit objectives** are objectives that are specific to individual units of an organisation.

[handwritten: good examples to compare public to private]

EXAMPLES OF OBJECTIVES	
Commercial	■ Increase number of customers by x% (sales)
	■ Increase market share by x% (sales)
	■ Derive 5% of revenues each year from new products (sales, research and development)
	■ Reduce number of rejects by x% (production)
	■ Organise annual appraisals for all staff (human resources)
	■ Inform all staff of new regulations (training)
	■ Provide monthly reports within x days (management accounting)
Public sector	■ Introduce x more places at nursery schools (education)
	■ Reduce response times to calls (ambulance, fire service)

Trade-off between objectives

3.5 When there are several key objectives, some might be achieved only **at the expense of others**. For example, a company's objective of achieving good profits and profit growth might have adverse consequences for the cash flow of the business, or the quality of the firm's products.

3.6 There will be a **trade-off** between objectives when strategies are formulated, and a choice will have to be made. For example, there might be a choice between the following two options.

Option A
- 15% sales growth
- 10% profit growth
- £2 million cash outflow
- Reduced product quality
- Reduced customer satisfaction

V

Option B
- 8% sales growth
- 5% profits growth
- £¹/₂ million cash inflow
- Same product quality
- Same customer satisfaction

3.7 If the firm chose option B in preference to option A, it would be trading off sales growth and profit growth for better cash flow, product quality and customer satisfaction. The long-term effect of reduced quality has not been considered.

Long-term and short-term objectives

3.8 Objectives may be long-term and short-term. A company that is suffering from a recession in its core industries and making losses in the short term might nevertheless continue to have a long-term objective of achieving a steady growth in earnings or profits. However in the short term its primary objective might be survival.

Primary and secondary objectives

3.9 Some objectives are more important than others. There is a **primary corporate objective** and other **secondary objectives** which are strategic objectives which should combine to ensure the achievement of the primary corporate objective.

    (a)   For example, if a company sets growth in profits as its primary objective, it will then have to develop strategies by which this primary objective can be achieved.

    (b)   Secondary objectives might then be concerned with sales growth, continual technological innovation, customer service, product quality, efficient resource management (eg labour productivity) or reducing the company's reliance on debt capital etc.

Alternative primary objectives   6/00

3.10 The primary objective for a company must be a financial objective based on earning profits, but there are different ways of expressing such an objective in quantitative terms.

Profitability

3.11 A company must make profits, but **profitability** on its own is not satisfactory as an overall long-term corporate objective.

    (a)   It **fails to allow** for the size of the **capital investment** required to make the profit.

    (b)   Since capital is often in restricted supply, **profitability** must be measured in terms of the scarce financial resources that a company will have at its disposal.

    (c)   Shareholders, as a group, should be interested in **maximising profits over time**, not short-term current year profits. In order to maximise profits over time, costs will have to be incurred today in order to generate returns in the future.

3.12 Another way of analysing productivity is by **value added**. The primary measure is the difference between revenue and the cost of bought-in materials and services. The value added is distributed to **employees** (as wages) **government** (as taxes), and **shareholders** (as dividends).

Return on capital employed (ROCE) or return on investment (ROI)

3.13 Some companies use an accounting ROCE as a prime objective. This measures the profit as a percentage of the investment (capital employed) needed to make the profit.

3.14 There are drawbacks in using ROCE.

    (a)   Capital employed is notoriously **suspect** as a financial measure.

    (b)   If ROCE were used, the company would find it difficult to balance short-term results against long-term requirements.

    (c)   The choice of ROCE as an objective also ignores the **risk of investments**. High risk projects might promise a high return if they succeed, but it may be safer to opt for a project with a lower return but a greater guarantee of success.

3.15 Ansoff suggested that return on capital employed should be the overall corporate objective, over the next 3 to 10 years, when forecasts can be made with reasonable accuracy. Beyond this period Ansoff suggested a **variety of long-term objectives** be pursued because they are more easily measurable and contribute towards the overall return.

EPS and dividends

3.16 **Earnings per share or dividend payments** are both measures which recognise that a company is owned by its shareholder-investors and the purpose of a company is the provision of a **satisfactory return** for its owners.

3.17 The main disadvantage of using EPS as an objective is that earnings and dividends do not relate shareholder profit or revenue to the amount of money invested by the shareholders. The shareholder is concerned with the **size** of the **return** he gets, but also with the **size** of the **investment** he must make to achieve the return.

Survival

3.18 **Drucker** suggested that the prime objective of a company is not simply financial, but is one of survival. He argued that there are five major areas in which to decide objectives for survival.

(a) A company needs to **anticipate** the **social climate** and economic policy in those areas where the company operates and sells. A business must organise its behaviour in such a way as to survive in respect to both.

(b) A business is a **human organisation** and must be designed for joint performance by everyone in it.

(c) Survival also **depends on** the **supply of** an economic product or service.

(d) A business must **innovate**, because the economy and markets are continually changing.

(e) Inevitably, a business must be **profitable** to survive.

Growth

3.19 It is arguable that a company should make growth its prime objective - growth in EPS, growth in profits, growth in ROCE or growth in dividends per share. There are some difficulties however, in accepting growth as an overall objective.

(a) **Growth of what**? 'Balanced growth' might be applicable in the short term. However, in the long run, some elements must be expected to grow faster than others because of the dynamics of the business environment.

(b) In the long run, growth might lead to **diseconomies of scale** so that inefficiencies will occur and the growth pattern will inevitably stagnate. The idea that a company must grow to survive is no longer widely accepted.

(c)   There is little reason why in theory companies should not pay all their earnings as **dividends** and have no growth. A practical consequence of such a policy would be that if no money was reinvested in the business, it would be overtaken by competitors.

(d)   **Growth is**, however, in the **interests** of **management** as it provides them with a career.

3.20   Growth is likely to be a prime objective for the following types of company.

(a)   Smaller companies since these will usually have a **greater potential** for significant rates of growth.

(b)   Larger companies which are seeking to achieve a **size** which will enable them to **compete** with other multinationals in world markets. Very big companies will probably only achieve significant growth through takeovers or mergers, rather than through internal growth.

Other objectives and goals

3.21   An organisation's leaders should also be formulating objectives for other aspects of their business, so that the strategic plans that are eventually made will conform to these objectives.

3.22   Goals for **products and markets** will involve the following type of decisions.

(a)   Whether the organisation wants to be the **market leader**, or number two in the market, or whatever

(b)   Whether the **product range** needs to be **expanded**. Whether the organisation relies too heavily on one product or one market

(c)   Whether there should be an **objective** to **shift position** in the market - eg from producing low-cost standard items for the mass market to higher-cost and higher-priced specialist products for individual segments of the market

(d)   Whether there should be a **broad objective** of modernising the product range or extending the organisation's markets

3.23   Goals for the **organisation structure** are particularly important for growing organisations. When companies get beyond a certain size, the old organisation may cease to be efficient.

Influences on objectives

3.24   Having established what an organisation's objectives might be, we now need to consider what influences the choice of objectives.

3.25   Influences are both internal and external. Internal influences include what the organisation was established to do, its **objects** The **views and attitudes** of owners and senior managers will be key influences on establishing objectives. The **level of return** they will regard as sufficient and the **degree of risk** that they are prepared to run are particularly important. The level of **financial resources available** will also be a key early influence.

3.26   Early **external influences** will include **anyone** who is **interested** in the organisation. Their potential influence must be carefully evaluated, since the business may need to please them.

There may however be conflicts between the need to obtain a return for the owners of the business, and the need to please external **stakeholders**.

3.27 The **competitive environment** within which the organisation operates will also be a key influence on objectives. It will act as a constraint on the business over certain lengths of time. However, the business must be alert for changes in the environment which will imply changes in objectives, both in terms of **market changes** and **technological changes** that will improve the efficiency of the production process.

3.28 To gain a more detailed understanding of the influences on objectives, we need to consider how organisations can be viewed as systems, which is the subject of the next section.

Exam Tip

The Specimen Paper asked for comparison of the objectives pursued in the private sector with those pursued in the public sector.

4 The systems approach to organisations 12/02

Key Concept

A **system** is 'an organised or complex whole' or 'an entity which consists of interdependent parts'.

4.1 The systems approach to organisation defines the organisation as a type of system.

System objectives

4.2 An organisation generally exists for a purpose, to which its activities are directed. However, organisations might have many goals.

(a) Hospitals exist to **cure the sick**.

(b) Some organisations have multiple or even conflicting goals: are prisons supposed to **protect society** or **reform offenders**?

(c) Profit-orientated organisations' objectives will differ from non-profit orientated organisations' objectives

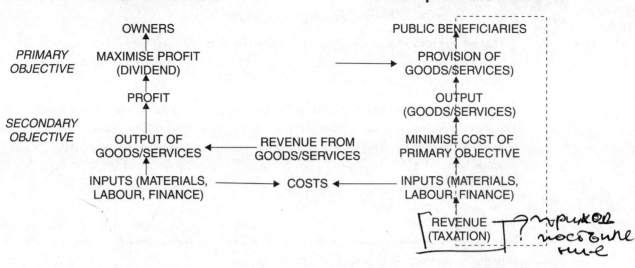

1. Profit orientated

2. Non profit-orientated

4.3 The differing objectives of systems will often be conflicting. Some form of **compromise** or **trade-off** between them must be reached. A system will not operate as efficiently as it should if these compromises are not reached in a satisfactory or optimal manner.

4.4 Restrictions on profit maximisation

- **Scarcity** of **key resources** such as cash or skilled labour
- **Technological constraints** limiting what goods and services can be produced
- **Economic constraints**
- **Political and legal constraints**
- **Responsibilities** towards society and for preserving the environment from pollution
- **Time**

The system boundary and the environment

4.5 Every system has a **boundary**, which defines what it is. The boundary will be expressed in terms of areas, or constraints that separate it from its environment. For example, a marketing department's boundary can be expressed in terms of who works in it and what work it does.

4.6 Anything which is external to a system belongs to the environment and not to the system itself. The environment exerts a considerable influence on the behaviour of the system; at the same time the system can rarely do much to control the behaviour of the environment.

Action Programme 1

If you were running a business, what factors in the business's environment might cause you particular concern?

4.7 In systems theory, a distinction is made between open and closed systems.

Key Concepts

A **closed system** is a system which is isolated from its environment and independent of it, so that no environmental influences affect the behaviour of the system, nor does the system exert any influence on its environment.

An **open system** is a system connected to a interacting with its environment. It takes in influences (or 'energy') from its environment and also influences this environment by its behaviour (it exports energy). An open system is a stable system which is nevertheless continually changing or evolving.

4.8 In practice, few systems are entirely closed. Many are **semi-closed**, in that the relationship with the environment is in some degree restricted.

4.9 The different types of system are described in the diagram below.

(a) **Closed system**

Shut off from its environment

(b) **Semi-closed system**

Predicted/controlled inputs from the environment → Relating to its environment in a controlled prescribed manner → Predictable/ controllable outputs

(c) **Open system**

Controllable inputs
Uncontrollable inputs
Unexpected inputs → Relating to its environment in both prescribed and uncontrolled ways → Both predictable and unpredictable outputs

4.10 On the other hand, social organisations such as businesses and government departments, are by definition **open systems**. Why? All social organisations are made up of human beings.

(a) Human beings participate in any number of social systems (family, friends), of which the work organisation is only one, although it is important.

(b) In most societies, human beings are exposed to a variety of influences from the social environment, such as advertising messages, family attitudes, government demands.

4.11 An organisation, or its management, might however try to limit the extent to which these external environmental influences are imported to the organisation's smooth functioning. For example, as we have discussed, organisations like to standardise work for the sake of predictability.

4.12 Business systems have some of the operational features of a semi-closed system. The inputs to a nuclear power station are controllable, predictable (uranium), as (we hope!) are its outputs (a steady supply of electricity).

Exam Tip

Open systems are particularly important in this paper.

Businesses as systems of transformation

4.13 In order to make profits businesses obtain **inputs** (resources) from the environment and transform them into **outputs** to the environment. The diagram below illustrates this process.

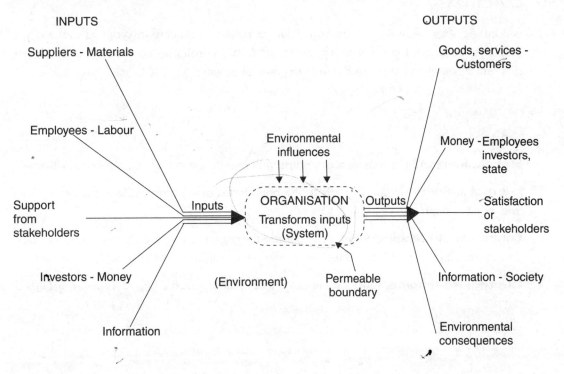

4.14 Inputs

- Materials, components and sub-components
- Labour
- Money
- Information and ideas
- Tangible property — *able to be touched clear and define*

4.15 Transformation processes

- Using people and machinery to make goods such as cars
- The provision of services (eg transport)
- The creation of knowledge to be more efficient

4.16 Outputs

- Goods and/or services
- Money (dividends, interest, wages)
- Information
- Environmental consequences of its activities (eg pollution, increased traffic)
- Social consequences of its activities

4.17 Sometimes this is known as the process of **adding value**. In other words the process of transformation ensures that the outputs are worth more in the customers' estimation than the inputs.

4.18 There are two points to note here.

(a) Customers **purchase value**, which they measure by comparing a firm's products and services with similar offerings by competitors.

(b) The business **creates value** by carrying out its activities either more efficiently than other businesses, or combined in such a way as to provide a unique product or service.

Stakeholders

4.19 For businesses, the motive of adding value to please customers in order to make a profit for investors seems clear cut. For many public sector organisations, the issue is not so clear cut, as different stakeholders exercise different degrees of power.

Key Concepts

Stakeholders are those people or groups with an interest in the organisation's activities.

Internal stakeholders exist **within** the boundaries of the organisation. They are employees and management.

Connected stakeholders are those outside the organisation, such as suppliers, customers and shareholders who have a direct interest in the organisation's activities.

External stakeholders include the state, local authorities, the public, pressure groups and so forth.

4.20 For many organisations, the principal stakeholders are diffuse. We shall discuss stakeholders in greater detail later in the Study Text.

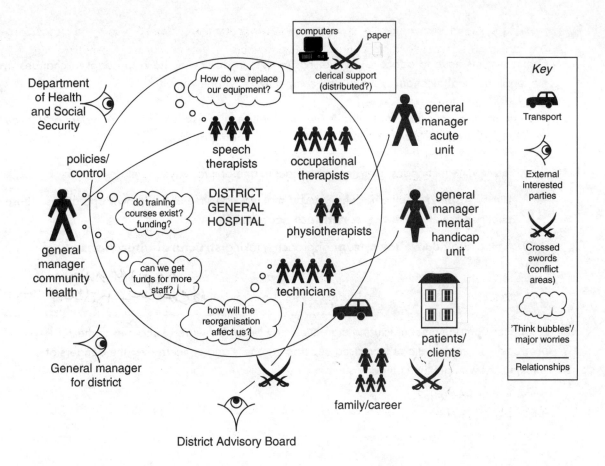

District Advisory Board

4.21 For now the diagram above illustrates the various elements of the system/organisation and the objectives of the people within it. (It is adapted from *Avison and Fitzgerald : Information System Methodologies*).

4.22 Note how certain objectives can come into conflict, for example the District Advisory Board's wish to re-organise facing opposition from technicians.

Subsystems

4.23 Every system can be broken down into **subsystems**. Separate subsystems interact with each other, and respond to each other by means of communication or observation. Subsystems may be differentiated from each other by:

- Function
- Space
- Time
- People
- Formality
- Automation

Action Programme 2

Demonstrate how each factor might have a major impact on organisational structure. For example, an organisation structured by function might have a production department, a sales department, an accounts department and a personnel department.

Adaptation

4.24 Social systems have to adapt to survive. Businesses, in particular, have to adapt to changes in the legal, political, economic, social and competitive environment.

4.25 If a system does not adapt and alter its own performance, it risks extinction. A system adapts by acquiring information about its environment and responding appropriately.

4.26 As the environment changes, a system may react in one of two ways.

(a) It may respond to external changes by making adjustments to its own operations. These changes are **short-term**, **functional** adaptations.

(b) It may also adopt a **long-term** approach, making **structural alterations**.

Action Programme 3

A tobacco company manufacturing cigarettes may become aware of changes in the environment symptomatic of increased health awareness and concern over the dangers of smoking. How might the company survive

(a) In the short term?
(b) In the long term?

Adapting to changes in inputs

4.27 Often, a business has to cope with changes in the input resources they consume. Frequently, such changes are **changes in costs**, relative to other costs.

Marketing at Work

In 1974 the price of oil quadrupled, and petrol prices and hence business costs went up. Various responses occurred.

- New oil fields were developed
- Cars were designed that used less petrol
- A number of ways of saving energy were invented

4.28 Other changes to inputs may be more long term, such as a slow increase in wages. To maintain competitiveness, firms will try and increase the efficiency with which labour is used, in order to minimise the impact of the cost rise.

Adapting transformation processes

4.29 Many firms have adapted the way they **transform inputs into outputs** to cut costs, and to use resources more efficiently, in the light of competitive pressures. Such changes include:

- Machinery and technology
- The use of information technology

■   A change in management structures

Business process re-engineering

4.30 Fundamental changes to systems design have been suggested by **business process re-engineering**.

Key Concept

Business process re-engineering (BPR), also known as **process innovation** and **core process re-design**, is the introduction of radical changes in business processes to achieve breakthrough results in terms of major gains in levels of performance plus reductions in costs.

4.31 The chief BPR tool is a clean sheet of paper. Re-engineers start from the future and work backwards. They are unconstrained by existing methods, people or departments. In effect, they ask, 'If we were a new company, how would we run the place?' Hammer points out that 'At the heart of re-engineering is the notion of discontinuous thinking - of recognising and breaking away from the outdated rules and fundamental assumptions that underlie operations.'

Adapting outputs

4.32 In market economies, businesses are supposed to adapt to changing customer needs, and even to anticipate them. Businesses and all organisations often have to adapt what they produce, in order to continue to add value for the customer. Any advertisement stating 'new, improved' is an example. We discuss the factors that cause customer needs to change in later chapters.

Value of the systems approach

4.33 Systems theory can be used to demonstrate how organisations can be managed, and how marketing enhances the organisation.

(a)   **Environment**

Systems theory emphasises the impact of **environmental factors** on a system. Customer needs are of particular importance.

(b)   **Dynamic factors**

Systems theory emphasises the **dynamic** aspects of organisation and what causes its sub-systems to develop.

(c)   **Relationships**

System theory focuses on **inter-relationships** between marketing and other departments, and between the organisation and its environment. It also may demonstrate how other parts of the organisation **(sub-systems)** pursue goals that are in conflict with those of marketing.

(d) **Feedback**

Marketing can give feedback on **outcomes** which enable management to compare them with objectives. These mean that management are less likely to take a simple A always causes B approach to marketing.

(e) **Appeal**

Systems theory has **imaginative appeal**. It is possible to draw the analogy between living systems and organisations (the 'organic analogy') and make some assumptions about how organisations are likely to behave on that basis. The analogy provides a framework for thinking about the organisation and designing its structure.

5 The contingency approach to organisations

5.1 **Contingency theory** holds that there is no universally best organisation structure, but that there could well be a best structure for each individual organisation, which will depend on **contingent factors** such as those below.

(a) **Age**

The older the organisation, the more **formalised** its **behaviour**. Work is repeated, so is more easily formalised. Organisation structure reflects the **age** of the **industry's** foundation.

(b) **Size**

The larger the organisation the more **elaborate** and **bureaucratic** its structure, the **larger** the **average size** of the units within it and the more **formalised** its behaviour (for consistency).

(c) **Technology**

The **stronger the technical system** the more **formalised** the work, and the more bureaucratic the structure of the operating core. We discuss technology below. The more **sophisticated** the technology, the more **elaborate** and **professional** the support staff will be (eg specialists who understand it).

(d) **Geographical dispersion**

An organisation on a single site will be organised differently from one in which there are several geographically separated units.

(e) **Personnel employed**

Formalisation, bureaucracy might be needed for a large, low-skilled work-force.

(f) **The environment**

(g) **The type of activities**

(h) **The business strategy**

(Mnemonic, using words in bold above: AS Ten Green PEAS)

The environment

5.2 The environment is a key contingency influencing organisation structure. Environmental uncertainty can arise from whether the environment is:

(a)   **Stable** (changes slowly and predictably) or **dynamic** (changes often, rapidly and unpredictably eg rapid technological innovation, consumer fashion)

(b)   **Simple** (relatively few environmental factors influencing what the organisation does) **or complex** (the firm is subject to many influences)

5.3   **Uncertainty in different industries.** Lawrence and Lorsch researched firms in three industries, plastics, industry foods and containers.

	Plastics	Industry foods	Containers
Environmental uncertainty	High	Moderate	Low
Degree of differentiation	High	Moderate	Low

5.4   Lawrence and Lorsch also argued that different departments in an organisation faced different levels of uncertainty. They investigated three divisions **within** each of the organisations under consideration (marketing, production and R&D – research and development). The degree of **environmental uncertainty** was found to differ between the divisions.

	Research & Development	Marketing	Production
Environmental uncertainty	High	Moderate	Low
Formality	Low	High	High
Time horizon	Long	Short	Short

5.5   Lawrence and Lorsch investigated how organisations coped with these contingencies. They identified two forces.

(a)   **Uniformity** is where all parts of the organisation operate in a **broadly similar** way. The same type of people are appointed ('So-and-So fits in'). Standard procedures are applied across the whole organisation.

(b)   **Diversity** means that different parts of the organisation behave in different ways. This is caused by the greater readiness of individuals to identify with **smaller work groups** than with an entire organisation, and the desire of subordinates to have more authority.

DIVERSITY

Goals   Time horizons   Decentralisation   Delegation   Formality   Interpersonal behaviour

group chosen to represent others

5.6   Lawrence and Lorsch referred to the degree of differentiation and integration.

(a) **Differentiation**

This is the degree to which the tasks and the work of individuals, groups and units are divided, **and** the degree to which there is a 'psychological distance' between managers in different departments.

(b) **Integration**

This is the quality of collaboration between departments.

5.7 Clearly, a highly differentiated organisation requires **integration devices** to function effectively. These include **committees,** liaison personnel, imposition of core values, and so on. The marketing department's role as an integration device is discussed in the next section.

6 Marketing and other functions

6.1 The marketing orientation is a philosophy of a business. Therefore it **cannot be restricted** to the people in the marketing department.

6.2 Typically, **marketing personnel** are responsible for:

- Researching customers' needs
- Assisting in the design of the product
- Suggesting a suitable pricing strategy
- Promotion: advertising, public relations etc
- Distribution: identifying how the product should be distributed
- Customer service: specifying service levels

6.3 These activities also involve other departments. In effect, the marketing department in a marketing orientated firm should:

- Champion the customer in the organisation
- Promote the organisation to the customer

6.4 **Involvement of other business functions in marketing**

Department	Activity
Finance	Credit terms
	Dealing with customers – invoicing payment
Production	Product manufacture; delivery times; quality
Human resources	Customer care training

Marketing and business orientation

6.5 The precise role of marketing will depend on the way the business is orientated.

(a) **Functional orientation**

If the business has a **functional** orientation, it will mean it is organised on the basis of **specialist roles**. The production function will be geared to producing products at low cost or on the basis of certain well-defined features. The key functions are likely to be finance and technical/design and marketing is likely to play only a small role. For businesses to be able to do without marketing, the demand for the product will probably have to exceed supply significantly.

Important

(b)   **Sales orientation**

A **sales** orientation involves an emphasis on the activities of **selling and promotion**. Rather than being based on function, this sort of organisation may be based on products with product managers managing specific products and developing skills in relation to promotion, pricing and distribution. The problem may be however that marketing may be merely a support function to sales, with little emphasis being placed on the needs of the customer. *no long term customer satisfaction*

(c)   **Marketing orientation**

A **marketing** orientation means the primary purpose is to fulfil the **customer's needs** and so maximise sales in this way rather than maximising sales by focusing on the mechanics of the selling process. The marketing department is obviously a key function in this kind of organisation, but the whole organisation has to be marketing orientated and to work towards the customer's needs. This has certain implications for the way the business is organised.

- Marketing involvement in senior management
- Delegation of decision-making to staff in contact with the customer
- Strong communications and information systems
- An emphasis on customer service in training and assessment

How to change the organisation's orientation

6.6   Marketing will have a significant role if the organisation is to change towards a marketing orientation. However change may be difficult, as **changes** in **missions** and **objectives** must be reflected in changing the way the entity is organised.

(a)   **Departmental differences**

Departmental goals may **conflict**, for example research and development's objective to develop new products may be ranged against production's objective of cost limitation.

(b)   **Timescale**

Marketing will also be aware that the **timescale** each department perceives as important will **differ**; the need for a few years work to break into particular markets will have to be considered against the desire of financial management for maximisation of short-term profits.

(c)   **Formality**

Differences in the degree of **formality** of departmental organisations may lead to internal culture clashes, for example the idea that only certain members of a department are permitted to deal directly with other departments. However a change in orientation will demand a significant degree of co-operation between departments.

6.7   To overcome these problems, **leadership** will be required from the most senior people within the organisation, and also **clear statements** of, *and* **emphasis** upon, the **mission** and **objectives** of the organisation. Marketing will have input into these and may play a proactive role itself in other ways: *clear statement of the importance upon the mission and objectives*

(a)   **Providing information**

Marketing can publicise the extent to which the organisation's objectives have translated into better performance in the markets and the problems which have been encountered.

draw out strength

(b) **Facilitating liaison**

For example, marketing can set up a system of departmental contacts, also running projects which involve a number of different departments.

(c) **Undertaking work**

For example, marketing can carry out SWOT analyses (see chapter 16) and provide a sounding board for how proposed changes will be perceived in the market.

(d) **Provision of training**

Training can cover issues such as telephone technique, and the presentation of areas that the customers see in the course of business.

These are all key aspects of a marketing department's **internal marketing**, the way it markets itself to other departments.

Exam Tip

The topics discussed in this section are important for exam purposes. You may be asked about the objectives of the marketing department, and how compatible they are (or how they conflict!) with those of the organisation.

Chapter Roundup

- A mission can contain both the organisation's values and its overwhelming commercial imperatives. It is sometimes embodied in a **mission statement**.

- Mission could be said to include four elements.

    - Purpose (why a company exists)
    - Strategy (commercial logic)
    - Values (basic beliefs and moral principles)
    - Policies and standards of behaviour

- **Objectives** might be included in the mission statement, depending on the type of mission statement used, but may be subsidiary to it.

- Objectives can be **corporate** and **unit, primary** and **secondary**, and **long-term** and **short-term**.

- The **systems approach to organisations** defines an organisation as a type of system, an **open, semi-closed** or **closed system**.

- The **contingency approach to organisations** holds that there is no universal best structure for organisations. What is best for an individual business will be dependent upon **contingent factors** (age, size, technology, dispersion, personnel, environment, activities, strategy).

- Marketing's role within an organisation will depend upon the organisation's **orientation** (functional, sales or marketing).

Quick Quiz

1   Which of the following is not a characteristic of mission?

    A   Rationale for existence
    B   General statement of future aims
    C   Long-term strategic direction
    D   Values

2   What are the four elements of mission?   *purpose strategy values policies and standards*

3   Which of the following would normally be contained in a mission statement?

    (A)   Nature of the business
    (B)   Methods of competition
    C   Financial targets
    (D)   Principles of business

4   Give six examples of corporate objectives.

5   *Fill in the blank*

    ...*System*........... is an organised or complex whole or an entity that consists of interdependent parts.

6   The outputs from an open system may be both predictable and unpredictable.

    True   ☑

    False   ☐

7   What is the difference between internal and connected stakeholders?

8   A marketing-orientated business emphasises the activities of sales and promotion

    True   ☐

    False   ☑

Internal stakeholders are those within the company eg employees, management. Connected stakeholders are those that have an interest in the company but are outside the boundary of that company.

Action Programme Review

1   (a)   The number of competitors in the marketplace and the strategies they adopt

        (b)   The products of competitors; their price and quality

        (c)   The strength of the domestic currency of the organisation's country of operation

        (d)   The structure of company and personal taxation

        (e)   Policies adopted by the government or ruling political body

        (f)   Social attitudes: concern for the natural environment

        (g)   The regulatory and legislative framework within which the company operates

2   (a)   Functional departments might include production, sales, accounts and personnel.

        (b)   Differentiation by space might include the geographical division of a sales function (subsystem) into sales regions (sub-subsystems).

        (c)   A production system might be subdivided into three eight-hour shifts.

        (d)   The hierarchy may consist of senior management, middle management, junior (operational) management and the workforce.

        (e)   There may be a formal management information system and a 'grapevine'.

        (f)   Some systems might be automated (sales order processing, production planning),while others may be 'manual' (public relations, staff appraisal).

3   (a)   In the short term the company may increase production of low tar brands or reduce the price of high tar brands.

        (b)   In the long term it may diversify into sectors that do not face threats from government.

Answers to Quick Quiz

1   B   A general statement of future aims is a company's vision.

2   ■   Purposes
     ■   Strategy
     ■   Values
     ■   Behaviour standards

3   A, B and D. C is wrong; a mission statement would not be quantified in this way.

4   Any six of:

     ■   Profitability
     ■   Market share
     ■   Growth
     ■   Cash flow
     ■   Return on capital employed
     ■   Risk
     ■   Customer satisfaction
     ■   Quality
     ■   Industrial relations
     ■   Added values
     ■   Earnings per share

5   A system.

6   True.

7   Internal stakeholders exist within the boundaries of the organisation (employees, managers)

     Connected stakeholders are those outside the organisation who have a direct interest in its affairs (suppliers, customers, shareholders).

8   False. A business with a **sales** orientation emphasises selling and promotion.

Now try illustrative questions 3 and 4 at the end of the Study Text

The marketing environment and change

3

Chapter Topic List
1 Setting the scene
2 The marketing environment
3 Environmental complexity and dynamism
4 Coping with change
5 Resistance to change

Learning Outcomes

☑ Explain the main elements of an organisation's marketing environment and discuss the significance of current and future environmental challenges

☑ Describe the interaction between the main elements of the marketing environment

☑ Appreciate the nature of environmental change in the various environments in which an organisation operates

☑ Understand the main features of environmental conditions such as turbulence, complexity and dynamism

Syllabus References

☑ Demonstrate the dynamic and complex nature of environmental change and its importance to the development of marketing strategy and planning

☑ Appreciate the potential significance of emerging environmental challenges to effective marketing in the present and future

Key Concepts Introduced

- ■ Environmental complexity
- ■ Turbulence
- ■ Environmental dynamism

1 Setting the scene

1.1 This chapter provides an introduction to the challenges that anyone involved in marketing is likely to face in the future, and how best to respond to those challenges.

1.2 In order to appreciate the impact of what the future may hold, we need to discuss the importance of change, and how best to respond to change. We focus first on the concepts of economic complexity and dynamism, and also turbulence which provide a guide on how to consider environmental changes.

1.3 Change can be very traumatic for certain people and resistance to change may well occur. In Section 4 of the chapter we consider how resistance to change happens.

2 The marketing environment

2.1 An organisation must **understand its environment** if it is to exploit changing market conditions and **target** its market successfully, the essence of a successful marketing strategy.

2.2 The **micro environment** includes all factors which impact directly on a firm and its activities in relation to a particular market in which it operates, and also any internal aspects of the organisation which influence the development of a marketing strategy.

2.3 The **macro environment** is concerned with broad trends and patterns in society as a whole which may affect all markets, but will be more relevant to some than others. Careful monitoring of the macro environment can enable an organisation to identify opportunities for and threats to its business and will enable it to adopt a proactive rather than a reactive approach in the action it takes.

2.4 The macro environment is large and complex. We shall look later in this Text in some detail at the ways in which **economic** factors, at home and abroad, **social** and **cultural** factors within families and larger groups, and **legal** and **political** considerations, can all affect the marketing of goods and services.

2.5 Developments in **technology** are happening at an ever-increasing pace. The rapid appearance of completely new products, such as the digital camera, and the obsolescence of those previously thought essential, presents a special challenge to marketers. The Internet is also having a profound effect.

2.6 The marketing concept will undoubtedly be increasingly affected by **ecological** issues. In the past there was a tendency to regard business activities as antithetical to 'greenness', but now it is being recognised that the two are complementary, and that one of the key factors in future business success will be the **sustainability** of business activity. This refers to the idea that resources which are used up must be replaced.

3 Environmental complexity and dynamism 12/03

Exam Tip

The changing environment is stressed in the syllabus, and you must ensure you are up-to-date with major developments that affect the marketing environment. Questions 1 and 2 in December 2003 both highlighted the changing environment.

3.1 The environment is so varied that many organisations will find it difficult to map its effects on them. A problem is that the environment is uncertain. Johnson and Scholes contrast the concepts of environmental **complexity** and environmental **dynamism**.

Key Concept

Environmental complexity relates to the uncertainties and variety of factors which impact upon an organisation.

3.2 **Complexity** arises from three factors.

- **Variety** of influences
- **Knowledge** needed
- **Interconnectedness** of influences

Complexity

Key Concept

Environmental dynamism describes the ability of an economy to grow rapidly and smoothly without the need for intervention.

3.3 An economy which has high economic dynamism is likely to be driven by significant powerful forces such as expanding global demand, increased use of information technology or deregulation. A dynamic economy is reflected in a **high annual rate of growth** in national income, which is likely to be related to a rapid growth in households' discretionary incomes.

3.4 An assessment of the relative uncertainty of the environment might be called for, and any changes identified. **Historical perspectives** are useful if the environment is stable, but dynamic environments require a more future-oriented perspective, including changing business and marketing strategies to take advantage of dynamic conditions.

3.5 Businesses are likely to have to take the following steps to adapt to environments that are complex and dynamic.

(a) **Flexibility in business planning**

This may imply a simpler management structure because of the need for immediate communication of change.

(b) **Awareness of the risks inherent in environmental conditions**

This emphasises the importance of risk analysis and contingency planning being built into future business strategy.

Marketing at Work

Singapore is an example of a dynamic economy. Its GDP has grown by an annual rate of about 8% over the past couple of decades, way ahead of the West European average of about 2% pa. Evidence of Singapore's dynamism is seen in the country's rising trade surplus, strong currency and rapidly rising standards of living for its people. As well as being about economic outcomes, economic dynamism can refer to a state of mind in which the people and institutions of a country have a determination to achieve economic growth. The entrepreneurial attitudes of the Chinese community in Singapore have contributed significantly to the country's recent economic success.

Marketers have contributed significantly to Singapore's economic success. The country has a long tradition of deregulation, in which the country's entrepreneurs have had to compete in order to survive against competition. A very good example of marketers' contribution is found in Singapore Airlines which is very market-orientated in the importance which it attaches to understanding and satisfying air travellers' needs. The airline has achieved significant market-led growth and a high level of profits, and has won numerous awards for its high levels of customer service.

Action Programme 1

How complex do you think the situations below are?

(a) A new product has just been introduced to a market segment. It is proving popular. As it is based on a unique technology, barriers to entry are high. The product will not be sold outside this market segment.

(b) A group of scientists has recently been guaranteed, by an EU research sponsoring body, funds for the next ten years to investigate new technologies in the construction industry, such as 'smart materials' (which respond automatically to weather and light conditions). This is a multi-disciplinary project with possible benefits for the construction industry. A number of building firms have also guaranteed funds.

Turbulence

Key Concept

Turbulence might be described as the degree of volatility in the environment.

3.6 The international business environment is not static and turbulence can arise from a number of sources.

(a) Changing governments or political instability. **Other political problems** such as terrorism are also sources of turbulence.

(b) There may be **massive changes** in **regional balances of power**, as a consequence of economic growth.

(c) The end of the Cold War has resulted in a **resurgence** of **nationalist sectarian** conflicts (eg in Bosnia) but more stability in other areas (eg central America).

(d) Exchange rates are less determined by trade than before; instead the capital markets are **global**: 'when New York sneezes, London catches a cold'. The Asian crisis of 1997, in which many Asian currencies and shares fell sharply in value, is an example.

Exam Tip

For the exam you must keep in mind when considering change how organisations are going to cope with it.

4 Coping with change

4.1 A number of issues need to be addressed if businesses are to cope successfully with a changing environment.

(a) **Environmental intelligence**

Clearly the possession of relevant environmental intelligence is a great help to any business seeking to deal actively with its environment. Businesses need to consider the **variety of information sources used,** the **reliability of what's available** and (importantly) the **speed at which data is obtained.**

(b) **Forecasting change**

We consider the forecasting techniques businesses use in detail in Chapter 16. For now, businesses need to consider a variety of possible options, the **best and worst case situations,** as well as the outcome they consider to be most likely. Often as well they should construct a forecast or a range of forecasts using **different assumptions** about the rate of change of key factors. **Plans** made should reflect the **outcomes** forecast, and also the **uncertainties** identified during the forecasting process. If uncertainties are significant, plans for dealing with difficulties may be required.

(c) **Organising for change**

A number of commentators have stressed the need for businesses to undergo regular fundamental re-organisations, to be able to cope better with a changing environment. Increasingly decisions will have to be taken away from a centralised head office function and **lines of communication simplified**, to ensure information is passed quickly to where it is needed.

(d) **Marketing change**

Managers need to consider the **internal marketing of change**, how change is presented to employees.

Suggested approach	Comment
Tell	The **people**: clearly, realistically, openly
Sell	The **pressures** which make change necessary and desirable The **vision** of successful, realistically attainable change
Evolve	The people's **attitudes, ideas, capacity** to learn new ways
Involve	The **people** where possible in planning implementation

(e) **Promoting a culture of change**

This implies not just suggesting changes that need to be made because a changing environment is anticipated, but creating a more outward looking organisation which actively seeks **new products**, **markets**, **processes** and **ways to improve productivity**.

5 Resistance to change

5.1 Arthur Bedeian cites four common **causes** of resistance to change.

(a) **Self-interest**

If the **status quo** is perceived to be comfortable, or advantageous to the individual or the group.

(b) **Misunderstanding and distrust**

Opposition can occur if the reasons for, or the nature and consequences of, the change have not been made clear. This aggravates uncertainty and suspicion about the perceived threat. This may well be aggravated by imposition of change without consultation.

(c) **Contradictory assessments**

Different individuals' evaluations of the likely costs and benefits of some change. Resistance arises from individuals' perceptions of the undesirability of change.

(d) **Low tolerance of change itself**

Differences in tolerance of ambiguity, uncertainty etc. This may arise because of bad past experiences of change or because of lack of experience of change.

5.2 Reaction to proposed change may range from the following.

- **Acceptance** (whether enthusiastic espousal, co-operation or resignation)
- **Indifference** (usually where the change does not directly affect the individual,
- **Passive resistance** (refusal to learn)
- **Active resistance** (deliberate spoiling)

5.3 Resistance to change has a number of manifestations.

(a) Symptoms of workforce resistance to change include **working-to-rule, absenteeism**, go-slows, deliberate errors, sabotage.

(b) Customer resistance to change may be important **entry barriers** in a market with customers sticking with goods or suppliers that they are used to, or which have served them well in the past.

Action Programme 2

Think of a company you know something about. How has it changed over the past few years in relation to new technology? How might it have to change over the next few years?

Chapter Roundup

- To cope with the varying and changing environment, organisations need to be able to cope with **economic complexity** and **economic dynamism** (the ability of an economy to grow rapidly).

- **Turbulence** relates to the degree of instability in the environment. Current causes of turbulence include the political situation in the Middle East and the economic problems in America.

- Resistance to change can be due to **self-interest, misunderstanding, contradictory assessment** or **intolerance** of **change**.

- Both **customers** and **employees** may **resist change**.

Quick Quiz

1   *Fill in the blanks*

    The marketing environment consists of the ...MACRO... environment and the ...MICRO... environment.

2   Define environmental complexity. *Defines as the uncertainties and varieties of factors wich impact upon an organisation*

3   *Fill in the blank*

    Environ. Dynamizm describes the ability of the economy to grow rapidly and smoothly without the need for intervention.

4   What steps will businesses have to take to adapt to environments that are complex and dynamic?

5   What is turbulence? *Turbulence is the degree of volatility in the environment*

6   What are the four causes of resistance to change described by Bedeian?

7   Which of the following factors influence the degree of complexity in a environment?

    A   Variety of influences
    B   Knowledge needed
    C   Whether the influence are macro or micro
    D   Interconnectedness of influences

8   When change is introduced, managers may find that many staff are indifferent to them.

    True   ☐

    False   ☐

Action Programme Review

1   (a)   The environment is **simple**, as the product is only being sold in one market. The environment is **dynamic**, as the product is still at the introduction stage and demand might be predicted to increase dramatically.

    (b)   The environment is **complex**, but **stable**. The knowledge required is uncertain, but funds are guaranteed for ten years.

2   –

Answers to Quick Quiz

1   Micro and macro

2   Environmental complexity arises from the uncertainties and variety of the factors that impact on an organisation.

3   Environmental dynamism

4   ■   Flexibility in business planning
    ■   Awareness of the risks inherent in environmental conditions

5   The degree of volatility in an environment

6   ■   Self-interest
    ■   Misunderstanding and distrust
    ■   Contradictory assessments
    ■   Low tolerance of change

7   A, B and D

8   True. This is most likely to happen if the changes do not affect the staff.

Now try illustrative questions 5, 6 and 7 at the end of the Study Text

Part B

The micro environment

The micro environment

4

Chapter Topic List	
1	Setting the scene
2	Defining the micro environment
3	Collecting data
4	Environmental scanning
5	Published statistics
6	Bought in data
7	External databases and the Internet

Learning Outcomes

☑ Demonstrate an understanding of the organisation's micro environment

☑ Identify the main features of the micro environment within which an organisation operates

☑ Access relevant sources of information on the micro environment

☑ Appreciate the role of information communication technology in an organisation's strategy for dealing with its micro environment

Syllabus Reference

☑ Demonstrate an awareness of key internal and external sources of information on the micro environment

BPP PROFESSIONAL EDUCATION

Key Concepts Introduced

- The micro environment
- Primary data
- Secondary data
- Internal data
- External data
- Database
- Real-time system
- Online system
- Internet

1 Setting the scene

1.1 The next few chapters of this Text deal with the micro environment. In these chapters we shall be particularly concerned with how organisations analyse their micro environment, and who is concerned with what the organisation is doing.

1.2 Marketing is about **allocating resources**. For the organisation to get the maximum benefit from its limited resources, it needs to ensure that the goods and services it produces are not wasted. The role of marketing is to **identify** and **anticipate customer needs** and wants so that the operation can use its skills and other resources to satisfy them.

1.3 Before we discuss the different elements of an organisation's micro environment in depth, we shall look briefly at what the micro environment is, and then discuss how **different information sources** can provide intelligence about the micro environment.

2 Defining the micro environment — 12/02, 12/03

> ### Key Concept
>
> The **micro environment** comprises all those individuals and organisations that affect the operations of a business on a day-to-day basis.

2.1 The following groups are important influences on how successful a business is:

- Customers
- Suppliers
- Intermediaries
- Competitors
- Employees
- Shareholders

2.2 We might need to remind ourselves of some of the underlying relationships between an organisation and the other organisations in its environment.

2.3 We have already mentioned that a business must generate profits. However, Drucker tells us that in order to generate profits it is necessary to **'create a customer'**. *or a cushmer need!*

2.4 The **market economy** based on **capitalism** contrasts with the centrally planned economy in which the State controls production, as in Soviet Russia up to the 1980s for example. A feature of market economies is that many firms compete with each other to create a customer. This is a spur to innovation and marketing activities, which Drucker holds are the distinguishing characteristics of business organisation.

2.5   *Elements of the micro environment*

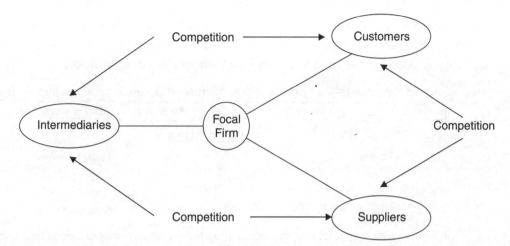

2.6   The diagram shows that the micro environment comprises not just those firms that an organisation **actually** does business with. It also includes those firms and individuals that an organisation could **potentially** do business with.

2.7   Therefore it includes not just our current customers, but potential customers who are probably currently being served by another organisation. Thus, an important element in understanding the micro environment is **competition** between organisations.

- ■   To get **customers**
- ■   To obtain **supplies**
- ■   To get access to the best **intermediaries**

2.8   In assessing competition, the various factors can be considered under these basic headings.

- ■   **Who are** the **competitors**, how strong are they?
- ■   What are the **characteristics** of the markets they compete in?
- ■   What are the **environmental influences** on the market?
- ■   How can the organisation maintain a **competitive advantage**?

2.9   For your *Marketing Environment* examination you need to have an understanding of the factors that affect the relationships between an organisation and its customers, suppliers and intermediaries. You need to know the basic factors that influence demand and supply.

Demand

2.10   Several factors influence the total market demand for a good. One of these factors is obviously its price, but there are other factors too. To help you to appreciate some of these other factors, you need to recognise that households buy not just one good with their money but a whole range of goods and services. The determinants of demand include:

- ■   The **price** of the good
- ■   The **price** of **other goods** (products and services)
- ■   The **size** of **households'** income
- ■   **Tastes** and **fashion**

- **Expectations**
- The **distribution** of **income** among households

Substitutes and complements

2.11 A change in the price of one good will not necessarily change the demand for another good. However, there are goods and services for which the market demand is inter-connected. These inter-related goods are referred to as either **substitutes** or **complements**.

(a) **Substitute goods** are goods that are alternatives to each other, so that an **increase** in the demand for one is likely to cause a **decrease** in the demand for another.

SUBSTITUTES

Coca Cola	V	Pepsi Cola
Tea	V	Coffee
Bus	V	Car
Terrestrial TV	V	Satellite TV

In this way the activities of competitors may have a major impact upon the demand for an organisation's products, even if the price and all other features of those products remain unchanged.

(b) **Complements** are goods that tend to be bought and used together, so that an *increase* in the demand for one is likely to cause an **increase** in the demand for the other.

COMPLEMENTS

Cups	Saucers
Bread	Butter
Cars	Components
Cars	Car servicing

Action Programme 1

If the ownership of domestic deep freezers increases, what do you think might happen to the demand for perishable food products? *the demand of frozen foods will increase*

Supply

2.12 The quantity supplied of a good depends, as you might expect, on prices and costs. More specifically, it depends on the following.

Price obtainable for the good	Prices of other goods	Cost of production	Changes in technology	Natural factors

SUPPLY

The micro and macro environments

2.13 In Part C of this Study Text we will look at the **macro environment**. You can distinguish the micro environment from the macro in terms of the directness of its effects.

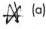 (a) The **micro** environment is about actual and potential transactions between a firm and its environment on a day-to-day basis.

 (b) The **macro** environment is about external forces which have a long-term impact upon the organisation's activities.

3 Collecting data

3.1 In sections 3 to 6 of this chapter we will discuss how marketing departments can make use of available data.

3.2 Data can be classified in various ways.

 Key Concepts

Primary data are data collected especially for a particular purpose, directly from the relevant source. Primary sources of consumer information, for example, would be the consumers themselves. Primary research is usually '**field research**', involving surveys, interviews, questionnaires, observation or experiments.

Secondary data are data which have already been gathered and assembled for other purposes or general reference. Secondary sources of consumer information would include published statistics and reports on consumer behaviour, books, Internet sites and so on. They are accessed by '**desk research**' which can often be carried out literally from the researcher's desk (given access to appropriate reference sources).

Internal data are data gathered within the organisation as a result of its operations, for example, information.

External data are data gathered from external sources, such as competitors' websites or government publications.

3.3 Desk research is the term used to describe the search for available data, usually as initial, exploratory research. Typical desk research activities include:

(a) Making use of **library sources**, such as journals, periodicals and recent academic books.

(b) Accessing the **organisation's information systems** and **records**, for information gathered by another department for a different purpose to the research in hand; internal data would include:

- **Production** data about quantities produced, materials and labour used etc
- Data about **stock**
- Data about **sales volumes**, analysed by sales area, salesman, quantity etc
- Data about **marketing** itself - ie promotion and brand data etc

- All **cost and management accounting data**
- **Financial management data** relating to capital tied up in stocks etc

(c) Tapping into industry internal **on-line databases**

(d) Buying in **data** and **reports prepared externally**, either as primary data for another organisation which is then syndicated, or as secondary data material for all users

Action Programme 2

Can you think of any limitations to desk research?

We shall discuss a systematic approach to developing an environmental information system in Part D of this Study Text. For now we shall list important sources of information that provide further details of the micro environment of a business.

4 Environmental scanning

4.1 Environmental scanning means keeping one's eyes and ears open to what is going on generally in the market place, especially with respect to competitors, and more widely in the technological, social, economic and political environment.

4.2 The result of environmental scanning is **market intelligence.** Its sources are:

- Financial newspapers, especially the *Financial Times* and the *Wall Street Journal*
- General business magazines, such as the *Economist* and *Business Week*
- Trade journals, such as *Campaign*
- Academic journals, such as *Harvard Business Review*
- Attending conferences, exhibitions, courses and trade fairs
- Making use of salesforce feedback
- Developing and making use of a network of personal contacts in the trade
- Watching competitors

Action Programme 3

Here is a small selection of headlines from *The Times* in the UK (5 August 2002)

(a) House prices show signs of slowdown
(b) Checks to make sure gold isn't tarnished
(c) Professions in insurance crisis

In each case, give examples of organisations that should think about the threats and opportunities that these stories indicate?

4.3 With regard to watching competitors, a **competitor intelligence system** needs to be set up to cope with a vast amount of data from:

- Financial statements
- Common customers and suppliers
- Inspection of a competitor's products
- The competitor's former employees
- Job advertisements

4.4 All this data needs to be compiled (eg clipping services, standard monthly reports on competitors' activities), catalogued for easy access, and analysed (eg summarised, ranked by reliability, extrapolating data from financial reports).

Action Programme 4

What information does your organisation hold on its competitors? How does it obtain that information? What does it use it for?

5 Published statistics

5.1 There is a wealth of published statistics which can be used by marketing departments. There are two prime sources - government and non-government.

5.2 The government is a major source of economic information and information about industry and population trends. Examples of UK **government publications,** many of which are available free online at **www.statistics.gov.uk**, are as follows.

(a) The **Annual Abstract of Statistics** contains data about manufacturing output, housing, population etc.

(b) The **Digest of UK Energy Statistics**.

(c) **Housing and Construction Statistics**. This is published quarterly.

(d) **Financial Statistics**.

(e) **Economic Trends**.

(f) **Census of Population**. The Office for National Statistics publishes continuous datasets including the **National Food Survey**, the **Household Survey** and the **Family Expenditure Survey**.

(g) **Census of Production** (annual). This has been described as 'one of the most important sources of desk research for industrial marketers'. It provides data about production by firms in each industry in the UK.

(h) **Department of Employment Gazette** (monthly) gives details of employment in the UK.

(i) **British Business**, published weekly by the Department of Trade and Industry, gives data on industrial and commercial trends at home and overseas.

(j) **Business Monitor**, published by the Business Statistics Office, gives detailed information about various industries.

(k) **Social Trends** is published annually.

5.3   Official statistics are also published by other government bodies such as the European Union, the United Nations and local authorities.

5.4   Non-government sources of information include the following.

(a)   Companies and other organisations specialising in the provision of economic and financial data (eg the **Financial Times** Business Information Service, the Data Research Institute, Reuters and the Extel Group)

(b)   **Directories and yearbooks**, such as Kompass or Kelly's Directory

(c)   **Professional institutions** (eg Chartered Institute of Marketing, Industrial Marketing Research Association, British Institute of Management, Institute of Practitioners in Advertising)

(d)   **Specialist libraries**, such as the City Business Library in London, collect published information from a wide variety of sources

(e)   **Trade associations**, trade unions and Chambers of Commerce

(f)   **Trade journals**

(g)   **Commercial organisations** such as banks and TV networks

(h)   **Market research agencies**

Action Programme 5

Most industries are served by one or more trade journals which can provide invaluable information on new developments in the industry, articles about competitors' products, details of industry costs and prices and so on.

Find out to what trade journals your organisation subscribes. Look through a number of them and note the type of information they contain and assess how that information may be used by both you and other members of your organisation.

6   Bought in data

6.1   The sources of data we have looked at so far have generally been free because they are in the public domain. Inexpensiveness is an advantage which can be offset by the fact that the information is unspecific and needs considerable analysis before being useable.

6.2   A middle step between adapting secondary data and commissioning research is the purchase of data collected by market research companies or business publishing houses. The data tend to be expensive but less costly than research.

6.3   There are a great many commercial sources of secondary data, and a number of guides to these sources are available.

- **The Blue Book** (ONS National Income and Expenditure)
- **Guide to Official Statistics**, The Stationery Office
- **Compendium of Marketing Information Sources**, Euromonitor
- **Market Search**

6.4 Commonly used sources of data on particular industries and markets include:

- Key Note Publications
- Mintel publications
- **Market Research GB**, Euromonitor

Exam Tip

Lack of knowledge of information sources is a very common weakness in exam scripts.

7 External databases and the Internet

Sources of information

7.1 As well as the paper-based sources of information described in the previous sections of this chapter, organisations can also use computer databases and, of course, access the Internet.

Key Concepts

A **database** is a collection of structured data. Any item of data can be used as the subject for enquiry.

A **real-time system** is a system where data is continually received and processed so that updating of data on the system is continuous and almost instantaneous.

An **online system** is a system that can be accessed by telephone at locations that are remote from the main computer.

7.2 The continual updating of real-time systems is of course their major advantage from the marketer's viewpoint. Up-to-date information about competitors and the general micro environment is readily available.

External databases

7.3 An organisation can obtain data from an **external database** operated by another organisation.

Online databases

7.4 Most external databases are online databases, which are very large computer files of information, supplied by **database providers** and managed by **host** companies. Access to such databases is open to anyone prepared to pay, and who is equipped with a personal computer plus a modem (to provide a phone link to the database) and communication software. These days an increasing number of companies offer free Internet access. Most databases can be accessed around the clock.

7.5 Providers of **database information** include the following.

- Directory publishers such as Kompass
- Market research publishers such as Mintel, Key Note and Frost & Sullivan
- Producers of statistical data, including the UK government and Eurostat
- Reuters Business Briefing
- FT Profile

7.6 As well as making information available, online searches can be **considerably more time-efficient** than searches of paper-based material. The structure of the database enables the user to access data quickly and to able to specify what data is required (for example, information about a specific competitor), rather than having to look through considerable amounts of paper-based data for little reward.

The Internet

Key Concept

The **Internet** is a world-wide network of powerful computers and telecommunications systems.

7.7 Internet usage has expanded considerably over the last few years with improved access and decreased cost. It is thought that in Britain use of the Internet is growing at between 10% and 15% per month.

7.8 Most companies of any size now have a site on the Internet available for access by customers or indeed competitors. A site is a collection of screens on the Internet providing information in text or graphic form.

7.9 The Internet is discussed in detail in Chapter 13. For now we shall mention briefly how according to Kotler, 'marketing is moving into . . . electronic marketing'.

(a) Buyers and sellers are communicating with each other over electronic devices, increasing the likelihood **of dialogue between seller and buyer** – after all, Internet websites can be **interactive**.

(b) Kotler suggests that customers can resort to Internet **'chat rooms to converse with other buyers** or owners about products and services in which they have an interest'. It cites an example when a group of customers clubbed together to negotiate a discount.

(c) The Internet will **increase the power of buyers,** by giving access to a larger number of suppliers, and information.

(d) Electronic marketing may pose a **threat to store-based retailing** particularly for those customers who prefer the extra convenience of home delivery.

Marketing at Work

The <u>CIM's website contains guidance</u> on creation of a business's website. The CIM emphasises the need for a strong purpose, identifying a target audience, ensuring you have sufficient internal resources to meet demand and careful site mapping.

Chapter Roundup

- An organisation's micro environment consists of itself and its current and potential **customers, suppliers** and **intermediaries**. The competition also has a key influence on the micro environment.

- There are various ways of **collecting data** about an organisation's micro environment.

Quick Quiz

1 Define the micro environment. *All those individuals and org. that affect the business on a day to day basis*

2 Who are the key constituents of the micro environment? *Customers suppliers Employees shareholders intermediaries competitors*

3 If the demand for a good goes up, the demand for a complement good will normally go down.

True ☐

False ☑

4 Match the following types of data with the description given.

(a) Primary data
(b) Secondary data
(c) Internal data
(d) External data

(1) Data gathered for general reference ⓓ
(2) Data gathered from within the organisation — ⓒ
(3) Data gathered directly for a particular purpose ⓐ
(4) Data gathered from sources maintained by others ⓑ

5 *Fill in the blank*

A database is a collection of *structured* data.

6 A system where data is continually received and processed so that updating of the data on the system is continuous and is almost instantaneous is called a:

A Direct-update system
B Online system
Ⓒ Real-time system
D Instant-update system

7 How else might competitors compete, other than over customers?

8 Give three examples of techniques that might be used in field research.

BPP
PROFESSIONAL EDUCATION

Action Programme Review

1   (a)   Domestic deep freezers and perishable products are complements because people buy deep freezers to store perishable products.

    (b)   Perishable products are supplied either as fresh produce (for example, fresh meat and fresh vegetables) or as frozen produce, which can be kept for a short time in a refrigerator but for longer in a freezer. The demand for frozen produce will rise (the demand curve will move to the right), while the demand for fresh produce will fall (the demand curve will move to the left).

    (c)   Wider ownership of deep freezers is likely to increase bulk buying of perishable products. Suppliers can save some packaging costs, and can therefore offer lower prices for bulk purchases.

2   The limitations of desk research are as follows.

    (a)   The data gathered is by definition not specific to the matter under analysis. It was gathered and prepared for another purpose and so is unlikely to be ideal.

    (b)   Because it was gathered for another purpose, the data are likely to require a fair amount of adaptation and analysis before they can be used.

    (c)   The data gathered are historical and may be some time out-of-date.

3   (a)   Property development companies, builders, mortgage providers, mortgage advisers, estate agents

    (b)   Gold and silver producers and buyers

    (c)   Accountants, solicitors, surveyors, insurance companies, insurance brokers, clients of professionals

It is a good idea to get into the habit of playing this game whenever you read a newspaper. One day you will spot a golden opportunity for your organisation that all competitors will miss.

4   –

5   –

Answers to Quick Quiz

1   The micro environment comprises all those individuals and organisations that affect the operations of a business on a day-to-day basis

2   ■   Customers
    ■   Suppliers
    ■   Intermediaries
    ■   Competitors
    ■   Employees
    ■   Shareholders

3   False. The demand for complements tends to rise or fall together.

4   (a)   (3)
    (b)   (1)
    (c)   (2)
    (d)   (4)

5   Structured

6   C   Real time system

7   Competitors may also compete to obtain supplies and gain access to the best intermediaries

8   Any three of:

    ■   Surveys
    ■   Interviews
    ■   Questionnaires
    ■   Observation
    ■   Experiments

Now try illustrative question 8 at the end of the Study Text

Stakeholders

5

Chapter Topic List
1 Setting the scene
2 The stakeholders of organisations
3 Internal stakeholders
4 Connected stakeholders
5 External stakeholders
6 The importance of stakeholders

Learning Outcomes

☑ Identify the various stakeholders that are interested in an organisation

☑ Appreciate the role of marketing in communicating with its publics

☑ Explain the importance of relationships between the organisation and its key stakeholders

☑ Assess stakeholder expectations

Syllabus References

☑ Describe the external and internal stakeholders that constitute the micro environment within which organisations operate and their importance to the marketing process

☑ Explain the nature of the interactions between the organisation and its various stakeholders

Key Concepts Introduced

- Stakeholders
- Internal stakeholders

- Connected stakeholders
- External stakeholders

1 Setting the scene

1.1 In this chapter we discuss the importance of those interested parties that can have an impact upon, and are affected by, an organisation's activities. These are its **stakeholders.**

1.2 We stressed in Chapter 4 the need for active analysis of the micro environment, and obviously stakeholder analysis is a vital part of this. Businesses need to understand.

- The **relative importance** of each stakeholder
- Their **actual** or **possible impact** upon the business
- Whether their **impact** is potentially positive, negative or neither
- The **interests** of each stakeholder group
- The **relationships** with each group of stakeholders
- How the business's **actions** affect stakeholders

Action Programme 1

Give four examples of an organisation's stakeholders.

Exam Tip

Be prepared to be asked about the stakeholders of a variety of organisations, not just businesses.

2 The stakeholders of organisations

Specimen paper, 6/03, 12/03

Key Concepts

Stakeholders are those people or groups with an interest in the organisation's activities.

Internal stakeholders exist **within** the boundaries of the organisation. They are employees and management.

Connected stakeholders are those outside the organisation, such as suppliers, customers and shareholders who have a direct interest in the organisation's activities.

External stakeholders include the state, local authorities, the public, pressure groups and so forth.

2.1 Very generally, a stakeholder can be understood as anyone who is affected by the decisions made by an organisation.

2.2 The diagram below illustrates the types of stakeholders an organisation might have.

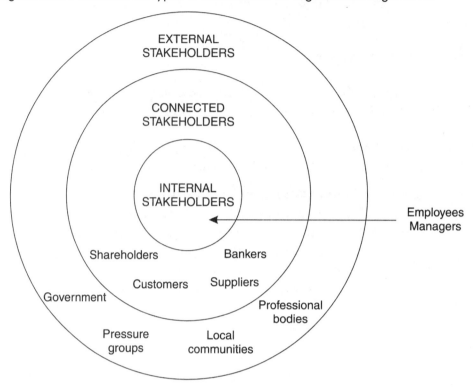

2.3 Stakeholder groups can exert influence on strategy. The greater the power of a stakeholder group, the greater its influence will be.

2.4 Each stakeholder group has different expectations about what it wants, and the expectations of the various groups will conflict.

2.5 There are two approaches to stakeholder theory for profit-orientated business organisations.

Strong view	**Weak view**
Each stakeholder in the business has a legitimate claim on management attention. Management's job is to balance stakeholder demands.	Satisfying stakeholders such as customers *is* a good thing - but only because it enables the business to satisfy its primary purpose, the long-term growth in owner wealth.

2.6 Problems with the strong stakeholder view

(a) Managers who are accountable to everyone are, in fact, **accountable to no-one**.

(b) Managers decide on the balance between different stakeholders - they will favour their own interests.

(c) It confuses a stakeholder's interest in a firm with a person's citizenship of a state.

(d) People have interests, but this does not give them rights.

2.7 A relationship in which **conflict** between stakeholders can be dramatic is that between managers and shareholders. The relationship can run into trouble when:

(a) Managers focus on maintaining the corporation as a vehicle for their managerial skills.

(b)   The shareholders wish to see radical changes to enhance their dividend stream and increase the value of their shares.

The conflict in this case can be seriously detrimental to the company's stability.

2.8   Shareholders may force resignations and divestments of businesses, while managers may seek to preserve their empire and provide growth at the same time by undertaking risky policies.

2.9   In practice an organisation's management may, consciously or unconsciously, do the following.

- **Identify who** their stakeholders are
- **Identify** their **respective importance**
- **Identify** their **power** (see below)
- **Assess how the business affects stakeholders**, and vice versa business
- **Identify stakeholders' interests**

2.10   How stakeholders relate to the management of the company depends very much on what type of stakeholder they are on the level in the management hierarchy at which they are able to apply pressure. Clearly a company's management will respond differently to the demands of, say, its shareholders and the community at large.

2.11   The way in which the relationship between company and stakeholders is conducted again is a function of the character of the relationship, the parties' **relative bargaining strength** and the philosophy underlying each party's objectives. This can be shown by means of a spectrum as follows.

Stakeholder mapping

2.12   Mendelow classifies stakeholders on a matrix whose axes are **power held** and **likelihood of showing an interest** in the organisation's activities. These factors will help define the type of relationship the organisation should seek with its stakeholders.

(a) **Key players** are found in segment D: strategy must be **acceptable** to them, at least. An example would be a major customer.

(b) Stakeholders in segment C must be treated with care. While often passive, they are capable of moving to segment D. They should, therefore be **kept satisfied**. Large institutional shareholders might fall into segment C.

(c) Stakeholders in segment B do not have great ability to influence strategy, but their views can be important in influencing more powerful stakeholders, perhaps by lobbying. They should therefore be **kept informed.** Community representatives and charities might fall into segment B.

(d) Minimal effort is expended on segment A.

2.13 Stakeholder mapping is used to assess the significance of stakeholders. This in turn has implications for the organisation.

(a) The framework of corporate governance and the direction and control of the business should recognise **stakeholders' levels** of **interest** and **power**.

(b) Companies may try to **reposition** certain stakeholders and discourage others from repositioning themselves, depending on their attitudes.

(c) Key **blockers** and **facilitators** of change must be identified.

2.14 Stakeholder mapping can also be used to establish **political priorities**. A map of the current position can be compared with a map of a desired future state. This will indicate critical shifts that must be pursued.

3 Internal stakeholders

3.1 Because employees and management (which includes the chairman and the board of directors) are so intimately connected with the company, their objectives are likely to have a strong and immediate influence on how it is run. Management and employees, key internal stakeholders, are interested in the following issues.

(a) **Organisation's continuation and growth**

The organisation is a place where management and employees spend a great deal of their time and energy. It pays them. Management and employees have a special interest in the organisation's continued existence.

(b) **Expectation and goals**

Managers and employees have certain **individual expectations** and goals which, it is hoped, can be harnessed, in part at least, to the goals of the organisation. These include security of income, interesting work and skills and career development.

3.2 The interests and expectations of internal stakeholders vary between cultures and change over time. In Japan, for example, a 'job for life' has until recently been accepted as a responsibility which organisations have held towards their workers. In the UK, employees are increasingly coming to expect short-term employment contracts, but expectations are rising in respect of such issues as mothers' rights to maternity leave.

3.3 Companies often face a dilemma in reconciling the needs of internal stakeholders with marketing needs. Providing crèche facilities for workers may satisfy the former but will it put the company at a price disadvantage in the market place?

3.4 On the other hand, satisfying the needs of internal stakeholders may actually help the **marketing effort**. Many enlightened work policies secure greater commitment and loyalty from workers. If the workforce is demotivated, a number of adverse consequences are possible.

- Low productivity
- High staff turnover leading to recruitment and training costs
- Increased militancy
- Presentation of a poor image to the customer, no 'happy smiling faces'

3.5 Many organisations are now practising what is called **internal marketing**. This applies the principles of marketing to employees as though they are internal customers. As with all external marketing, employers need to consider the diverse range of needs that employees seek to satisfy at work, and aim to meet them. Communication of a company's values are a key part of internal marketing.

Marketing at Work

United Biscuits' statement of responsibility to its employees:

'To achieve the dynamic morale and team spirit based on mutual confidence without which a business cannot be successful, people have to be cared for during their working lives and in retirement. In return we expect from all our staff loyalty and commitment to the company. We respect the rights and innate worth of the individual. In addition to being financially rewarding, working life should provide as much job satisfaction as possible. The company encourages all employees to be trained and developed to achieve their full potential.

United Biscuits takes a responsible attitude towards employment legislation and codes of practise, union activities and communications with staff. We place the highest priority on promoting and preserving the health and safety of employees. Employees, for their part, have a clear duty to take every reasonable precaution to avoid injury to themselves, their colleagues and members of the public.'

The Board of Directors: co-ordinating internal and some connected stakeholders

3.6 At the top of the chain of command in any organisation is a body of people with decision-making powers. A local council, a board of trustees or a board of directors all have powers delegated to them by another body - the voting population, the settlor and beneficiaries and the shareholders in each case respectively. The quality of this body's decisions is therefore subject to review but for practical purposes a board should 'run' the organisation.

3.7 In many UK companies, the Board provides both functions with **executive directors** who run the business, and **non-executive directors** who are supposed to keep watch on the shareholders' behalf. So, in theory, then the board is an institution combining internal and connected stakeholders. If it is not to be a rubber stamp for executive management, it must include non-executive directors with **real influence**.

4 Connected stakeholders

4.1 Connected stakeholders include the following.

Shareholders

4.2 Shareholders look for a **return** on their **investment**, whether in the short or long term. As shareholders own the business, this is a commercial organisation's prime objective (at least in the UK). Some shareholders are concerned with a corporation's ethical performance, hence the growth of investment funds designed to avoid certain companies.

4.3 Shareholder involvement, particularly institutional shareholder involvement, has been encouraged by the recent interest in **corporate governance** in many countries. Other reasons, particularly **large remuneration** for **directors**, have led to increased shareholder pressure. The most potent weapon shareholders have is to sell their shares, as the falling share prices that will result may encourage a takeover bid.

Bankers

4.4 Bankers and other financiers are also interested in a firm's overall condition, but from the point of view of the security of any loan they make. A bank is keen to minimise the risk of interest not being paid, or of its security being poor.

4.5 If financiers are unhappy, they can limit or withdraw credit facilities, and thus leave a business with insufficient funds to fulfil its objectives.

Suppliers

4.6 Suppliers will expect to be paid and will be interested in future business.

4.7 If the relationship with suppliers deteriorates because of a **poor payment record**, suppliers can limit or withdraw credit and charge higher rates of interest. They can also **reduce their level** of **service,** or even switch to supplying competitors.

4.8 Major suppliers will often be key stakeholders, particularly in businesses where **material costs** and **quality** are significant. Supplier co-operation is also important if organisations are trying **to improve their management of assets** by keeping stock levels to a minimum; they will need to rely on suppliers for reliability of delivery.

4.9 The position of suppliers will depend on the **level of competition** they themselves face. If supply arrangements appear to be complicated or are often disrupted, organisations may consider taking these arrangements in-house.

Distributors

4.10 The main interest of distributors are for **reliable supply, improvements in quality** and **support** on marketing. Distributors can stock **competing brands** and can delay payments for goods received.

4.11 **Problems with distribution arrangements** can also threaten sales.

4.12 As with suppliers, most businesses are seeking to **develop relationships** with their distributors. Not only does this assist businesses' asset management, distributors can enhance the product by the ways in which they sell it, and the after-sales service. They can also provide important **market intelligence**.

Consumers

4.13 Consumers have increasingly high expectations of the goods and services they buy, both from the private and public sectors. These include not just low costs, but value for money, quality and service support.

4.14 In theory, if consumers are not happy with their purchases, they will take their business elsewhere next time. The consumer is thus sovereign and if suppliers do not cater for their complex set of needs and expectations, they will lose business. With increasingly competitive markets, consumers are able to exercise increasing levels of power over companies as individuals.

4.15 More sophisticated analysis of consumer behaviour has also enhanced the importance of consumers. Dissatisfied customers are more likely to make their views known than satisfied customers. Moreover businesses now believe that normally the costs of retaining existing customers are **significantly less** than those of obtaining new customers. The implications of this will be discussed many times during your CIM studies.

4.16 Consumers are increasingly evaluating goods and services not just on the basis of how they will perhaps satisfy their immediate material needs, but also how they will satisfy their **deeper moral needs**. For example, a shopper may prefer one brand of baked beans not for its taste but because the manufacturer supports a good cause of which the consumer approves. Marketing managers must be alert to the ever-changing social concerns of buyers and seek to accommodate these within their marketing mix.

4.17 Organisations can respond to consumer concerns by having systems in place for dealing with customer comments and criticisms.

(a) **Customer panels** (focus groups) or visits to customers

(b) A written **customer services policy** (a customer charter)

(c) Giving staff in **contact** with **customers** the **authority** to deal with complaints or problems

(d) **Formal procedures** for dealing with **customer complaints** including staff dedicated to responding to comments or criticisms

Limitations of consumer power

4.18 It is however true that in a number of markets consumers do not have complete sovereignty over suppliers.

(a) **Lack of competition**

In many markets, **competition** is **very limited** and consumers cannot realistically take their business elsewhere. Even if there are large numbers of competitors, there may be little differentiation between products in respect of the moral concerns of consumers.

(b) **Limited knowledge**

Consumer sovereignty may also be limited by the **limited knowledge** that consumers have of a product. How many people are capable of fully evaluating the tangible qualities of CD players (let alone the moral and social credentials of their manufacturers)?

(c) **Unfair contracts**

Consumers have been subject to **unfair contracts**, as they do not have the resources to evaluate properly the choices put to them. For example, a consumer is often not in a position to judge the safety of one product as opposed to another.

(d) **Redress**

In the past, it has not always been easy for consumers to **get redress**. A large company is better able to absorb the costs of a legal action than an individual consumer.

4.19 In short, consumerism arose because in many FMCG (fast-moving consumer goods) industries, the bargaining power of the consumer is low.

4.20 Because of the limitations of consumer sovereignty described above, a number of means are available for the protection of consumers' wider interests. We shall discuss these in later chapters of this Text.

5 External stakeholders

5.1 External stakeholder groups – the government, local authorities, pressure groups, the community at large, professional bodies – are likely to have quite diverse objectives and have a varying ability to ensure that the company meets them.

(a) The **government** has an interest in tax revenue, compliance with legislation and required development.

(b) **Local authorities** are also interested, because companies can bring local employment and affect the local environment (eg by increasing road traffic).

(c) **Professional bodies** are interested to ensure that members who work for companies comply with professional ethics and standards.

(d) **Pressure groups** deal with a variety of issues.

Marketing at Work

Increasingly the stakeholders of charities are being given the rights to be consulted, and trustees must report on contacts with stakeholders. Recently the Charity Commission in the UK emphasised that trustees must state whether they have consulted stakeholders (major funders, members, beneficiaries and donors) about payments to trustees, and must also disclose the results of the consultation.

Many charities are of course proactive in communicating with stakeholders and have made efforts to explore a number of channels of communication. The anxiety disorder charity No Panic for example runs its support and recovery groups by teleconferencing.

Action Programme 2

A key document in communication with stakeholders is a charity's annual report. What do you think are the key elements in a charity's annual report?

5.2   The government at local and national level is a very important stakeholder and, **in theory** reflects the values of the people which it represents. Consider the following examples of the reasons why government bodies take an interest in the activities of commercial organisations.

(a)   The **spending patterns** of companies on capital equipment can have significant macroeconomic effects.

(b)   Government often looks to private companies to relieve it of **responsibilities**, eg in respect of the employment of disabled people.

(c)   A profitable business sector results in greater **tax collection potential** for governments.

5.3   The actions of organisations can affect the core social values of a culture. Consider the following examples.

(a)   Does **advertising** of luxury goods create a greater sense of alienation by poorer members of society who will never be able to afford them?

(b)   Does the use of **foreign languages** (eg American terms in England; English in France) threaten the cultural identity of a nation?

(c)   Do **newspapers** have a duty to represent the interests and views of all sections of society?

5.4   Strategies for dealing with different external stakeholders will vary. Businesses may find it easier to negotiate with an external stakeholder who has a number of interests than it would be to negotiate with one whose interest is only one issue. Local stakeholders may be best dealt with by local management, whereas stakeholders with national or international concerns may be best dealt with on a business-wide or even industry-wide basis.

Action Programme 3

Stakeholders can also be split up into primary and secondary stakeholders. What do you suppose would be the differences between the two groups?

6 The importance of stakeholders 6/03

6.1 We have discussed in this chapter the pressures that stakeholders can exert. Organisations must thus identify the relative importance of the different classes of stakeholders. This means considering the degree of **power** stakeholders have, and their degree of **interest** in the organisation.

6.2 Once this analysis has been undertaken, organisations have to decide how best to deal with stakeholder concerns.

Responding to stakeholder power

6.3 As we have seen **shareholders** can influence and constrain the management of a company at a number of different levels. When deciding on the company's objectives, management actions will be directed to maximise **long term owner value**.

6.4 However in order to fulfil the company's mission and maximise long-term owner value, management activities will be influenced to a greater or lesser extent by *other* stakeholders.

(a) **Customers' demands** will **dictate decisions** for investment in new products, development of existing ones and setting-up of new outlets. They will also affect the standards adopted for quality control. The extent to which they can be enticed away by competitors' products will affect the planned advertising spend.

(b) **Suppliers' and distributors' demands** will **affect the timing** and **amount** of production.

(c) **Employees' attitudes and objectives** will greatly affect the organisation and co-ordination required to put production plans into effect. Construction of departments and work groups, job design, workflow and the amount of training undertaken will all be matters in which management will have to take employees' views into account.

(d) **Legislation, regulations and the community at large**. At the planning level management discretion can be constrained both by legal requirements designed to protect the community as a whole and the potential consequences of popular anger.

Exam Tip

In the exam you may be asked to identify the most important stakeholder interests for your own or another organisation. For example, question 2 in June 2003 asked about the stakeholders of a charity.

Action Programme 1

You now have a chance to put Mendelow's classification (see above) into practice. Select an organisation, think what stakeholders are interested in it and assess their relative power and interest. Justify your measurements of power and interest.

Chapter Roundup

- **Stakeholder analysis** identifies the various parties interested in an organisation and its activities. These include:

  - **Internal** stakeholders (eg employees and managers)

  - **Connected** stakeholders (eg shareholders, bankers, customers and suppliers)

  - **External** stakeholders (eg government, concerned with the organisation's activities in a wider social context)

Quick Quiz

[handwritten: shareholder, customers, suppliers bankers, distributors]

1   Give five examples of connected stakeholders.

2   Match the descriptions with the letters in Mendelow's grid.

Level of interest

	Low	High
Low Power	A	B
High	C	D

- Keep informed *B*
- Keep satisfied *C*
- Need minimal effort *A*
- Must find strategy acceptable *D*

3   What is the most powerful weapon shareholders have in their dealings with the company?

4   *Fill in the blank*

    A [handwritten: customer charter] .... is a written customer services policy.

5   What is the strong view of stakeholder theory for profit-centred organisations?

6   What is the weak view of stakeholder theory for profit-centred organisations?

7   What is internal marketing?

    A   The marketing department
    B   the principles of marketing to employees as if they were customers
    C   The promotion of the interests of internal stakeholders
    D   The activities of the staff shop

8   What are the main requirements of distributors as connected stakeholders?

Action Programme Review

1   In a sense we are all stakeholders, but more specific examples are shown in the diagram in paragraph 2.2 of this chapter.

2   Ian Mathieson, a partner in the Chartered Accountants Pannell Kerr Foster, highlighted the following elements as being important in a good annual report:

■   The trustees' report should explain the charity's strategy, policies and performance, demonstrating how resources are used, outlining successes and setbacks and giving a balanced message. The report should also set out the planning processes and organisational structure, and indicate the charity's plans for the future.

■   A key policy which the report should highlight is the charity's risk management policy. Being able to demonstrate a sound risk management policy and its links to other key policies can appeal to potential donors.

■   Mathieson points out that although stakeholders expect to see innovative and informative annual reports, charities shouldn't be looking to spend large sums on glossy publications. Good means of demonstrating what the charity does include case studies, comments from stakeholders and users, and statistics presented in a reader-friendly way (through charts and graphs)

There is no single ideal report as charities differ significantly in the work they do. 'All charities are unique and have a different message to communicate.' However readers of the report who haven't been actively involved, should be able to understand from the annual reports what charities have achieved.

3   **Primary stakeholders** are stakeholders who participate in the organisation's primary activities. For organisations producing goods or services, primary stakeholders would include employees, customers and suppliers.

Secondary stakeholders are those individuals and groups who do not participate in the primary activities. They are however affected by the organisation's secondary impacts and involvements – those over and above its primary activity of producing goods or services for consumption. Examples of secondary stakeholders include local communities, pressure groups, the media, government and general public.

4   Criteria which you might have considered:

(a)   Who the members of each group of stakeholders are

(b)   How much power they can exercise over the organisation

(c)   What claims the individuals have on the organisation

(d)   How significant the concerns of individuals are and the extent to which the concerns are being addressed

Answers to Quick Quiz

1
- Shareholders
- Bankers
- Customers
- Suppliers
- Distributors

2
A Need minimal effort
B Keep informed
C Keep satisfied
D Must find strategy acceptable

3 The right to sell their shares and hence possibly cause share prices to fall.

4 A customer charter.

5 Each stakeholder in the business has a legitimate claim on management attention. Management's job is to balance stakeholder demands.

6 Satisfying stakeholders such as the customer is good only because it enables the business to satisfy its primary purpose, long-term growth in owner wealth.

7 B The principles of marketing to employees as if they were customers.

8
- Reliable supply
- Quality improvements
- Support in marketing

Now try illustrative question 9 at the end of the Study Text

Pressure groups

6

Learning Outcome

☑ Recognise and assess the impact of key trends in business ethics on the marketing function

Syllabus References

☑ Explain the significance of the range of pressure groups interested in the organisation and their potential impacts

☑ Specify the role of marketing in managing these pressure groups

Key Concepts Introduced

■ Pressure group   ■ Consumerism

1 Setting the scene

1.1 Society has expectations of business organisations, in particular that they behave in a socially responsible way.

1.2 Balancing the needs for **social responsibility** with the need to make profit for shareholders can be a difficult problem to reconcile. Although the organisation has pressures from external financial stakeholders to maximise sales and profits, other external stakeholders have different ends in mind.

1.3 We therefore discuss in the rest of the chapter those outside influences that are concerned with what they see as an organisation's social duties. We give examples of pressure groups and then discuss in detail the role of consumer pressure groups. We then move on to consider the issues of environmentalism and market failure, and show how organisations may be influenced by pressures arising from these issues.

2 Pressure groups 6/03

Key Concept

A **pressure group** is a group of people who have got together to promote a particular cause. An alternative name is a <u>cause group</u>. The term is also used to mean any interest group.

2.1 Stakeholders may be unable to exercise any sovereignty over an organisation, whether as a consumer, employee or member of the public at large. In these circumstances, individuals may seek to influence an organisation by joining a **pressure group**.

Exam Tip

Pressure groups are of more importance in some sectors than to others, but they will be very important in the Marketing Environment exam.

2.2 Interest and pressure groups arise from two causes.

■ The failure of parliamentary representatives to air important concerns
■ The inevitable fact that different groups in society have different interests

2.3 Pressure groups have an interest in matters of public policy, but do not aspire to control the machinery of government. There are many thousands of groups ranging from major umbrella groups to small purely local groups, often established for a specific purpose.

(a) <u>**Cause** groups (or **promotional** groups) promote a distinct cause or issue (eg CND, Greenpeace, Howard League for Penal Reform).</u> Sometimes the word *pressure group* is used here.

(b) **Interest groups** (or **defensive** or **sectional** groups), defend the wide interests of groups in society such as mineworkers (NUM), business firms (CBI) or consumers.

Action Programme 1

Compare the websites of a cause and interest group of your choice. Are there major differences in areas such as the information they give about themselves, the press coverage quoted of their activities, items of special interest such as specially-commissioned surveys, and any products they offer?

2.4 Some of these groups have other activities than trying to influence government and might regard political activity as only one of their many roles. Some of the major charities, such as Oxfam, do good work and also try to influence government policy. A group can have one of two sorts of relationship with government.

(a) **Insider groups** are regularly consulted by government as a matter of routine in areas of policy. In fact, some insider groups *expect* to be consulted. Note that insider groups do not necessarily support the government of the day. The British Medical Association, for example, although not always supporting government policy on the NHS, is still regularly consulted.

(b) **Outsider groups** do not have a direct link to government. Some of their activities are to **promote interest** in their cause outside government (eg in the media) so that the issue is raised in the public arena and to **gain credibility** in the eyes of the public and recognition of their importance by the government, so that their pronouncements are taken seriously.

2.5 The role of pressure groups is controversial.

(a) Some argue that the existence of a pressure group means that **power** is **diffused widely**, and that they are an informal check on ever-increasing power of the state. They also help protect minorities.

(b) Others argue that some pressure groups (eg business interests) are far **more influential** than others (eg some supporters of rail transport believe that 'the road lobby' has undue influence on UK transport policy) and that this is anti-democratic.

(c) In the US some people argue that lobbying by the National Rifle Association against firearm restrictions has impeded gun control legislation, which might have helped reduce the US's high murder rate.

Action Programme 2

There has been increased concern with the costs caused by traffic congestion in large cities. Some, like Singapore, have responded by *road pricing*. Drivers are charged for using certain roads at certain times. Think of as many interested parties (including government institutions) as you can who would favour or oppose such a move.

2.6 Pressure groups may either encourage or try to discourage a policy.

Marketing at Work

Examples of two contrasting pressure groups in Britain are the Countryside Alliance and the Hunt Saboteurs Association. The main press focus on the Countryside Alliance has been on its opposition to the proposed ban on hunting. As well as marches, the Association has also tried to increase understanding and support for hunting with dogs by campaigns and information packs. The Alliance is also investigating legal challenges to any proposed ban on hunting, including challenges under the Human rights legislation and problems over contract law.

Over time the Alliance's remit has widened to cover 'the real rural agenda'. This includes other country sports, such as angling and fishing. As well as campaigns, the Alliance provides members with advice on recent legislation and practical skills, for example shotgun technique courses.

Wider rural concerns of the Alliance include the production of food; the concern is that smaller businesses are being edged out due to inappropriate regulations and failure by businesses and consumers to buy local products. ' (We) believe that food production in Britain does not need special exemptions or subsidies. It needs sensible regulation and an ability to compete in the marketplace. Consumers who demand higher standards, in terms of food safety, environmental protection and animal welfare must be willing to pay for the true cost of this food production.'

The Hunt Saboteurs Association's website is rather more narrowly-focused. It is designed to arouse strong reactions from users by including graphic pictures of animal suffering. It also includes quotes allegedly made by leading huntsmen that do not portray them in a good light. Apart from these the site is focused on sabotage operations, covering not just hunts, but also dealing with traps and snares and angling. The main support service offered is legal advice, with details of how saboteurs have fared when charged with offences under public order legislation, and also contact details should saboteurs find themselves in difficulty.

Action Programme 3

See if you can find your own examples of two opposing pressure groups, and compare and contrast the techniques they use.

2.7 The Sunday trading issue was an interesting example as a number of different interest groups combined in a campaign for a mutual objective.

2.8 The main pressure groups reflecting economic interests are as follows.

(a) **Businesses**: Employers' organisations. These can be supplemented by smaller more specified trade associations in particular industries, which gang together to promote common interests (eg newspapers to oppose tax on the press).

(b) **Professional associations** are groups of people who do the same type of job or use similar skills such as accountants and doctors. Professional associations are generally involved in setting standards of skill and enforcing adherence to good practice (for example, through disciplinary schemes) who do the same type of job or use similar skills.

(c) **Trade unions** are similar to professional associations, in that they represent people who work.

(d) **Consumers' associations** represent people as consumers, in other words, campaigning for the interests of consumers on issues such as product pricing, safety and quality. Consumer associations have campaigned for labelling on food, for example.

How to influence government

2.9 Pressure groups influence government in a number of ways, depending on whether they are insiders or outsiders.

Insiders

2.10 Pressure groups can influence national governments in various ways.

2.11 The UK government has itself issued details on how to influence government - in this case the EU.

2.12 Of particular importance is the need to influence the decision making processes of the European Commission. EU regulations, for practical purposes, take priority over national law. They are arrived at after a great deal of negotiation, and for this reason alone, are difficult to change. It is therefore much better to influence the **drafting process** of new regulations than to try and get them changed once they have been implemented.

2.13 The DTI has published a leaflet *(Brussels can you hear me?)* which recommends the following approach to influencing EU decision making.

(a) **Get in early**

A business should make its views known in the drafting stage. (Often it is helpful to work with officials rather than ministers.)

(b) **Work with others**

'A spread of opinion carries more weight than a lone voice.' UK businesses should thus work with European trade associations and to encourage firms in other countries to lobby their own governments too.

(c) **Think European**

A firm's lobbying will be much more effective if it can be demonstrated that the issue is relevant to the single market programme, or the EU's other aims. (Also, at national level, demonstrating that your idea is in line with existing government policy will help.)

(d) **Be prepared**

There are a number of sources of information about the Community's activities. It is important to monitor what is going on, and the issues that are being dealt with by the Commission. (The same is true for government.)

2.14 The UK government also recommends that having a **long-term presence** in Brussels can be of immense benefit, given that the lobbying process can be a long standing one. Moreover, a business might be in a position of **initiating** the legislative process if it has unique information about a particular trading issue.

Outsiders

2.15 Some interest groups can act as both insiders **and** outsiders. When not walking up and down the corridors of power, members of an interest group can do the following to influence government policy.

(a)   They can try and influence public opinion and the legislative agenda by **advertising**. The RSPCA advertised (unsuccessfully) for a dog registration scheme in the UK. This was more than just an appeal for donations: the advertising was specifically designed to change government policy.

(b)   Few organisations can afford expensive press advertising. However there are other ways of getting publicity: demonstrations, petitions, direct action and public relations.

2.16 These methods may or may not have a direct impact. If the action is public, ministers might not wish to be seen to lose face by submitting. However, they can create a climate of opinion to which politicians can later respond. The adoption of *environmental* issues by politicians is the result of many years of campaigning by pressure groups.

Marketing implications

2.17 Many of the tactics used against governments can be used against businesses (eg feeding stories to the media, marches and so on).

2.18 Some pressure groups are unremittingly hostile to certain businesses, and their aim is to extinguish them altogether. For example, businesses exporting veal calves have faced pressure group hostility. In such cases, all businesses can do, other than rely on the law, is exercise important public relations issues. The nuclear power industry, for example, is very well placed to exploit, in advertisements, public concern about global warming and environmental pollution.

2.19 Other pressure groups have more restricted aims, and may be amenable to negotiation. A firm might set considerable PR benefit from this as well as advice.

2.20 A firm has a number of basic responses.

■   **Ignore** the **pressure group**
■   **Deal** with the **pressure group**, and take some of its ideas on board
■   **Employ** a **pro-active public relations** and **advertising policy**
■   **Sue for libel** – but McDonald's has found that this can be a public relations disaster

2.21 The firm's response will be conditioned by:

(a)   The **number of interests of the pressure groups**

A multi-interest pressure group may be more open to negotiation than a single-issue pressure group, but expertise in a variety of fields may be needed for effective negotiation with a multi-issue group.

(b) **Nature of the interests**

An economic pressure group will be concerned with tangible economic benefits; a social or environmental group with less tangible benefits, which may be difficult to measure.

(c) **Implications of continuing conflict**

This particularly means how a conflict might escalate.

3 Consumer groups

Key Concept

Consumerism is a term used to describe the increased importance and power of consumers. It includes the increasingly organised consumer groups, and the recognition by producers that consumer satisfaction is the key to long-term profitability.

3.1 Consumerism is an attempt to even up the relationship between individual consumers and large powerful corporations. The basis of consumerism is often taken to be President Kennedy's Consumer Bill of Rights which highlighted four basic rights.

The right to safety

3.2 The right that a product be **safe to use** is covered by legislation in many countries. The main problem is that research may reveal that there are, in fact, specific risks to consumers in using certain products that were at one time thought to be safe, for example cigarettes. The future may also reveal damage to the wider environment, for example the effect of leaded petrol on the earth's atmosphere.

The right to be informed

3.3 This means that **instructions on products** should be **sufficient**, and there should be **clear labelling** of the ingredients that should be used in foodstuffs. This right also covers information about **purchase terms** (excessive small print could be called unfair.) It places an obligation on advertisers to make sure that adverts for products are factually correct and are not misleading.

The right to choose

3.4 In theory this should encourage **competition**, but if of course there is competition, marketers will be trying to influence consumer choice. Therefore the right to choose could be seen as less important provided customers are fully informed; however the right to choose might also be interpreted as the right to choose without being unduly pressurised, thus discouraging unsolicited marketing and pressurised selling.

The right to be heard

3.5 An alternative description might be the right to give **feedback**, particularly the right to make complaints and know that those complaints will be quickly and fairly answered.

Consumer safety

3.6 Many countries have legislation punishing businesses that supply consumer goods that do not comply with safety requirements.

Fair trading

3.7 A large number of countries have officers or departments who have the authority to promote fair trading and competition, and act against restrictive practices. Their roles might include:

(a)   Various functions in relation to **monopolies, mergers, restrictive practices** and **uncompetitive practices**

(b)   Review of the carrying on of the **commercial supply** to consumers of goods and services

(c)   **Issuing licences**

(d)   Collation of evidence of **harmful practices** which may adversely affect the interests of consumers

(e)   Taking action against persons who persist in **conduct detrimental** to the consumer

(f)   Encouraging **relevant associations** to prepare **codes of practice**

Consequences of consumer protection legislation

3.8 Consumer protection legislation might appear to be an onerous burden on businesses. Product standards act as additional guidelines.

3.9 Although managers might complain about the extra costs there are a number of wider issues to be considered.

(a)   Does consumer protection legislation **impede business performance**?

(b)   Does consumer protection legislation **put business** at a **competitive disadvantage** from overseas competitors?

3.10 Such costs are very hard to quantify but there are a number of salient features which might be noted, which limit the competitive impact of such legislation.

(a)   **Overseas competitors in the domestic market**

Products sold in the local market are subject to local law. The fact that they are imported does not exempt them from consumer protection legislation in the UK. Overseas producers may be at a disadvantage, being less familiar with the UK market and practice. At the very least, there is no obvious gain.

(b)   **Domestic businesses in overseas markets**

Domestic businesses are subject to the laws regarding consumer protection prevalent in the overseas markets.

There might indeed be burdens, but they are shared equally.

3.11 If the effect of consumer protection legislation enhances business's best practice, then **overall**, there may even be a benefit. After all, the USA, where the consumer movement first started, was the birthplace of consumerism. Germany, whose export performance is generally impressive, has had some of the most exacting product quality regulations in Europe.

Self regulation

3.12 The use of law to regulate the relationship between buyers and sellers can often seem like a case of using a sledgehammer to crack a nut. Instead, many organisations regulate their dealings by **voluntary codes of conduct**.

3.13 A voluntary code of conduct is a statement by an organisation of the standards by which it seeks to do business. Codes are usually developed by a trade association and individual members incorporate the code into the dealings they have with their customers.

3.14 Voluntary codes usually include a mechanism for **resolving disputes** through arbitration.

3.15 Many countries have bodies promoting advertising standards. In Germany for example, the *Zentrale zur Bekämpfung unlauteren Wettbewerbs e.V.* deals with issues of misleading advertising and unfair competition, whilst the Deutscher Werberat deals with issues of taste and decency. The European Advertising Alliance brings together national advertising self-regulatory organisations ('SROs') and organisations representing the advertising industry in Europe.

Marketing at Work

One of the more unusual recent (December 2003) adjudications of the UK's Advertising Standards Authority concerned a hard-hitting campaign by the charity Barnardo's. The campaign consisted of a number of photographs of babies, one with a cockroach crawling out of its mouth, another with a syringe in its mouth, and a third with a meths bottle in its mouth. The caption to the last of these read 'Baby Amy is two minutes old. Poverty has already mapped out her future. Poverty is waiting to destroy Amy's hope and joy and is likely to lead her to a future of alcoholism.'

Barnardo's argued that the advertisements were intended to draw attention to child poverty, stating in support that 86% of people did not know that one in three children in the UK lived in poverty. They stated that the advertisements showed the reality of child poverty and reflected the nature of their work, which was often distressing. Barnardo's believed that people would be more shocked about discovering the facts about child poverty than by their advertisements. A hard-hitting campaign was justified for the same reasons as tough anti-smoking or drink-driving campaigns were allowed.

However the Advertising Standards Authority upheld complaints that the advertisements were distressing and likely to cause widespread offence, even though it believed that the illustrations were stylised and clearly not realistic representations.

3.16 Possible sanctions that these bodies might employ include:

(a) **Published disapproval**

The organisations publish reports which detail public complaints and decisions in respect of the complaint.

(b) **Media recommendations**

The organisations will have power to recommend to media owners that certain advertisements or advertisers should not be accepted on their books.

Marketing at Work

In May 2001 the UK's Advertising Standards Authority published its adjudication on complaints by the Daily and Sunday Express papers and various members of the public against Associated Newspapers, publishers of the rival titles the Daily Mail and Mail on Sunday. The complaint related to a mailing campaign by Associated Newspapers at the time the Express papers were acquired by Richard Desmond, a publisher of various adult titles. The mailing was headlined: 'The Daily and Sunday Express have been acquired by a pornographer. Do you really want an X-rated paper in your home? Open this envelope to find out how you could save over £20 and read a paper you and your family can be proud of.'

The ASA upheld complaints that:

(a) The advertising was unsubstantiated and misleading. The ASA considered that the background of Richard Desmond did not mean that the Express titles would become X-rated. It asked the advertisers to make it clear in the future that they were merely expressing their opinion.

(b) The advertising was denigratory. Associated Newspapers argued that the mailing merely reflected their opinion. However the ASA considered that the advertisement unfairly denigrated the editorial integrity of the Express titles, and asked Associated Newspapers to change its approach in future.

Consumer protection organisations

3.17 As well as government bodies, there are voluntary associations.

3.18 An example of such a body is the Consumers' Association of Canada (CAC). The Association is an independent, not-for-profit, volunteer-based, charitable organisation. Its mandate is to inform and educate consumers on marketplace issues, to advocate for consumers with government and industry, and work with government and industry to solve marketplace problems.

3.19 CAC focuses its work in the areas of food, health, trade, standards, financial services, communications industries and other marketplace issues as they emerge.

3.20 CAC members serve on various industry committees, and the Association has also been active in a number of areas:

- Standards for services
- Food labelling
- Health care services
- Merger issues

- Electrical safety standards
- International trade
- Gasoline pricing
- International standards
- Harmonization of provincial legislation
- Pensions insurance
- Utility sector privatization
- Airlines

Marketing at Work

Recent projects of the CAC have included the Food Tips project where the CAC worked together with key partners in the food, literacy, and health sectors. The Food Tips were written in plain language to help consumers with lower literacy skills shop smart and eat well.

CAC has also been collaborating with a number of health care and health professional associations to design and test a set of symbols that could replace standard instructions that are found on containers of medication.

3.21 Some industries may have panels of individuals appointed to represent the consumer interests. This is particularly true of **utilities** such as public transport.

3.22 There are also a number of private groups which aim to protect consumer interests in various ways.

(a) Campaigners for the maintenance and improvement in the **quality of specific products**, for example campaigners promoting real ale (cask beer) over keg beer

(b) Groups lobbying for **legal changes** to protect the public, for example anti-smoking groups

(c) **Relatives/friends of disaster victims** lobbying for changes to prevent future disasters

Action Programme 4

Consumerism has been called 'the shame of marketing' (Drucker). Is this a fair statement?

3.23 Sometimes, consumer sovereignty and protection organisations fail to protect the wider interests of consumers. In these circumstances, consumers sometimes turn to pressure groups. These are a few examples in which consumers have been successful in applying pressure to seek changes in business practices.

(a) Consumers began **boycotting** Shell **filling stations** in large numbers, leading the company to reverse its policy on a controversial environmental subject concerning the disposal of an oil drilling platform.

(b) For many years, some consumers **boycotted** goods made in **South Africa** in protest at the undemocratic government of that country.

(c)   Pressure was applied to **change** the **Nestlé company's** practice of exploiting the market for processed milk in developing countries.

3.24 Developments such as the Citizens' Charter aim to specify precisely the levels of service that consumers of public sector services can expect. The aim is to make providers of public services more responsive to what users demand.

(a)   Note that some users or consumers of public services may not be in a position to pay for them directly (eg the dependent elderly). As consumers, their **needs** should **be specified**.

(b)   It may not be possible for consumers to find an **alternative supplier** of utility services.

Impact on marketing

3.25 Organisations need to understand how consumer groups can influence the industry environment. Working with consumer groups can have significant advantages, even the **positive endorsement** of products by the groups. A failure to respond to concerns can lead to **boycotts** not just of the products concerned, but also all other products sold by the organisation. Animal welfare groups have targeted organisations' whole product ranges rather than just those products which have been tested on animals.

Marketing at Work

Alcoholic versions of soft drinks – so-called 'alcopops' – have caused considerable controversy recently, particularly because the products seem to be directed mainly at young people.

As reported in *Marketing Business*, the need for tighter controls over the marketing of alcopops has led to action by the drinks industry itself. A code of practice has been introduced by The Portman Group, which is an organisation founded by the major UK drinks producers to promote sensible drinking and to reduce misuse of alcohol.

The code of practice complements and is consistent with all other relevant self-regulatory codes, and it helps to control the industry without the burden of new legislation. The provisions of the code are wide-ranging and cover the naming, packaging and merchandising of drinks.

An example of its operation is that of the marketing of Carlsberg-Tetley's 'Thickhead' drink, which was held by the Portman Group to be in breach of industry guidelines and to be a 'serious misjudgement'. Very soon, Carlsberg-Tetley responded by agreeing to change the label.

Chapter Roundup

- **Social responsibility** echoes the fact that businesses have a wider input on the physical and social environment than simply an economic one.

- The extent to which **social responsibility** is desirable is controversial. The discussion in part is determined by the wider social and political context.

- The members of **pressure groups** are people who have come together either because they come from a similar area of society with common interests, or because they wish to promote an issue or cause.

- Pressure groups campaign in favour of or against existing policies, or bring new issues to the attention of policy makers.

- **Consumer groups** represent consumers' interests. They exist to ensure that products give good value. They promote safeguards for consumers against unethical business practice.

- Public concern with the environment may have several impacts upon business, including demands for **environmentally friendly products** and the effect of **bad publicity.**

- **Market failure**, the failure of the free market mechanism to produce the most efficient allocation of resources has a number of causes:

  - Market imperfections
  - Differences between social and private costs
  - The existence of public goods
  - The need to consider non-market goals

Quick Quiz

1   Match the type of pressure group with the description.

   (1)   Cause group (a)   Promotes wide issues
   (2)   Interest group   (b)   Promotes a specific issue

2   Give three examples of ways in which pressure groups can influence government.

3   What are the four steps that the UK government has recommended be used to influence European Union decision-making?

4   Which of the following method would be least likely to be used by an outsider pressure group to influence government policy?

   A   Advertising
   B   Petitions
   C   Demonstrations
   Ⓓ   Serving on government committees

5   What is consumerism?   *B the team use to describe the increasing power of consumers.*

6   Which of the following rights were part of US President Kennedy's Bill of Consumer Rights?

     A   Safety   *all*

     B   Choice

     C   Information

     D   Hearing

7   What are the main methods used by advertising standard bodies to enforce their views?

8   What did Drucker describe as the 'Shame of Marketing'?

Action Programme Review

1   –

2   Here are some possible suggestions. (Please note that the list below does not claim to represent the policies and practices, whether stated or informal, of any of the organisations mentioned.)

Possibly for

- Emergency services (lower congestion means fast trips to fires etc)
- Local authorities of congested areas (eg City of Cambridge)
- Environmental groups (eg Friends of the Earth) who wish to reduce pollution
- Public transport organisations
- Tax raising authorities
- Technology companies (for design contracts)

Possibly against

- Motorists' associations (eg AA and RAC)
- The car industry generally
- Petrol companies (reduced motoring means fewer sales)
- Many individual motorists
- Residents associations worried about traffic being diverted
- Civil liberties organisations (as people's movements might be tracked)

3   –

4   The marketing concept deals with the identification of customer needs and their satisfaction at a profit. Consumerism arose in reaction to poor quality, unethical marketing and pricing strategies, and sharp practice. If these did not exist, consumer groups would not be necessary.

That said, magazines like *Which?* do a valuable service in spreading information, in that they rigorously analyse the *product* and *price* elements of the marketing mix.

Furthermore, the individual consumer is powerless in the face of a large corporation. Only by pooling their interests can consumers get effective redress against bad business practice.

Answers to Quick Quiz

1   (1)   (b)
     (2)   (a)

2   Any three of:

   ■   Employing lobbyists
   ■   Making politicians directors
   ■   Going on committees
   ■   Donating to political parties

3   ■   Get in early
     ■   Work with others
     ■   Think European
     ■   Be prepared

4   D   Serving on government committees would imply the group was an insider pressure group

5   A description of the increased importance and power of consumers

6   All of them

7   ■   Publishing disapproval of conduct

     ■   Making recommendations that certain advertisers or advertisements should not be accepted

8   Consumerism

Now try illustrative question 10 at the end of the Study Text

The industry environment

7

Chapter Topic List	
1	Setting the scene
2	Competition for customers
3	Industry structure and competitive behaviour
4	Regulation of competition
5	Monitoring competitors

Learning Outcomes

☑ Analyse the competitive environment within an industry

☑ Understand the impact of competition policies on the organisational/marketing environment

☑ Undertake a competitor analysis

☑ Evaluate factors impacting upon market share

Syllabus References

☑ Explain the importance of monitoring competitors and industries and how the organisation assesses their strategic and marketing implications

☑ Examine the impact of competition policies on the organisation and its marketing environment

Key Concepts Introduced

■ Competitive forces   ■ Oligopoly

■ Barriers to entry   ■ Cartel

BPP
PROFESSIONAL EDUCATION

- Fragmented industry
- Monopoly
- Perfect competition
- Price discrimination
- Concentrated industry
- Emerging industry

1 Setting the scene

1.1 In the last chapter on the micro environment we discuss the influences of an industry within which the organisation operates, and in particular the impact of competition.

1.2 We start off by discussing how competition works. Michael Porter described five basic **competitive forces** which apply in most situations. We then go on to discuss how much the competitive environment can depend on the industry and market structure.

1.3 National governments and the EU have attempted to regulate certain practices that appear to be contrary to the public interest, and we discuss what these practices are, and how regulation works, in section 4 of this chapter.

1.4 Lastly we consider how an organisation might respond to the competitive environment it faces, both in **analysing competitors** and **formulating its own strategy**. The strategic issues introduced here will be developed in much more detail in your studies for later CIM papers.

Exam Tip

The Specimen Paper asked for an explanation of why firms should monitor their industry environment.

2 Competition for customers   Specimen paper, 12/02

2.1 Are the people who buy our products customers with a choice, or are they captive?

2.2 Any organisation wishing to expand or move into a market must consider whether the market is growing or has the capacity to grow. For example, the UK market for mineral water was more or less established by Perrier in the 1980s. As public doubts about the quality of the water supply increased, a number of other bottled waters were offered for sale (eg Malvern) together with own-brands, created by supermarkets.

2.3 The characteristics of the market also need to be investigated. Michael Porter (*Competitive Strategy*) makes a distinction between two groups of characteristics.

(a) **Environmental factors** characterise the nature of competition in one industry compared with another – for example, in the chemicals industry compared with the clothing retail industry. They make one industry as a whole potentially more profitable than another.

(b) Factors that characterise the **nature of competition** within a particular industry. These relate to the competitive strategies that individual firms might select.

2.4 Porter suggests that there are five basic **competitive forces** which influence the state of competition in an industry and can be used as the outline for a **structural analysis** of an industry.

Key Concept

Competitive forces are 'the structural determinants of the intensity of competition' which collectively determine the profit (ie long-run return on capital) potential of the industry as a whole.

2.5 Competitive force analysis indicates the likely size of profits, and the long-term prospects, in particular the **degree of future competition**. It thus provides a basis for developing future strategy.

PORTER'S COMPETITIVE FORCES
The **threat** of new **entrants** to the industry
The **threat** of **substitute products** or services
The **bargaining power** of **customers**
The **bargaining power** of **suppliers**
The **rivalry** amongst current competitors in the industry

Source: adapted from Porter (*Competitive Strategy*)

The threat of new entrants (and barriers to entry)

2.6 A new entrant into an industry will bring extra capacity. The new entrant will have to make an **investment** to break into the market, and will want to obtain a certain market share. The strength of the threat from new entrants is likely to vary from industry to industry, depending on two factors.

(a) **Strength of the barriers to entry**

   The stronger the barriers, the less likely entry is.

BPP PROFESSIONAL EDUCATION

(b) **Response of existing competitors to the new entrant**

If a new prospective entrant thinks that firms which are already in the industry would respond to a new competitor by reducing their prices and starting a price war, the new entrant would be more likely to think twice before deciding to make its entry into the market.

Key Concept

Barriers to entry are the factors which make it difficult for a new entrant to gain a foothold in an industry.

2.7 Barriers to entry can be categorised as follows.

There's always a gap!

INDUSTRY PRODUCT-MARKETS

FIRM'S PRODUCT - MARKET

Scale economies necessary for profit

Existing cost advantages

Existing product differentiation requires expensive promotion

Existing firms have best acess to distribution

Switching costs discourage customers from seeking new suppliers

Economies of scale

2.8 High fixed costs (ie costs that do not change how many goods you produce) imply a **high breakeven point** (number of units sold to cover fixed costs). Profit might depend on the ability to achieve a high volume of sales. If significant economies can be obtained by producing above certain volumes of output, existing firms in the industry will have a big cost advantage over a new entrant.

Product differentiation

2.9 Existing firms in an industry may have built up a good brand image and strong customer loyalty over a long period of time, through advertising, product quality and so on.

2.10 Moreover a firm might develop a **variety of brands** to 'crowd out' the competition. This creates a barrier to entry, because new entrants would have to spend heavily to overcome the existing brand loyalties and to build up a brand image of their own. These high 'start-up' losses might deter would-be competitors, given that the chances of eventual success in the new market might be fairly slim anyway.

Capital requirements

2.11 The amount of capital that a new entrant needs to invest varies from one industry to another. In some industries, for example, capital requirements are low, whereas in other industries, a substantial investment might be required. When capital requirements are high, the barrier against new entrants will be strong, particularly when the investment would possibly be high-risk.

2.12 Investment in IT may be a further example. On the other hand IT can be used to leap over certain entry barriers. An example is the use of telephone banking, which may obviate the need to establish a branch network.

Switching costs

2.13 Switching costs are the costs that a customer would have to incur by switching from one supplier's products to another's. The costs are not just financial: **time** and **inconvenience** are costs in this context. The consequences of a switch might include the following.

- Buying **new ancillary equipment** compatible with the equipment of the new supplier
- Loss of the existing supplier's **after-sales service**
- Risk that the new supplier will be **less reliable** than the existing supplier

2.14 When customers think that switching costs would be high, there would be a strong barrier to entry against new competitors in the industry. IS/IT may also tie customers and suppliers into the same distribution channel.

2.15 Switching costs also apply to retailers and distributors as well as to consumers. It might cost a consumer nothing to switch from buying one brand of frozen peas or one make of car to buying another, but the potential costs for the **retailer** or **distributor** might be high. How reliable will the new supplier be in providing fresh stock on demand?

Access to distribution channels

2.16 Distribution channels are the means by which a manufacturer's products reach the end-buyer. In some industries new distribution channels are difficult to establish, and existing distribution channels hard to gain access to. This is a universal complaint of Western countries trying to export to Japan.

Marketing at Work

Food products in the UK are largely sold through supermarket chains, and it can be difficult for a new producer to get supermarket organisations to agree to stock the product.

As retailers become more powerful, they are placing more and more demands on food producers: failure to comply can mean exclusion from the channel of distribution.

Cost advantages of existing producers, independent of economies of scale

Existing cost advantages

2.17 Barriers to entry may exist when existing firms in an industry have certain cost advantages over new entrants which are nothing to do with economies of scale. These would include the following.

(a) **Patent rights**, these however expire after a certain time, but this time does give the firm a breathing space

(b) **Experience** and **know-how** (eg cost benefits obtained through the learning curve factor)

(c) **Government subsidies**

(d) **Access** to **sources** of raw materials on favourable terms, such as a long-term low-price supply contract

2.18 Entry barriers are not static.

(a) They can be **raised** by a **number of measures**, such as maximising early sales demand to increase the cumulative volume needed to be profitable. A firm can increase the perception of risk.

(b) Entry barriers might be lowered by **changes** in the **environment**, in particular by cost-reducing technological changes, which a new entrant can invest in straightaway, and so compete more effectively against established firms in the industry. New entrants might be able to identify novel distribution channels for products or services.

② The threat from substitute products

2.19 The products or services that are produced in one industry are likely to have substitutes that are produced by another industry. Substitutes offer different ways of meeting the same customer need.

2.20 For example, you may need to go to Paris from London. Crossing the English channel, **railway travel** is a **substitute** for flying or going by car-ferry. Note that they are different ways of meeting the same need. (The ferry companies compete with each other, but they are not substitute products. They offer the **same** type of service.)

2.21 When firms in an industry are faced with threats from substitute products they are likely to find that demand for their products is relatively **sensitive to price**. A significant threat is any improvement in the price-performance characteristics of these substitutes.

 Marketing at Work

An example of substitute products is provided by the metals industry. For many years 'tin cans' were made out of steel: however, aluminium, which is thinner and lighter, has replaced in many applications.

In response to this, the steel industry has developed new alloys of steel, which it hopes will enable it to fight back in this significant market.

③ **The bargaining power of customers.**

2.22 Customers want better quality products and services at a lower price. If they succeed in getting what they want, they will force down the profitability of suppliers in the industry. The profitability of an industry is therefore dependent on the strength of the bargaining power of its customers, which is dependent upon a number of factors.

CUSTOMER BARGAINING POWER	
Purchases are substantial % of sales	Customer will be in a strong position
Purchases are high % of total purchases by customer	Customer will be a weaker position if most of purchases come from one supplier or industry
Level of switching costs	IT can raise switching costs in cash terms and operational inconvenience
Nature of products	Suppliers may increase bargaining power by creating a strong brand which customers feel obliged to have
Level of profits	Customers making low profits need low cost suppliers
Takeover threat	Possibility that customers may take over sources of supply if supplier charges too much
Knowledge of customers	Level of awareness customers have, or the skills of their purchasing staff
Product quality	If quality is important, customers are less likely to be price-sensitive, and industry might be more profitable

④ **The bargaining power of suppliers**   12/03

2.23 Just as customers can influence the profitability of an industry by exerting pressure for higher quality products or lower prices, so too can suppliers influence profitability by exerting pressure for higher prices.

2.24 The ability of suppliers to get higher prices depends on the following factors.

- **One or two dominant suppliers** to the industry may be able to charge monopoly prices.

- The **suppliers** may be **threatened** by new entrants, or by substitute products.

- The suppliers may have **other customers** outside the industry, and do not rely on the industry for the majority of their sales.

- The **suppliers' products** may be vital to the customers' business.

- The supplier may produce a **differentiated product** which buyers need to obtain.

- **Switching costs** for buyers may be high.

Marketing at Work

Wickes, the timber, building materials and home improvement products group has made electronic trading a core part of the company's IT operations.

Wickes receives around 60% of its invoices electronically. Early receipt of invoices via EDI into the company's in-house invoice processing application allows prompt identification of problems and mismatches.

Wickes also uses EDI to send orders to its suppliers. The retail sites provide order information on a daily basis for consolidation. The consolidated orders are then transmitted to suppliers overnight and are ready for processing the following morning. Order lead times are reduced, slower paper-based ordering is eliminated and accuracy is better.

The current competitors can be intensive, act tous

Rivalry amongst current competitors in the industry

2.25 The intensity of competitive rivalry within an industry will affect the profitability of the industry as a whole. Competitive actions might take the form of price competition, advertising battles, sales promotion campaigns, introducing new products for the market, improving after-sales service or providing guarantees or warranties. *Less profits*

might take the form of price competition advertising battles, promotion campaigns, after sales & services, guarantees, warranties, all that will affect the profitability of the industry as a whole

Strength of competition

2.26 The intensity of competition will depend on the following factors.

Whether there is a large number of equally balanced competitors

2.27 Industries with a large number of firms are likely to be very competitive. When the industry is dominated by a small number of large firms, competition is likely to be less intense, or is restricted.

The rate of growth in the industry

2.28 When firms are all benefiting from growth in total demand, their rivalry will be less intense. Rivalry will be greater when firms are competing for a greater market share in a total market where growth is slow or stagnant, especially where the costs of leaving the market are high.

Whether fixed costs are high

2.29 If fixed costs are high, and variable costs are a relatively small proportion of the selling price, firms will often compete on price, and sell at prices above marginal cost, even though this will mean a failure to cover fixed costs and make an adequate returning the longer run. In the short run any contribution towards covering fixed costs is better than none at all.

Ease of switching

2.30 Whether buyers can switch easily from one supplier to another will influence competition. Easy switching will encourage suppliers to compete (eg Coke and Pepsi).

Capacity and unit costs

2.31 A supplier might need to achieve a substantial increase in output capacity, in order to obtain reductions in unit costs eg by acquiring labour-saving equipment.

The difficulty that competitors may have in guessing each other's intentions

2.32 When one firm is not sure what another is up to, it may well respond to the uncertainty by formulating a more competitive strategy.

High strategic stakes

2.33 If a firm has put a lot of capital and effort into achieving certain targets and has made success in the industry a prime strategic objective, the firm will be likely to act very competitively in order to ensure that its targets are achieved. Japanese firms allegedly place market share as a high strategic objective, and will act keenly to achieve it.

Exit barriers

2.34 Just as there are barriers to entry into an industry, so too are there barriers to exit which make it difficult for an existing supplier to leave the industry.

INDUSTRY				
Firm				

| EXIT BARRIERS | Fixed assets with low break-up value | Cost of redundancy payments | Effect on rest of group | Reluctance of managers | Government pressures |

EXIT

Exam Tip

Although you need to know about Porter's five forces, you will not be expected to undertake a five force analysis in the exam.

BPP
PROFESSIONAL EDUCATION

Competitive strategies – a summary

2.35 Competitive advantage or **competitive edge** is anything which gives one organisation an edge over its rivals in the products it sells or the services it offers. Much of the competitive advantage which an organisation might hope to achieve, however, is provided by the nature/quality/price of its products.

(a) One company's products might have a definite edge over its rivals because it is better in **quality**, or cheaper in **price**.

(b) Where rival products are much alike (eg petrol, many processed foods etc) competitive advantage may be sought by creating a superior **brand image** and making the product **seem different** and more desirable than a rival producer's similar product.

2.36 The type of competitive strategy which a firm adopts will depend on the competitive strategies adopted by rivals and will have implications for product design and quality, pricing and advertising.

(a) **Cost leadership strategy**

This seeks to achieve the position of lowest-cost producer in the industry as a **whole**. By producing at the lowest cost, the manufacturer can compete on price with every other producer in the industry, and earn the highest unit profits.

(b) **Differentiation strategy**

This is based on the assumption that competitive advantage can be gained through particular **characteristics** of a firm's products or brands. The customer is prepared to pay more for this distinguishing characteristic.

DIFFERENTIATION

Colour differences | Size differences | Different wrappings | Different variations for different market segments | New gimmicks on old products | Back up services

2.37 Differentiation can take place in other ways. Businesses can be flexible as to the **means of payment** they allow (credit terms, smartcards etc) for example.

Focus strategy

This is where a firm concentrates its attention on one or more particular segments or niches of the market, and does not try to serve the entire market with a single product. The firm will focus on a particular type of buyer or geographical area.

2.38 Examples of how information technology can support each of these strategies are shown in the following table.

Strategy	How IT can support the strategy
Cost-leadership	By facilitating reductions in cost levels, for example by reducing the number of administration staff required.
	Allowing better resource utilisation, for example by providing accurate stock information allowing lower buffer inventories to be held.
	Using IT to support just-in-time and advanced manufacturing systems.
Differentiation	Differentiation can be suggested by IT, perhaps in the product itself or in the way it is marketed.
	Publishing is an example with the move from paper-based products to electronic.
Focus	IT may enable a more customised or specialised product/service to be produced.
	IT also facilitates the collection of sales and customer information that identifies targetable market segments.

Marketing at Work

Competitive Advantage through IT - Information Technology at Otis

Otis' success derives from being an effective user of information technology. The company's competitive advantage stems from three main developments – OTISLINE, REM and the use of fuzzy logic.

OTISLINE

The 'freephone' OTISLINE, in addition to its original purpose of improving customer service, has helped in areas like elevator maintenance, new equipment sales, marketing of elevator services. Otis has used OTISLINE in foreign markets to **increase the barriers to entry for its competitors** seeking to enter those same markets.

Otis now possesses the ability to access service information from both independent service companies and its own regional offices. This serves as a **database for customer files** as well as a **depository for all maintenance activities** for elevators under service contracts.

REM

REM is a PC-based system designed to monitor elevator performance from a distant location, 24 hours a day, that controls selected standard functions in order to spot problems in advance and to **avoid breakdowns**.

It is a **preventive** system that is programmed with predefined parameters that when deviated from initiates a warning signal which if unattended, could lead to a breakdown. Otis is able to recognise potential problems without alerting the customer and perform the necessary maintenance quickly. Technicians **can access elevator maintenance information as they are working** upon the problem without having to completely shut down the elevator beforehand.

Fuzzy Logic

Neural networks and artificial intelligence are used to identify peak hours of usage and the elevator can respond accordingly. Using weight and frequency, **elevators decide for themselves** where they should be at certain times of the day, thus greatly **reducing waiting time** (2 minutes to 30 seconds).

As a technology-based development, fuzzy logic is **copied relatively easily by competitors**, thus effectively eliminating Otis' competitive advantage in this area.

2.39 Drawbacks to a focus strategy

(a) The market segment might **not be big enough** to provide the firm with a profitable basis for its operations.

(b) The segment's needs may eventually become **less distinct** from the main markets.

(c) **Competitors** can move into the chosen segment (as the Japanese have done into the luxury car market previously dominated by BMW and Mercedes).

3 Industry structure and competitive behaviour

3.1 Although the five competitive forces are at work in any industry, the balance of power between the different competitors in an industry can vary.

(a) An industry might be populated by a number of **small scale competitors**. An example in the UK is hairdressing: there are few large 'chains' of hairdressers; most hairdressing salons are independent.

(b) On the other hand an industry might be **dominated** by a **small number** of large competitors.

(c) There may be a combination: few **leading companies** may **dominate** the market, but **smaller ones** might **exist** as well. The fast-food industry in many countries features major chains such as McDonalds as well as independent outlets (for example, fish and chip shops and kebab shops).

Fragmented industries

Key Concept

A **fragmented industry**, according to Porter is 'populated by a large number of small and medium-sized companies.' Moreover, a fragmented industry is characterised by 'the absence of market leaders with the power to shape industry events.'

3.2 This corresponds to market structure known as perfect competition.

Key Concept

Perfect competition is a situation where there is a large number of firms, each with a very small share of the market, producing a homogeneous product, with firms and consumers possessing perfect information, and with free entry to, and exit from, the industry.

3.3 Characteristics of perfect competition

- There is a **large number** of **buyers** and **sellers** in the market.
- **Individual firms** are 'price takers', unable to influence the market price individually.

- **Producers** and **consumers** act **rationally** and have the same information.
- The **product** is **homogeneous**: one unit of the product is the same as any other unit.
- There is **free entry** into and exit of firms out of the market.
- There are **no transport** or **information gathering** costs.

3.4 Perfect competition acts as a useful theoretical benchmark against which we can:

(a) **Judge or predict** what firms might do in markets where **competition** shows some or most of the **characteristics of being perfect**

(b) **Contrast the behaviour** of firms in markets that are imperfect

Action Programme 1

Think about the market for a particular product – say, motor cars. To what extent is this market 'perfect'?

3.5 Long-run equilibrium will, occur in the industry when there are no more firms entering or leaving the industry because no new firm thinks it could earn profits by entering and no existing firm thinks it could do better by leaving. In the **long run**, equilibrium will occur when the **revenue from selling an extra unit equals its cost and its price.**

3.6 **Reasons for fragmentation**

- **Barriers** to **entry** are **low**: it is easy to set up in business.
- There are **few economies of scale** to be had by a large firm.
- **Small scale businesses** may be **more flexible** in coping with erratic demand.
- A **large firm** in a fragmented industry **cannot use** its **size** when dealing with suppliers.
- Being too large might lead to **higher overhead costs**.
- **Local image** and **reputation** are important.
- The **market** itself might be **fragmented**, as buyers can have a variety of different tastes.
- **Government** can forbid concentration.
- If **standards** are **enforced locally**, this can encourage fragmentation.

3.7 A fragmented industry can be consolidated into one with fewer companies as follows.

(a) **Technology may change**.

(b) **New standard product**

A standard product might be preferred to the previous custom-made variety for a number of reasons. Fast food chains such as McDonalds or Spud-u-like offer a consistent standard, and customers might welcome this lowering of the risk of disappointment.

(c) **Separate cause of fragmentation and deal with it**

Many big publishing companies have a large number of smaller **imprints**, with their own characteristics. (The BPP Holdings plc group, in addition to offering training, publishes a number of different imprints which serve different markets in different ways).

(d) **Consolidation**

Some industries **consolidate naturally** as they age.

Concentrated industries

Key Concept

A concentrated industry is dominated by a small number of large firms, which are able to exercise a significant influence over the market as a whole.

3.8 This corresponds to the market structure known as oligopoly.

Key Concept

Oligopoly is a market dominated by a few suppliers.

3.9 The essence of oligopoly is that **firms' production decisions are interdependent**. One firm cannot set price and output without considering how its rivals' response will affect its own profits. How an oligopolist will actually set his output and price depends on what assumption firms make about their competitors' behaviour.

3.10 **Reasons for concentration**

- It is **cheaper** to **produce in bulk** (ie where there are economies of scale).
- The amounts of **money needed** to stay in the business are **large**.
- Entry **barriers** are **high**: in other words it is hard to set up in business.
- The service does **not depend uniquely** on the **skills** of a particular individual.
- A large firm can benefit from an **integrated distribution network**.
- **Customers' needs** are **fairly standard** in the market.
- There are **economies of scale** in marketing distribution, purchasing etc.
- The company has **proprietary product technology**.

3.11 The importance of industry concentration is that there is nearly always a **'market leader'** who can significantly influence:

- The way business is done
- Relationships with sources of supply
- Distribution
- Pricing

Price leadership and price wars in concentrated industries

Key Concept

Cartel is an association of suppliers formed for the purpose of co-operating on the fixing of variables such as price or output levels.

3.12 A price cartel or price ring is created when a group of oligopoly firms combine to agree on a price at which they will sell their product to the market.

3.13 Each oligopoly firm could increase its profits if all the big firms in the market charge the same price as a monopolist would, and split the output between them. This is known as **collusion**, which can either be tacit or openly admitted.

3.14 The success of a price cartel will depend on:

(a) Whether it **consists** of **most or all** of the **producers** of the product.

(b) Whether or not there are **close substitutes** for the product. For example, a price cartel by taxi drivers might lead to a shift in demand for transport services to buses, cars and trains.

(c) The **ease** with which **supply** can be **regulated**.

(d) The **price elasticity** of **demand** for the product. An attempt to raise prices might result in such a large a fall in demand that the total income of producers also falls. *that would*
Depend on the demand of a product.

(e) Whether **producers** can **agree** on their individual shares of the total restricted supply to the market. This is often the greatest difficulty of all.

The monopoly market

3.15 Monopoly is the opposite of perfect competition.

Key Concept

In a **monopoly**, there is only one firm, the sole producer of a good which has no closely competing substitutes.

3.16 In monopoly the firm can earn **supernormal profits** in the long run as well as in the short run, because there are **barriers to entry** which prevent rivals entering the market.

Price discrimination

Key Concept

The term **price discrimination** refers to a situation in which a firm sells the 'same' product at different prices in different markets.

Action Programme 2

Have you come across price discrimination in practice?

When?

3.17 Three basic conditions are necessary for price discrimination to be effective and profitable.

(a) The seller must be able to **control the supply** of the product. Clearly, this will apply under monopoly conditions. The monopoly seller has control over the quantity of the product offered to a particular buyer.

(b) The seller must be able to **prevent** the **resale** of the good by one buyer to another.

Services are less easily resold than goods while transportation costs, tariff barriers or import quotas may separate classes of buyers geographically and thus make price discrimination possible.

(c) There must be **significant differences** in the willingness to pay among the different classes of buyers.

Marketing at Work

Some German companies have reported losing lucrative home markets because the Internet has made it easier for customers to access and compare prices from other suppliers.

Geographical price discrimination is becoming harder to sustain in an age where 'a shopper with a credit card and computer can sit at home and order from around the world'. The Internet has therefore increased competition, and is used by many organisations as a competitive weapon.

Emerging industries

An **emerging industry** is a new, or re-formed, industry. It can be created by technological innovation, changes in costs, social and economic changes.

3.18 Examples, of new, new-ish and emerging industries include the following.

- Electronic publishing (ie 'books' transferred to CD-ROM) and interactive television
- Waste recycling (in some countries)
- Virtual reality applications

3.19 The problems with emerging industries include the following.

- The **technology** is uncertain.

- Customer requirements are not known.

- New industries start with **high costs**, but these fall eventually.

- **Newly formed companies** are in a **good position** to get into the industry.

- **Consumers** need to be **informed** about what the industry can offer in order to be interested in new products or services.

- Some new industries receive **subsidies**.

- Early **barriers** to **entry** include technology, access to materials, problems obtaining funds.

3.20 In an emerging market, even the approach to competitors differs. Licensing can encourage competition. This helps build the market, and in any case, it is rarely feasible to maintain a monopoly in the long run. In the 1950s, Pilkington licensed its revolutionary glass making technology to its competitors.

4 Regulation of competition   Specimen paper, 12/03

4.1 The government, through legislation, can significantly influence the nature of relationships between a firm and members of its micro environment. Legislation can be used, for example, to control the price at which goods or services are sold to customers, or to allow a supplier access to a market which economic and technical barriers had previously excluded it.

4.2 A good example of competition regulation is the UK's **Competition Act 1998**. The Act prohibits:

(a) Certain agreements or concerted practices which have as their object or effect the **prevention, restriction** or **distortion** of **competition** within the United Kingdom

(b) The **abuse** of a **dominant position** in a market if it may affect trade within the United Kingdom

4.3 The **Director General of Fair Trading** enforces these provisions; he can give directions for bringing any infringement to an end and impose penalties of up to 10% of turnover.

4.4 The Competition Act also established the Competition Commission. The Commission has two aspects to its work:

(a) Preparation of **reports**

(b) The **appeals tribunal** which will hear appeals against decisions made under the prohibition provisions of the new Competition Act 1998

4.5 The investigations being carried out by the Competition Commission in 2002 included the following:

(a) Possible monopoly in the supply of prescription-only veterinary medicine
(b) The level of termination charges made to other operators by mobile phone companies
(c) The level of charges levied at the three biggest London airports by BAA plc

4.6 The **Enterprise Act 2002** includes provisions to reform UK competition law. In provisions expected to come into force during 2003, criminal sanctions for operating a cartel are introduced with a maximum penalty of five years in prison for those found guilty of dishonestly operating deliberate agreements to fix prices, share markets, limit production and rig bids.

Marketing at Work

A good example of a situation where a merger was allowed to proceed with safeguards in place was the merger of the two largest companies involved in the UK's ITV television network, Carlton Communications and Granada. In its report in October 2003 the Competition Commission accepted the companies' views that the merger would remove disfunctionality in the ITV network. The Commission believed that the merger would benefit viewers, through better programme quality and choice, and independent producers. Provided safeguards operated effectively, advertisers would also benefit through a stronger, more competitive, ITV.

The Commission were particularly concerned about the impact on the remaining small ITV companies. In response Carlton and Granada agreed a package of safeguards proposed by the ITC. The merged company would also give the other regional licensees the option to roll over existing airtime sales contracts.

The Commission was also worried about the sale of Carlton's and Granada's advertising airtime and in particular the share for discount deals with advertisers and media buyers. The Commission allowed advertisers a fall-back option, enabling them to renew the terms of their 2003 contracts without change (automatically adjusted, should viewing figures fall). The Commission considered, as an alternative remedy, the two companies divesting their sales houses, and running these as independent entities. However the Commission felt that the merged company might still be able to exercise excessive influence on the demerged sales houses, and it seemed unrealistic to divorce the broadcasting company from its principal source of income.

EU competition law

4.7 Anticompetitive practices which affect only the trader within one member state of the European Union (EU) are subject only to national legislation. However, where such practices may affect free trade between member states, the EU rules on competition come into force. EU rules prohibit 'all agreements between undertakings, decisions by associations of undertakings and concerted practices which may affect trade between member states and which have as their object or effect the prevention, restriction or distortion of competition within the common market'.

4.8 **Mergers** must be notified to the Commission when:

(a) All the undertakings concerned achieve combined aggregate worldwide sales revenue of **more than 2.5 billion euros**.

(b) In each of at least three Member States, combined aggregate **sales** of more than **100 million euros**.

(c) In **each** of these **three Member States**, at least two of the firms concerned should exceed **25 million euros in sales**.

(d) Each of at least two of the companies concerned boast **aggregate EU-wide sales** of more than **100 million euros**.

Quotas

4.9 Member states of the EU are prevented from restricting competition by the fact that any form of **quota** is strictly controlled. A quota is a restriction which limits the import, export or through-transit of goods by reference to quantity or value.

Article 85 – restrictive agreements, decisions and concerted practices

4.10 This prohibits all agreements between businesses, decisions of associations of businesses and concerted practices which **affect** trade between members and **prevent, restrict or distort** competition. Any such agreement or decision shall be void. There then follows a list of activities of particular concern eg fixing prices, limiting production, sharing markets, discriminatory conditions of trading.

4.11 Any agreement may be 'justified' (subject to certain conditions) and the prohibition declared to be inapplicable if it contributes to **improving production** or **distribution** or promotes technical or economic progress, while allowing consumers a fair share of the resulting benefit.

Article 86 – abuse of dominant position

4.12 Any **abuse** by one or more businesses of a dominant position within the common market or in a substantial part of it shall be prohibited as incompatible with the common market so far as it affects free trade between member states; the list of particular abuses is similar to that set out in Article 85. Where a group of inter-related companies is involved, their conduct jointly may infringe Article 86.

4.13 A business will enjoy a **dominant position** where it has **power** to **hinder** the maintenance of effective competition on the relevant market by allowing it to behave independently of its competitors and customers and ultimately of consumers a dominant position itself is not reprehensible – only an **abuse** of it is an infringement.

Competition in the USA

4.14 The USA has some of the strongest laws on competition in the industrialised world, reflecting the practice in the USA of resolving many conflicts in court.

4.15 In the past they have been used against companies such as Microsoft and against AT&T, the monopoly telephone supplier. During the 1980s AT&T lost its hold over local calls, as seven regional telephone companies were set up under court supervision. AT&T became the long distance supplier and faced more competition in that field.

4.16 However, Congress subsequently modified the law to allow local companies and long-distance operators to compete with each other. The result has been the consolidation of the industry into three giant telecoms operations.

4.17 Moves against other companies have been less successful. IBM was threatened by actions in the 1970s, but these made little headway before being thrown out in 1982. IBM's position was instead undermined by the development of personal computers and networked office systems.

4.18 Critics of the US approach claim that in many fields government intervention is irrelevant, as technology changes too quickly. In addition laws have not been enforced consistently over time, but only when political fashion has dictated.

4.19 Other criticisms of competition legislation include its failure to take into account social needs other than competition, for example the preservation of employment. In addition the attempts by domestic firms to compete abroad may be undermined by fierce competition at home. Firms may not be able to obtain the returns they need for activities such as innovation and research and development, which will improve their prospects overseas.

Regulations governing specific industries

4.20 In many countries regulators are given significant authority over specific industries. Utilities are one common example; their supply is a necessity for daily life, and their providers may hold a national or regional monopoly.

4.21 In practice, the regulators of these industries do have considerable power.

(a) They can specify **minimum** level of **services**.

(b) They can **limit the increases in prices** the companies can change their customers. For example a utility might only be allowed to increase prices by the retail price index less a percentage. This is to encourage efficiency.

(c) They can **encourage greater competition** in the industry by adjudicating over uncompetitive practices, referring the issue to the competition authorities, or restructuring the industry.

Other government influences on competition in an industry

4.22 As a buyer, controller and supplier in a mixed economy, the government can bring considerable pressure to bear on competition within an industry.

(a) The government can influence the **timing and extent of structural changes** within an industry. Direct influence can take the form of 'full-blown regulation of such key variables as entry to the industry, competitive practices or profitability' (Porter).

(b) Governments can **influence** an **industry's structure** in indirect ways, such as the imposition of minimum product quality and testing standards.

(c) Governments might impose **policies** which keep an **industry fragmented**, and prevent the concentration of too much market share in the hands of one or two producers.

(d) In some industries, governments **regulate** the **adoption** of **new products**. In the pharmaceuticals industry new drugs or medicines must undergo stringent testing and obtain government approval before they can be marketed.

(e) **Subsidies** from the government to firms in an industry can take the form of cash grants, tax incentives or other incentives (eg rent-free government factories).

(f) Government policy can affect the position of products in one industry with respect to the position of **substitute products**. More stringent **safety regulations** on one type of product might weaken its competitive position against substitute products.

Exam Tip

The Specimen Paper asked for reasons why firms should not collude with competitors.

5 Monitoring competitors   Specimen paper

5.1 The purpose of analysing competitors is to try and assess what they will do. This will enable the organisation to respond accordingly. Competitive advantage is about **relative** competitive position. Competitors are sometimes used as benchmarks.

5.2 We discussed in Chapter 4 the sources that can be used to obtain information about competitors. The increased importance of information technology means that organisations have to consider carefully how they should monitor competitors and what they are aiming to achieve.

Competitor analysis

5.3 Aspects of competitor analysis

- What are the **competitor's future goals**?
- What **assumptions does the competitor hold** about the industry and its place in it?
- Is the competitor **competing on price**?
- Is the competitor **offering a different product**?
- Is the competitor **concentrating on one set of customers**?
- **What are the competitor's capabilities** (ie its strengths and weaknesses)?

Future goals

5.4   Useful information about the competitor's goals

- What are the business's **stated financial goals**?
- What **trade-offs** are made between long-term and short-term objectives?
- What is the competitor's **attitude to risk**?
- Do **managerial beliefs** (eg that the firm should be a market leader) affect its goals?
- **Structure**: for example, do marketing staff have more power than finance staff?
- What **incentive systems** are in place?
- What are the **managers** like? Are they united? Do they have a favourite strategy?
- To what extent does the business **cross-subsidise** others in the group?
- What is the purpose of the business: to raise money for the group?

Assumptions

5.5   Other questions relate to each competitor's assumptions (accurate or otherwise) about:

- Itself and its **position** in the industry
- The **industry as a whole** (eg does the competitor consider the industry is in decline?)

5.6   Assumptions:

- **Indicate the way** in which the competitor might **react**
- **Explain biases or blind spots** in how the competitor's managers see the environment

5.7   Useful information about competitor assumptions

- What are the competitor's **perceptions** of its **relative position** (in terms of cost, product quality) in the industry?

- Is there a particularly strong **'emotional' bond** with particular products and markets?

- Are there **cultural or regional differences** that influence the actions of managers?

- What does the competitor believe about the **future demand** for the industry?

- Does the competitor accept the industry's **'conventional wisdom'**?

- In addition a **career analysis** of key managers can be informative. An accountant in charge is likely to have different priorities from a marketer.

Current strategy

5.8   Analysing the competitor's current strategy covers:

■ Products	■ Overall costs
■ Distribution	■ Financial strengths
■ Marketing and selling	■ Organisation
■ Operations	■ General managerial skills
■ Research and engineering	■ Managerial ability
■ Prices	■ Stakeholder relationships

Capabilities

5.9 Analysis should identify the competitor's:

- **Core or distinctive strengths**
- **Ability to expand in a particular market**

Other information

5.10 Information would include:

- Market share
- Sales volumes and margins
- Discounts
- Major changes in the internal environment (eg boardroom disputes)
- New product development plans
- Relationships with stakeholders, or potential relationships (eg exclusive rights)

Competitor response profiles

5.11 All these are combined in a **competitor response profile**. This indicates:

- The **competitor's vulnerability** to environmental forces, competitors' actions etc
- **The 'battleground'**, invading a competitor's position in a low-priority product range

Competitor information systems

5.12 A successful CIS needs to follow six steps.

- **1: Decide** what **information** is **required**
- **2: Design appropriate data capture systems** and collect the data
- **3: Analyse** and evaluate the **data**
- **4: Communicate** the resulting information
- **5: Incorporate** the information and conclusions reached **into strategy**
- **6: Feedback** results so that the information system may be refined

Action Programme 3

Jot down a list of items of information obtained from an environmental analysis of competitors.

Who they think they are
Distribution
Loyalty to Product
Frequency in updating Product
How do they see the MKT Place
Management System.
Costs
Prices
Marketing budget
Long term Plan
Stakeholders.

Chapter Roundup

- A business has to deal with **competitors** and **potential competitors** if it is a business. Competitors compete for the same resources and customers.

- Porter holds that the structure of competition in an industry is determined by the following forces.

    - Barriers to entry
    - The threat of substitute products and services
    - The bargaining power of customers
    - The bargaining power of suppliers
    - The rivalry amongst current competitors

- **Different industry structures** occur in different industries.

    - **Fragmented industries** are characterised by a large number of small firms.
    - **Concentrated industries** are characterised by a small number of large firms.
    - **Emerging industries** are characterised by greater uncertainty.

- The object of UK **competition law** is to protect the public interest by ensuring that the beneficial effects of competition can be exercised.

- Competition in the UK is regulated by the **Office of Fair Trading** and the **Competition Commission**. The objects of the competition legislation are to protect the **public interest** and regulate **anti-competitive practices**.

- Organisations can adopt various competitive strategies

    - **Cost leadership** (being the lowest cost producer within an industry)

    - **Differentiation** (emphasising the **particular characteristics** of a firm's products or brands)

    - **Focus strategy** (concentrating on niches, either **products** or **market segments**)

- **Competitor analysis** involves analysing **competitors' goals, assumptions** about the industry and their position in it, current **strategies** and likely **responses.**

Quick Quiz

1   List Porter's five competitive forces.

2   Give five examples of barriers to entry. —

3   Fill in the blank

A .... strategy is based on the assumption that competitive advantage can be gained through particular characteristics of a firm's products of brands.

4   Which of the following is not a competitive strategy?

    A   Cost leadership
    B   Price promotion
    C   Differentiation
    D   Focus

[Handwritten annotations: threat of new entrants; new substitute product of service; bargain power of customers; bargain power of supply; Economies of Scale. established distribution. Brand Loyalty. Switching costs.]

5   Fill in the blank.

     A .... industry is populated by a large number of small and medium-sized companies.

6   Oligopoly is a market where there is a large number of firms, each with a small share of the market.

     True   ☐

     False ☐

7   What is a cartel?

8   Give six aspects of competitor analysis.

Action Programme Review

1   (a)   There is a huge number of buyers, and many sellers too. For any given model of car, a particular dealer is likely to be a price taker.

     (b)   Communication is generally good. Product features are well known and list prices are freely available. And discount levels too are widely commented on, in the press and by word of mouth.

     (c)   Consumers don't always act rationally. A car which appeals to a buyer's self-image, or snobbishness, may command a higher price than another apparently similar model.

     (d)   The product is very far from homogeneous.

     (e)   Entry to the market is not easy, whether we are talking about manufacturers of motor cars (very high start-up costs), or dealers.

     (f)   Transport costs are *not* absent. On the contrary, significant geographical price differentiation is possible because of the high transport costs involved.

2   You might have thought of:

     (a)   Telephone calls (different prices for peak and off-peak calls)
     (b)   Rail travel (there are many different tickets you can buy for an identical journey)
     (c)   Package holidays (more expensive during school holidays)

3   (a)   Who are the existing competitors? How much of the market do they hold in each segment of the markets (eg in each particular region or country)?

     (b)   Who are potential competitors? How soon might they enter the market?

     (c)   How profitable are existing competitors? What is their EPS, dividend yield, ROCE etc?

     (d)   What do the goals of each competitor appear to be, and what strategies have they adopted so far?

     (e)   What products/services do they sell? How do they compare with the organisation's own products or services?

     (f)   How broad is their product line? (eg Are they 'up-market high quality, or down-market low quality, low price and high volume producers?)

     (g)   What is their distribution network?

(h)   What are their skills and weakness in direct selling, advertising, sales promotions, product design?

(i)   What are their design skills or R & D skills? Do they innovate or follow the market leader with new product ideas?

(j)   What are their costs of sale and operational capabilities, with respect to:

    (i)   Economies of sale

    (ii)   Use of advanced technology equipment

    (iii)   Patents, trademarks, know-how

    (iv)   Quality control

    (v)   Location

    (vi)   Transportation costs

    (vii)   Labour skills and productivity

    (viii) Supply advantages (ie special access to raw materials at a low cost)

    (ix)   Industrial relations and industrial disputes

    (x)   Reliability in servicing customers

(k)   What are their general managerial capabilities?

(l)   Financial strengths and weaknesses. What is the debt position and financial gearing of each competitor? Do they have easy access to sources of new finance? What proportion of profits do they return in the business in order to finance growth?

(m)   How is each competitor organised? How much decentralisation of authority do they allow to operating divisions, and so how flexible or independent can each of the operating divisions be?

(n)   Does the competitor have a good spread or portfolio of activities? What is the risk profile of each competitor?

(o)   Does any competitor have a special competitive advantage – eg a unique government contract or special access to government authorities?

(p)   Does any competitor show signs of changing strategy to increase competition to the market?

Answers to Quick Quiz

1 ■ Threat of new entrants
  ■ Threat of substitute products
  ■ Bargaining power of customers
  ■ Bargaining power of suppliers
  ■ Rivalry amongst current competitors

2 Any five of

  ■ Economies of scale
  ■ Product differentiation
  ■ Switching costs
  ■ Capital requirements
  ■ Access to distribution channels
  ■ Other cost advantages

3 Differentiation

4 B Price promotion

5 Fragmented

6 False. The description is of perfect competition. Oligopoly is a market dominated by a few suppliers.

7 An association of suppliers that fixes prices or output levels.

8 ■ Future goals
  ■ Assumptions
  ■ Competition on price
  ■ Differentiation of product
  ■ Concentration on certain customers
  ■ Capabilities

Now try illustrative questions 11 and 12 at the end of the Study Text

Part C

The macro environment

The macro environment

Chapter Topic List	
1	Setting the scene
2	Defining the macro environment
3	Macro environmental factors
4	The environmental set
5	Sources of environmental information
6	Information on the UK economy
7	Information on international markets

Learning Outcomes

☑ Appreciate the importance of the macro environment to the marketer

☑ Access relevant sources of information on the macro environment

Syllabus References

☑ Appreciate the importance of the macro environment to the marketing process

☑ Awareness of key sources of information on the macro environment

Key Concepts Introduced

■ The macro environment   ■ Environmental set

1 Setting the scene

1.1 In this chapter we introduce the concept of the macro environment. The macroenvironment consists of the general forces which are impacting, or will be impacting upon a company's micro environment.

1.2 Clearly the number of possible factors that could have an impact upon an organisation is quite daunting. We therefore start off by providing a general framework for analysis of the environment. We shall discuss each of the most significant factors briefly here and in more detail in the succeeding chapters.

1.3 As with the micro environment, it is important for an organisation to know about the **possible sources of information** it can use. We discuss in general terms the sources of information about macro-factors, and then go into more detail about how information on the UK economy and world markets can be obtained.

Exam Tip

Bear in mind that the exam is set months in advance of being sat. Macro environmental issues that were topical a year or so before you are due to sit your paper might therefore form the basis of a question.

2 Defining the macro environment 12/03

2.1 Remember that the **micro** environment comprises all those organisations and individuals with which a business unit interacts, whether directly or indirectly.

Key Concept

The **macro environment** is concerned with general forces in the environment which may one day affect a company in its micro environment.

2.2 To illustrate the contrast between the micro and macro environments, customers and potential customers are real individuals existing in a company's **micro** environment. However, **demographic** change is one of those more abstract phenomenon in a company's **macro** environment which won't directly affect the company's customers today, but may do at some time in the future.

2.3 However, sometimes there is overlap. For example, government bodies feature prominently in most organisations' micro environment (eg as customers; as tax collector). But government bodies also create legislation which indirectly affects the environment in which a business operates.

2.4 An organisation can easily monitor its micro environment, but it can be quite critical that it adequately monitors its macro environment. Macro environmental analysis involves:

- **Identifying** the key factors in the environment
- **Forecasting** what is likely to happen to each of the factors in the future
- **Responding** to environmental change

Political-Legal
Economical
Social
Technological

Factors in the environment

2.5 There are any number of models for describing **general** environmental factors. One in common use in the UK is SLEPT which stands for:

- Social-cultural
- Legal
- Economic
- Political
- Technical (or Technological)

PEST WITH AN L

2.6 SLEPT analysis is widely used in the UK for discussion of the general environment, so we shall use this framework. The sector approach conflates general with specific environmental conditions.

2.7 A variation of SLEPT which is commonly used is PEST:

- Political/legal
- Economic
- Social
- Technical/Technological

+ NATURAL ENVIRONMENT

2.8 In addition, the natural environment is seen by many people as becoming an increasingly important element of organisations' macro environment. 'Environmentalism' is a concept which does not divide neatly into 'micro' and 'macro' environmental elements.

Other classifications

2.9 An alternative model, STEEPLE, gives equal prominence to **environmental** and **ethical** issues.

2.10 Richard Daft (*Organisation Theory and Design*) proposed an alternative arrangement of ten 'sectors' in the environment, in no particular order, as follows.

- Financial resources sector
- Industry sector
- Government sector
- Human resources sector
- Technology sector

- Market sector
- Economic conditions sector
- Socio-cultural sector
- International sector
- Raw materials sector

Remember, FIGHT ME SIR.

3 Macro environmental factors

Social change and social trends

3.1 Social change involves changes in the nature, attitudes and habits of society. Social changes are continually happening, and trends can be identified.

(a) **Rising standards of living**

These may result in wider ownership of consumer and luxury goods, which have implications for those industries.

(b) **Society's attitude to business**

Increasing social obligations and responsibilities are being heaped on to companies in many countries, not least with respect to ethical conduct (towards customers, employees etc).

3.2 Jones classified the social factors in a slightly different way, as follows.

(a) **Underlying factors**

These include population trends; education policy and the educational standards of the workforce; and attitudes to acquiring skills.

(b) **People at work**

The labour market, trade unions and work attitudes are all important. In these areas organisations are at the mercy of legislation and political pressures.

(c) **Individuals and society**

This category of social factors includes challenges to the existing social order, involvement by junior employees in decisions taken within their organisation, the social responsibility of employers to their employees, income and wealth distribution, and spending patterns.

Demography

3.3 One of the most important social changes is that related to population numbers and composition. Demography is the study of population and population trends.

Cultural changes

3.4 Each society has a certain culture (its own attitudes and ways of doing things). Within each society, there are many culture groups. Examples are as follows.

- **Ethnic** and **racial cultures**
- Religious cultures
- Classes
- The way business is conducted in each country

Marketing at Work

Cultural change might have to be planned for. An example is suggested by Japan. Since World War II, Japanese employees have been famed for their work ethic. The company came first. Holidays would be sacrificed for extra work and people rarely changed jobs. This cultural ethic was helpful in reconstructing Japan after the devastation of war.

However, Japan's growing prosperity has meant that the work ethic is declining as the new generation wants more leisure time and so on. People are less averse to changing jobs. Japanese companies might be able to plan for this change by forcing employees to take holidays or investing in leisure businesses.

The political and legal environments

3.5 Many **economic** forecasts ignore the implications of a **change in government policy**, irrespective of whether or not there is a **change of government**. This limits their value.

(a) At national level, politics is significant as the political process includes **legislation**.

(b) Politics at international level also has a direct bearing on organisations. **European Union directives** affect all countries in the EU.

(c) The government and supra-national institutions control much of the economy. The **government** is the nation's **largest supplier**, **employer**, **customer** and **investor**. The slightest shift in political emphasis can decimate a particular market almost overnight (for example, aerospace and defence).

(d) For a variety of reasons, nations want to have **national champions** in particular industries. The shipping and airline industries have been particularly affected by the desire and insistence of many countries to have their own fleets.

3.6 Political **change** complicates the task of predicting future influences, and planning to meet them. Some political changes cannot easily be planned for.

3.7 Marketing managers must be constantly aware of the legal implications of their actions. The amount of law affecting marketers, both directly and indirectly, is increasing in most countries. Here are some examples of the ways in which a marketing manager needs to be aware of the law.

- **Customers** are gaining **more rights** in their dealings with a supplier.
- Similarly, **employees** are gaining **more rights**.
- **Advertisers** are increasingly **restricted** in the claims they can make.
- **Governments** in most countries have **passed laws** against anti-competitive practices.
- The **law** is often **resorted to** in disputes between manufacturers and their distributors.

Marketing at Work

Marketing managers who run foul of the law can cost their organisations a lot of money.

The Hoover company found itself facing claims for compensation from thousands of angry customers after a sales promotion involving offers of free flights went disastrously wrong.

3.8 As well as the law, there is an increasing amount of quasi-law which affects marketers. This is based on voluntary codes which do not normally have the full sanction of legal punishment, but companies find it in their interest to abide by them.

The economic environment

3.9 The state of the economy affects all organisations, both commercial and non-commercial. The rate of growth in the economy is a measure of the overall change in demand for goods and services. Growth is an indication of increases in demand. For example, an increase in Gross National Product per head of the population might result in a greater demand for:

- Private cars and less demand for public transport
- Domestic consumer goods, such as dishwashers and compact disc players
- Services (eg restaurant meals or holidays abroad)

OTHER ECONOMIC INFLUENCES	
Regional or national level	The rate of inflation
	Unemployment and the availability of manpower with appropriate skills
	Interest rates and availability of credit
	The balance of trade and foreign exchange rates
	Taxation levels and incentives
	Government subsidies
	Public expenditure (and public sector procurement policies)
Rate of inflation, unemployment and so on.	Comparative growth rates, inflation rates, interest rates and wage rates in other countries
	The extent of protectionist measures against imports
	Freedom of capital movement between different countries
	The development of international economic communities, such as the European Union, and the prospects of international trade agreements between countries
	The levels of corporate and personal taxation in different countries
	Relative exchange rates
	Economic agreements

3.10 The state of the economy or more often the forecast state of the economy will influence the planning process for organisations which operate within it.

(a) In times of **boom** and increased demand and consumption, the overall planning problem will be to **identify** the **demand**.

(b) Conversely, in times of **recession**, the emphasis will be on **cost-effectiveness, continuing profitability, survival** and **competition**.

3.11 Economists can contribute to the strategic planning process with economic forecasts and information about economic trends.

Economic trends: regional, national and international

3.12 Three levels of economic trend analysis need to be considered: regional (area) trends, national trends and international trends.

The natural environment

3.13 Physical environmental conditions are important for organisations in the following ways (in addition to obvious factors like earthquakes and the weather and pressure groups).

(a) The physical environment is a source of **resource inputs**. Managing physical resources successfully (eg oil companies, mining companies) is a good source of profits. If resources are scarce or valuable, this is doubly important.

(b) The physical environment presents **logistical problems** or opportunities to organisations. Proximity to road and rail links can be a reason for siting a warehouse in a particular area.

(c) The physical environment is also under the **control** of **other organisations**.

(i)   Local authority town planning departments can influence where a building and necessary infrastructure can be sited. Zoning regulations prohibit the siting of commercial developments in some residential districts.

(ii)   Governments can make regulations about some of the organisation's environmental interactions. Pollution legislation is an example.

The technical environment

3.14 Technological change is rapid, and organisations must adapt themselves to it.

3.15 Organisations that operate in an environment where the pace of technological change is very fast must be flexible enough to adapt to change quickly and must plan for change and innovation, perhaps by spending heavily on research and development. We discuss the technical environment in more detail in Chapter 13.

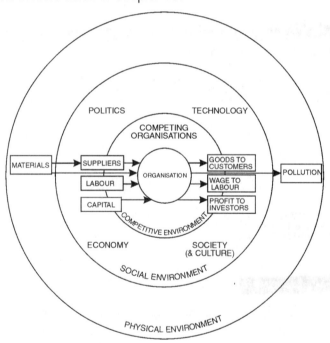

Action Programme 1

Carry out a macroenvironmental analysis on your employer, taking into account the SLEPT factors and also the natural environment. You'll find that marketing personnel are a good source of information; after all, they have to find out what customers are after.

4 The environmental set

Key Concept

A firm's **environmental set** includes those factors in the environment which affect it but over which it has limited control.

4.1 A feature of a **public house's** environmental set might include at any one time:

- **General economic conditions** (can people afford to go out drinking?)

- **Local conditions** (eg the closure of a nearby business might reduce the numbers of regular customers)

- **Social trends** leading to a cut in the number of drinkers

- **Government policy** (to raise money by taxing alcohol)

4.2 Set elements can change. For example, the pub's would fall if another pub opened nearby. This might prove to be more urgent in any one year than the long-term decline in drinking, even though this latter trend is an important factor.

4.3 A factor may be a critical factor in the environmental set of one organisation, but irrelevant to another (eg the state of the economy may be critical to an estate agency, but almost irrelevant to an undertaker).

4.4 An organisation should consider how each of the key macroenvironmental factors which make up its environmental set are likely to affect it.

Opportunities and threats

4.5 In terms of SWOT analysis (Strengths/Weaknesses/Opportunities/Threats), an external appraisal of the environment identifies profit-making opportunities which can be exploited by the company's strengths. It also anticipates environmental threats (such as a declining economy, competitors' actions, government legislation or industrial unrest) against which the company must protect itself. (SWOT analysis is covered in Chapter 16.)

5 Sources of environmental information

5.1 Part D of this Study Text will discuss in some detail the process of marketing research. For now we list some sources of information about the macroenvironment that may be helpful background in the next few chapters. These include newspaper, trade journals, government publications and databases.

5.2 It is easy to be overwhelmed by the volume of environmental information on offer, and the variety of data that must be used. The temptation to ignore these factors completely might be understandable especially as managers are more concerned with short-term issues relating to immediate production.

5.3 However, some sort of scanning of environmental information sources is essential. In a large company, this can be done by the **strategic planning department**, if there is one. In a small company, everybody involved might keep an eye open for relevant environmental changes.

5.4 Managers can easily read about a topic in the paper. However it is not always easy to ensure that relevant environmental information is acted upon, especially if it is not something that requires an immediate reaction.

5.5 One way of ensuring that wider environmental issues are not overlooked is a type of **scanning exercise**. At regular intervals, an individual deputised to the task reports to managers on developments in the firm's environment.

5.6 Organisations should look **routinely** and **continuously** to obtain macro environmental data. With developments in information technology (for example, the development of Mintel online services and McCarthy CD ROM databases), increasing volumes of information are becoming available. Competitive advantage will go to companies who not only collect such data, but are able to *process* it and make appropriate responses.

Environmental data

5.7 McNamee lists various areas of environmental information that ought to be included in a database for strategic planners. These are briefly described below.

Economic data

5.8 **Economic data** includes details of past growth and predictions of future growth in GDP and disposable income, the pattern of interest rates, predictions of the rate of inflation, unemployment levels and tax rates, developments in international trade etc. The sources of macro economic data are outlined in detail below. This is used to discern future demand and spending patterns.

5.9 Industry data including **sales volume**, **product facilities** and **technological changes** will also be important.

Political data

5.10 **Political data** (on what influence the government is having on the industry) comes from the mainstream media, unless the firm has inside knowledge and contacts in the government. One of the advantages of lobbying is not only to influence government but to get an early indication of policy.

Legal data

5.11 What are the likely implications of recent legislation, what legislation is likely to be introduced in the future, and what implications would this have? Legal data also comes mainly from the mainstream media. In addition, there are specialist publications) indicating the significance of recent case law. Other firms specialise in certain types of information.

Social data

5.12 What are the changing habits, attitudes, cultures and educational standards of the population as a whole, and customers in particular? Social data comes from an enormous variety of sources. Governmental publications may be helpful. Surveys conducted by market researchers are also a useful source, although not publicly accessible.

Natural environment data

5.13 Data about the resources available to businesses is important, but businesses also need to consider how concerns about the natural environment may act as present constraints or future limitations. Knowledge about the activities and campaigns of pressure groups can be important. There is overlap with the political environment, as businesses will need to gauge how the government is responding to green concerns.

Technological data

5.14 We discuss some approaches to technological forecasting and data sources in Chapter 13.

Public databases

5.15 You can now access large volumes of generally available information through databases held by public bodies. A variety of such services are available.

   (a)   Some newspapers offer computerised access to old editions, with search facilities looking for information on particular companies or issues.

   (b)   A variety of public databases are also available for inspection.

   (c)   Some databases have been designed specifically for marketing users such as ACORN.

Exam Tip

Don't forget the websites listed in the front of this book; they are excellent sources on a large number of topics.

6 Information on the UK economy

UK statistical sources

6.1 Here, we summarise important sources of statistical information on the UK economy, on the UK in a European context and on the UK in a world context. Similar sources are available for other countries.

6.2 The **Office for National Statistics** website **www.statistics.gov.uk** provides an initial starting point and covers a range of official statistics. (Most of the statistical sources below are available free from the ONS website as PDF files. A quick way to reach them is to search (for example, for *Regional Trends*) at www.google.co.uk, specifying 'pages from the UK'.)

UK STATISTICAL SOURCES	
Annual Abstract of Statistics	Major annual statistics of government departments under eighteen headings, generally over a ten-year period up to the previous calendar year.
Bank of England Quarterly Bulletin	Statistics on assets and liabilities of banks and building societies and on the money supply, government debt, exchange rates and interest rates.
Business Monitor	Summary statistics on the annual Census of Production, with a two - to three-year time lag.
Business Ratio Reports	Annual analyses of accounting ratios for 12,000 leading companies.
Economic Trends	Tables and charts showing trends in the UK economy.
Labour Market Trends	Data on the labour market, including earnings and retail prices.
Financial Statistics	Financial data for the latest month or quarter. Includes financial accounts for the various sectors of the economy.
Monthly Digest of Statistics	Monthly data on output of a wide range of industries. Statistics on components of national income and expenditure, demography, the labour market and various social issues.
National Income and Expenditure	Also called 'The Blue Book'. The most comprehensive source of data on national income, output and expenditure and their components.
Regional Trends	Detailed regional data including economic, social and demographic indices, based on the UK Standard Planning Regions.
Social Trends	Detailed data on household wealth, income and expenditure, and demographic and social trends.
United Kingdom Balance of Payments	Also called 'The Pink Book'. The prime source of data on the balance of payments broken down into its various components.

Other information

6.3   Other useful sources of information and articles on the economy include bank reviews and the National Institute Economic Review. The NIER comments on the state of the UK economy and the world economy. It provides useful comparisons between the UK and competitors, for example regarding labour costs, productivity and education.

Interpretation of statistical sources

6.4   Naturally, statistics need to be interpreted cautiously. Many sources are not published until they are out of date, although the internet has made publication faster for many statistics. Some statistics may be of doubtful reliability. The uses made of statistical data by governments in the management of the economy and by businesses in marketing and planning are considered in the next chapter.

7 Information on international markets

7.1 Companies can obtain considerable help and advice in its attempts to research foreign markets. Informal contacts may be made with a variety of organisations including the following.

- Overseas agents and distributors
- Banks
- Trade and professional organisations
- Government departments
- Foreign embassies and consulates
- Academic institutions

UK in a European context

7.2 Among the statistical sources on Europe, the following publications are of particular interest.

Economic Survey of Europe	This annual publication presents data by individual country and also by geographical groupings, including the Eastern bloc. Identifies and analyses trends in industry, investment, consumer spending, national output and trade.
European Economy	This is published three times a year, together with a statistical supplement giving annual economic indicators, by the Commission of the EU. An annual report on the economic situation within the EU is included in each November issue.
Eurostat	The Statistical Offices of the European Communities provide annual publications giving major economic indices and these are available from The Stationery Office under the heading **Eurostat**.

UK in a world context

7.3 Statistical sources relating to worldwide economic issues include the following.

World Economic Outlook (IMF)	Provides and analyses short and medium-term projections for individual countries. Includes discussion of key policy issues.
UN Statistical Yearbook	Includes a wide variety of indices.
World Economic Survey (United Nations)	Analyses fluctuations in various world economic indicators. Covers problems and prospects for developed and developing economies and the international trade outlooks.
Monthly Digest of Statistics	Includes regular statistical series, plus special statistics compiled on specific issues. Areas covered include demography, earnings, prices, human resources and production.

7.4 Others commonly consulted sources on international markets are listed below.

(a) The **Bank of England** and the major UK banks have published booklets on trade prospects for various countries.

(b) The major 'serious' **newspapers** produce periodic surveys on various countries.

(c)   The **Economist Intelligence Unit** produces reports on various industries, countries and long term developments.

(d)   Most **major trade associations** and **Chambers of Commerce** hold data on trade fairs, visits and market intelligence for various countries.

(e)   There are numerous **trade directories** for overseas markets including Kompass, Dun and Bradstreet, Kluwer and Croner.

(f)   The **EU** and **OECD** produce numerous reports on trade statistics and prospects for member countries.

(g)   The **Department of Trade and Industry** and the Overseas Trade Services provide many publications, statistical summaries and intelligence reports.

(h)   The **Confederation of British Industry** produces a monthly report on foreign markets.

(i)   Many Anglo-foreign **Chambers of Commerce** and major Chambers of Commerce based on foreign countries provide regular market reports.

(j)   The **Office for National Statistics** produces regular data on international trade.

(k)   Many **reference libraries** subscribe to syndicated market research and abstract services including Emerald, Key Note, Mintel and Euromonitor.

7.5   Among the more commonly available and used data sources are the following.

- Guide to Official Statistics
- Monthly Digest of Statistics
- Overseas Trade Statistics

7.6   Various international bodies including the United Nations, the European Union, the European Coal and Steel Community, the Organisation for Economic Co-operation and Development and the International Monetary Fund also produce publications.

Action Programme 2

As you progress through your CIM studies, it will be very helpful to have information about countries with different marketing environments. We recommend that you have files on three contrasting countries. Collect background data on your chosen countries, watch out for relevant news items and review key political, social, economic and technological developments.

Exam Tip

The marking guide for the June 2003 paper emphasised 'The syllabus gives equal weight to all the various macro environments and examiners should recognise that a detailed knowledge of one is no longer required. Emphasis should be on the significance of the environment and its implications for marketers'.

Chapter Roundup

- There are a variety of ways of classifying the forces at work in the **macro environment**. (Social, legal, economic, political, natural, technological).

- Before answering a question on the macro environment, you should think about the possible relevance of the following.

    - **Economic change** at a regional, national or international level (eg trade developments)
    - The **political environment** and government influence (new legislation)
    - **Social and cultural changes** (eg changing attitudes)
    - The **law** and changes in the law
    - Changes in the size and make-up of the **population**
    - **Technological change**

- There are a number of statistical sources on the UK and international economy which businesses should **scan**.

Quick Quiz

1   Define the macro environment. *ENViRonment that is concerent with The factors that are out of the control of the organisa-tion and one day may Have effect on its micro environment*

2   *SOciaL*
    LeGaL
    EcoNOMical
    PoliticaL
    TecHNOLogicaL

    =

3   *FinanciaL*
    IDustRy
    Government
    Human Resources
    TecHNOLogy
    MaRket
    economic
    SociaL -cuLtuRaL
    InternatinaL
    Raw material

    =

4   Give four examples of demographic factors that may impact upon an organisation.

5   Fill in the blank *environmental set*
    .... includes those factors in the environment that affect a firm but over which it has limited control.

6   Give three examples of sources of information about international markets.

7   What are the main economic influences affecting a business at a regional or national level?

8   Which of the following types of law might impact upon a business?

   A   Criminal
   B   Tort
   C   Contract
   D   Health and safety
   E   Consumer protection
   F   Employment

Action Programme Review

1   Did you remember to prioritise the factors? Which are the most important?

2   –

Answers to Quick Quiz

1   The macro environment is concerned with general forces in the environment which may one day affect a company in its micro environment.

2   Socio-cultural
     Legal
     Economic
     Political
     Technological
     (and don't forget Natural!)

3   Financial resources sector
     Industry sector
     Government sector
     Human resources sector
     Technology sector
     Market sector
     Economic conditions sector
     Socio-cultural sector
     International sector
     Raw materials sector

4   Any four of:

   ▪   Household structure
   ▪   Sex
   ▪   Age
   ▪   Class
   ▪   Employment
   ▪   Geographical distribution

5   The environmental set

6 ■ Overseas agents
   ■ Banks
   ■ Trade ad professional organisations
   ■ Government and department
   ■ Foreign embassies and consultants
   ■ Academic institutions

7 ■ The rate of inflation
   ■ Unemployment and the availability of labour
   ■ Interest rates and availability of credit
   ■ Balance of trade and foreign exchange rates
   ■ Taxation levels and incentives
   ■ Government subsidies
   ■ Public expenditure

8 All of them

Now try illustrative question 13 at the end of the Study Text

The social and cultural environments

9

Chapter Topic List	
1	Setting the scene
2	Demography
3	The demographic profile of the UK
4	Demography and human resources
5	Demography and product markets
6	Social structure
7	Culture
8	Lifestyle and health

Learning Outcome

☑ Recognise and assess the potential impact of key trends in the social and cultural environments on the marketing function

Syllabus Reference

☑ Explain the social, demographic and cultural environments, and in general terms, their influence on and implications for marketing

Key Concepts Introduced

- Demography
- Rate of Natural Increase in population
- Class
- Culture
- Socialisation
- Lifestyle

1 Setting the scene

1.1 In this chapter we describe how social and cultural factors can influence marketing.

1.2 A key influence on the social environment is what is happening to population. We therefore start by discussing **demography**, the study of population. This involves studying a population's rate of growth or decline, its geographical and social distribution and its age structure (ie the proportion of young, middle aged and elderly people in the population).

1.3 You should realise that demographic developments not only affect the **pattern of demand**, but also the **availability of resources** to meet that demand. In section 4 of this chapter we describe how organisations can respond to the strains on available labour resources caused by demographic change.

1.4 We then move on to discuss **social class**. Social class is fundamentally an economic issue, with cultural connotations. We shall discuss how social class is reflected in income and buying decisions.

1.5 Lastly in this chapter we consider **culture**, the system of beliefs, values and behaviour in a group of people. It defines ways of behaving acceptably in given situations. Culture is acquired at home (from parents, television etc) and at school (from teachers and peers). The acquisition of culture, language and so on is referred to as socialisation. Values learnt can affect consumer behaviour in a number of different ways.

1.6 All of these factors are important in analysing and segmenting markets.

Exam Tip

A widely drawn question on the Specimen Paper asked for a discussion of the marketing implications of three social or lifestyle changes.

2 Demography   6/03

Key Concept

Demography is an 'analysis of statistics on birth and death rates, age structures of populations, ethnic groups within communities etc' (Bennett, *Dictionary of personnel and human resources management*).

2.1 The **purposes** of studying population and trends within it are as follows.

- People create a **demand** for goods and services.
- **Economic growth** should **exceed population** growth for enhanced standards of living.
- **Population** is a **source of labour**, one of the **factors of production**.
- **Population** creates **demands** on the **physical environment** and its resources.
- The structure of the population has implications for how markets are **segmented**.

Population size

[handwritten: 60,600,000 UK]
[handwritten: 50,763,000 england]

2.2 There is some argument that a country has an optimum **population size**. Why might a country's population size be important?

(a) **Importing of labour**

If a population is too small, the country will have to **import labour** to exploit its resources or provide services. A population below a certain size might make it hard to achieve economies of scale.

(b) **Demand for resources**

A population that is too large might create, **excessive demand** on food and resources and more demand for **educational resources**, housing and public services than the state or the private sector are able to supply.

(c) **Supply of labour**

Population size might determine **supply of labour** in relation to other factors of production (eg land, capital).

Causes and measurement of changes in the rate of population growth

2.3 What might be most important is the **rate of change** in population size. Note that countries with **large** populations may have a slow rate of population growth. In the 20th century, the population of European countries has increased significantly. However, as a proportion of global population, it has decreased, as the populations of countries in Asia and Latin America, for example, have grown much faster.

2.4 Changes in the rate of population growth are caused by the following factors.

■ Changes in the **birth rate**, or fertility rate; the birth rate can fluctuate sharply in the short run, with temporary 'baby booms' and falls in the rate of new births

■ Changes in the **death rate** or mortality rate

■ **Emigration** and/or immigration

Key Concept

The **Rate of Natural Increase in population** (RNI) is the birth rate minus the death rate.

[handwritten: Since 1901 with there is been more birth than deaths in the UK and the population has grown]

2.5 The long-term growth in the world's population has been due mainly to the **reduction** in the **death rate**. In earlier times, the world's population growth was lower because although the birth rate was high, so too was the death rate. Improved medicine and medical practice has reduced loss of life through disease and the death of new-born children and of mothers in childbirth. *[handwritten: Due to natural change]*

2.6 The reasons for recent population growth or decline are cultural, technological and economic. The higher rate of population growth in **less developed countries** compared with developed countries has arisen due to a high birth rate as well as a declining death rate.

2.7 Population increase can put immense stress on infrastructure (eg water, sewage), but also provides a labour force. It is projected that by 2025, with anticipated migration, over 60% of the world's population will be living in urban areas. Failure to meet the aspirations of the population can lead to political unrest. Economic growth and encouragement of people to have fewer children (if they are no longer needed as an insurance policy for the future) become political priorities.

FEATURES OF GROWING AND FALLING POPULATIONS	
Growing populations	**Falling populations**
Fast economic growth required	More productive techniques needed to maintain output
Overcrowding	Difficult to achieve economies of scale
More resources for capital investment required	Greater burden on young
Increased market stimulating investment	Changing consumption patterns
Labour mobility	

2.8 Governments can **indirectly** influence population size by:

- **Subsidising children** (eg through child allowances, generous maternity and leave)
- **Publicising birth control**, and offering cheap provision of it

2.9 Population size will be generally a more important factor than income per head for companies seeking to develop in worldwide markets for **essentials** or **low-cost products**.

Age structure and distribution

2.10 In our discussion of population growth we mentioned the **age structure** of the population. The effect of greater life expectancy is that a larger proportion of the population will be senior citizens (say 65 years or over) and unlikely to be working.

(a) A country with an **expanding population** will have **larger proportions of children and old people**, and **lower proportions of people of working age**.

(b) A country with a **declining population** will eventually have a **large proportion of old people** and **reducing proportions of people of other ages.**

2.11 The **working population must create a country's economic wealth**. With more people at retirement age, and also more young children, the proportion of the population which is working will be lower, and the proportion which is non-working and dependent on the working population will be higher.

2.12 From a **demand perspective**, the following are typical implications for marketing of an ageing population.

(a) Holiday tour companies may find increased demand for cruise holidays relative to demand for family beach holidays.

(b) Durability may replace fashionability as key design attributes.

(c) Distribution systems may favour home delivery at the expense of large out-of-town stores, if people are unable or unwilling to drive.

If the country has an expanding population the demand for the product that appeal to older groups or families with young children will increase

2.13 Marketers should not overlook the **supply implications** of an ageing population.

- If a company has relied on a young work force, will these continue to be available?
- If so, at what price?
- Should the company consider recruiting older people instead?

Marketing at Work

In the UK Saga is a very good example of a company that is focused on the mature population. Saga is exclusively for people who are 50 or over and provides a range of services specifically designed for them. Initially Saga specialised in holidays outside peak season, but has now branched out into publishing, insurance, home shopping, financial services and radio stations.

Saga holidays are a mix of holidays to popular destinations and some less obvious places; the company runs a number of holidays to Latin America, for example. Many holidays focus on particular interests, for example opera, heritage and gardens. The company also runs holidays for singles. The Saga magazine has articles on a wide range of subjects, ranging from First World War survivors to students at Oxford University who are grandparents, and also the ten sexiest women over 50.

Saga is increasingly trying to target its campaigns, and increase cross-selling to customers, as well as considering customer acquisition and retention. Customised mailing appealing to the right person at the right time can be used to cut mailing costs and also improve mailing results.

Geographic distribution

2.14 Another important feature of demography is the **location** of the population. A country may suffer the problems of overpopulation in some areas and underpopulation in others.

Action Programme 1

The (fictitious) Republic of Guarana in Latin America is undergoing a number of major changes. Now a democracy, it has re-established links with Western providers of capital, who are investing in the country, to extract its unique resource of Vrillium. In particular, large numbers of Vrillium mines have been opened in the San Serif valley. This comprises about 10% of the country's land area and is the site of Guarana's elegant capital Bosanova. This new economic activity is welcome. The mines and related industries will spur rapid economic growth. Bosanova has a population of 50,000. 80% of Guarana's population are peasant farmers. The prices of their crops on world markets have plummeted and the government of Guarana is alarmed at the growing rural poverty, especially as the population is increasing and agriculture is primitive and inefficient. The government has little money to invest in the countryside.

What consequences do you think the developments will have for Guarana?

2.15 Demography also deals with the effect of **concentration** and **dispersal** of population in particular areas. Industrialisation has traditionally meant a shift from the countryside to the towns. In some countries people are moving away from big cities to suburbs or smaller towns and are commuting elsewhere to work.

(a)   The region from which the workers have moved will suffer a **distortion** in the **age structure** of its population, with fewer people of a working age and so a much larger proportion of dependants. The region is therefore likely to sink even further into depression and relative poverty.

(b)   Eventually, the region might become **virtually depopulated**. This appears to be happening in parts of Scotland and, on a more localised basis, in ex-mining towns in England where coal pits have been closed down. City centres also face a fall in population.

Gender

2.16 Sex is important in population studies. The work roles played by males and females in different societies vary, even within the industrial world. In different societies, women and men have distinct purchasing and social powers.

Ethnicity

2.17 Only a few societies are homogenous, with populations of one culture and ethnic background. Japan is an example, although the population includes descendants of Koreans. On the other hand, a society like the USA has a population drawn from a variety of different areas.

2.18 Ethnicity is interesting to demographers, insofar as it acts as a marker for other social factors. The local authority of an area with a population drawn from a variety of ethnic backgrounds will have to take note in its education provision, if, say, English is not widely spoken.

Problems with evidence

2.19 Businesses need to be aware of the **limitations of the statistics** that they use. National income averages may mask differences that are significant from the marketer's viewpoint, for example the existence of fast-growing, high-income sectors of the population. Marketers also need to be aware of the definitions used; the number of people classified as middle-class could significantly differ depending on whether middle-class is defined as people owning a refrigerator or owning a television.

Exam Tip

In the exam you may be asked how demographic changes affect specific types of business.

3   The demographic profile of the UK

3.1   In this section we use the example of the UK to show how demographic change may have implications for marketing activity.

Collecting the figures

3.2   Many important facts about a country's demographic profile are collected by government to aid planning. Every ten years, the UK government conducts a **census**. Originally this was undertaken as a population count alone, but recently additional information about the population has been requested.

3.3   The UK government publishes various statistics every year, as a result of its various data collection exercises. Two examples are the **Annual Abstract of Statistics** and **Social Trends**. Both contain population data, although **Social Trends** goes into more detail about people's habits. Summary Census information can also be viewed at **www.statistics.gov.uk**. Some data comparisons from the past and projections into the future are given below.

Population size

3.4   The population of the UK as a whole has grown significantly since the turn of the century, but this growth is **expected to level off**.

Population of the United Kingdom

	2021 projected '000s	2001 '000s	1996 '000s	1991 '000s	1901 '000s	% change 1901–2001
England & Wales	55,527	52,042	52,010	51,100	32,528	60
Scotland	4,993	5,062	5,128	5,107	4,472	13
Northern Ireland	1,724	1,685	1,663	1,601	1,237	36
United Kingdom	62,244	58,789	58,801	57,808	38,237	54

As you can see, the last century has seen a significant increase, particularly in England & Wales. The increase is projected to continue, but relatively slowly.

Gender distribution

3.5   There is a slightly greater number of women than men in the UK population. Women generally have a longer life expectancy than men, and there are more males below the age of 65 than females.

Age structure

3.6   The age structure of the population is of particular concern to planners and business organisations. In 1961, 12% of the population were 65 or over. This is expected to rise to 24% by 2031.

3.7 It can be seen that, while the **working** population is fairly constant as a percentage, there is a shift in the relative proportion of elderly and young dependants. This has been occurring since 1961 and continued in the 1990s. This shift is important for the following reasons.

(a) The elderly dependants have **different needs** (for long-term health provision, for example) to younger people whose needs are for education and so on. Planners must take this into account when allocating resources for social provision.

(b) The elderly, as a **market segment**, are likely to be increasingly important.

(c) The decline in the number of young people will mean that organisations might have to change their **recruitment policies** or **production methods**. There will be fewer young people, and more competition for them.

3.8 The age structure, as with population size generally, depends on birth rates and death rates. Importantly, of course, the age structure depends not only on the **current** birth rate, but also on that of previous years. For example, there was an increase in the numbers of births immediately following World War II and another, as these baby boomers themselves had children, in the 1960s.

Action Programme 2

Choose an organisation, and describe how recent changes in the number of young people in the population will impact upon its marketing activities.

[handwritten: Travel agent will have the need to provide product in this case hotels with child care, playgrounds and child activities]

Ethnicity

3.9 Ethnic minorities form around 5% of the UK's population, although about half the UK's ethnic minority population lives in London and the South-East (comprising 9% of the population there as opposed to 1% in the north). *Social Trends* reports that ethnic minority populations are younger (around one in three under 16 as opposed to one in five otherwise) than the average population.

Regional distribution

3.10 As well as changes in aggregate population numbers, there are changes in where people choose to live and work. Different regions may have different birth and death rates. In aggregate, these differences can have a significant influence on social provision (eg schools, hospitals) and infrastructure (eg roads).

3.11 Over the last twenty years or so there has been a shift from cities and built-up areas to non-metropolitan regions. This can be caused by differing birth and death rates in the various regions, or internal or external migration.

3.12 Some of these trends may reverse over the next few years. There is pressure from government on local authorities in South-East England to build more homes, and create new or greatly expanded towns. There is also pressure to build on 'brown field' sites (sites of previous development) in cities.

Family

3.13 Demographic information is also used to map the social units in which people live (eg family size). Some trends in the UK are as follows.

(a) More and more people **live alone**, with one-person households accounting for 30% (6.5 million) of all **households** in 2001 (compared to 12% in 1961). This fact was marked in some advertising for a bank's mortgage service. Instead of featuring couples buying a house, it featured an individual buying a flat.

(b) At 2001, **married couples** made up 50.7 per cent of the adult population and 45% of households. However, the percentage of married couples in the population is declining. Marketers and advertisers have been criticised for advertising which does not reflect the realities of family life in the UK, but an idealised version of it.

(c) Almost 30% of households in England and Wales contain **dependent children** and one in nine have children under five years old.

(d) 9.6% of households in England and Wales are lone-parent and over 90% of these are headed by a woman. Two thirds of **lone-parent households** have **dependent children** and the remaining third contain only **grown up children**.

Summary

3.14 The UK population is increasing slowly. In aggregate, the age structure is shifting towards a higher proportion of elderly people. Urban areas have had stable or falling populations, whereas numbers are growing in rural counties and small towns. There is a slow increase in single person households, but most people live as part of larger units.

4 Demography and human resources

4.1 Demographic influences have a long-term influence on an organisation's supply of human resources and hence its policies towards its **human resources management** (HRM). This section uses the example of the UK.

4.2 Increasing population size would appear, superficially, to offer a larger labour market to employers. On the other hand if increasing population is largely caused by a fall in the death rate, this will merely mean that, unless state retirement ages are changed, there are more people around who do not belong to the labour force.

4.3 In many countries, **women** are **increasing** their participation in the labour force. The increasing participation of women is related to:

(a) An increase in the availability of part-time jobs
(b) Male unemployment arising from the decline of traditional heavy industries
(c) The growth of the service sector
(d) An increase in the average age at which women have children

4.4 The HRM implications of long-term demographic changes can easily be overwhelmed by fluctuations in the business cycle. In the UK recession in the 1990s, 'the easing of the labour market for IT specialists, accountants and other specialisms was very marked' (Connock, **HR**

Vision). To ignore demographics and other long-term trends in HR planning however, is an example of short-termism.

4.5 Organisations must also consider **education trends** such as the proportion of school leavers going into higher education. This will impact upon the base of potential recruits with the right qualifications. Any other changes, such as a decline in engineering and technology graduates, should also be considered carefully.

4.6 Population trends and trends in education are thus the crucial influences on the **supply** of labour. However, it is often asserted, even in times of high unemployment, that there is a skills shortage. This probably means that there is not the **right mix** of skills on supply to satisfy the demand. Stephen Connock believes that jobs will grow in IT services, health services, and multi-skilled occupations.

Coping with demographic and education trends

4.7 Stephen Connock suggests six steps by which organisations can cope with these demographic and educational trends. In effect this is a form of segmentation.

Step 1. **Establish** the **labour market** the organisation is in (eg young people, part-time workers)

Step 2. **Discover** the **organisation's catchment areas** (ie location of potential recruits)

Step 3. **Discern** the **supply side trends** in the catchment area labour force (eg how many school leavers are expected? What is the rate of growth/decline of local population?)

Step 4. **Examine education trends** in the area

Step 5. **Assess** the **demand** from **other employers** for the skills you need

Step 6. Assess whether some of your **demand** can be **satisfied** by a supply from **other sources**

4.8 Organisations will need proper 'resourcing strategies' to make sure their demand for labour is properly met.

4.9 **Older workers** are a possible labour market. This was a feature of the mid-1980s, when some companies in the retail sector targeted older workers (over-40s and over-45s) because of their:

- Skills and experience
- High regard for customer service
- Stabilising influence on younger staff
- Contribution to better staff retention rates

4.10 **Women returners**. There are a number of factors determining a woman's return to work.

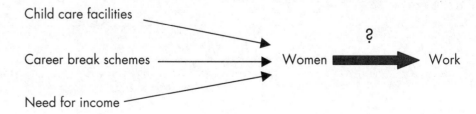

5 Demography and product markets

5.1 Businesses must remain aware of the changes in demographic profile. Some changes are predictable, others less so.

(a) A **baby boom** will result in increased demand for infant and children's goods.

(b) The **consequences of earlier baby booms** will result in many people reaching their peak earning potential at the same time.

(c) **Changes in government policy** may have a sufficient impact on the geographical distribution of the population, including pressures to build in certain areas and on certain types of land.

(d) **Changes** in **working patterns** are likely to affect both the workforce employed (more women, more part-time workers) and a wide variety of goods and services, for example financial services with flexible payment plans because of decreased security in the labour market.

5.2 Changes in the age structure of the population, as appear to be the case in the UK, offer new opportunities for firms wishing to segment the market according to age.

Marketing at Work

The effect of demography on product markets can be seen in products which are universally available.

(a) **Holidays**

About 60% of the population of Britain take at least one holiday each year. In the past, some holidays have been designed for the youth market (eg Club 18-30). Holidays designed with the needs of the retired in mind seem increasingly likely.

(b) **Health**

Life expectancy at birth in the UK has increased from 45.5 years (men) and 49 (women) in 1901 to 75 and 80 by the year 2000. By 2000, men of 65 could expect to live to age 81 while women could expect to live to age 84. The latest (2001) forecasts project an increase of two further years by 2021. The number of elderly residents of both local authority and private sector homes had increased from under 200,000 in 1980 to over 250,000 in 1991. This trend is almost certain to continue.

5.3 An example of a use of demography in marketing is **family life cycle** (FLC). This is a summary of demographic variables.

	Age
+	Marital status
+	Career status
+	Whether have children
Family life cycle	

5.4 Family life cycle is able to identify the various stages through which households progress. Particular products and services can be target marketed at people who occupy specific stages in the life cycle of families.

(a) **Single adulthood**

Individuals may have high disposable income; although they are at a low point on the career ladder, they will have few financial commitments. They will be able to indulge in activities such as attending concerts or dining out. With no family responsibilities, there may be little planning for the future.

(b) **Young married couples with no children**

Again this is a prosperous period with two incomes and no costs of children. They may have the income to afford luxury purchases such as overseas holidays or fashionable clothing. However, there may be more concern about the future, for example taking out mortgages or pensions.

(c) **Married couple with dependent children**

Disposal income may fall as children consume resources of money and also time, thus leaving less time for other lifestyle activities.

(d) **Empty nesters**

These middle-aged people whose children have grown up and left home were the marketer's holy grail. Having no responsibilities and with mortgages paid off, they were seen as a wealthy market. In practice, matters have not worked out like this.

Marketing at Work

A survey published early in 2001 by Andersen Consulting and Online Insight, *Beyond the Blur: Correcting the Vision of Internet Brands* suggested that many e-marketing initiatives were ill-aimed. Marketers 'were looking in the mirror instead of at their target audience.'

The survey suggested that many companies could achieve much better returns if they concentrated on consumers aged 35 or older who comprise about 10% of the population but who comprise 70% of online purchasers.

The best ways to reach this public were to:

(a) Provide a satisfying experience for the customers rather than bombarding them with heavy unfocused advertising

(b) Recognise that different customers had different needs, and therefore move websites away from the 'one size fits all' category

In addition repeat buying in e-commerce tended to be skewed towards older consumers.

The survey also found that a third of website customers were not motivated by price; they were concerned with website speed, ease of use, security and brand selection.

Action Programme 3

What do the findings of this survey suggest about the best approach to targeting older consumers?

6 Social structure

6.1 A society is a large agglomeration of people, deployed in a variety of complex social relationships. The term **social structure** can be used to describe these relationships.

6.2 To say that a society has a social structure implies that it can be aggregated into groups:

(a) Whose members share certain things in common

(b) Which, more importantly, have relationships of superiority or inferiority in relation to, or influence over, other groups

Action Programme 4

Here is a quotation from *The Wealth of Nations* by Adam Smith.

'... the common wages of labour depends upon the contract made between those two parties [workmen and master] whose interests are by no means the same. The workmen desire to get as much, the masters to give as little as possible... We rarely hear, it has been said, of the combinations [trade unions] of masters, though frequently of those of the workmen... Masters are always and everywhere in a sort of tacit, but constant and uniform combination not to raise the wages of labour above their actual rate ... [and] ... sometimes enter into particular combinations to sink the wages of labour even below this rate. These are always conducted with the utmost silence and secrecy ... Such combinations, however, are frequently resisted by a contrary defensive combination of workmen ... They are desperate, and act with the folly and extravagance of desperate men who must either starve or frighten their masters into immediate compliance.'

What can you tell about the social structure of the society outlined in the quotation?

Key Concept

Class is a term used in many different contexts in the UK.

(a) **Subjective** definitions of class relate to the way in which people consider themselves. (A MORI poll reported in The Times on 21 August 2002 showed that 68% of the UK population considered themselves to be working class, though by objective definition only 49% fall into that category.)

(b) **Objective** measures of social class consist of selected demographic (mainly socio-economic) variables: income, education and **occupation** are the most common.

6.3 In practice, class strata or divisions are commonly derived from the specific demographic factors of **wealth/income** (economic resources), **educational attainment**, and **occupational status**. Max Weber argued that **status** is a dimension which can overlap class boundaries determined by these narrow criteria.

6.4 Social groups are most commonly divided into strata or **classes**, with each class sharing a common level of status.

6.5 Shared values, attitudes and behaviour are characteristics of a social class, as distinct from those of a higher or lower class: research has been able to relate consumption behaviour to class standing. Social classes can be used n market segmentation exercises.

6.6 Social grade definitions vary.

(a) There are two-category schemes, such as the following.

Producers of goods and services	Managers and organisers
Blue-collar	White collar
Lower-class/working class	Middle class

(b) Five or six category schemes include the JICNAR social grade definitions (A-E) which correspond closely to what are called Social Classes I-V on the Registrar General's Scale.

Registrar General's Social Classes	JICNAR Social grades	Social status	Characteristics of occupation
I	A	Upper middle class	Higher managerial/professional eg lawyers, directors
II	B	Middle class	Intermediate managerial/administrative/ professional eg teachers, managers, computer operators, sales managers
III (i) non-manual	C_1	Lower middle class	Supervisory, clerical, junior managerial/ administrative/professional eg foremen, shop assistants
(ii) manual	C_2	Skilled working class	Skilled manual labour eg electricians, mechanics
IV	D	Working class	Semi-skilled manual labour eg machine operators
V			Unskilled manual labour eg cleaning, waiting tables, assembly
	E	Lowest level of subsistence	State pensioners, widows (no other earner), casual workers

(c) Some definitions also add a seventh stratum: upper class, consisting of the aristocracy (titled landowners) and the very wealthy (through ownership or investment). This stratum undoubtedly still exists in the UK, and this 1% of the adult population is reckoned to own around one quarter of the wealth of Britain!

6.7 'Social class' should be used in marketing or planning with caution, for the following reasons.

(a) **Definition**

It is not exactly or consistently defined.

Class = ?

- *Economic interest?*
- *Status?*
- *Wealth?*
- *Background?*
- *Access to power?*
- *Educational achievement*

(b) **Social changes**

Social mobility may make it difficult to use the concept in a meaningful way. People commonly perceive themselves to be in a different class to that in which they are objectively classified, and/or may aspire to membership of a higher class.

(c) **Dual income families**

Conventional gradings take into consideration the occupation of the head of the household, but with **dual-income families**, **fluctuating** family/household **patterns**, the **mobility** of **labour** and changes in employment circumstances (eg redundancy or insolvency), this may give a rather misleading picture.

(d) **Cause and effect**

People in the same social class have **many things in common**, for example similar standards of housing or similar access to educational opportunity. However these cultural characteristics are the consequences of social class rather than the causes of it. People's lifestyles are arguably a reflection of their **economic condition** in society, not the reason for their position.

6.8 Because of criticisms of the above classification, more sophisticated measures of socio-economic and group membership have been devised. Housing type and ownership are particularly important methods of segmentation for many types of good. The use of this method is made much easier by the major categorisation scheme for all housing types in the UK, known as ACORN (A Classification Of Residential Neighbourhoods), which enables precise target marketing based on housing type to be conducted by suppliers.

Educational attainment

6.9 **In many industrialised countries** it is likely that more and more people will achieve some form of educational or work-related qualification.

6.10 There is some evidence to suppose that social classes replicate themselves. There is also a definite correlation between an individual's **academic attainments** and the **occupational status** of the individual's father. In other words, if your father, or the breadwinner of the household, was a member of class B, it is likely that you will be too.

Socio-economic position, income and wealth

Action Programme 5

'Comparing people's income is a simple matter. All you need to do is compare income after direct tax and social security contributions to see how well off people are.'

What's wrong with this statement?

6.11 The exercise above indicates some of the problems collecting and presenting data relating to wealth and living standards. Some households are **taxed more than** they **benefit**, and others **benefit more** than they are **taxed**. Let us look at some UK figures for 1995-96, comparing the poorest 20% to the wealthiest 20%.

	Bottom 20%	Top 20%	All
	£	£	£
Original income (wages, pensions)	2,430	41,260	17,200
Gross income (original income + cash benefits)	7,340	42,450	20,450
Disposable income (after tax, NIC, etc)	6,210	31,980	16,170
Post-tax income (after interest taxes)	4,280	26,890	12,820
Final income (after education, NHS, school meals etc)	8,230	29,200	15,920

6.12 Income can be related to occupational groupings as follows.

Occupation of household head	Poorest 20%	Richest 20%
Professionals	-	13
Employers and managers	2	32
Intermediate and junior non-manual	2	21
Skilled manual	6	18
Semi-skilled manual	4	4
Unskilled manual	2	1
Retired	43	8
Unoccupied	39	2
Other	2	1
	100	100

Nearly half of the households in the richest 20% are headed either by professionals or managers.

Buying patterns

6.13 Buying behaviour is an important aspect of marketing. Many factors influence the buying decisions of individuals and households. Demography and the class structure are relevant in that they can be both **behavioural determinants and inhibitors**.

(a)   **Behavioural determinants**

These encourage people to buy a product or service. The individual's personality, culture, social class, and the importance of the purchase decision (eg a necessity such as food or water, or a luxury) can predispose a person to purchase something.

(b) **Inhibitors**

These are factors, such as the individual's income, which will make the person less likely to purchase something.

6.14 Socio-economic status can be related to buying patterns in a number of ways, both in the amount people **have to spend** and **what they spend it on**. It affects both the **quantity** of **goods** and **services supplied**, and the **proportion** of their **income** that **households spend** on goods and services. Let us compare, using the 1991 UK census figures, household expenditure by head of household where the head is in the professional group with the unskilled manual group.

Household expenditure

Item	Professional % of total purchases	Unskilled manual % of total purchases
Housing	17.8)	17.9)
Fuel, light, power	3.2) 36.4	6.1) 45.0
Food	15.4)	21.0)
Alcohol and tobacco	4.1	8.5
Clothing and footwear	5.8	5.4
Household goods and services	13.3	12.5
Motoring; fares	18.5	14.7
Leisure	17.7	9.5
Other	4.2	4.4
	100.0	100.0

6.15 As you can see, the **wealthier professionals** spend less of a **proportion** of their total income on food and housing, and more on leisure, than do unskilled manuals. This does not imply they spend any less in absolute terms of course: they just have more available to spend on other things.

6.16 The effect of social class on leisure and services is an example of how discretionary spending varies from class to class. In 1991, over 80% of members of social class AB took at least one holiday, compared to under 60% of class C2. In classes DE, over half took no holiday at all.

7 Culture 6/03, 12/03

Key Concept

Culture is 'the sum total of the beliefs, knowledge, attitudes of mind and customs to which people are exposed in their social conditioning. Through contact with a particular culture, individuals learn a language, acquire values and learn habits of behaviour and thought'.

7.1 **Culture** is a much broader concept than the sense in which it is most often used by people to refer to classical aesthetic or artistic pursuits.

7.2 As suggested by our definition above, culture embraces the following aspects of social life.

(a) **Beliefs and values**

Beliefs are what we feel to be the case on the basis of objective and subjective information (eg people can believe the world is round or flat - some beliefs are truer than others). Values are beliefs which are enduring, general and accepted as a guide to culturally appropriate behaviour. They shape attitudes and so create tendencies for individuals and societies to behave in certain ways.

(b) **Customs**

Customs are modes of behaviour which represent **culturally accepted ways** of behaving in response to given situations. There are various types of social behavioural norms. Keith Williams (**Behavioural aspects of marketing**) identifies four.

EXAMPLES OF CUSTOMS	
Folkways	Appropriate patterns of behaviour; violations are noticed but not severely punished
Conventions	Accustomed or habitual standards of behaviour such as social etiquette
Mores	Significant social norms such as monogamy and taboos, for example, against pornography or prostitution
Laws	Formal recognition of mores considered necessary in interests of society, with penalties against violation

(c) **Artefacts**

Culture embraces all the physical tools designed by human beings for their physical and psychological well-being. Works of art, technology, products, buildings etc are all physical manifestations of social existence. Some of these physical objects may be **symbolic** of other things. A **logo** stands for the company, for example.

(d) **Rituals**

A ritual is a type of activity which takes on symbolic meaning, consisting of a fixed sequence of behaviour repeated over time. **Ritualised** behaviour tends to be public, elaborate, formal and ceremonial – like religious services, marriage ceremonies, court procedures, even sporting events.

7.3 The learning and sharing of culture is made possible by **language** (both written and spoken, verbal *and* non-verbal).

7.4 **Symbols** are an important aspect of language and culture. Each symbol may carry a number of different meanings and associations for different people. The advertiser using slang words or pictorial images must take care that they are valid for the people he wants to reach - and up-to-date.

7.5 Some consumer researchers talk about the **transfer of cultural meaning** at different stages of the marketing process. The culturally constituted world produces products which are invested with cultural meaning or significance by advertising and fashion or, indeed, consumers.

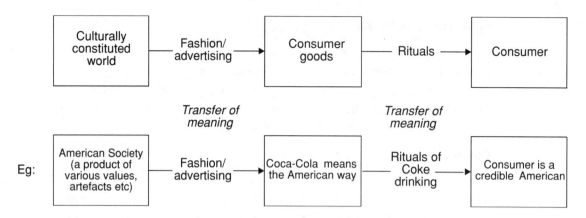

7.6 Knowledge of the culture of a society is clearly of value to businesses in a number of ways.

(a) Marketers can **adapt** their **products** and **appeals accordingly**, and be fairly sure of a sizeable market.

(b) Marketers can also plan to participate in the **teaching process** that creates culture. Mass media advertising, in particular, is an important agent by which cultural meanings are attached to products, people and situations.

(c) Human resource managers may need to tackle **cultural differences** in recruitment. Some ethnic minorities have different body languages; which may be hard for some interviewers to interpret.

Action Programme 6

Schiffman & Kanuk (*Consumer Behaviour*) gives the following summary of American core values and their relevance to why people are motivated to buy products or services. Consider how far they are applicable to *your* social culture.

Value	General features	Relevance to consumer behaviour
Achievement and success	Hard work is good; success flows from hard work	Acts as a justification for acquisition of goods ('You deserve it')
Activity	Keeping busy is healthy and natural	Stimulates interest in products that are time-savers and enhance leisure time
Efficiency and practicality	Admiration of things that solve problems (eg save time and effort)	Stimulates purchase of products that function well and save time

Value	General features	Relevance to consumer behaviour
Progress	People can improve themselves; tomorrow should be better than today	Stimulates desire for new products that fulfil unsatisfied needs, ready acceptance of products that claim to be 'new' or 'improved'.
Material comfort	'The good life'	Fosters acceptance of convenience and luxury products that make life more comfortable and enjoyable.
Individualism	Being oneself (eg self-reliance, self-interest, self-esteem)	Stimulates acceptance of customised or unique products that enable a person to 'express his or her own personality'.
Freedom	Freedom of choice	Fosters interest in wide product lines and differentiated products.
External conformity	Uniformity of observable behaviour; desire for acceptance	Stimulates interest in products that are used or owned by others in the same social group.
Humanitarianism	Caring for others, particularly the underdog	Stimulates patronage of firms that compete with market leaders.
Youthfulness	A state of mind that stresses being young at heart and a youthful appearance	Stimulates acceptance of products that provide the illusion of maintaining or fostering youthfulness.

7.7 Culture in a society can be divided into **subcultures** reflecting social differences.

(a) **Class** *Netto – WORKING CLASS D–E*
Marks & Spencer classes A–C,
People from different social classes might have different values reflecting their position in society. These values might relate to attitudes to work, or the value of education. Different classes might dress differently.

(b) **Ethnic background** *Nat west POLISH account*

Social Trends makes a distinction between **white** ethnic groups and all others (within the white group, there are also many ethnic minorities). Even though most people from minority ethnic backgrounds may have been born in the home country, they can still be considered a distinct cultural group.

(c) **Religion**

Religion and ethnicity are related in that most Muslims in the UK, for example, come from Pakistan, Bangladesh or Africa. Even within the white population, religion can be a marker of ethnicity. Many Roman Catholics, for example, might well have Irish ancestry or connections. Values and lifestyles are affected by religions (the prohibition of eating certain kinds of food, for example).

(d) **Geography or region**

Even in such a small country as England, there are distinct regional differences. Speech accents most noticeably differ, but there are also perceived variations in personality, life style, eating and drinking habits between the North and South, or the South West and South East - and even between West and East London! Some regions, such as Yorkshire, have a particularly strong self-image and loyalty to local products.

(e) **Age**

Age subcultures vary according to the period in which individuals were socialised to an extent, because of the great shifts in social values and customs in this century. Age subcultures also vary through each individual's life. Each individual progresses through the **'teen'** or **'youth'** (14-24 year old) **subcultures**, which are the most strongly bonded and identifiable groups. The elderly are another **distinct subculture**.

(f) **Sex**

There are some subcultures related to sex. Some products, for example, are targeted directly to women or to men. The homosexual community, also, might be considered a subculture in its own right.

(g) **Work**

Different organisations have different corporate cultures, in that the shared values of one workplace may be different from another.

7.8 The exclusivity of subcultures should not be exaggerated, since each consumer is simultaneously a member of many subcultural segments.

Action Programme 7

(a) Find at least one example of marketing targeted at a segment of each of the above subcultures.

(b) Visit shops or look through magazines that are not targeted at the subcultures into which you happen to fit. Make a note of the differences you see.

Acquiring culture: the socialisation process

Key Concept

Socialisation is the process by which we acquire sufficient knowledge of a society and its ways to be able to function and participate in it.

7.9 As a learning process, socialisation may function through the following means.

(a) **Instrumental conditioning**

Children try out various social behaviours. These are reinforced either positively (with satisfaction, approval or rewards) or negatively (with failure, disapproval or punishment) in order to shape a child's behaviour. Adults adjust their own behaviour in the same way, when confronted with approval, acceptance, rejection or embarrassment.

(b) **Cognitive learning**

The child develops a 'map' of various situations in which behaviour succeeds or fails, gathering information for use in later situations when there is a particular goal to be achieved or problem to be solved. A range of options or principles is learned, rather than particular responses.

(c) **Imitation of observed behaviour**

Imitation is a common behaviour in animals as well as humans, usually based on curiosity or observed reinforcement of the behaviour.

(d) **Identification**

This involves the adoption of the perceived values and attitudes of the model person, usually in an attempt or aspiration to become like him.

(e) **Role experimentation, exploration**, or **role play**

Children explore not only their own roles, but those of others by 'trying out' some of those roles. (Children play at being nurses or doctors, policemen, parents or whatever.) Adults also play at occupying unaccustomed roles, in social situations, and are often encouraged to do so in training for managerial or other interpersonal jobs.

Action Programme 8

Identify two commercial situations where socialisation is relevant.

8 Lifestyle and health   Specimen paper

Key Concept

Lifestyle refers to distinctive ways of living adopted by particular communities or sub-sections of society.

8.1 Lifestyle is a manifestation of a number of behavioural factors, such as motivation, personality and culture. When the numbers of people following it are quantified, marketers can **assign** and **target products** and promotion upon this particular target lifestyle group.

8.2 One simple example generalises lifestyle in terms of four categories.

(a) **Upwardly mobile, ambitious**

People seek a better and more affluent lifestyle, principally through better paid and more interesting work, and a higher material standard of living. Persons with such a lifestyle will be prepared to try new products.

(b) **Traditional and sociable**

Compliance and conformity to group norms bring social approval and reassurance to the individual. Purchasing patterns will therefore be conformist.

(c) **Security and status seeking**

Safety and ego-defensive needs are stressed. This lifestyle links **status, income and security**. It encourages the purchase of strong and well known products and brands, and emphasises those products and services which confer status and make life as secure and predictable as possible. These would include insurance, membership of motoring organisations. Products that are well established and familiar inspire more confidence than new products, which will be resisted.

(d) **Hedonistic preference**

The emphasis is on enjoying life now and the immediate satisfaction of wants and needs. Little consideration is given to the future.

8.3 The **green movement** has become part of many lifestyle segments. Companies segment some market clients according to whether they are 'pale' or 'dark' green in their attitude to the environment and therefore how significant environmentally friendly product attributes will be to the purchasing decision.

8.4 Lifestyle segmentation seeks to classify people according to their **values, opinions, personality characteristics, interests and so on.** The relevance of this concept is bound up in its ability to introduce various new dimensions to existing customer information. These include customers' disposition towards savings, investment and the use of credit, general attitude to money, leisure and other key influences.

8.5 Lifestyle segmentation attempts to discover the particular unique life style patterns of customers, which will give an **insight into their preferences** for various products and services. Strategists who use this segmentation tool will be better able to direct their marketing energies to meet the future needs of these identified groups.

Health issues

8.6 There have been significant changes in the UK in attitudes to diet and health. Most obvious has been a decrease in smoking from 46% of all over 16s in 1972 to 30% in 1990.

8.7 In addition there has been an increase in vegetarianism, and 'green consumerism'. This includes a concern with 'organic food' now found in many supermarkets. The increased consumption in poultry is caused, not so much by concern with health, but more by its relative fall in price resulting from battery farming techniques. Sugar has been replaced by artificial sweeteners.

8.8 Sport is a health issue, but has a wider significance in that the 'provision of sporting and recreational facilities has been recognised by the police, probation officers and social workers as being beneficial in reducing crime, particularly in the inner cities' *(Social Trends)*.

8.9 The impact of health on businesses is as follows.

(a) **Increasing market** for **sports-related goods** (even though, as in the case with training shoes, sporting goods might be purchased as fashion accessories).

(b) **Increasing concern** with **employee health** and the effect of ill-health on productivity. Some employers provide gyms and physical recreation facilities. Others offer counselling programmes to employees who are alcohol abusers.

(c) The **developing** of **new food products** with certain characteristics (eg for 'healthy eating'). Some supermarket chains have Healthy Eating programmes.

Marketing at Work

'The place with nothing' has been suggested as an advertising slogan for the Philippines' new luxury resort. The resort is devoted to health and relaxation and offers yoga, blood-cell analysis, and massage and cleansing regimes. Many cottages have their own gardens, but there are a number of places in the communal grounds where visitors can relax quietly. The resort claims that its restaurant is the only restaurant in the world devoted to raw food, although guests who are tired of it have the option of the local McDonalds down the road.

The resort has won an international reputation despite having 'no televisions, no telephones, no refrigerators in the rooms, no all-you-can-eat seafood buffet, no smoking and absolutely no nightlife.' It seems to appeal in particular to tired and stressed city dwellers seeking calm.

Far Eastern Economic Review

Chapter Roundup

- **Demography** is the study of population and population trends. It is relevant to businesses as long-range trends in the population affect the demand for goods and services and the supply of labour.

- **Population size** can affect overall economic activity and the exploitation of natural resources. The **rate of population change** also affects government investment decisions and infrastructural plans.

- Many industrialised countries are **ageing societies**. In other words, whilst the population is still growing in absolute terms, this is in fact because people are living longer. A greater proportion of the population is elderly. At the same time these trends to fluctuate, as the result of the working through of 'baby booms' and so on.

- Demography affects **regional policy**. In the UK there has been a shift out of the major conurbations.

- The characteristics of the population are also changing, with an increasingly qualified and skilled labour force. The job for human resources managers is to tap the labour market in the most effective way.

- The **social structure** of the population can be analysed in a number of ways, on the basis that there is a correlation in the activities of certain groups. Class is not always easy to define but there are significant differences in income, education and wealth in different segments of the population.

- **Culture** is a word which denotes beliefs, values, rituals, artefacts and habitual ways of behaving.

- A culture influences the basic assumptions governing people's behaviour. It is purposeful, learned, shared, cumulative and dynamic.

- Culture, like language, is acquired through the process of **socialisation**. This is the process by which the individual acquires sufficient knowledge of society and its ways to be able to function and participate in it.

- **Lifestyle** refers to the **ways** in which people **live** and their life **preferences** and **objectives**.

Quick Quiz

1   The Rate of Natural Increase in population = ?

2   Which of the following is not a feature of a growing population?

    A   Overcrowding

    B   Labour mobility

    C   Difficulties in achieving economies of scale

    D   Requirement for fast economic growth

BPP PROFESSIONAL EDUCATION

3   *Fill in the blank*

.... is the sum total of the beliefs, knowledge, attitudes of mind and customs to which people are exposed in their social conditioning.

4   Give five examples of subcultures

5   *Fill in the blank*

....................refers to distinctive ways of living adopted by particular communities

6   Give three examples of objective measure of class.

7   What is an 'empty nester'?

8   Which of the following are lifestyle categories?

A   Upwardly mobile and ambitious
B   Hedonistic preference
C   Affluent grey
D   Intermediate non-manual

Action Programme Review

1   Here is one possible answer. The existence of the new wealth will encourage:

(a)   Mass urbanisation
(b)   Potential rural depopulation

as the new industries will encourage peasants to move in from the land in the hope of a better life. Bosanova's resources will become more and more strained. At the same time it is possible that, without parallel increases in agricultural efficiency, the ageing rural workforce, who cannot move, will become less productive.

2   –

3   You need to consider not just age but also the life experiences of the ageing population. For instance, many people now in their early or middle fifties benefited from the expansion in higher education in the 1960s, and marketers have to take these increased education levels into account. Overall fitness levels may also have increased with the result that older consumers may be more interested in 'adventure holidays than recliner chairs'.

The article in the *Financial Times* that covered the survey suggested the following steps.

(a)   Carefully acknowledging age without drawing too much attention to it

(b)   Not automatically using the opposite advertising messages to those used in the 'yoof' market

(c)   Taking into account how older consumers see and wish to portray themselves; sales of toiletries, cosmetics and clothing have increased significantly among the over-50s

4   There are two groups distinct from, but connected with, each other: masters and workmen, with masters in a position of superiority when it comes to wealth and power. This position is held in relation to the workmen. You are also told that the relationship between the two groups is **necessarily** antagonistic (traditionally held to be a Marxist view). Many would dispute this and

would say that it is in the interest of both groups to co-operate. The example shows that a society can have groups who have relationships with each other, without necessarily having the same interests.

5   Unfortunately the issue is not that simple. Firstly, there is indirect taxation, particularly VAT. Households on different incomes are more or less exposed to this. Secondly, there is the issue of mortgage interest relief, which is not available to people renting their accommodation. Thirdly, there are additional social benefits such as education. It is hard to combine all these factors together.

6   –

7   –

8   (a)   In marketing, children are socialised as consumers, through advertising on television, pocket money and so on.

     (b)   In human resources, individuals joining an organisation often have to be socialised into the corporate culture. There might be various rituals on starting work.

Answers to Quick Quiz

1   Birth rate minus death rate

2   C   Difficulties in achieving economies of scale is a characteristic of a declining population

3   Culture

4   Any five of:

■   Class
■   Ethnic background
■   Religion
■   Geography
■   Age
■   Sex
■   Work

5   Lifestyle

6   ■   Income
     ■   Education
     ■   Occupation

7   Middle-aged person whose children have grown up and left home

8   A and B. These categories are simply aspects of a person's views and aspirations. C and D are objective categories which could be used as social classes.

Now try illustrative questions 14 and 15 at the end of the Study Text

The economic and international environments

10

Chapter Topic List	
1	Setting the scene
2	Economic policy objectives
3	National income
4	Economic growth, unemployment and inflation
5	The business cycle
6	Fiscal and monetary policies
7	The international environment

Learning Outcomes

☑ Recognise and assess the potential influence of the business cycle on the marketing function

☑ Recognise and assess the potential impact of government economic policy on the marketing function

Syllabus Reference

☑ Explain the economic and international environments and, in general terms, their influence on and implications for marketing.

Key Concepts Introduced

- National income
- Gross domestic product
- Gross national product

- Indirect taxation
- Monetary policy
- Supply side economics

■	Actual economic growth	■	Comparative advantage
■	Business cycle	■	Exchange rate
■	Fiscal policy	■	Floating exchange rates
■	Direct taxation	■	Balance of payments

1 Setting the scene

1.1 In this chapter we consider various aspects of the economic environment which organisations face.

1.2 We firstly describe certain key aspects of economies, including in section 5 the business cycle, which is a key influence on economic policy. In section 6 we briefly discuss how governments go about managing the economy.

1.3 The other aspect of this chapter is the **international environment**. Even firms based in and selling solely in domestic economies will face competition from imports. Moreover government policies designed to affect the exchange rate and the balance of payments can have other economic consequences as we shall see in section 7 of the chapter.

1.4 Businesses need to anticipate changes in economic conditions and government policies. It is not always easy to do so. Moreover the effect of any changes on the markets in which the marketer is interested may be delayed.

2 Economic policy objectives   Specimen paper

2.1 Before we discuss the most important aspects of an economy's performance, and the various ways in which governments attempt to control the economy, we shall start off by briefly discussing the main **aims** of economic policy. The following sections should be read with these aims in mind.

2.2 Among the aims of a government's economic policy may be the following.

(a) **To achieve sustainable growth in national income per head of the population**

Growth implies an increase in national income in real terms. The idea of sustainable growth implies that the fluctuations of the business cycle are avoided and that output grows on a steady upward trend. **This is the most important goal**.

(b) **To control price inflation**

This has become a central objective of economic policy in many countries in recent years.

(c) **To achieve full employment**

Full employment does not mean that everyone who wants a job has one all the time, but it does mean that unemployment levels are low, and involuntary unemployment is short-term.

(d) **To achieve a balance between exports and imports**

The wealth of a country relative to others, a country's creditworthiness as a borrower, and the goodwill between countries in international relations might all depend on the achievement of an external balance over time. Deficits in external trade, with imports exceeding exports, might also be damaging for the prospects of economic growth.

The changing emphasis of economic policy

2.3 The emphasis on different policy objectives has changed in line with political, social and economic events. The objective of **full employment** was central to policy in developed countries following the Second World War. Later, other macro economic objectives came to the fore. Explicit policy commitments have been made by governments at different times in different countries to the objectives of **low inflation, balance of payments equilibrium** and sustainable development of the economy.

2.4 **Sustainable development** describes a pattern of growth at a local or a national level which is stable over the long term and is unlikely to be a victim of its own success. Sustainability implies that there will always be **sufficient natural, financial** and **human resources** available to meet future growth. Sustainable development has been particularly used to describe growth which does not destroy the natural resources which are vital to further production.

2.5 To try to achieve its intermediate and overall objectives, a government will use a number of different policy tools or policy instruments.

2.6 These policy tools are not mutually exclusive and a government might adopt a mix of policies to achieve its economic objectives. As will become clearer when we look at different policy objectives, conflict may arise between different objectives, meaning that choices have to be made.

Exam Tip

A Specimen Paper question covered government economic objectives, indicators of their success and marketing implications of an objective.

3 National income

3.1 Three key measures of economic activity are:

- National income
- Gross national product (GNP)
- Gross domestic product (GDP)

Definition of national income

Key Concept

UK **national income** as 'the sum of all incomes of residents in the UK which arise as a result of economic activity, that is from the production of goods and services. Such incomes, which include rent, employment income and profit, are known as factor incomes because they are earned by the so-called factors of production: land, labour and capital' *(Office for National Statistics (ONS)).*

3.2 National income is also called **net national product**.

3.3 The terms 'income' and 'product' are just two different aspects of the same circular flow of income. The term 'net' means 'after deducting an amount for capital consumption or depreciation of fixed assets' from the gross figure.

Gross domestic product (GDP)   12/00

3.4 National income is largely derived from economic activity within the country itself. Domestic economic activity is referred to as total **domestic income** or **domestic product**. It is measured gross.

Key Concept

Gross domestic product (GDP) refers in the UK to the total value of income/production from economic activity within the UK.

Gross national product (GNP)

3.5 'Some national income arises from overseas investments while some of the income generated within the UK is earned by non-residents. The difference between these items is **net property income from abroad**.' *(ONS).*

Key Concept

Gross national income or **gross national product (GNP)** is the gross domestic product (GDP) plus the net property income from abroad - or after subtracting the net property income from abroad, if it is a negative value.

The relationship between GDP, GNP and national income

3.6   The relationship between GDP, GNP and national income is therefore as follows.

	GDP
plus	Net property income from abroad
equals	GNP
minus	Capital consumption
equals	National income (net)

Action Programme 1

Which of the following may cause an increase in national income?

(a)   A rise in exports

(b)   An increase in saving

(c)   A fall in consumer spending

Measuring national income

3.7   Total spending, consists of consumption spending, government spending, investment spending, spending by foreigners on our goods and services minus spending by us on foreign goods and services. This is often symbolised as $C + I + G - S - T + (X - M)$ (the circular flow of national income) where:

   C = consumption expenditure

   I = investment expenditure

   G = government expenditure

   S = savings

   T = taxation

   X = expenditure on our exports by foreigners

   M = expenditure by us on imports

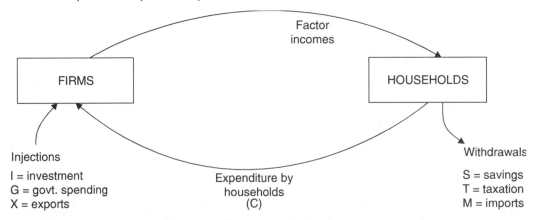

3.8   If a government is planning its economic policy, and wishes to increase the country's GDP and GNP, it might wish to turn its attention to any of these items, ie:

   ■   Trying to increase consumer spending, C

   ■   Trying to increase private investment, I

   ■   Deciding to increase government spending, G and/or I

   ■   Trying to improve the balance of payments on overseas trade, (X – M)

3.9 Although technically national income has a particular definition, generally you will find all these measures (GDP, GNP and NI) loosely referred to as 'national income'.

3.10 Calculating the national income serves several purposes:

- **Measuring** the **standard** of **living** in a country (national income per head)
- **Comparing** the **wealth** of different countries
- **Measuring** the **change** in **national wealth** and the standard of living
- **Ascertaining long-term trends**
- **Assisting central government** in its **economic planning**

National income and inflation

3.11 Inflation is a particular problem in using national income as a measure of national wealth. Price inflation increases the **money value** of national income.

3.12 We should be careful not to interpret this as meaning that there is more economic activity going on in our economy. All that has happened is that the prices of the things we are measuring have increased. To see if there has been any **real** change in the level of activity we must deduct any influence due to inflation.

Problems with making comparisons

3.13 When evaluating international marketing opportunities, national income figures can be useful to the marketer. It is therefore important to appreciate the factors to consider when analysing comparative data.

3.14 The national income figures say **nothing** about the **distribution of income** in the country.

3.15 When comparing countries there is also the problem of **converting national income** calculated in one currency to that of another. This is not necessarily as straightforward as it sounds and may make conclusions about such comparisons difficult to reach.

3.16 Simpler and more direct comparisons are sometimes used for making international comparisons. One way of doing this is to select a **number of products** which are widely in demand. Examples might be television sets and motor cars. Measurements can then be obtained of:

- The average number of cars or TV sets per household or per head of the population
- How long it takes an average worker to earn enough in wages to buy a car or a TV set

3.17 However, this kind of comparison is also problematic, since cars and televisions (to take our examples above) are of limited use or value to some people and in some cultures.

3.18 William Nordhaus and James Tobin proposed a **'measure of economic welfare'** (MEW) to give more useful comparisons of people's welfare. The MEW adjusts GNP for various items.

  (a)   Items **added** are allowances for **leisure** and **non-marketed goods**, for public amenities such as roads, and for private durable goods such as jewellery and furniture.

  (b)   Items **subtracted** are expenditure on **'regrettables'** such as defence and commuting, various **'disamenities'** such as pollution, and an allowance for the benefits of education, since these arise later in enhanced labour earnings.

(c)   To ensure that a **per capita** figure is arrived at, further deductions are made to reflect the extra capital and current output required to meet any increase in population.

The level of investment in the economy

3.19 The total or aggregate amount of investment spending in a national economy is a sign of the strength of the economy. New investment will increase output and so national income. A change in the level of investment spending is a major reason for the upswings and downswings in economic activity which we call business cycles.

Private sector investments

3.20 Private sector investment will come from **retained profits**, **new issues of shares**, or **borrowing**. However, in an economic recession profits might be low, and investors might lack confidence in a recovery, so that new shares issues are impossible on a large scale.

Public sector investment

3.21 Public sector investment might be financed by higher taxation, or by an increased deficit between government income and expenditure, that is, a higher **public sector borrowing requirement (PSBR)**.

(a)   Public sector spending should have **socially valuable** 'spin-off' effects, such as improved roads, sewers and public buildings.

(b)   However, a high PSBR, meaning large government borrowings, might force up **interest rates** in the capital markets and **'crowd out'** private sector investment, by making it too expensive for firms to borrow and invest profitably.

4 Economic growth, unemployment and inflation

12/02

Economic growth

4.1   Economic growth may be measured by increases in the **real** gross national product (GNP) per head of the population.

Key Concepts

Actual economic growth is the annual percentage increase in national output. **Potential economic growth** is the rate at which the economy would grow if all resources (eg people and machinery) were utilised.

Actual growth

4.2 **Actual** growth in the long run is determined by two factors.

- Potential output
- **Aggregate demand**, the total spent on domestic goods and services

общунност

Potential growth

4.3 The **causes of growth in potential output** are the determinants of the **capacity of the economy** (the supply side) rather than actual spending (the demand side).

(a) There may be increases in the **amount of resources** available such as the discovery of new natural resources, change in the size of the working population and invention of new technology and methods.

(b) Increases in the **productivity of resources** may result from technological progress or changed labour practices, for example.

Factors needed for sustained economic growth

4.4 **Sustained economic growth** depends heavily on an adequate level of **new investment**, which will be undertaken if there are **expectations of future growth in demand**.

the factors afecting economy growth are ① increase on investment ③ technological progress ② Natural resources

Natural resources

4.5 The rate of extraction of natural resources will impose a limit on the rate of growth. Production which uses up a country's natural resources, such as oil, coal and other minerals, depletes the stock of available resources; it is therefore in a sense **disinvestment**.

Technological progress

4.6 Technological progress is a very important source of faster economic growth.

- The same amounts of the factors of production can produce a higher output
- New products will be developed, thus adding to output growth

4.7 There can be technical progress in the labour force. If workers are better **educated** and better **trained** they will be able to produce more. For example, if there is a fault in the production process, a skilled worker will be able to deal with it quickly, whereas an unskilled one might have to call for a superior instead.

4.8 If technological progress is labour saving, then **unemployment will rise** unless there is either a simultaneous expansion of demand or a reduction in hours worked by each person, in which case there is no productivity increase associated with the technological progress.

4.9 Technological progress may therefore stimulate growth but at the same time conflict with the goal of full employment. A further consequence of this could be that those people in work would benefit from economic growth in the form of higher wages, but those people put out of work by the new technology would be left with a lower income.

the technological factor of economy growth conflict in some cases with the economy goal of full employment, if the technological progress been made that may stimulate unemployment

External trade influences on economic growth

4.10 An improvement in the **terms of trade** (the quantity of imports that can be bought in exchange for a given quantity of exports) means that more imports can be bought or alternatively a given volume of exports will earn higher profits. This will boost investment and hence growth.

Exam Tip

The terms of trade is a concept you should grasp for the exam.

4.11 The rate of growth of the rest of the world is important for an economy that has a large foreign trade sector. If trading partners have slow growth, the amount of exports a country can sell to them will grow only slowly. This limits the country's own opportunities for investment and growth.

Advantages and disadvantages of economic growth

4.12 Economic growth should mean that the population as a whole will be able to **raise** its **standard of living** in material terms, and that there should also be an **improvement** in **economic welfare.** A country with economic growth is more easily able to provide a welfare state service without creating intolerable tax burdens on the community.

4.13 There are potential disadvantages to growth, however.

(a) Growth implies **faster use** of **natural resources**. Without growth, these resources would last longer.

(b) Much economic activity tends to create **pollution**, such as acid rain and nuclear waste. It leads to emissions which threaten to produce disruptive climatic changes through an increase in the greenhouse effect. It results in more roads, cultivated farmland, new and larger towns, and less unspoilt countryside.

(c) There is a danger that some sections of the population, unable to adapt to the demands for new skills and more training, will not find jobs in the developing economy.

some unskilled people will not find jobs due to demand of new technological knowledge

Action Programme 2

Which of the factors listed above have contributed most to your own company's economic growth over the last few years? Have there been any significant problems with growth?

Unemployment

RESULTS OF UNEMPLOYMENT	
Loss of output	Unemployed labour is not producing anything, and therefore total national income is less than it could be.
Loss of human capital	Unemployed labour will gradually lose their skills through lack of practice.
Increasing inequalities in income	The unemployed poor become poorer.
Social costs	Unemployment can result in personal suffering and distress, and possibly increases in crime.

4.14 Unemployment may be classified into categories.

(a) **Frictional unemployment**

Frictional unemployment occurs where there is a shortage of a given type of worker in one region, but a surplus of the same type in another (for example, clerical staff may be plentiful in Wales but in short supply in London). In general, it takes time to match prospective employees with employers, and individuals will be unemployed during the search period for a new job.

(b) **Seasonal unemployment**

This occurs in certain industries, for example building, tourism and farming, where the demand for labour fluctuates in seasonal patterns throughout the year.

(c) **Structural unemployment** ~ Borpupa

This occurs where long-term changes in the conditions of an industry occur.

(d) **Technological unemployment**

This is a form of structural unemployment, which occurs when new technologies are introduced.

(e) **Cyclical or demand-deficient unemployment**

Domestic and foreign trade go through cycles of boom, decline, recession, recovery, then boom again, and so on. During recovery and boom years, the demand for output and jobs is high, and unemployment is low. During decline and recession years, the demand for output and jobs falls, and unemployment rises to a high level.

4.15 A government can try to create jobs or reduce unemployment by:

- **Spending** more **money directly** on **jobs** (for example, hiring more civil servants)
- **Encouraging growth** in the **'private sector'** of the economy
- **Encouraging training** in job skills

Action Programme 3

Is unemployment a bad thing for businesses?

Inflation

4.16 An economic policy objective which now has a central place in the policy approaches of the governments of many developed countries is that of stable prices. Why is a high rate of price inflation harmful and undesirable?

RESULTS OF INFLATION	
Redistribution of income and wealth	Those with economic power may gain at expense of the weak, particularly those on fixed incomes
Balance of payments	If the rate of inflation is higher than in trading partners, exports become relatively expensive, imports relatively cheap and balance of trade and employment will suffer
Uncertainty in value of money	Resource allocation and decision-making are harder and businesses may defer long-term decisions
Resource costs of changing prices	Substantial labour time is spent on planning and implementing price changes, and customers have to spend more time making price comparisons

[handwritten margin note: Because the Demand exceeds supply to try and prevent it prices will rise]

4.17 **Demand-pull inflation** occurs when the economy is buoyant and there is a high aggregate demand which is in excess of the economy's ability to supply.

(a) Because aggregate demand exceeds supply, **prices rise**.

(b) Since supply needs to be raised to meet the higher demand, demand for factors of production will increase, and so factor rewards (wages, interest rates, and so on) will also rise.

(c) Since aggregate demand exceeds the output capability of the economy, demand-pull inflation can only exist when unemployment is low.

4.18 **Cost-push inflation** occurs where the costs of factors of production rise regardless of whether or not they are in short supply. This appears to be particularly the case with wages: workers anticipate inflation rates and demand wage increases to compensate, thus initiating a wage-price spiral. Interest rate rises can also add to the rate of inflation, because mortgage costs will rise.

4.19 **Import cost-push inflation** occurs when the cost of essential imports rise regardless of whether or not they are in short supply.

4.20 A further problem is that once the rate of inflation has begun to increase, **expectational inflation** may occur. This means that, regardless of whether the factors that have caused inflation are still persistent or not, inflation will be expected. To protect future income, wages and prices will be raised by the expected amount of future inflation. This can lead to the vicious circle known as the **wage-price spiral**, in which inflation becomes a relatively permanent feature because of people's expectations that it will occur.

Control of inflation: various approaches

4.21 The best way of controlling inflation will depend on the causes of it. In practice, it may be difficult to know which cause is most significant. The table below sets out various policies designed to control inflation.

ANTI-INFLATION POLICIES	
Perceived cause of inflation **Demand-pull**	**Policy to control inflation** Take steps to reduce demand in the economy, perhaps by ■ higher taxation, to cut consumer spending ■ lower government expenditure (and lower government borrowing to finance its expenditure) ■ higher interest rates
Cost-push	Take steps to reduce production costs and price rises ■ de-regulate labour markets ■ encourage greater productivity in industry ■ apply controls over wage and price rises (prices and incomes policy)
Import cost-push	Take steps to reduce the quantities or the price of imports. Such a policy might involve trying to achieve either an appreciation or depreciation of the domestic currency
Growth of the money supply	Take steps to try to reduce the rate of money supply growth, perhaps by ■ cutting the Public Sector Borrowing Requirement ■ funding the PSBR by borrowing from the non-bank private sector ■ trying to control or reduce bank lending ■ trying to achieve a balance of trade surplus ■ maintaining interest rates at a level that might deter money supply growth
Expectations of inflation	Pursue clear policies which indicate the government's determination to reduce the rate of inflation

5 The business cycle   6/03

Key Concept

Business cycle is the periodic fluctuation of levels of economic activity, for example output and employment.

5.1 The **business cycle** (or **trade cycle**) is the continual sequence of rapid growth in national income, followed by a slow-down in growth and then a fall in national income. A sustained fall in national income is an **economic recession**. After the recession comes growth again, and when this has reached a peak, the cycle turns into recession once more.

5.2 The understanding of business cycles can be crucial in many sectors, especially the capital goods sector, an **investment** in capital goods represents an **expensive anticipation** of future rewards.

5.3 Four main phases of the business cycle can be distinguished.

THE BUSINESS CYCLE	
Depression	Heavy unemployment Low consumer demand Over-capacity (unused capacity) in production Prices stable, or even falling Business profits low Business confidence in the future low
Recovery	Investment picks up Employment rises Consumer spending rises Profits rise Business confidence grows Prices stable, or slowly rising
Boom	Consumer spending rising fast Output capacity reached: labour shortages occur Output can only be increased by new labour-saving investment Investment spending high Increases in demand now stimulate price rises Business profits high
Recession	Consumption falls off Many investments suddenly become unprofitable and new investment falls Production falls Employment falls Profits fall. Some businesses fail Recession can turn into severe depression

5.4 Recession tends to occur quickly, while recovery is typically a slower process. The diagram below can be used to help explain how this is so.

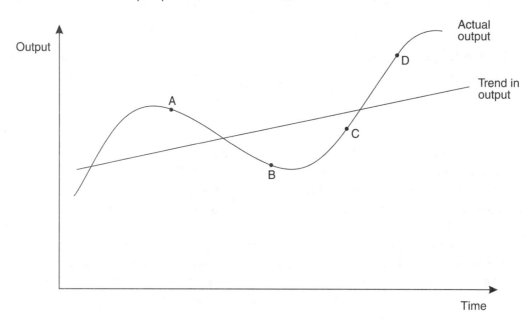

5.5 At point A the economy is entering a recession. In the recession phase, **consumer demand falls and** many investment projects already undertaken begin to look unprofitable. Eventually, in the absence of any stimulus to aggregate demand, a period of full **depression** sets in and the economy will reach point B.

5.6 Recovery can be slow to begin because of the **effect of recession** on **levels of confidence**. It can take some time for confidence to return, and initial moves towards expansion of activity are likely to be tentative.

5.7 At point C the economy has reached the **recovery phase** of the cycle. Once begun, the phase of recovery is likely to quicken as confidence returns.

5.8 As recovery proceeds, the output level climbs above its trend path, reaching point D, which is the **boom phase** of the cycle.

Consequences of the business cycle

5.9 Wide fluctuations in levels of economic activity may be damaging to the overall economic well-being of society. The inflation and speculation which accompanies boom periods may be inequitable in their impact on different sections of the population, while the bottom of the trade cycle may bring high unemployment. Governments generally seek to stabilise the economic system, trying to avoid the distortions of a widely fluctuating trade cycle, for example by maintaining a stable level of prices.

5.10 Forecasting the pattern of the business cycle is very difficult in practice. The cycle is affected by such things as oil prices and international political stability, all of which are themselves difficult to predict.

5.11 Businesses must identify those measures which tend to give **advance warning** of movements in the business cycle such as **leading indicators** (a combined measure including share prices, house building and interest rates) and **trend measures**.

Action Programme 4

(a) Compare the ability of large and small businesses to:

    (i) Survive recessions
    (ii) Benefit from booms

(b) How important is the feel good factor in marketing?

6 Fiscal and monetary policies

Fiscal policy

Key Concepts

Fiscal policy is government policy on taxation, public borrowing and public spending.
Direct taxation is taxation of incomes.
Indirect taxation is taxation of products and services, for example value added tax.

6.1 Fiscal policy leads to action by the government to spend money, or to collect money in taxes, with the purpose of influencing the condition of the national economy.

6.2 A government might intervene in the economy by:

(a) **Spending more money** and financing this expenditure by borrowing

(b) **Collecting more in taxes** without increasing spending

(c) **Collecting more in taxes** in order to **increase spending**, thus diverting income from one part of the economy to another

6.3 Fiscal policy is concerned with government spending and taxation.

6.4 If government spending is increased, expenditure in the economy will rise and so **national income** will **rise**.

6.5 If government taxation is increased expenditure and national income will fall. A government might deliberately raise taxation to take inflationary pressures out of the economy.

6.6 Fiscal policy can be used to reduce unemployment and provide jobs. For example:

■ More government spending on **capital projects**
■ **Government-funded training schemes**
■ **Taxation** of companies on the basis of the numbers and pay levels of employees

6.7 Government spending, however, might create inflationary pressures, and inflation tends to create more unemployment. Fiscal policy must therefore be used with care, even to create new jobs.

Marketing implications of fiscal policy

6.8 Marketers are interested in fiscal policy for a number of reasons.

(a) The **overall level of taxation** affects the level of aggregate demand in the economy.

(b) **Taxation of specific groups** may affect the spending power of particular market segments.

(c) **Taxation of specific products** may have a serious impact on a specialised business. Whisky manufacturers are lobbying for a reduction in indirect taxes.

(d)   There is **uncertainty** about the time lag between the implementation of economic policies and their effect. For example, the speed with which tax cuts affect consumer spending will depend upon consumer confidence.

(e)   If policy objectives are set at the same time each year, there is scope for lobbying for favourable tax treatment of certain types of product.

Action Programme 5

The burden of an indirect tax must either be borne by the producer or passed on by the producer to consumers. If a producer passes on the whole of the burden, what does that tell you about the demand for his product?

Monetary policy

Key Concept

Monetary policy is the regulation of the economy through control of the monetary system by operating on such variables as the money supply, the level of interest rates and the conditions for availability of credit.

6.9   Monetary policy can be used as a means towards achieving the ultimate economic objectives for inflation, the balance of trade, full employment and real economic growth.

6.10   To achieve these ultimate objectives of economic policy, the authorities will set intermediate objectives for monetary policy.

6.11   In the UK, the ultimate objective of monetary policy in recent years has been principally to **reduce** the **rate of inflation** and to reduce it to a sustainable low level. The intermediate objectives of monetary policy have related to the level of interest rates, growth in the money supply, and the exchange rate for sterling.

Marketing effects of monetary policies

6.12   Marketers should be clear about how targets and indicators will impact on their marketing efforts.

(a)   What do **targets** for interest rates mean for new house sales? What do indicators of actual interest rates imply for the success that government is having in implementing its policy?

(b) What does **movement in the exchange rates** mean for the competitiveness of exporters?

(c) What do **targets and indicators** of Gross Domestic Product imply for aggregate demand in the economy?

(d) What is the **time lag** between changes in interest rates and their impact upon the domestic economy?

Supply side economic policies

Key Concept

Supply side economics is an approach to economic policy making which advocates measures to improve the supply of goods and services (eg through deregulation) rather than measures to affect aggregate demand.

increasing the ~~demand~~ supply of goods and services by investing in production

6.13 Supply side economists argue that by putting resources to work an economy will automatically generate the additional incomes necessary to purchase the higher outputs, that is **supply creates its own demand**.

6.14 The main propositions which characterise supply side economics are as follows.

(a) The predominant long-term influence upon output, prices, and employment are the **conditions** of **aggregate supply**.

(b) Left to itself, the **free market** will **automatically generate** the **highest level** of **national income** and employment available to the economy.

(c) Inflexibility in the labour market through the existence of trade unions and other restrictive practices retain wages at **uncompetitively high levels**. This creates unemployment and restricts aggregate supply.

(d) The rates of **direct taxation** have a major influence upon aggregate supply through their effects upon the incentive to work.

(e) **Government only has a limited role** in the economic system. Demand management can only influence output and employment 'artificially' in the short-run, whilst in the long-run creating inflation and hampering growth. Similarly state-owned industries are likely to be uncompetitive and accordingly restrict aggregate supply. Political pressures on the level of tax will mean that **growth** generated by the government is unlikely to be sustained in the long-term.

6.15 There are a number of steps governments can take to improve supply flexibility in the labour market.

■ Privatisation of state monopolies, allowing for price competition
■ Abolition of restrictions on wages and other regulations limiting competitiveness
■ Limitations on the power of trade unions
■ Removal of distortions in the tax and benefit systems
■ Encouragement of training, labour mobility and innovation

6.16 Certain recent changes, for example the minimum wage and fairness at work, have allegedly reduced flexibility within the economies of European Union countries.

Marketing effects of supply side policies

6.17 For marketers, an emphasis on supply side economics brings opportunities and problems.

(a) Opportunities are made available to firms to **reduce** their **input prices** (eg lower labour and telephone costs).

(b) On the other hand, liberalisation of markets has put **many companies** under **great pressure** to **reduce their own costs**.

Action Programme 6

(a) Draw up a checklist of key economic indicators and detail the sources of information you would use.

(b) Use these indicators to analyse the current economic situation in your country.

[handwritten: PRODUCTION employement GDP Interest rates]

7 The international environment

Comparative advantage

7.1 International trade:

■ Enables countries to **specialise**
■ Serves as a means of **developing political links** with other countries
■ **Increases competition** and possibly efficiency of production
■ **Creates larger markets**, with the potential for economies of scale in production

7.2 Comparative advantage is important in international trade.

Key Concept

Comparative advantage is the principle that economic agents are best employed in activities which they carry out relatively better than other activities.

(a) A country normally exports goods which it can **produce most efficiently**, that is, at lowest cost relative to other countries, and it normally imports goods in which other countries are relatively more efficient. This is called the principle of comparative advantage.

(b) When countries exchange goods on the basis of **comparative advantage**, they all gain. The source of the gain is that worked output is larger when each country specialises in goods it can produce most efficiently.

7.3 Free international trade makes it possible to enjoy the benefits suggested by the principle of comparative advantage. However, there are other advantages to the countries of the world in encouraging free international trade.

(a) **Raw materials**

Some countries have raw materials surplus to their needs and others have a deficit. A country with a surplus (for example, of oil) can take advantage of its **resources to export them**. A country with a deficit of raw materials must either import them or accept restrictions on its economic prosperity and standard of living.

(b) **Competition**

International trade **increases competition** amongst **suppliers** in the world's markets. Greater competition reduces the likelihood of a market for a good in a country being dominated by a monopolist. The greater competition will force firms to be competitive.

(c) **Bigger markets**

International trade creates larger markets for a firm's output, and so some firms can benefit from **economies of scale, expand from limited domestic markets** or **spread their risks** by engaging in export activities. **Economies of scale** improve the efficiency of the use of resources, reduce the output costs and also increase the likelihood of output being sold to the consumer at lower prices.

(d) **Political factors**

There are **political advantages** associated with international trade because the development of trading links provides a foundation for closer economic and political links. An example of closer links based on trade is the European Union and its development of a Single Market in Europe.

(e) **Consumers**

From the consumer's point of view, international trade should provide **greater choice, lower prices** and better quality products all resulting from increased competition.

Trading blocs

7.4 Countries in various regions have entered into closer economic arrangements such as NAFTA (USA, Canada, Mexico), the EU, Mercosur (Brazil, Argentina, Uruguay, Paraguay, Bolivia and Chile.)

7.5 However, there are limits to trading blocs.

(a) **Free movement of capital** between the world's major financial centres has increased over recent years. Of course, the current turbulence in Asia has led some politicians to question this arrangement. However, one of the causes of international financial crises has been **weak systems of banking and financial regulation**.

(b) Trade on a **global scale** is becoming **liberalised**, as discussed below.

(c) Some of the world's markets offering the **greatest potential for growth** (eg India and China) are not part of a trading bloc.

(d) **New technology**, such as the Internet, makes it harder to police trade barriers in some areas.

International trade liberalisation: the WTO

7.6 Since 1945, the major industrial nations, and now developing countries also, have sought to increase trade. The fall of communism and the failure of state control of trade have added to the pressure for free trade.

7.7 The WTO (World Trade Organisation) was formed in 1995 as successor to the former General Agreement on Tariffs and Trade (GATT). China became a WTO member in 2001.

(a) **Membership** of the WTO requires **adherence to certain conditions** regarding competition in the home market.

(b) **Membership rules are slightly less onerous for 'developing countries'**, which can maintain some protectionist measures, although this is a matter of dispute.

International influences on the organisation's domestic conditions

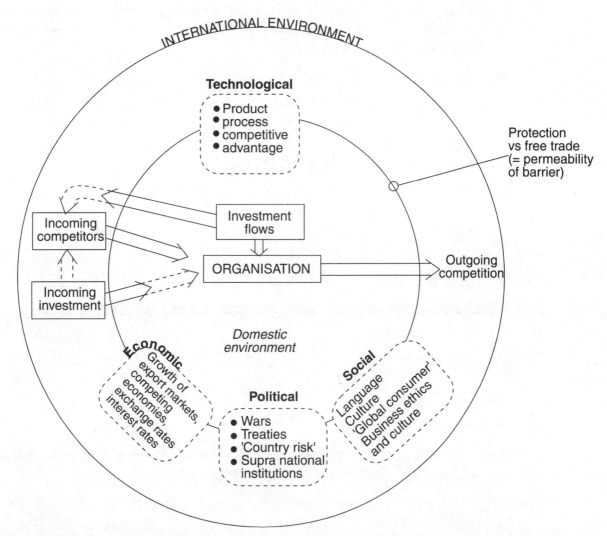

7.8 The diagram demonstrates the following.

(a) In times of increasing free trade, firms (unless they have overwhelming competitive advantages in their national markets) can expect incoming competition. That said, the possibility of **competing abroad** is also available.

(b) **Investment flows** can also **go two ways**. A firm can attract investment from overseas institutions. Competing firms from overseas can receive investments from domestic institutions.

(c)   The **barrier** between the **domestic environment** and the international environment is **relatively permeable**, depending on the **product** and the **openness** of the market for the product or the economy

Exchange rates

Key Concept

Exchange rate is the price of a currency expressed in terms of another currency.

7.9   The exchange rate between two currencies is determined by the interaction of demand and supply conditions. Demand and supply of a particular country's currency are derived from the country's balance of payments position.

(a)   If it is a **surplus** country where

$$\begin{array}{ccc} \text{Value of exports} & & \text{Value of imports} \\ \text{+ capital inflows} & > & \text{+ capital outflows} \end{array}$$

then demand relative to supply will be rising. The foreign exchange markets will therefore tend to quote the **currency** at a **higher exchange rate**.

(b)   If it is a **deficit** country, the **supply** of its currency will be **rising** relative to demand for it and so the forex markets will tend to quote the **currency** at a **lower exchange rate**.

Fixed exchange rates

7.10 A fixed exchange rate system is theoretically possible but not often found in practice.

Floating exchange rates

Key Concept

Floating exchange rates are exchange rates which are allowed to fluctuate according to demand and supply conditions in the foreign exchange markets.

7.11 Floating exchange rates are at the opposite end of the spectrum to fixed rates. At this extreme, exchange rates are completely left to the free play of demand and supply market forces, and there is no official financing at all. The ruling exchange rate is, therefore, at equilibrium by definition.

7.12 In practice, governments seek to combine the advantages of exchange rate stability with flexibility and to avoid the disadvantages of both rigidly fixed exchange rates and free floating.

Managed (or dirty) **floating** refers to a system whereby exchange rates are allowed to float, but from time-to-time the authorities will intervene in the foreign exchange market:

- To use their official reserves of foreign currencies to buy their own domestic currency
- To sell their domestic currency to buy more foreign currency for the official reserves

7.13 Movements in exchange rates can create risks for importers and exporters, for example where prices are agreed in advance in a foreign currency. Speculation in the capital markets often has a much bigger impact short-term than changes in supply and demand. While exchange rates remain volatile, international trading companies can do a number of things to reduce their risk of suffering losses on foreign exchange transactions, including the following.

(a) Many companies buy currencies **forward** at a fixed and known price.

(b) **Dealing in a hard currency** may lessen the risks attached to volatile currencies.

(c) **Operations can be managed** so that the proportion of sales in one currency are matched by an equal proportion of purchases in that currency.

(d) The marketing and sales department can insist on **invoicing in the domestic currency**. This means that the customer bears all the foreign exchange risk, however this may be an unacceptable arrangement. Furthermore there is the risk that sales will be adversely affected by high prices, reducing demand.

(e) **Outsource activities** to the local market. Firms which have invested made efforts to obtain many of their inputs, subject to quality limits, from local suppliers. Promotional activities can also be sourced locally.

(f) Marketers can try and aim at **segments** in the market which are not particularly price sensitive. For example, many German car marques such as Mercedes have been marketed in the US on the basis of quality and exclusivity. This is a type of strategy based on differentiation focus.

The balance of payments

Key Concept

Balance of payments is the statistical accounting record of all of a country's external transactions in a given period.

7.14 Because of the principle of comparative advantage, international trade can be beneficial to all countries that take part in it. However, it can present countries with balance of payments problems arising from a persistent mismatch in the flows of exports and imports, resulting in surpluses or deficits in the value of goods and services exchanged.

7.15 **Problems with deficits** include the following.

(a) **Effect on growth**

Since a trade **deficit represents a leakage** of income from the national economy, there is a danger that **economic growth diminish**es unless internally generated growth can compensate for this.

BPP
PROFESSIONAL EDUCATION

(b)   **Exchange rates**

A persistent trade deficit is likely to put **downward pressure** on the **exchange rate** as confidence in the currency is weakened and as demand for it, relative to other currencies in general, falls.

(c)   **Domestic consequences**

A depreciating exchange rate will mean that the **price of imports** in domestic terms will be **rising**, putting pressure on **domestic inflation** with consequent knock-on effects for wage demands and unemployment.

7.16   Problems can emerge with persistent surpluses.

(a)   **Overheating**

A trade surplus represents an injection into the national economy which may result in an **overheating** of the economy if domestic production is already at full capacity. Overheating will tend to reflect itself in **upward pressure on prices** as total demand for goods (domestic and foreign) exceeds total domestic supply.

(b)   **Exchange rates**

Surpluses are likely to put **upward pressure** on the **exchange rate** which will push up the price of exported goods in foreign countries. This gives rise to the possibility that the surplus will decline.

7.17   Where trade is out of balance, governments can take a number of measures to restore the balance.

(a)   **Transport restrictions**

Governments can discourage imports through **quotas**, controls or taxes (although this would doubtless lead to retaliatory action). Some argue that the imposition of product standards testing is a form of control. It might be illegal under EU rules or other treaty obligations (eg WTO).

(b)   **Giving support to exporters**

This may take a number of forms such as export monopolies, advice (as provided by the government). Export credit insurance reduces the risk, and hence the return that might have to be earned.

(c)   **Devaluing the currency**

Devaluation makes exports cheaper and increases their value.

(d)   **General fiscal and monetary policy**

Economic policy can reduce the overall level of activity in the economy. While (a), (b) and (c) are **expenditure switching** policies, which transfer resources and expenditure away from imports and towards domestic products, this is an **expenditure reducing** policy.

(e)   **Arising interest rates**

This will increase the value of the currency, to make imports cheaper.

(f)   **Supply side measures**

In the long term, **supply side measures** can encourage exports.

7.18 Naturally, marketers should be alert to the problems as well as opportunities which such measures pose.

(a) **Unpredictable impacts**

As with other economic policies the **magnitude** and **timing** effects of a change in policy may be uncertain, and affected by confidence factors not just in domestic but also in foreign markets.

(b) **Effect on exporters**

Recent British experience suggests that an increase in the exchange rate may do more damage to exporters than an equal decrease would help them. This may emphasise the need for measures to be taken quickly to counter the effect of an increase in exchange rate, for example a **cut in prices** or **increased marketing activity**. Export subsidies are very rare, but it is common for governments to **promote exports** in other ways.

(c) **Effect on costs**

Import quotas/tariffs **raise prices of material inputs**. This increases costs of production, and hence the price that has to be charged to earn a profit. It might also stimulate domestic manufacturers to start up production (**import substitution**).

Marketing at Work

Although motivated by the desire to combat terrorism, Australia's prime minister, John Howard, has been attempting to improve trading relationships with America on the back of his support for the war against Iraq.

However many critics have accused Howard of seeking to develop the wrong markets, claiming that good economic relations with Asia are much more important for the Australian economy. Former Prime minister, Paul Keating, has accused Howard of 'crawling up under the US armpit'. He argues that America will benefit far more from Australian sectors such as the media being open to American conglomerates than Australia's export trade will benefit from access to US markets. 'If we ask for the right to sell just one hamburger patty in the US, we'll be struck down by the first xenophobic congressman we meet appealing to the farm lobby.'

Statistics appear to support Keating's view; trade with Asia accounts for around 60% of Australia's overseas trade, trade with the USA only around 10%. Australian companies have however been unwilling to make significant investments in Asia, deterred by legal problems, corruption and the threat of terrorism. However companies that have invested in more developed markets have often struggled to achieve satisfactory returns. Australia may also be vulnerable if trading relations between China and other Asian countries improve, leading to Australian businesses competing on less advantageous terms.

Far Eastern Economic Review, 5 June 2003

Action Programme 7

Choose a country that is a significant trading partner of your own country, and obtain information about its key economic indicators from the websites given at the start of the chapter. From this information, and from relevant recent press coverage, assess how that country's economic prospects are likely to impact upon your own country's trade with it.

Action Programme 8

A balance of payments crisis in your country has made policy action inevitable. You have been delegated the task of preparing a two-page submission to the responsible government minister on the case for and against expenditure switching, and expenditure reducing policies, making clear the impacts of each for domestic and international marketers.

Chapter Roundup

- The primary aim of economic policy is to provide a **stable economic framework** from which sustainable growth can be achieved. Other objectives include **control** of **inflation** and **unemployment** and **balancing trade**.

- There are various ways of defining **national income**; one way is to say that it equals the sum of expenditure (consumption + investment + government) + exports – imports.

- The periodic rise and fall of trading activity over a number of years is known as the **business cycle** or **trade cycle**.

- Changes in national income begin with a small change in expenditure, leading to a larger eventual change in national income, due to the **multiplier effect**.

- Changes in national income can be explained partially by the **accelerator principle** which is that changes in investment spending are proportionally greater than changes in consumption spending, and therefore investment spending is more susceptible to bigger downturns and upturns.

- Trade cycles are explained in Keynesian economies as the combined effect of the **multiplier** and the **accelerator**.

- **Monetary** and **fiscal policy** should be used in conjunction with each other.

- A government must decide how it intends to raise tax revenues, from direct or indirect taxes, and in what proportions tax revenues will be raised from each source. **Fiscal policy** provides a method of managing aggregate demand in the economy.

- The reality of economic management tends to be complex.

  - The behaviour of economic agents (consumers, producers and others) may be **unpredictable** and **unstable**.

  - There are often **considerable lags or delays** between policy actions and their effects.

- The international marketer always operates in a wider **economic context**, and part of that context relates to trade and funds flows arising out of the general economic relationships between the exporting countries and other countries.

- The principle of **comparative advantage** suggests that countries with a comparative cost advantage in producing particular goods should partly or completely specialise in producing those goods.

Quick Quiz

1   Give four examples of aims of economic policy.

2   Which of the following would not lead to an increase in a country's national income?

    A   Increase in consumer spending
    B   Increase in imports
    C   Increase in private investment
    D   Increase in government expenditure

3   *Fill in the blank*

    ~~Multiplier~~ .... is the ratio of the change in income to the change in expenditure that caused it.

4   Match the following classifications of unemployment to the reasons given for them arising.

    (a)   Frictional
    (b)   Seasonal
    (c)   Structural
    (d)   Technological
    (e)   Cyclical

    (1)   Introduction of more advanced production processes
    (2)   Demand differs at different times of the year
    (3)   Occurs during decline and recession years
    (4)   Long-term changes in industry conditions
    (5)   Regional shortages and surpluses

5   What is the difference between demand-pull and cost-push inflation?

6   What are the four phases of the business cycle?

7   Competitive advantage is the principle that economic agents are best employed in activities that they carry out relatively better than other activities.

    True   ☐

    False ☐

8   Give four examples of factors influencing the level of a country's exchange rate.

Action Programme Review

1   Only (a). Both (b) and (c) are reductions in national income.

2   –

3   Various arguments have been advanced to suggest high unemployment can provide benefits for businesses. The threat of unemployment it is suggested limits wage rises, means that there is a greater pool of people to recruit from, and means that workers are likely to work longer hours and be more acquiescent.

    However, there are also some substantial downsides. In many sectors uncertainty, caused by the threat of unemployment, hits demand and thus hits sales. Additionally evidence suggests that where redundancies have occurred, the remaining employees often are not grateful to be kept in work, nor motivated to work harder, but are unsettled, and spend time looking for new jobs themselves because of the deterioration in atmosphere and the feeling that they will be next to be made redundant. If a culture is created where people expect to change jobs regularly, staff who make the move first may well be those with the most marketable skills whom businesses can least afford to lose.

An example quoted in the *Financial Times* in April 2001 of a company where staff and general cost reduction caused major problems was Marks & Spencer. To fulfil market expectations during the 1990s, staff numbers were limited or reduced, store enhancements were restricted, and relationships with suppliers squeezed. As a result, earnings matched market expectations for a while but eventually: 'Customers started to notice that value for money was not quite as good as it could have been. That you had to wait to get the attention of a sales assistant. That the shops were dowdy and so was the some of the merchandise. These impressions accumulated. Gradually the positive Marks and Spencer anecdotes were replaced by negative ones. Suddenly the company's reputation fell off a cliff. And so did its profits.'

4   (a)   (i)   A recessionary stage in the business cycle implies that the key indicators of economic activity are showing lower levels of activity. Lower spending by consumers results in lower spending by firms, which in turn leads to depressed prices for the goods and services provided by individuals and firms.

Large firms are able to manage successfully periods of recession in a number of ways. If they are large and diversified, they may be able to shift resources away from areas of contraction towards those of growth (eg some export markets may continue to grow despite a recession in the domestic market). Larger firms may also have the financial strength to see them through a recession until the level of economic activity picks up. This may be lacking with the smaller firm. Furthermore, large well-resourced firms may be able to exploit a recession by investing in new equipment while prices are low. New capacity would then be ready for when an upturn in demand occurred. Finally, large firms may be in a strong position to require their suppliers to bear part of the burden of a recession, for example by requiring them to extend their credit period or to reduce their selling prices.

The main advantage which small firms have over their larger competitors is flexibility. Small firms often operate with equipment which is older and less capital intensive. With lower fixed costs, running at below full capacity can be less of a problem than for a larger capital intensive firm.

(ii)   Much of what was said above can also be said about large and small firms' abilities to benefit from boom conditions.

Larger firms may have the capital resources which allow them rapidly to exploit a growing market. They may also be in a better position to collect information which will identify for them where, when and how sectors of the economy are booming. Large firms are often able to keep large stockpiles of goods which are built up during a recession and which can be made available to cater for a sudden boom in the economy.

The principal advantage of small firms is again their flexibility. There may be fewer bureaucratic delays in recruiting new staff and investing in new capacity when an upturn in demand seems imminent.

(b)   The business cycle measures what is actually happening to levels of economic activity. It is also important to understand individuals' and companies' confidence and expectations of economic prosperity – the so-called feel good factor. There is evidence that private and company buyers postpone many capital purchases when they are unsure about the ability to support financially such investments in the future. Hence many marketers seek to understand how people feel about the future as an indicator of future demand for their products.

5   Demand for the product must presumably be changed little by an increase in prices, at least in the opinion of the producer. Otherwise he would fear to pass on the tax burden by increasing his prices as this would lead to a fall in revenue.

6   –

7   –

8   The country is facing a balance of payments crisis as a result of imports exceeding exports.

Two alternative methods of alleviating the crisis are considered here: switching government spending between expenditure headings; and reducing government expenditure in total. The pros and cons of each approach are considered below.

Expenditure switching policies would involve government switching expenditure between sectors, for example between the household and company sectors. It may decide to switch spending away from sectors which consume resources (for example, welfare benefits) to sectors which generate resources (for example, expenditure on essential infrastructure).

Benefits

(i)   Total government expenditure is not cut, and so negative multiplier effects are minimised.

(ii)   Positive multiplier benefits may result from directing resources to sectors with a high multiplier effect.

(iii)   The government may invest in industries which can produce goods to substitute for imports.

(iv)   Investment in infrastructure may lower firms' costs, thereby improving exports.

Disadvantages

(i)   The policy may not address a fundamental problem of a government spending beyond its resources.

(ii)   There is no guarantee that investment in new production facilities will help to reduce imports, or help to increase exports.

(iii)   The process may take a long time to have any effects.

With *expenditure reducing policies*, the government cuts its total expenditure.

Benefits

(i)   The international financial community may see spending reductions as a sign of good economic management, thereby strengthening the exchange rate.

(ii)   Government interest costs to service its debt are reduced.

(iii)   The government will have less need to borrow on international money markets.

(iv)   The deflationary effects of cutting expenditure may be to cut total consumption, including consumption of exports.

Disadvantages

(i) Expenditure cuts cause social costs to rise.

(ii) Expenditure on vital infrastructure may be cut, thereby preventing firms' production costs from falling.

(iii) A deflationary effect could cut government tax revenues, makings its borrowing requirement even greater.

Answers to Quick Quiz

1
- Achieving sustainable growth
- Controlling inflation
- Achieving full employment
- Achieving a balance of payment equilibrium

2   B   Increase in imports

3   Multiplier

4   (a)   (5)
    (b)   (2)
    (c)   (4)
    (d)   (1)
    (e)   (3)

5   Demand-pull inflation occurs because of an excess demand which factors of production cannot supply. Cost-push inflation occurs when the costs of factors of production increase irrespective of demand levels.

Look up Demand pull inflation and cost push inflation

6
- Depression
- Recovery
- Boom
- Recession

7   False. The definition given is of comparative advantage.

8   Any four of:

- Balance of payments position
- Comparative inflation rates
- Comparative interest rates
- Speculation
- Government policy

Now try illustrative questions 16 and 17 at the end of the Study Text

The political and legal environments

Chapter Topic List

1	Setting the scene
2	The state and the public sector
3	State influences over economic activity
4	State influences over organisations
5	Influences on government policy
6	Principles of business law
7	Contract law
8	The law of tort
9	The law of agency
10	Data protection
11	Trade descriptions
12	Intellectual property
13	Marketing and the legal environment

Learning Outcome

☑ Recognise and assess the potential influence on, and implications for, the marketing function of key trends in the political and legal environments

Syllabus Reference

☑ Explain the political and legislative environments, and in general terms, their influence on and implications for marketing

Key Concepts Introduced

- Political party
- Interest group
- Contract
- Agent

1 Setting the scene

1.1 In this chapter we discuss the influence of the political and legal environment on marketing.

1.2 Firstly we discuss the role of the state and **state influences** over economic activity. The state can influence activity through its own role as consumer and investor. Secondly the state can affect organisations by providing, or restricting or forbidding certain activities.

1.3 Lastly in this part we deal with the **influences** on what **policies** are adopted by the state, particularly focusing on the roles of **political parties**.

1.4 The second part of this chapter deals with certain important aspects of the legal environment. Marketing managers need to be aware of the law for a variety of reasons.

(a) **Customers** are gaining more **rights** in their dealings with a supplier.

(b) Similarly, **employees** – a major cost to most businesses – are gaining more **rights**, affecting the marketing department's ability to be flexible and to keep costs down.

(c) **Advertisers** are increasingly **restricted** in the claims they can make in their advertising.

(d) Governments in most countries have passed laws to prevent companies developing **anti-competitive practices**.

(e) Certain types of legislation, for example **health and safety** can impose significant costs on businesses but can also mean that the barriers to entry in the industry are high.

(f) The **law** is often resorted to in disputes between manufacturers and their distributors.

(g) **Increased regulation** can help certain businesses, for example trademarks or patent protection.

1.5 In this chapter we deal with various aspects of business law. What is important is how traditional principles can be modified, generally in favour of the **consumer**. Thus the law of contract can be modified to provide protection against unfair terms. Law may also provide general protection to the consumer by means of fair trading and trade descriptions legislation. Data about consumers is governed by data protection legislation in many countries.

1.6 A further means of regulation is voluntary codes of conduct, and these are particularly important for advertising.

2 The state and the public sector

2.1 The modern state, in other words the institutions of government, has a large number of historical and philosophical antecedents. Some key features of the modern state are as follows.

(a) It has **complete sovereignty** in a defined territory, unless it cedes some of this sovereignty.

(b) It has **legislative** and **coercive** powers.

(c) It can **raise taxation** and **distribute** the **proceeds**.

(d) In theory, it is supposed to be **above sectional interests**.

(e) The state's **actual autonomy** is **limited**.

   (i) The effects of **international economic trends** are often out of its control.

   (ii) The authority of the state is often delegated to **supra-national institutions** like the European Union (EU) or is constrained by treaty.

2.2 Various reasons have been given for the growth of the public sector and public spending.

(a) The impact of **industrialisation and urbanisation**, leading to pressures for increased government intervention in the economy and society

(b) **Demographic pressures**, particularly the substantial increase in the proportion of old people, who place major demands on social service of all kinds

(c) **Electoral pressures**, as parties compete for public support by promising better services

(d) **Pressures** from **public sector bureaucrats** and **professionals** to maintain and expand services

(e) **Pressures** from **clients**, users and associated pressure groups to improve services

(f) The **welfare state**, with guaranteed benefits, was designed for a society in which most people had **paid** employment, not one with high levels of unemployment

2.3 Critics suggest that there are in-built tendencies in the public sector towards the proliferation of **bureaucracy** and increased **public spending**, because of the absence of the discipline of the market.

2.4 The size of the public sector has been the subject of considerable political and ideological controversy.

Privatisation

2.5 Over the last 20 years however various areas of the public sector (eg water, gas, electricity, telecommunications) have been delivered to the private sector in a process of **privatisation**. Reductions in public sector borrowing and expenditure resulting from privatisation have financed tax cuts in various countries. Privatisation has also been held to encourage competition, but criticism has been levelled in some cases as public utilities were sold off as private monopolies.

Action Programme 1

Which publicly provided services have you used up until now? What benefits do you think:

(a)   You have gained from using them?

(b)   You will have gained in 40 years time?

(c)   Your neighbour gains from using them?

3   State influences over economic activity

3.1   The state influences activity through:

- Its **taxation** and **interest policies**
- **Public spending** on **goods and services**
- **Regulation**

3.2   The rationale for state intervention as a whole has two main elements, which are now briefly described.

(a)   **Equity**

An equitable distribution of resources is one which is regarded as fair.

(b)   **Market failure**

We have already seen how state action can be used against imperfect competition and externalities.

4   State influences over organisations

4.1   Government economic policy affects organisations in the following ways. The variety of influences are outlined in the following diagram.

Action Programme 2

List the ways in which the policies of government and local government have affected your employer:

(a) Directly

(b) Indirectly in the past year

5 Influences on government policy

5.1 Government policy is determined by a variety of factors:

- Past decisions
- Existing resources and projected future resources
- Promises made to the electorate

5.2 The apparatus of government is headed by ministers who, unlike the civil servants advising them, are elected, and whose jobs as ministers can be terminated every so often by the electorate.

Political parties and interest groups

Key Concept

A **political party** is an organisation whose members:

(a)   have some shared values or interests

(b)   have shared views as to how society should be run

(c)   are prepared to work together to ensure that they achieve control over policy making and the apparatus of government

5.3   Political parties determine what the government will do (eg raise indirect taxes as opposed to income tax), and are important, but not the only, players in the process by which policy is developed. A political party aims to take over the whole of government, and to be in charge of a variety of public policy areas from crime prevention to arts sponsorship. It is this **universality of ambition** that distinguishes a political party from a special interest group.

Interest groups and pressure groups

Key Concept

An **interest group** represents the various points of view on a number of issues held by defined social groupings.

5.4   An interest group would like to **influence** the government. It represents people who share certain objectives. A **pressure group** promotes **particular issues**. In practice, this distinction is hard to maintain.

Media and lobbyists   12/02

5.5   Professional **lobbyists** also apply external pressure to the political system. Many trade associations, for example, employ lobbyists to get their message across to influential members of the government.

5.6   The **media** are also a source of pressure on governments. In many countries, the opposition of powerful media can be sufficient to force a government to change its policies.

5.7   However, the power of the media can be a matter of debate. It is sometimes argued that newspapers are a declining influence, and that most people get their news from television. Television news is required to be balanced in the UK. There is no doubt that the ability to perform well on TV is an essential political skill. Politicians and the government often react to media pressure (eg over directors' pay).

5.8 Political parties in democracies have become much more adept in their use of **advertising** and **public relations**. Public relations is now a vital part of the normal political routine, with **spin doctors** employed to give events a gloss favourable to the party.

Political parties and business

5.9 Although political parties have universal ambitions, this does not mean that they are immune to sectional interests. In the reasonably near past, it was relatively easy to identify the relationship between political parties and interest groups. Socialist and labour parties represented the organised working class, and others represented business and capital.

5.10 The relationship between a party's philosophy and its attitudes to business is no longer a simple one. In part, this is because a new consensus seems to have emerged on the value of market-based policies.

(a) **Work place regulation** (such as the Social Chapter of the Maastricht Treaty) is supported, in most of Europe, by parties of both left and right.

(b) Free trade promotes competition, but many pro-business governments do not wish to see **their** businesses affected. Some EU governments have, in the past, been hostile to Japanese investment in the UK. However, the single European market is designed to promote competition.

Policies and decision-making

5.11 In the UK the party in power gives some sort of direction to government policy and state activity. This political direction, in the UK at least, is exercised much in the manner of the captain on the bridge of a large ship.

(a) Many things will go on as they have before and the political masters will do little to interfere with them (eg the rule that in the UK cars are driven on the left).

(b) Even when a government does wish to change policy, there are usually **extensive consultations** with experts in the Civil Service, interest groups and so on.

(c) Some policies have a **long time scale**, and implementing them is a slow and cumbersome exercise, like turning round a ship.

5.12 Politics is also about **compromise**, arising out of negotiation with different interest groups, and so political decision-making on a national scale cannot really be compared to the decision-making framework in a business. This is because governments do not exist to make a profit.

6 Principles of business law

6.1 The amount of law affecting marketers, both directly and indirectly, is increasing in most countries.

6.2 As well as the law, you need to know about the increasing amounts of quasi-law which affects marketers. This is based on **voluntary codes** which do not normally have the full sanction of a legal punishment, but companies find it in their interest to abide by them.

6.3 In this section, we are going to start by describing the basic **types** of law that affect marketers. We will look at more specific applications later.

6.4 The legal environment consists of **laws made by parliaments case law** (precedents developed by the courts) and **quasi-laws**, such as government-sponsored codes of conduct and rules developed by trade associations. European Union countries also face an increasing body of legislation from the European Commission.

Exam Tip

When dealing with questions about legislation, try to think what the legislation is trying to achieve. At a simple level of course, legislation lays down what is permitted and prohibited for individuals and businesses. There may also be other, more specific, aims including enforcement of fair dealing, settlement of disputes, and balancing the interests of the consumer or business against the wider interests of society.

7 Contract law

7.1 One of the most important areas of law for business is the law of contract. The discussion that follows is based on the **common law** of the UK.

Key Concept

A **contract** is a legally binding agreement that defines a relationship between two parties.

The essentials of a contract

7.2 The courts will usually look for the evidence of three elements in any contract before they will be prepared to uphold that contract or award a remedy.

(a) The parties must have an **intention** to **create a legally binding relationship** between themselves.

(b) There is an **agreement** made by **offer** and **acceptance**.

(c) There is a **bargain** by which the obligations assumed by each party are supported by **consideration** (value) given by the other.

7.3 A party is said to be in breach of contract where, **without lawful excuse**, he does not perform his contractual obligations precisely.

Remedies available for breach of contract

7.4 A party has a number of remedies when the other party is in breach of contract, including damages (compensation for loss caused by the breach).

The terms of the contract

7.5 As a general principle the parties may by their offer and acceptance include in their contract whatever terms they prefer. But the law may modify these express terms in various ways.

(a) The terms must be sufficiently **complete** and **precise** to produce an agreement which can be binding. If they are vague there may be no contract.

(b) To be enforceable, terms must be validly **incorporated** into the contract.

Court interventions

7.6 There has been strong criticism of the use of **exclusion** (or exemption) **clauses** in contracts. In those conditions the seller may try to **exclude** or **limit** his **liability** for failure to perform as promised, for breach of contract or for negligence — or he may try to offer a 'guarantee' which in fact reduces the buyer's rights.

7.7 Courts have sought to protect the consumer from the harsher effects of exclusion clauses in two ways.

(a) An **exclusion clause** must be **properly incorporated** into a contract to have legal effect.

(b) **Exclusion clauses** are **interpreted strictly**; this may prevent the application of the clause.

Statutory intervention

7.8 The Unfair Contract Terms Act (UCTA) 1977 in the UK applies to clauses excluding or limiting liability in contract or tort and is a good example of how governments in various countries have tried to legislate.

7.9 The Act uses two techniques for controlling exclusion clauses - some types of clauses are **void**, whereas others are subject to a **test of reasonableness**. The main provisions of the Act are as follows.

Main provisions	
Exclusion of liability for negligence	A person cannot, by reference to any contract term, restrict his liability for death or personal injury resulting from negligence. In the case of other loss or damage, a person cannot restrict his liability for negligence unless the term is reasonable.
Standard term contracts and consumer contracts	The person who imposes the standard term, or who deals with the consumer, cannot unless the term is reasonable: (i) restrict liability for his own breach or fundamental breach; or (ii) claim to be entitled to render substantially different performance or no performance at all.

Main provisions	
Unreasonable indemnity clauses	A clause whereby one party undertakes to indemnify the other for liability incurred in the other's performance of the contract is void if the party giving the indemnity is a consumer, unless it is reasonable.
Guarantee of consumer goods	The terms of a 'guarantee' of goods cannot exclude or restrict liability for loss or damage caused by defects of the goods.
Sale and supply of goods	Any contract for the sale or hire purchase of goods cannot exclude the implied condition that the seller has a right to sell or transfer ownership of the goods.
Misrepresentation	Any attempt to exclude liability for **misrepresentation** must satisfy a test of reasonableness.

The test of reasonableness

7.10 To be reasonable, the term must be fair and appear reasonable to the average person. The burden of proving reasonableness lies on the person seeking to rely on the clause.

Action Programme 3

Do you remember the essential elements of a contract?

8 The law of tort

8.1 Also referred to as the law of negligence, this principle of law can affect all dealings which an organisation has with others, and not just those with whom it has a contractual relationship.

8.2 If a person suffers personal injury or damage to property by a defective product he may be able to recover **damages** for **negligence** from the manufacturer under the common law of tort (discussed below).

8.3 To succeed in an action for negligence the plaintiff must prove three things, that:

(a) The **defendant** owed him (the plaintiff) a **duty of care**.

(b) There was a **breach** of that **duty** by the defendant.

(c) As a foreseeable consequence the plaintiff suffered **injury, damage** or (in some cases) **financial loss** (although pure loss of profits cannot be recovered).

Duty of care; product liability   12/03

8.4 The law of negligence applies in **product liability** cases where physical injury or damage results from failure to take proper precautions. However, if there is a reasonable opportunity of avoiding the injury by intermediate inspection or by routine precautions, there is no duty to a plaintiff who could have avoided it by these means.

8.5 A company may therefore owe a duty of care, including a duty to avoid injury, to all users and others who come into contact with its products. For example, a toy company selling a dangerous toy may be in breach of a duty of care not only to people who buy its toys, but also to anyone who eventually uses them.

8.6 A further area in which the duty of care has been developing is the duty of care owed by retailers to customers. Several retailers in various countries, Macdonalds being the best-known example, have been sued for selling hot drinks which customers have subsequently spilled and scalded themselves. As a result businesses have posted warnings on the cups or on the machines that vend the drinks.

9 The law of agency

9.1 Organisations frequently use other individuals or organisations to perform functions on their behalf. Within the environment of a firm, agency law is particularly important in governing the conduct of a firm in relation to its employees and intermediaries. The former is often referred to as a **principal**, the latter as **agents.**

Key Concept

An **agent** is a person authorised to act for another (the principal) and bring that other person into legal relations with a third party.

9.2 The relationship of principal and agent is usually created by mutual consent. The consent (with one exception) need not be formal nor expressed in a written document. It is usually an **express** agreement, even if it is created in an informal manner.

9.3 Although businesses involved in handling advertising for customers are commonly known as **advertising agencies**, this is not the case in reality. In fact they are principals in their own right. They are solely liable to the media owners (eg newspapers, TV) for payment for advertising space. If the agency becomes insolvent, the media owners cannot seek payment from the customer whose products were being advertised. If the advertiser becomes insolvent, the agency must still pay the media owners.

9.4 When an agent agrees to perform services for his principal for reward there is a contract between them. Even if the agent undertakes his duties without reward he has obligations to his principal. The term **fiduciary duty** is often used. The agent owes to his principal a duty not to put himself in a situation where his own interests conflict with those of the principal.

Commercial agents: EC directive

9.5 Potentially far-reaching changes to agency law were introduced by the Commercial Agents (Council Directive) Regulations 1993, which implement the provisions of an EC directive on commercial agents.

9.6 A commercial agent is a self-employed intermediary who has **continuing authority** to negotiate the sale or purchase of goods on behalf of his principal or to negotiate and conclude such transactions on behalf of and in the name of his principal.

market leasing

DUTIES OF COMMERCIAL AGENTS AND PRINCIPALS	
Agents	Principals
Act in good faith	Act in good faith
Supply all necessary information	Supply all necessary information
	Provide all necessary documentation
	Tell agent of all acceptances, refusals and failures to execute contracts
	Notify agent if volume of commercial transactions will be significantly lower than expected

10 Data protection

10.1 In 1995 the European Parliament adopted a new *Directive on Data Protection*, with two main purposes.

(a) **To protect individual privacy**

The directive applies to all personal data, in any form.

(b) **To harmonise data protection legislation**

This means in the interests of improving the operation of the single European market, there can be a **free flow of personal data** between the member states of the EU.

The directive has wide implications. A new **Data Protection Act** came into force in 1998 in the UK.

10.2 Some important features of the new legislation are as follows.

(a) It spells out the **conditions under which processing is lawful**. This was not at all clear under the previous legislation.

(b) Everyone has the right to go to court to seek redress for **any breach** of data protection law, rather than just for certain aspects of it, as at present.

(c) Filing systems that are structured so as to facilitate access to information about a particular person fall within the legislation. This includes systems that are **paper-based** or on **microfilm** or **microfiche**. Personnel records, in particular, are likely to be caught by the Act in future.

(d) Processing of personal subject's data is **forbidden** except in the following circumstances.

■ With the subject's **consent**, by free, specific and informed agreement
■ As a result of a **contractual arrangement**
■ Because of a **legal obligation**
■ To **protect the vital interests** of the subject
■ Where processing is in the **public interest**
■ Where processing is required to exercise **official authority**

(e) The processing of **'sensitive data'** is forbidden, unless express consent has been obtained or there are conflicting obligations under employment law. Sensitive data includes data relating to racial origin, political opinions, religious beliefs, physical or mental health, sexual proclivities and trade union membership.

(f) If data about a data subject is **obtained from a third party** the data subject must be given the following information.

■ The identity of the **controller** of the data
■ The **purposes** for which the data are being processed
■ **What data** will be disclosed and **to whom**
■ The existence of a right of subject **access** to the data

(g) Data subjects have a right not only to have a **copy of data** held about them but also the right to know **why** the data is being processed and **what is the logic** behind the processing.

11 Trade descriptions

11.1 Trade descriptions legislations require businesses to describe what they sell accurately and fairly.

11.2 UK rules provide a fairly comprehensive list of what constitutes a trade description.

(a) Quantity, size or gauge of goods

(b) Method of manufacture, production, processing or reconditioning

(c) Composition

(d) Fitness for purpose, strength, performance, behaviour or accuracy

(e) Any other physical characteristics not included in the preceding paragraphs

(f) Testing by any person and the results of testing

(g) Approval by any person or conformity with a type approved by any person. For example, this would cover a statement that the item had qualified for the 'kitemark' of the British Standards Institute

(h) Place or date of manufacture, production, processing or reconditioning

(i) Person by whom manufactured, produced, processed or reconditioned

(j) Other history, including previous ownership or use

11.3 There are three offences under the UK's legislation:

■ Applying a **false trade description** to **goods** and supplying or offering to supply any such goods

■ Making **false statements** relating to **services, accommodation or facilities**

■ Making **misleading statements** as to the price of goods or other types of misleading statements that are not actually false

11.4 The motor trade has featured in a number of cases under the UK legislation, particularly in respect of the mileage and condition of used cars. The travel industry has also fallen foul on various occasions of the rules relating to service, accommodation or facilities.

11.5 Trading standards officers have responsibility for enforcing trade description legislation and various other laws including those relating to food standards, weights and measures and consumer credit.

12 Intellectual property

12.1 In most countries it is deemed to be in the public interest that *ideas* in general should be allowed to be exploited. However the law has developed to provide protection to certain specific categories of industrial and intellectual property.

Patent	Monopoly right to exploit an invention for a stated period of time
Trademark	Distinctive word, name or other mark used to indicate a connection in the course of trade between goods and services and their owner
Copyright	Protection for authors, artists, composers etc from being deprived of their rewards by unauthorised copying of their works

12.2 Generally unlike patents and trademarks, copyright does not require registration but comes into effect automatically when a work is created.

12.3 As well as attaching to artistic works, copyright may also attach to original industrial designs.

Action Programme 4

Give examples of what you would think would be registrable trademarks.

Marketing at Work

The lax enforcement of intellectual property legislation can cause problems for companies trading in certain markets. Britain's Imperial Tobacco group has had difficulties with its operations in Indonesia. A provincial trader, Sumatra stole the trademark of its premier cigarette brand, Davidoff, and Imperial Tobacco had major problems enforcing its rights.

The problem lay not in the law, which was strengthened about 10 years ago, but in the reluctance of the courts to enforce the law. Eventually Imperial needed a decision by the Indonesian Supreme Court to enforce its rights The lower courts had refused to consider evidence that the sale of the trademark to Sumatra was fraudulent, and ignored claims that Sumatra was not actively using the trademark as it was required to do by Indonesian law.

Imperial Tobacco's problems could have had serious consequences for the Indonesian economy as a whole. Not only had Imperial Tobacco planned to invest in a hi-tech factory generating hundreds of jobs, but Imperial's problems might have deterred other companies from investing even though 2003 was designated by the Indonesian government as the year of investment.

Far Eastern Economic Review 22 May 2003

13 Marketing and the legal environment   12/03

13.1 The political and legal environment can affect businesses in many ways. At the most basic level governments seek to provide **stability**, and a lack of stability will seriously jeopardise the business environment, with external parties not willing to invest in, or do business with, countries where the government is unstable or there is significant political violence.

13.2 As far as more specific policies are concerned, we discussed above how policy in many areas only changes slowly over time. Industries and organisations must however be alert for likely changes in policy. Marketers must be political realists and understand politicians' hidden agendas which may be quite different to their stated objectives. They must also be aware of the **wider implications** of policy shifts. Although John Major's Citizen's Charter was ridiculed in some quarters, it helped draw more attention to the importance of consumer interests in the UK.

13.3 Businesses also need to consider the impact of changes in how powers are **devolved** outside central government. In America state legislatures have been described as 'the forum for the ideas of the nation.'. Directly elected mayors also wield considerable power in major cities.

13.4 Businesses need to be aware of the wider social consequences of legislation changes and how they affect issues that are discussed in other chapters in this book. For example legislation against sexual discrimination has had an impact on the opportunities women are offered, and through its effect on their working lives, has had wider impacts on their lifestyle choices.

13.5 One aspect of minimising problems from governmental intervention is social and commercial good citizenship, complying with best practice and being responsive to ethical concerns. Often what is considered good practice at present is likely to acquire some regulatory force in the future. In addition, compliance with voluntary codes, particularly those relating to best practice or relations with consumers, can be marketed positively.

Exam Tip

Question 1 in December 2003 asked about the impact of changes in the legal environment on the food industry.

Marketing at Work

An example of the development of good practice has been the corporate governance codes published during the 1990s in the UK. The first committee to report, the Cadbury committee, was set up in response to concerns raised over the circumstances surrounding a number of high-profile corporate collapses. The committee published a code of best practice; listed companies were obliged under Stock Exchange rules to state whether they comply with the Code and give reasons for non-compliance.

Subsequently the Greenbury report reinforced Cadbury by giving more detailed recommendations on directors' remuneration and the Hampel report reviewed the recommendations of Cadbury. The Stock Exchange published a Combined Code combining the recommendations of the three reports. Developments are also taking place in guidelines on specific aspects of corporate governance, for example the Turnbull report on risk management.

13.6 By contrast businesses that fail to comply with the law run the risk of **legal penalties** and accompanying **bad publicity**. Companies may also be forced into legal action to counter claims of allegedly bad practice that is not actually illegal; as the McDonalds case demonstrates, even a victory in such an action cannot prevent much bad publicity.

13.7 Of course compliance with legislation may involve **extra costs**, including the extra procedures and investment necessary to conform to safety standards, staff training costs and legal costs. However these costs may also act as a **significant barrier to entry**, benefiting companies that are already in the industry.

13.8 The issues of legal standards and costs have very significant implications for companies that trade internationally. Companies that meet a strict set of standards in one country may face accusations of **hypocrisy** if their practices are laxer elsewhere. Ultimately higher costs of compliance, as well as costs of labour may mean that companies **relocate** to countries where costs and regulatory burdens are lower.

13.9 Companies may wish to take all possible steps to avoid the bad publicity resulting from a court action. This includes implementing systems to make sure that the company **keeps abreast** of **changes in the law**, and staff are kept fully informed. Internal procedures may be designed to minimise the risks from legal action, for example human resource policies that minimise the chances of the company suffering an adverse judgement in a case brought by a disgruntled ex-employee. Contracts may be drawn up requiring **binding arbitration** in the case of disputes. Ultimately businesses may prefer the costs of settling cases out of court, rather than the direct and indirect consequences of court action.

An active approach

13.10 As well as compliance, businesses also need to consider how they can actively influence policy. Influence may be by the industry or an individual business.

(a) **Initial influence**

Industry influence is perhaps most important during the **early stages** of legislation when as we have seen legislation may be built upon good practice. Industry concerns may also be an important influence upon the **fiscal policy**.

(b) **Comments**

Later in the legislative programme, when more specific proposals have been published businesses affected directly by the legislation may be given the chance to **comment** in detail.

(c) **Lobbying**

Whilst legislation is going through legislature, members may be **lobbied**, although we have seen above that lobbying of this sort has had much bad publicity in certain countries because of the cash for question scandals.

(d) **Enforcement**

When the legislation is in place, governments may require the help of businesses to **enforce** it. In any event governments regularly seek **feedback** on legislation through formal bodies such as Deregulation Taskforces or more informally.

Exam Tip

In the exam, you may wish to answer questions in the light of your own country's legislation. You will however need to understand how your own country's legislation deals with the issues that we have discussed in the context of UK legislation.

Action Programme 5

Which laws have most impact on your day-to-day work?

Chapter Roundup

- **State intervention** in **economic activity** is justified by the need to ensure equity and to correct market failures arising from **imperfect completion**, **imperfect information**, **externalities** and **public goods**.

- The state contains a **variety of institutions** serving a number of purposes. The relationships between the state and other areas of the public sector are characterised by varying degrees of **regulation and control**.

- The role of regulation has changed in recent years. Some formerly-run government activities are now in the private sector. Regulation has decreased in some areas, but increased in others (EU rules).

- Government influences business indirectly through its **conduct of economic policy** affecting investment and demand, and directly through **company law**, **corporation tax** and **indirect taxes**. The government can also be a **major buyer** from, or **supplier to**, particular industries.

- Under the **law of contract**, a valid contract is a legally binding agreement, formed by the mutual consent of two parties. The three essential elements of a contract are **offer** and **acceptance**, **consideration** and **intention** to enter into **legal relations**.

- As a general rule, the parties to a contract may include in the agreement whatever terms they choose. This is the principle of **freedom of contract**, which the law seeks to protect. However, certain contractual terms are regulated by statute, particularly where the parties are of unequal bargaining-strength.

- **Data protection** legislation requires data users to register with the Data Protection Registrar.

- Businesses must be aware of the **priorities** of central and local government, and can influence policy by **lobbying** and **feedback**.

Quick Quiz

1   *Fill in the blank*

    Interest Group. represents the various points of view on a number of issues held by defined social groupings.

2   Give five reasons for the growth of the public sector and public spending.

3   How does government social policy impact upon an organisation?

4   Which of the following is not an essential element of a contract?

    A   Intention to create legal relations
    B   Offer and acceptance
    C   Quantum meruit
    D   Bargain for consideration

5   What branch of law is concerned with breaches of the duty of care leading to injury?

6   Which of the following are remedies for breach of contract?

    A   Damages ✓
    B   Specific performance
    C   Force majeure
    D   Decision
    E   Reasonable indemnity

7   A commercial agent is a self-employed intermediary who has continuing authority to negotiate the sale or purchase of goods on behalf of his principal.

    True   ☐

    False ☐

8   What in the context of data protection legislation is sensitive data?

Action Programme Review

1   *Hint.* Consider education, street lighting, health, policing, roads.

    You pay taxes *now* to fund current benefits for yourself and others, in the hope that other people will do the same for you in future. Other people's taxes may well have paid the salaries of your teachers, for example. Your taxes pay the salaries of other people's teachers now.

2   –

3   There are three essential elements of a contract. An agreement must be reached as a result of an offer and acceptance. The agreement must contain an element of value, known as consideration (although a gratuitous promise is binding if made by deed). The parties to the agreement must intend to create legal relations.

4   (a) *Devices* (eg the Mercedes three-pointed star).
    (b) *Names* (eg 'Esso').
    (c) *Words* known or invented (eg 'Crest'; 'Kodak').
    (d) *Letters* (eg 'BPP').

(e)   *Numerals* (eg '4711').

(f)   *Smells* (which computers can now depict graphically to establish their uniqueness).

(g)   *Colour combinations,* although a trade mark is usually registered for use in any colour.

(h)   *Sounds,* such as the cavalry charge jingle of the Direct Line red telephone on wheels.

(i)   Some *three-dimensional figures,* such as the Rolls Royce *Spirit of Ecstasy* silver lady.

(j)   *Three-dimensional shapes,* such as the traditional glass Coca-Cola bottle.

5   –

Answers to Quick Quiz

1   An interest group

2   Any five of:

- Consequences of industrialisation
- Consequences of urbanisation
- Demographic pressures
- Electoral pressures
- Pressure from those employed in public sector
- Pressures from users and interest groups
- Consequences of welfare state

3   Through its impact on:

- Workplace regulation
- Employment law
- Labour supply
- Skills
- Education

4   C   Quantum meruit is a remedy against breach of contract.

5   Tort

6   A, B and D

7   True

8   Data relating to racial origin, political opinions, religious beliefs, physical or mental health, sexual proclivities and trade union membership

Now try illustrative questions 18 and 19 at the end of the Study Text

The natural environment

12

Chapter Topic List
1 Setting the scene
2 Environmental issues
3 Green marketing

Learning Outcome

☑ Recognise and assess the potential impact of key trends in the natural environment on the marketing function

Syllabus Reference

☑ Explain the natural environment and, in general terms, its influence on and implications for marketing

Key Concepts Introduced

- The green movement
- Sustainability
- Private costs
- Social cost
- Private benefit
- Social benefit
- Externality
- Public good

1 Setting the scene

1.1 Issues relating to the natural environment have already had a considerable impact on marketing policies and this influence is expected to increase in the future. In the past there has been a tendency to regard marketing, and business activities in general, as incompatible with 'green' principles, but it is now recognised that the two can be complementary.

1.2 In this chapter we highlight the concerns about the natural environment that have become important over the last few years. We show how pressures from environmental groups have impacted upon businesses, and also show how green issues have linked in with the concepts of social responsibility, sustainability and externalities.

1.3 We go on to consider how green issues have affected marketing practice, and how 'green' marketing might differ from conventional marketing.

Exam Tip

As issues relating to the natural environment have been given more emphasis in the new syllabus, this area is likely to be important in exams over the next few years.

2 Environmental issues   12/02, 12/03

2.1 Much of the concern about companies' responsibilities focuses on their attitude towards environmental concerns of the public. The environment has come to people's attention for a number of reasons.

(a) The **entry** into **decision-making** or political roles of the generation which grew up in the 1960s, where ecological issues became aired for the first time, has affected the political climate.

(b) The growth in prosperity after World War II has encouraged people to feel that **quality of life**, as opposed to material production and consumption, is no longer a luxury.

(c) **Expansion of media coverage** (eg of famines) and wider discussion of long-term environmental trends (eg the impact of global warming on the weather) has fuelled public anxiety. This has been particularly true in relation to third world issues such as rain forest destruction and drought.

(d) Some **notable disasters** (eg Chernobyl, oil slicks caused by the Exxon Valdez accident and the Gulf War) have aroused public attention.

(e) **Greater scientific knowledge** is available about the effect of productive activity on the environment. For example, it has only recently been possible to measure the hole in the ozone layer and assess its causes.

(f) **Longer-term cultural shifts** against the ideals of science and rationality have encouraged the idealisation of a 'natural' way of life. (Appeals to nature are common in advertising.)

BPP PROFESSIONAL EDUCATION

2.2 It is possible to identify several ways in which the public concern with environmental issues will impinge on business.

- Consumer demand for products which appear to be **environmentally friendly**
- Demand for **less pollution** from industry
- **Greater regulation** by government
- Demand that businesses be charged with the **external cost** of their activities
- Possible requirements to conduct **ecological** (or environmental) **audits**
- Opportunities to develop products and technologies which are **ecologically friendly**

Marketing at Work

The increase in the use of recycled and recyclable packaging materials over recent years are examples of business recognising its responsibilities toward resource sustainability. The material usually carries a statement declaring it is or can be recycled. This demonstrates that organisations recognise that being considered a relatively 'green' organisation is advantageous to them.

Action Programme 1

In recent years 'green' issues have come into considerable prominence. How have such issues affected the way in which products are marketed?

The green movement

Key Concept

The **green movement** is concerned with the way the human race interacts with and effects the environment. A major focus of this is concern about the damage to nature and living things which has come about as a consequence of exploitation of natural resources.

2.3 A major concern is with the study of **ecology** (the systems of plant and animal life, and the relationships between them). Major environmental themes include the following.

- The ecology is a web of complex interconnected living systems.
- Everything, including pollution, goes somewhere into this system.
- The balance of nature reflects a natural wisdom which is benign.
- All exploitation of nature will ultimately have a cost.

Which environmental issues will impact upon businesses?

Marketing at Work

Acid rain was linked to large-scale damage to forests throughout northern Europe, and acidification of water supplies and fish-bearing lakes and rivers. However, it has not been possible to establish direct responsibility, and so Swedish foresters or Finnish farmers have not been able to claim from British industrialists or Russian power stations.

The impacts on the environment led to political pressures to constrain the effects of industrial production.

However, it is now clear that there is no link at all between UK industry emissions and Scandinavian forest blight.

Action Programme 2

Can you think of some examples of environmental issues which have caused concern in recent years? Was any of the concern actually justified?

Green pressures on business

2.4 Pressure for better environmental performance is coming from many quarters. **Consumers are demanding a better environmental performance** from companies. In recent surveys, it has been demonstrated that around three-quarters of the population are applying environmental criteria in many purchase considerations.

2.5 **Green pressure groups** have increased their influence dramatically since the late 1980s. Membership of the 13 largest green groups in the UK has grown to over 5 million.

2.6 Groups have typically **exerted pressure** through **three main types of activity**.

Activity	Comment
Information based	Gathering and providing information, mounting political lobbies and publicity campaigns.
Direct action	Varying from peaceful protests and the usually legal activities of organisations such as Greenpeace, through to the terrorism of more extreme organisations.
Partnership and consultancy	Groups work with businesses to pool resources and help them improve environmental performance (eg the farming consultancy of the RSPB).

2.7 **Employees** are increasing pressure on the businesses in which they work - partly for their own safety and partly to improve the public image of the company.

2.8 **Environmental legislation** and regulations are growing. Pressure from the green-influenced vote has led to mainstream political parties taking these issues into their programmes. Most western countries now have laws to cover land-use planning, smoke emissions, water pollution and the destruction of animals and natural habitats.

2.9 The **media** has played a part in **spreading awareness** of environmental issues. Large scale disasters and issues such as global warming have become common themes for newspaper and television features.

2.10 **Environmental risk screening** has become increasingly important. Companies have become responsible for the environmental impact of their operations. As a consequence, many are now checking out the environmental, as well as the business and financial profile, of enterprises which they wish to acquire.

Marketing at Work

Direct action by consumers can have a very immediate impact. Monsanto thought that investment in genetically modified (GM) products would be seen as helping Third World farmers by increasing yields. However, they failed to take on board the fact that these farmers usually save seed from one crop to sow the following season. This would not be possible with GM crops.

Bad publicity portrayed Monsanto as exploiting, rather than helping, the Third World. In addition, inadequately addressed environmental concerns about the effect of GM crops on nature, led to a consumer boycott of GM products, trial crops being destroyed and a tumbling share price. The final straw was the news that Monsanto's UK staff canteen was GM free!

Social responsibility and sustainability

2.11 Social responsibility is based on two ideas.

(a) **The moral and ethical responsibilities of businesses**

Businesses must work within a society **on which they depend** for continued existence. While businesses control many of the resources available to society, the majority of the population actually contribute to the production of wealth, and natural justice demands that they share in its benefits. Society should not be asked to solve and pay for those problems which businesses cause, without help from those businesses. Businesses and business people are also socially prominent, and must be seen to be taking a lead in addressing the problems of society.

(b) **The benefits to business of 'enlightened self-interest'**

In the long term, a business's concern over the possible damage which may result from its activities will safeguard the interests of the business itself. In the short term, responsibility is good for the image of the company. In addition, as pressure for legislation grows, 'self regulation' can avoid potentially disadvantageous campaigns.

2.12 Opponents of these ideas argue that social responsibility is not part of a company's remit, since it should only be concerned to protect the interests of its shareholders.

2.13 A company's responsibility to society involves the following elements.

- Economic responsibilities
- Legal responsibilities
- Ethical responsibilities (eg product safety, labelling)
- Discretionary responsibilities (eg corporate donations to charity)

2.14 The degree of morality and legality involved in the social responsibilities of a company may take a number of different forms.

	Moral	Immoral
Legal	Body Shop	Arms sales?
Illegal	Whistle blowing?	Drugs

2.15 Many modern companies are publishing the terms under which they choose to operate as a **code of ethics**, although this may well be published under different titles (such as a code of conduct, principles of conduct, guidelines, operating principles, company objectives or a staff handbook).

Marketing at Work

DuPont is trying to reverse the adverse publicity for GM organisms. It has rebranded itself as a life sciences company and looks positively to the future of GM foods.

It has invested heavily in social responsibility, working hard in a think tank project to eradicate the guinea worm, a water-dwelling parasite in Africa that causes ulcers on legs and feet. DuPont eventually perfected a nylon with a weave that acts as a filter. As a result the number of sufferers has decreased from three million to 100,000 people.

With this background, it is trying to change people's concerns about GM foods. The chairman and chief executive, Chad Holliday, regularly invites environmentalists to the DuPont headquarters so he can listen to their views. As a result, DuPont have had no problems with environmental protesters.

Key Concept

Sustainability involves developing strategies so that the company only uses resources at a rate which allows them to be replenished (in order to ensure that they will continue to be available). At the same time emissions of waste are confined to levels which do not exceed the capacity of the environment to absorb them. In relation to the development of the world's resources, policies based on sustainability seek to:

- Pursue equity in the distribution of resources
- Maintain the integrity of the world's ecosystems
- Increase the capacity of human populations for self-reliance

Market failure

2.16 **Market failure** occurs when a **free market mechanism** fails to produce the optimum allocation of resources. Market failure arises in several ways.

- **Imperfections** in a market
- **Divergence** between **private costs** and **social costs** (externalities)
- The **existence of public goods**
- The need to consider **non-market goals**, such as 'social justice'

2.17 The other principal causes of market failure are considered below.

Social costs and private costs

2.18 In a free market, suppliers and households make their output and buying decisions for their own private benefit, and these decisions determine how the economy's scarce resources will be allocated to production and consumption. Private costs and private benefits therefore determine what goods are made and bought in a free market.

> ### Key Concepts
>
> (a) **Private cost** measures the cost **to the firm** of the resources it uses to produce a good.
>
> (b) **Social cost** measures the cost **to society as a whole** of the resources that a firm uses.
>
> (c) **Private benefit** measures the benefit obtained directly by a supplier or by a consumer.
>
> (d) **Social benefit** measures the total benefit obtained, both directly by a supplier or a consumer, and indirectly (at no extra cost), to other suppliers or consumers.

2.19 When private benefit is not the same as social benefit, or when private cost is not the same as social cost, an allocation of resources which reflects private costs and benefits only may not be socially acceptable.

2.20 An example of a situation where private and social costs differed would be where a firm produces a good, and during the production process, pollution occurs.

(a) The **private cost** to the firm is the **cost of** the **resources** needed to make the good.

(b) The **social cost** consists of the private cost plus the **additional disadvantage suffered** by other members of society.

2.21 An example of a situation where private benefit and social benefit differed would be where customers at a café in a piazza benefit from the entertainment provided by professional musicians, who are hired by the café.

(a) The customers of the café are paying for the service, in the prices they pay, and they obtain a private benefit from it.

(b) At the same time, other people in the piazza, who are not customers of the café, might stop and listen to the music. They will obtain a benefit, but at no extra cost to themselves. They are **free riders**, taking advantage of the service without contributing to its cost.

(c)   The social benefit from the musicians' service is greater than the private benefit to the café's customers.

Externalities

Key Concept

Externality is the name given to a difference between the private and the social costs, or benefits, arising from an activity.

2.22   Less formally, an externality is a **cost** or **benefit** which the market mechanism fails to take into account. One activity might produce both harmful and beneficial externalities.

Action Programme 3

Much Wapping is a small town where a municipal swimming pool and sports centre has just been built by a private firm. Which of the following is an external benefit of the project?

(a)   The increased trade for local shops
(b)   The increased traffic in the neighbourhood
(c)   The increased profits for the sports firm
(d)   The increased building on previously open land

Public goods

Key Concept

A **public good** is a good whose benefits cannot be restricted to particular customers. Consumption of a good is non-rivalrous, meaning that consumption by one person does not deprive others of the good.

2.23   Some goods, by their very nature, involve so much spillover of externalities that they are difficult to provide except as **public goods** whose production is organised by the government.

2.24   The consumption of public goods by one individual or group does not significantly reduce the amount available for others. Furthermore, it is often difficult or impossible to exclude anyone from its benefits, once the good has been provided. As a result, in a free market individuals benefiting from the good would have no economic incentive to pay for it.

2.25   Defence and the machinery of justice are perhaps the most obvious examples of public goods. It is not practicable (or desirable) for individuals to buy their own defence or legal systems.

Merit goods and demerit goods

2.26 The existence of market failure and of externalities suggests that government must intervene to improve the allocation of resources. Another possible reason for intervention is to increase the consumption of what are termed **merit goods**. Such goods are considered to be worth providing in greater volume than would be purchased in a free market, because higher consumption is in the long-term public interest. Education is one of the chief examples of a merit good.

2.27 On the other hand, many governments want to see **less** consumption of certain **demerit goods**, such as tobacco.

Pollution policy

2.28 One area often discussed in relation to externalities is that of pollution, for example from exhaust gas emissions or the dumping of waste. If polluters take little or no account of their actions on others, this generally results in the output of polluting industries being greater than is optimal.

2.29 If polluters were forced to pay, say a **tax** for any externalities they impose on society, producers would almost certainly change their production techniques so as to minimise pollution. Consumers would choose to consume less of those goods which cause pollution.

2.30 Many industrialised countries have also imposed environmental legislation. Companies might have to face a variety of measures designed to deal with the pollution.

(a) **Government fees**

German chemical companies face a charge on each tonne of hazardous waste disposed of, a levy on carbon dioxide emissions, and a charge on sold waste in landfill. This can add significantly to operating costs.

(b) **Government regulations**

Fines might be imposed for persistent breach of pollution guidelines, and pollution might be monitored by government inspectors.

(c) **Tradeable permits**

One means of regulating pollution is the tradeable pollution permit. Every year, the state issues pollution permits to each company for a certain price. A total number of permits are allocated each year, representing the total amount of emissions permitted. These permits can be sold. Therefore, it might be cheaper for a company to reduce its pollution than do nothing, as the cost could be recouped by the revenue gained by selling the permit.

Marketing at Work

Commercial packaging is regulated in Germany. Much packaging should be recyclable, and companies are responsible for disposing of their packaging. While packaging may be an obvious regulatory target, the consequences of not using packaging might be severe.

In Russia the introduction of packaging increased the life of each loaf, which meant that fewer had to be produced to meet demand, and waste of food and energy was reduced.

INCREASED REGULATION

Change production
ahead of legislation

Switch to products
combating threats of
externalities

Relocate business to
lower regulation country

2.31 An example of a product which has had increased sales because of publicity about externalities is sun-tan lotion. The damaging effect of CFCs on the ozone layer led to increased concern about sunlight-induced skin cancer. Lotions are now marketed on the basis of how much protection against radiation they give.

Environmental management systems

2.32 **Environmental management systems**. By the early 1990s, it was clear that, for many major companies, environmental protection had become a key strategic issue. The 1990s saw a flood of environmental legislation relating to the following issues.

- Product standards
- Plant design standards
- Waste reduction and recycling
- Civil liability for environmental damage
- Environmental impact studies
- Packaging
- Eco-labelling

2.33 Emphasis is moving away from 'end of pipe' pollution control to **preventing problems at source**. Faced with growing legislation and public pressure, companies have begun to develop new standards themselves, called **environmental management systems**.

2.34 **Potential benefits of environmental management systems**

- Reduced insurance premiums
- Easier conformance with environmental legislation
- Reduced fines for infringing regulations
- Cost savings through more efficient resource use
- Improved public relations
- Reduced likelihood of environmental accidents
- Increased staff motivation
- Improved ability to attract and retain staff   (Grayson, 1992)

2.35 More and more large companies, particularly consumer goods producers, have given a board member responsibility for the environment, and have produced an environmental policy statement. The following statement was produced by the Yamaha Corporation of America.

Environmental commitment policy

Earth exists not only for those of us who currently live on it, but also for our descendants. We must live in a way that will ensure a future for our children. It is, therefore, our duty to protect our valuable environment so that all living creatures can continue to live on this planet.

Yamaha's objective is to contribute to the enhancement of the quality of life around the world and through various activities including the music business.

We have to be aware that corporate activities are deeply related to the environment, and we at Yamaha acknowledge our responsibility to nature. We are dedicated to enriching people's lives and helping to preserve the environment as we live together harmoniously in society.

The Principles of Yamaha's Corporate Environmental Activities Include:

■ Make efforts to develop technology and provide products that will be as sensitive as possible to the earth's animals, plants, and environment

■ Promote energy-saving activities and make effective use of resources in the areas of research and development, production, distribution, sales and service

■ Promote pollution prevention and waste minimization activities

■ Endeavour to follow environmental rules and regulations, encourage environmental protection activities, and ensure the well-being of employees and citizens by practicing sound environmental management

■ Promote continuous improvement methodologies utilizing a Corporate Environmental Compliance Team to monitor business practices and recommend to management methods for improving processes

■ Encourage environmental awareness to all employees so environmental factors are considered in its decision-making processes

---

 Action Programme 4

Environmental matters are often in the news. Over (say) the next month, cut out items from (good) newspapers or make notes from any relevant TV or radio items or programmes which are concerned with environmental matters. Consider the implications for the marketing function of the business, government department etc concerned.

---

3 Green marketing·

3.1 'Green marketing' brings a new factor into the traditional concerns of the modern business person.

3.2 The strongest reason for bringing the environment into the business equation is the consumer, and the need to make responsiveness to, and responsibility for, the consumer the central principle of marketing activity.

3.3 The **consumer must be the driving force** behind changes in marketing and business practices. If new practices do not meet consumer needs, they will fail.

3.4 **Green consumption** can be defined as the **decisions** related to consumer choice **which involve environmentally-related beliefs**, values, attitudes, behaviour or choice criteria. The following evidence indicates that this is important.

- Surveys indicate increased levels of environmental awareness and concern
- Increasing demand for, and availability of, information on environmental issues
- Green product concepts and green substitute products
- Value shifts from consumption to conservation
- Effective PR and marketing campaigns by environmental charities and causes

3.5 The consumer demand for products which claim ecological soundness has waxed and waned with initial enthusiasm replaced by cynicism as to 'green' claims.

(a) **Marketing advantages**

Companies like Body Shop have cleverly exploited **environmental friendliness** as a marketing tool. Supermarkets now stock bleaches or cleansing products which are supposed to be 'kind to nature'.

(b) **Bad publicity**

Perhaps companies have more to fear from the impact of **bad publicity** relating to the ecological effect of their activities than positive environmental messages. An example from the USA was the consumer campaign to boycott tuna from companies whose methods of fishing endanger the lives of dolphins. This has led to changed fishing techniques.

(c) **Limits to willingness to change**

Consumers may not want to **alter aspects of their lifestyles** for the sake of environmental correctness. For example, vehicles are a prime source of carbon dioxide emissions, and simple ways to reduce pollution would be a lowering of speed limits or reduction in car usage. While this has been implemented in the USA, it appears to be out of the question in Europe. In the UK, encouraging a switch to public transport to restrict car usage is controversial.

(d) **Education of consumers**

Finally, consumers may be **imperfectly educated** about environmental issues. For example, much recycled paper has simply replaced paper produced from trees from properly managed (ie sustainably developed) forests. A recent debate, in the USA, relates to the ecological friendliness of disposable nappies. Manufacturers argue that the total effect on the environment of disposable nappies is less than that of the non-disposable kind. They argue that the environmental impact of washing (in terms of energy use, water pollution and so on) is greater than that of making and disposing a disposable nappy.

3.6 In order to maintain good public relations, some companies may have to educate consumers as to the relative environmental impact of their products.

Action Programme 5

Make a list of all the products or services you can think of which use 'green-ness' as a major selling point.

Green marketing principles

3.7 Green marketing begins from the premise that marketing as such is not environmentally unfriendly. The products and services being marketed will necessarily become greener, to reflect more general awareness of the need to counter the effects of environmental degradation.

3.8 There are a number of possible barriers to green marketing.

(a) **Costs**

Costs are likely to be incurred in developing more environmentally friendly products and services.

(b) **Technical and organisational**

Technical and organisational barriers have to be overcome. For instance, in developing practical applications of green energy sources, and in reshaping organisations and their workforces into new ways of carrying out their roles and promoting new attitudes to their jobs.

(c) **Conflicts between objectives**

Many of the problems which will need to be addressed are **complex** and there are **conflicts** between the alternatives available. How do we choose between fuels which create acid rain, and those which produce atomic waste? What about the human consequences of dismantling environmentally unfriendly industries in areas where there are no alternative sources of employment?

(d) **International implications**

Many of the policies pursued by a particular enterprise will have implications for the environment in countries beyond **national boundaries**.

(e) **Lack of visibility**

Changes which promote beneficial effects, eg on the ozone layer, may well be resisted as they have **no visible effects.**

(f) **Timescale**

The fact that problems are generally created, and have to be treated, over a relatively **long time scale** creates difficulties in promoting policies and mobilising groups to implement them.

3.9 The main problems faced by those seeking to implement these green policies include the **lack of certainty** about the **nature** of the problem and about the **effectiveness** of the remedies proposed. In some cases, companies have introduced supposedly environmentally friendly policies and products simply as a means of paying token allegiance. One possible consequence of this is **moral fatigue**. The public may become tired of the whole idea, or sceptical about the truth of claims to greenness.

Developing the policies

3.10 Green marketing requires that managerial principles are related strictly to customer satisfaction. This requires a **green managerial orientation**.

- Rethinking the balance between efficiency and effectiveness
- Rethinking attitudes to and relationships with customers
- Rethinking the balance between our needs and our wants
- Redefining customer satisfaction
- Refocusing onto the long-term objective, rather than shorter or medium-term
- Rethinking the value chain
- New corporate culture

Processes for green marketing

3.11 While a process for green marketing can follow the same framework as a conventional marketing process, differences will occur in four areas.

- **Information** which is fed into the process
- **Criteria** against which performance is measured
- **Values** against which objectives are set
- **Extent** to which the process needs to involve the **whole** organisation

Marketing information

3.12 At the heart of green marketing is an appreciation and thorough understanding of the ways in which the company **impacts** on the **customer**, **society** and the **environment**. An **audit** of company performance in these areas is required. Customer needs, and their sensitivities to environmental issues, need to be researched, along with the activities, strategies and policies of competitors. A typical model of analysis, such as the SCEPTICAL list below, could be applied to green issues.

S ocial factors

C ultural factors

E conomic factors

P hysical environment

T echnological factors

I nternational factors

C ommunication and infrastructure factors

A dministrative and institutional factors

L egal and political factors

For each area, we can examine which 'green issues' are raised for the company in question.

Marketing planning

3.13 Marketing plans need to be re-considered in the light of **environmental priorities**.

- Financial, strategic product/market and technical objectives
- Markets

- Strategies and action plans - eg market share, customer satisfaction, competitor comparisons
- Performance and technical aspects of product performance and quality

Performance

3.14 All these aspects have to be fitted within a view of the company's **performance taking account of environmental responsibilities**. In addition, the **traditional criteria** for **evaluating success or failure**, and the parameters within which they operate, will have to be **re-drawn**.

Time

3.15 **Timescales** have to be **lengthened** considerably, since products are now evaluated in terms of their long-term effects, as well as the impact of the processes used in their production.

Judging success

3.16 Green marketing evaluates the marketing mix in terms of **four Ss**.

S atisfaction of customer needs

S afety of products and production for consumers, workers, society and the environment

S ocial acceptability of a product, its production and the other activities of the company

S ustainability of the products, their production and the other activities of the company

Competitors and suppliers

3.17 Since greenness will be an important **competitive factor**, it will be important for companies to have information about their performance in comparison with major competitors and to be assured that their suppliers are meeting green standards.

A model of the green marketing process

3.18 The green marketing process requires the **matching** of those **internal variables,** which the company can control, with the **structures of the operating environment** which the commercial decision-maker faces. Peattie (1992) describes these as internal and external **green Ps** to be used as a checklist to diagnose how well the company is succeeding in living up to targets for green performance.

Marketing at Work

Being able to predict problems can produce great strategic advantages, but also some odd results. The problem of CFCs from aerosols and their effects on the ozone layer was known from the early 1970s. Johnson & Johnson abandoned the use of them in their products back in 1975.

Consumer reactions to the problem began in the late 1980s. The firm was well prepared, but found themselves in a very strange position, having to attach 'ozone friendly' labels to products which had been modified more than ten years before!

3.19 This example illustrates green marketing problems very well. **Action is vital at the time when public perceptions threaten a product**.

3.20 Resistance to green marketing within many companies is likely to remain strong. It may be necessary for marketers to **market internally** ideas for these changes. New products, new communications strategies and messages, new clean plant and technology, new appointments of staff skilled in these areas, and very broad changes in organisational culture will all have to be sold to powerful individuals and groups within organisations.

3.21 Green marketing needs to be accepted not just into the present policies of the company, but in the way it plans and acts far into the future. Companies must institutionalise the ideas and to **change the company's culture**.

- Build a basis for understanding by disseminating information
- Formulate systematic plans for the implementation of green marketing

- Set aside resources
- Require demonstrations of managerial commitment
- Encourage participation and contributions throughout the company
- Sustain an internal PR programme creating a healthy response to green ideas

Action Programme 6

Consider the environmental impact on marketing in the following contexts. You may want to investigate each of these areas and discuss them with fellow students or colleagues.

(a)   Primary industries (eg food production)
(b)   Consumer goods manufacturing
(c)   Industrial or business-to-business production
(d)   Retailing
(e)   Service providers
(f)   Not-for-profit sector
(g)   Small businesses

Chapter Roundup

- Environmental issues have become more important over the last 10-20 years, with the emergence of the green movement and green economics.

- Environmental issues will have direct and indirect impacts on both marketing practices and on businesses in a more general sense.

- **Green marketing** practices must overcome a variety of barriers. A new **'green' orientation** is required in obtained marketing information, marketing planning and creating a green marketing process.

Quick Quiz

1   Give three examples of ways in which green pressure groups have exerted pressure on businesses.

2   What are the two ideas upon which social responsibility is based?

3   *Fill in the blank*

    .... involves developing strategies so that the company only uses resources at a rate that allows them to be replenished.

4   Private costs – social costs = ?   *the cost that business pays to buy it's goods the social cost that social groups has to pay by the businesses action*

5   A public good is a good produced by the public sector.

    True ☐

    False ☑

6   List five benefits of an environmental management system.

7   *Fill in the blanks*

    s *afety*

    s *atisfaction*

    s *ocial* *acceptability*

    s *ustainability*

    are the four Ss of green marketing.

8   Give three examples of ways in which governments have attempted to deal with pollution.

Action Programme Review

1   Every stage of a product's life is affected by environmental issues - how it is made, what it made of, how it gets to the customer, what it is used for, what is the effect of its use, and how it is disposed of. 'Green' issues have affected the **product** itself ('ozone-friendly', 'dolphin-friendly'), its **packaging** (recyclable), its *price* (organically produced vegetables are more expensive, for example), and its **promotion** (BMW used the appealing idea that their cars are almost totally recyclable for the next generation of car drivers).

2   Similar alarms have been expressed about **ozone depletion**. Alternatives to CFCs are being developed to act as solvents in the electronics industry and coolants in refrigerators. The use of CFCs for blowing polystyrene foam (used as insulation by the building industry) has been banned in some countries and is being phased out in many others.

    Recycling is already widespread and the demand for products and packaging made from recycled materials, or from materials which can be recycled, is increasing steadily. Car manufacturers such as Mazda and Citroen are using plastic components to reduce vehicle weight and recycling used components.

    In addition to these concerns about the impact of production and consumption on the environment, there are also related concerns about the ways in which these affect **human and**

animal welfare. The mistreatment of animals in food production, and concern of the inhumanity of certain kinds of animal husbandry techniques, has produced a strong reaction amongst consumers. Vegetarianism is on the increase, and this has had a significant impact on the demand for meat. There has also been an impact on the sales of cosmetics and other products in which animals are used in product testing.

The above can have a very direct impact on aspects of marketing. You might also have thought of problems relating to waste, food scares, climatic changes, energy resources and social issues in general.

3   Item (b) is an external cost of the project, since increased columns of traffic are harmful to the environment. Item (c) is a private benefit from the firm. Item (d) would only be an external benefit if a building is better for society than the use of open land, which is unlikely. Item (a) is correct as the benefits to local shops are additional to the private benefits of the sports firm and as such are external benefits.

4   –

5   The possibilities are endless! A few examples:
- The Body Shop cosmetics
- 'Environmentally friendly' detergents
- No 'CFC' aerosols
- Organic produce
- Ethical investments

6   –

Answers to Quick Quiz

1
- Gathering information
- Direct action
- Partnership and consultancy

2
- The moral and ethical responsibilities of business
- The benefits to business of enlightened self-interest

3   Sustainability

4   Externalities

5   False. It is a good whose benefits cannot be restricted to particular customers.

6   Any five of:

- Reduced insurance premiums
- Earlier conformance with legislation
- Reduced fines
- Cost savings
- Better public relations
- Reduced likelihood of environmental accidents
- Increased staff motivation
- Improved ability to attract and retain staff

7 ■ Satisfaction of customer needs
   ■ Safety of products
   ■ Social acceptability of products
   ■ Sustainability of products

8 ■ Fees
   ■ Regulations
   ■ Permits

Now try illustrative question 20 at the end of the Study Text

The technical and information environments

13

Chapter Topic List	
1	Setting the scene
2	Technology, industry and society
3	Technology and growth
4	Technology and organisations
5	Technology and employment
6	Developments in technology
7	Developments in communications
8	The Internet
9	Technology and marketing

Learning Outcome

☑ Recognise and assess the influence on, and implications for, employment, organisations, the marketing function and communications, of trends in the technical and information environments

Syllabus Reference

☑ Explain the importance of the technical and information environments and their actual and potential impacts on organisations, employment, marketing and communications

Key Concepts Introduced

- Technology
- Decision support systems
- Computer Telephony Integration
- Electronic Data Interchange

1 Setting the scene

1.1 This chapter emphasises how important the technological environment is in marketing. First we discuss what technology actually means – not just equipment but the way in which equipment is used and the organisation of people and machines in work processes. Technology has some direct impacts on marketing including determining how **goods are supplied**, how marketers **communicate** and how markets operate.

1.2 As well as having some direct impacts, technological innovation is a key factor in **economic growth**. However, its effect on the economy is not easy to predict. It is clearly not the only factor that influences economic growth, and its influence is uncertain, since the precise usefulness of an invention cannot always be predicted in advance. The marketer will try to influence how technology is diffused.

1.3 Technology can have various other indirect influences, including influences on an organisation and employment patterns, and we discuss these in the last two sections of this chapter.

1.4 The second half of the chapter is given to examples of specific technological developments which are of significance to the marketer, particularly developments in communication technology. The Internet, which we have mentioned earlier, is very important in this context.

1.5 Lastly we draw the chapter together by summarising the most important effects of technological developments on the marketing environment.

2 Technology, industry and society

What is technology?

2.1 A simple answer to the question 'what is technology?' would include vague references to advanced machines, computers and so on, but the word can also denote simple objects like the wheel. Technology can also refer to the ways in which these objects are developed.

2.2 You can see that **apparatuses** are used in **techniques**, and techniques are co-ordinated by **organisations**. Organisations represent the whole social and technical structure, for example the division of labour.

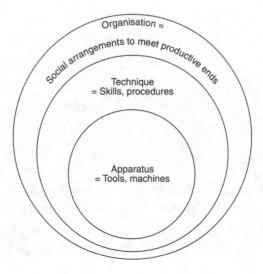

2.3 Buchanan and Huczynski, quoting Langdon Winner, note three uses of the word 'technology'.

Key Concept

Technology consists of the apparatus (eg tools, equipment; techniques (ways of using tools, work methods); organisation (social arrangements for productive ends).

2.4 Technology thus implies both tangible objects and social relationships. Both of these are **invented**. Technology (in the sense of apparatus and technique) changes the way people work, and so inevitably it is part of the surrounding social system.

2.5 In practice, technology's effects are varied. McLoughlin and Clark argue that technology generates its own imperatives and skills.

(a) Technology reduces complex tasks needing manual or **action-centred** skills (with significant exceptions like the construction industry).

(b) Technology generates more **intellective** skills (ie problem-solving, data interpretation).

Riding a bike is exercising an action-centred skill. Understanding market research reports is an intellective skill.

2.6 The **technological determinist** argument states that **technology alone has an internal dynamic which dictates** how work is done. This means that technology in work is so powerful that it is beyond human control, and is not influenced by social factors. For example, technological change generates more technological change: organisations are forced to use new technologies as a result of competitive pressures. However there are some choices offered to users.

(a) **Equipment design**

One issue concerns the amount of **control** built into the machine. Examples from aircraft design indicate that pilot boredom (and hence errors) result if humans are given too little to do, or cannot intervene.

(b) **Innovation**

Technical innovation is promoted for a variety of reasons, not only to do with the production process. Much information technology has been used to increase management information.

(c) **Work organisation**

There are still choices in the way in which **work is organised** around the technology.

Process re-engineering

2.7 Investment in technology can be wasted, if the fundamental processes of the business remain unaltered. In other words, the **apparatus** might change and even the **techniques**, but not the **organisation** behind it.

2.8 This might be a reason why, despite all the investments in information technology, the productivity of office workers has not matched the dramatic improvements in manufacturing productivity in recent years.

3 Technology and growth

3.1 Economists use the **production possibility curve** to describe the choices which are made in conditions of scarcity. This means that, if an economy's total output is limited, society will have to make sacrifices, producing one type of good (say, food) rather than other goods. The significance of technology is that it enables the economy to produce more goods and services in total than before. Thus it involves economic growth, with the production possibility 'frontier' moving from AB to CD.

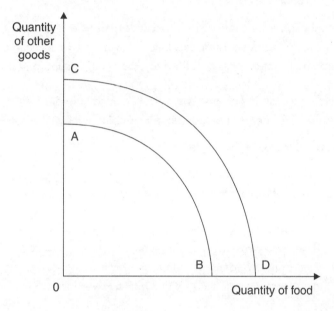

3.2 The history of the past 200 years has been one of enormous economic growth. The UK, for example, is now able to support a population which in the early 19th century would have been inconceivable.

Technological change

3.3 David S Landes *(The Unbound Prometheus)* states: 'The Englishman of 1750 was closer in material things to Caesar's legionaries than to his own great-grand-children'. Landes mentions the role of technology in economic growth as follows.

(a)   **Quantitative** gains in **productivity** (ie more outputs per unit of input) have occurred.

(b)   'Modern technology also ... turns out **objects** that could **not** have been **produced** in any circumstances by the craft methods of **yesterday**.'

(c)   'Finally to this army of new and better products ... should be added the great range of exotic products ... now available at reduced prices thanks to **improved transportation**'.

3.4 'These material advances have in turn provoked and promoted a large complex of economic, social, political and cultural changes which have reciprocally influenced the rate and course of technological development'. These changes have included the following.

(a) **Industrialisation** (eg movement of labour and resources from agriculture to industry)

(b) **Modernisation** (urbanisation, reduction in death rates, centralising government and so on)

Some people cite post-industrialisation as a development. Increases in manufacturing productivity release resources for the service sector of the economy.

Importance of technical change

3.5 The significance of technological change is manifold.

(a) Schumpeter, an economic theorist, argued that '**fundamental technical innovations** undergo the long-term pattern of booms and contractions which has characterised the Western economy as a whole'.

(b) 'Technical change is central to the **maintenance** of the vitality of the modern economy. It is not simply that innovation leads to growth and wealth; innovation is indispensable if the economy is not to stagnate' (Yearley, *Science, Technology and Social Change*).

3.6 If technological progress is **labour-saving** (technical advance that uses less labour and the same amount of capital per unit output), then unemployment will rise unless there is either:

(a) A simultaneous expansion of demand

(b) A reduction in hours worked by each person, in which case there is no productivity increase associated with the technological progress

3.7 Technological progress may therefore **stimulate growth** but at the same time **conflict** with the goal of **full employment**. A further consequence of this could be that those people in work would benefit from economic growth in the form of higher wages, but those people put out of work by the new technology would be left with a lower income.

3.8 Almost every activity in a modern industrial society has developed in some way through technological change.

Marketing at Work

The UK used to be a predominantly agricultural society, with most people subsisting by earning their living on the land, or in small towns. In 1850 in the UK, over half the labour force were in some way involved in agriculture. Now it employs about 283,000. This results from staggering increases in productivity brought about in many ways by technology, in its broadest sense. The **organisation** of agriculture into larger farms has provided economies of scale.

The combine harvester replaced teams of labourers with scythes and the tractor replaced the horse-drawn plough. Technology has also been evident in the development of fertilisers (although these have had some harmful effects on the soil quality). Modern techniques in biotechnology are breeding new strains of crops (and animals), for their particular qualities.

3.9 Information technology has changed from a specialised industry dominated by a few companies whose 'product' included machines, software and lucrative service contracts, to one in which there is a huge number of almost identical products trying to win on a number of competitive strengths.

Marketing at Work

In the UK, cinema attendances were once well over 20 visits per person per year. This number fell to 1.5 by 1990 (when there were 88.7 million cinema visits). This has largely been caused by television, a new technology, which, like IT, has also reduced in cost since its invention.

Television itself has been subject to competition from video and DVD. New technology has also greatly increased the number of television channels potentially available. In March 2004 the magazine *Total TV guide* listed over 90 satellite, digital and cable channels in addition to the five terrestrial channels. Of the channels listed, 14 were dedicated film channels.

3.10 The impact of **recent** technological change also has potentially important social consequences.

(a) Whereas people were once collected together to work in factories, **home working** will become more important.

(b) Certain sorts of skill, related to **interpretation of data** and **information processes**, are likely to become more valued than manual or physical skills.

(c) Technology increases manufacturing productivity, so that more people will be involved in service jobs. These require greater **inter-personal** skills (eg in dealing with customers).

A cautionary perspective

3.11 Technology, or investment in it, in the narrow sense, cannot on its own promote economic growth. The first application of **steam** power was invented, not in 18th century England, but almost 2,000 years before: there was, however, no 'use' for it. Societies with large pools of slave labour had little need for 'labour-saving' inventions.

3.12 In the UK, the industrial revolution not only depended on technological advances but also:

(a) A **single market** (England) which encouraged scale economies

(b) An **efficient system** of **raising finance** (London was a major financial centre, and also the centre of a large global network)

(c) A **workforce** for whom **employment** in a **factory** was a **better existence**, economically, than trying to earn a living from the land

Action Programme 1

The Republic of Rukwa is a largely agricultural society. For foreign exchange, it is dependent on the exports of kwat. Kwat is a grain which can only be grown in Rukwa's climate. It is, however, widely in demand in Western markets as a 'health' food. Kwat is grown by peasant farmers on small plots of land on banks of the River Ru. At present, the harvested Kwat is transported by ox-drawn barges down the River Ru to port Ruk for export. The process is slow, owing to bottlenecks on the river. Rukwa has no other natural resources. The government is thinking of several alternatives to ease this situation.

1   Build a high speed road, and use foreign loans to buy lorries and four-wheel drive vehicles for farmers

2   Build a railway, with imported steel and engines

3   Widen the River Ru at key points, and purchase outboard motors for the barges

What do you think is right or wrong with all these options?

A diffusion model of innovative technology

3.13 Innovation in the market place can take many forms, from radically new products incorporating new technology to changes in packaging. The diffusion of innovation model normally applied to consumers is as follows.

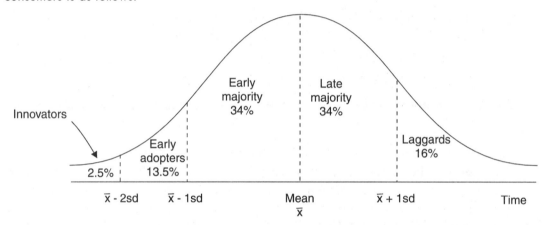

DIFFUSION MODEL	
Innovators	These are eager to try new ideas and products and often in close contact with change agents like sales staff and other opinion leaders. Often perceived to be risk takers, prepared to try and willing to pay often premium prices for 'being the first'.
Early adopters	They too are willing to change and are often opinion leaders themselves. They are likely to have greater exposure to the mass media than later adopters and certainly more willing to change. They are likely to seek out information actively about new products in specialist journals etc.
Early majority	A more conservative segment who tend to purchase a new product just ahead of the average time, but who will have given it some thought before the purchase.
Late majority	These are slower than the average and sceptical about new products. They are very cautious purchasers likely to need some persuading.
Laggards	These are the smaller group of traditionalists actually unwilling to change. They may actually be forced to change only when their previous choice is obsolete and no longer available.

Diffusion and marketing strategy

3.14 Marketers usually want to ensure a **rapid diffusion** or rate of adoption for a new product. This allows them to gain a large share of the market prior to competitors responding. A **penetration** policy associated with low introductory pricing and promotions designed to facilitate trial are associated with such a strategy.

3.15 In some markets, particularly where research and development cost has been high, where the product involves 'new' technology or where it is protected from competition perhaps by patent, a **skimming** policy may be adopted. Here price is high initially, usually representing very high unit profits. sales increase in step with price reductions, in line with available capacity or competitors' responses.

3.16 How far this applies to new technologies, however, is uncertain. Businesses must create customers for the new technology.

(a) In industry markets, the **diffusion process** will be **enhanced** if customers can be convinced of the technology's success, if it does not involve unacceptable risk.

(b) Companies might wish to ensure **rapid adoption** of the technology, and so raise barriers to entry to imitators or competitors. Again this might require creating customer need.

(c) However, as the example of the laser above demonstrates, it is **not easy to know** the possible **applications of a new technology** and how a customer can be created.

Marketing at Work

It is not possible to offer a general law as to whether technological change and the diffusion of innovation supports a particular industry structure, as there are so many contradicting examples. Take the example of personal computers. There is a much greater choice of brand of PC on the market. The computer industry which was dominated by IBM has fragmented. However, many computers share common technology, both in hardware (Intel) and in software (Microsoft).

In these cases, the old computer industry has been effectively split into at least two. Proprietary software (which only runs on one machine) is no longer desirable. Some commentators however argue that here is a real danger of near monopoly; **Microsoft** has been accused of trying to squeeze out competitors, by its use of patents. The Windows updates have been promoted heavily - perhaps to make it hard for competitors to keep up.

4 Technology and organisations

4.1 How important is technology to organisation structure? Or to be more precise, how important are the configuration of apparatus and technique to organisation structure? Is the structure of an organisation determined by its technology?

The socio-technical systems view

4.2 Joan Woodward developed the 'socio-technical systems' view that the **structure** of organisations and **nature** of management depended on the **nature** of the technology used within the organisation.

4.3 This categorisation also describes a rising scale of technical complexity, in other words, process production is more complex than mass production, which is more complex than unit production. By 'technical complexity' she meant the extent to which the **production** process is **controllable** and its **results predictable**.

Technology and centralisation

4.4 There is a continuing debate between whether organisations should be centralised or divisionalised. Decentralisation enables the firm's resources to be organised around a **product**, or a particular **market segment**.

   (a) Centralisation has the advantages of specialisation (more efficient labour division) and economies of scale.

   (b) Decentralisation has the advantage that operations are **close to the customer**.

4.5 **Technology**, especially information technology, can render this debate redundant. It enables both **more centralisation** and **more decentralisation at the same time**.

4.6 Many organisations now see **information** as a corporate resource, even a source of competitive advantage.

4.7 New applications of information technology make it much easier for senior managers to review and **control** the operations of the organisation. Senior managers can be given, through executive information systems, a much more detailed look at operations. The information processing function of middle management is partly redundant.

4.8 At the same time, IT enables certain activities to be **decentralised**. A desktop computer connected to a network or central database gives the user access to the corporate information resource, on the spot. If a customer is applying for a loan, for example, on expert system embodied in software can give the user an answer there and then, without having to pass the request through a layer of bureaucracy.

4.9 The way in which IT departments developed, until the advent of the microcomputer, also favoured centralisation. A large mainframe requires one site, and operating units would hand in their data for processing and output. Recent technological developments have devolved information systems to operating departments, as that one implication of IT is no longer centralised. Central control is still maintained through common standards and, more importantly, a unified resource of data.

5 Technology and employment

5.1 Technological development perhaps has three different effects on employment.

- It **requires new skills**, so creates new jobs for the new machinery
- It **destroys old jobs** and replaces people with machinery (for good or ill)
- It **increases productivity**, so freeing up resources and labour for other activities

Action Programme 2

Provide an example of each of the effects listed in 5.1.

5.2 Technological development then affects **employment patterns** over the whole economy, as new industries and activities develop.

5.3 Technology also affects, as we have seen, the type of work done.

- Machinery sometimes demands certain types of work organisation
- Technology requires new skills

5.4 Shoshana Zuboff, in her book *In the Age of the Smart Machine* reviews the far-reaching effects that **information technology** and **computerisation** will have on work and future management practice. She begins by examining what computerisation actually does. For example, assume that a complicated production process has now been computerised. What effects does this have on the way that the process is controlled?

(a) **Automation**

The process has been **automated**. Effectively, this means that tasks are performed with the minimum of human judgement and intervention and according to set routines.

(b) **Informating**

The process has been **informated**. As the process is controlled by computer, human beings can only monitor it **indirectly** by observing the data that the computer displays on, say, a VDU screen.

5.5 How might this affect management?

(a) **Skills needed**

Effective production control in a computerised environment depends on the **ability** of the workforce to **interpret** and **manipulate** abstract data, and to do this they need an overall theoretical knowledge of the system. A critical, questioning attitude towards data presented on the screen is needed also.

(b) **Decision making**

Dealing with problems thrown up by data on a screen requires an ability to discuss them in a co-operative way, and so decisions may be arrived at by **consensus**. Traditional management practice requires that managers control information, and that managers alone take decisions.

BPP
PROFESSIONAL EDUCATION

(c) **Employee empowerment**

Information technology itself is becoming more **user friendly**, which may lead to **employees gaining more control** over their own work. With the growth of database technology, routine transactions can be taken over by the machines, so that human beings can be freed to make use of the wealth of information easily available.

(d) **Cost cutting**

Computerisation has largely been seen as a means of **cutting costs**. Cost savings are easily identified. However, Zuboff argues that few organisations consider that information, intelligently used, can be a means of **adding value**.

Other effects on work operations

5.6 Zuboff's argument is that information technology can both liberate as well as control. However, there are other features relating to people's working lives that might also be briefly considered.

(a) **Redeployment**

Technology, by automating routine operations, might mean that staff are **redeployed elsewhere**. A much-touted example is the desire of UK banks to push more employees into 'sales' or 'customer service' type jobs. This might have the effect of eventually restoring the degree of social interaction in office jobs.

(b) **Expert systems**

Technology might be used to **support up front operations**, devolving decision-making. This has been mentioned in the context of delayering. The organisation hierarchy, as it were, is on computer. **Expert systems**, in particular might have this effect. An expert system is a computer system which contains a base of knowledge, which it can use to answer queries. (Expert systems have been used for medical diagnosis, for example). Expert systems contain a knowledge base, a sort of question and answer session and a program to display reasoning.

The future of work

5.7 There is always a risk in crystal gazing. Many of the assumptions about **technological unemployment** have failed to materialise. Technology has created new jobs and released labour resources for other socially or economically desirable activities.

5.8 It might be interesting, however, to examine briefly one view of how work might develop in future. In his book *The Work of Nations,* Robert B Reich (an advisor to US President Clinton) argues the following.

5.9 Reich believes that the 'global corporation' will be a reality. In other words, Reich believes that corporations will take their activities from place to place, without concern for nationality.

5.10 A result of advanced technology is the value put (in Zuboff's phrase) on intellective skills. Reich assumes, in a view similar to Zuboff, that the workforce will be divided.

WORKFORCE

Routine production service workers	In-person service workers	Symbolic – analytic workers
Factory line workers	Office cleaners	Software designers
Online data processors	Nurses	Investment bankers
	Retail sale workers	Architects
	Taxi drivers	Consultants
		Academics

5.11 The output of routine production (manufactured goods) can be traded internationally, as can the output of symbolic-analytic work.

5.12 Reich argues that the proportion of routine production workers will fall, as factories automate or relocate, and the (US) workforce will comprise mainly in-person service workers, with about 20% of the workforce as symbolic analysts.

(a) Reich argued that global economic and technological change will put **symbolic analysts** in a **dominant position**. They will earn the most wealth.

(b) **Routine producers**, confronted with an immense and rapidly growing pool of semi-skilled and unskilled labour worldwide, find their **incomes slipping** and their jobs disappearing.

(c) **In-person service workers** will **face competition** from workers in routine production industries.

5.13 In short, Reich argues a growing disparity of incomes between the symbolic analysts and the rest. He assumes a gradual deskilling of many jobs, as the labour market for routine producers becomes global. Surplus routine producers might migrate to in-person service jobs, thus creating competition there and driving down wages.

6 Developments in technology   6/03

6.1 Recent developments in technology have made significant changes to the business and information environments within which organisations operate.

Marketing at Work

A key technological development that is currently being tested by various companies is a mobile phone containing a credit card.

The new development is risky since there is no method of including the card that seems significantly better than all other possibilities. One method being investigated is having the phones emit an infrared beam directly to a cash register; another is having a special chip in the phone that can be scanned; another just involves the use of text messaging.

The Japanese credit card company, Nicos, has linked up with mobile network provider NTT DoCoMo, in an attempt to develop the infrared system. The main obstacle they face is the preference of the Japanese for cash purchases; 5.6% of personal spending is by credit or debit card compared with 31% in the United States. As cell phone penetration is high in Japan (approaching 80%), including a credit card as one of the phone's facilities may make credit card use seem much more natural.

A further option being investigated is turning mobile phones into credit card acceptance terminals. This may have particular potential in developing markets such as India with many small shop or stall keepers who have previously found the cost of installing a traditional credit card terminal to be too high.

Developing this sort of project is much easier in Japan because of the close relationships between network providers and handset manufacturers.

Despite the risks, the potential benefits are huge. These developments are good for credit-card companies because it's easier for customers to buy on credit; mobile phone companies benefit because the phones become more of an essential; for consumers credit card use is more interactive and they don't have to carry as much around.

Far Eastern Economic Review, 14 August 2003

Production systems

6.2 Production management information systems provide information to help with the planning and control of production. One application which is frequently computerised is **production planning**, involving the provision of a production plan to meet the requirements of customers and stockists. Computer systems are also being used in an increasing number of contexts in advanced manufacturing environments.

6.3 **Stock control systems** or modules range from simple **batch processing** systems that update a stock file from daily movement records, to **online (real-time)** systems providing instant, up-to-date information on stock availability. A good stock control system should reduce working capital that would otherwise be tied up in stocks.

Point of sale devices

6.4 More and more large retail stores are introducing **Electronic Point of Sale (EPOS)** devices using bar coding, which act both as cash registers and as terminals connected to a main computer. This enables the computer to produce **useful management information** such as sales details and analysis and stock control information **very quickly**.

6.5 The provision of immediate sales information (for example, which product sells quickly), perhaps analysed on a branch basis permits great speed and flexibility in **decision-making** (certainly of a short-term nature), as consumer wishes can be responded to quickly.

6.6 Many retailers have now introduced Electronic Funds Transfer at the Point of Sale systems (EFTPOS). These are systems for the electronic transfer of funds at the point of sale. Customers in shops and at petrol stations can use a plastic card (usually a credit card or debit card) to purchase goods or services, and using an EFTPOS terminal in the shop, the customer's credit card account or bank current account will be debited automatically. EFTPOS systems combine point of sale systems with electronic funds transfer.

Office support systems

Decision support systems

Key Concept

Decision support systems are usually taken to mean systems which are designed to produce information in such a way as to help managers make better decisions.

6.7 **Decision support systems (DSS)** are a form of management information system. Managers use decision support systems to **assist in making decisions** when there is **uncertainty** about the likely **impact of different actions**. DSS range from fairly simple information models based on spreadsheets to expert systems.

6.8 Decision support systems **do not make decisions**. The objective is to allow the manager to consider a number of **alternatives** and **evaluate them** under a variety of potential conditions. Managers using these systems often develop scenarios to refine their understanding of the problem and their possible actions.

Executive information systems

6.9 An **executive information system (EIS)** provides senior executives with access to key facts and figures related to business performance. An **EIS** is therefore **likely to have the following features**.

(a) Provision of **summary-level data**, captured from the organisation's main systems (which might involve integrating the executive's desktop PC with the organisation's mainframe)

(b) A facility which allows the executive to **'drill down'** from higher levels of information to lower

(c) **Data manipulation facilities** (for example comparison with budget or prior year data, trend analysis, 'what-if?' functionality)

(d) Graphics and templates for **user-friendly presentation** of data

Expert systems

6.10 Expert systems are computer programs which allow users to benefit from existing knowledge and information. An expert system is a program that **relies on a database holding a large amount of specialised data**, for example on legal, engineering or medical information, or tax matters. The user keys in certain facts and the program uses its information on file to produce a decision about something on which an expert's decision would normally be required.

6.11 Expert systems **can give factual answers to specific queries**, but they can also indicate to the user what a decision ought to be in a particular situation, and in this respect, expert systems can be a form of decision support system for managers.

7 Developments in communications

Specimen paper, 12/02

7.1 Some people referred to the 1990s as the 'telecom revolution' in the same way as the 1980s were regarded as the computer revolution. External applications of IT revolve around developments in this field.

ISDN

7.2 An important recent development is the spread of **Integrated Services Networks (ISDN)** which in effect will make the entire telephone network **digital**. It will therefore be possible to send voice, data, video and fax communications from a single desktop computer system over the telecommunication link, **without using a modem**.

7.3 Data can be transmitted at least **twice as fast** over ISDN than over normal tele-communications.

7.4 Advantages of ISDN (besides speed and cost savings on call times) are that:

(a) Computer **networks can be extended** to small branch offices.

(b) **More than one service** can be sent over the link **at the same time.** For example it would be possible, for architects to use one telecommunications link to view building plans on a PC, and also to discuss them on a handset.

Fax

7.5 Fax has largely **superseded** older systems such as telex and the computerised equivalent 'teletex' (not to be confused with 'teletext').

7.6 The latest fax machines can also be used as **scanners** to scan data into a PC, as **printers** for PC output and as **photocopiers**. Faster machines are being developed that will cut down the time to send an A4 sheet from six seconds to one to two seconds.

7.7 Alternatively a PC can be fitted with a **fax modem**, allowing data to be transmitted directly from the PC without going through a separate fax machine.

7.8 However, users of PCs fitted with fax modems may easily forget that when they switch off their machine at the end of the day, it will **not be able to receive fax messages**, unlike a stand-alone fax machine, which tends to be left on-line 24 hours.

Electronic mail (E-mail)

7.9 E-mail reduces the need to send letters or faxes, place memos in pigeon-holes or despatch documents by courier.

7.10 Typically information is posted by the sender to a central computer which allocates disk storage as a **mailbox** for each user. The information is subsequently collected by the receiver from the mailbox.

(a) Senders of information thus have **documentary evidence** that they have given a piece of information to the recipient and that the recipient has picked up the message.

(b)   Receivers are **not disturbed** by the information when it is sent (as they would be by face-to-face meetings or phone calls), but collect it later at their convenience.

7.11   Each user will typically have **password protected access** to his own inbox, outbox and filing system. He can prepare and edit text and other documents using a **word processing** function, and send mail using **standard headers and identifiers** to an individual or a group of people on a prepared **distribution list**.

7.12   E-mail systems may serve one department or the whole organisation. It is also possible to connect an e-mail system to outside organisations.

Voice mail

7.13   Voice mail (or v-mail) systems enable the **caller's message to be recorded** at the recipients voice mail box (similar to a mail box in an e-mail system).

7.14   The main **advantage** of the system is that it only requires a telephone to be used. No typing or keying in is necessary. A voice mail message is basically a **spoken memo**; for the person sending the message it is much more convenient than typing it or having it typed and then faxing it.

7.15   Voice mail can be used for different situations.

■   To contact sales representatives **in the field**
■   To **leave messages** in departments in different time zones
■   In organisations where employees might be **working away** at a client's premises

Computer Telephony Integration (CTI)

Key Concept

Computer Telephony Integration (CTI) systems gather information about callers such as their telephone number and customer account number or demographic information (age, income, interests etc).

7.16   The information is stored on a customer database and can be **called up and sent to the screen** of the person dealing with the call, perhaps before the call has even been put through.

7.17   Thus sales staff dealing with hundreds of calls every day might **appear to remember individual callers** personally and know in advance what they are likely to order. Order forms with key details entered already can be displayed on screen automatically, saving time for both the sales staff and the caller. Alternatively a busy manager might note that an **unwelcome call** is coming in on the 'screen pop' that appears on her PC and choose to direct it to her voice mail box rather than dealing with it at once. As another example, a bank might use CTI to **prompt sales people** with changes in share prices and with the details of the investors they should call to offer dealing advice.

7.18 Radio networks for portable telephone communications, also known as **cellular phones**, started up in the late 1980s and boomed in developed countries in the 1990s, as you are no doubt aware from the deluge of advertising on television and radio.

7.19 Again, **digital** networks have been developed and are now operating alongside earlier transmission systems. These are better able to support data transmission then the older analogue networks, with **higher transmission speeds** and less likelihood of data corruption. This means that a salesperson out on the road, say, can send or receive a fax simply by plugging a lap-top PC into a mobile handset. A combined **palmtop** computer and cellular phone is already on the market.

Mobile communications

7.20 In theory it is now possible to do any kind of office activity **outside** the office, on the move, although **limitations in battery power** (a technology lagging far behind others described in this book) impose restrictions.

7.21 The mobile services available are increasing all the time. Here are some examples.

(a) **Messaging services** include voice mail, short message service and paging services.

(b) **Call handling services** include call barring, conference calls and call divert.

(c) **Corporate services** include integrated numbering (a single contact number for both the phone on their desk and for their mobile), and virtual private networks that incorporate mobile phones as well as conventional desktop phones, so that users can dial internal extension numbers directly.

(d) **Internet access** is possible, although the speed of transmission when downloading information is relatively slow at present, but improving.

(e) **Dual mode handsets** will allow users to use both cheap cordless technology when in the office and cellular technology when outside.

Teleconferencing

7.22 Teleconferencing involves people who are in different locations being linked by telecommunications equipment which may include video as well as audio links. Obviously, there are potential savings in cost and time compared with conferences which involve the participants travelling to a single location.

7.23 Audiographic teleconferencing, also called electronic whiteboarding or screen sharing, uses both audio and data connections. A computer screen shared at different sites is used as a 'electronic blackboard'. Some systems permit sharing of software.

Electronic data interchange

Key Concept

Electronic Data Interchange (EDI) is a form of computer-to-computer **data** interchange, and so another form of electronic mail.

7.24 Instead of sending reams of paper in the form of invoices, statements and so on, details of inter-company transactions are sent via telecom links, **avoiding the need for output** and paper at the sending end, and **for re-keying of data** at the receiving end.

7.25 The general concept of having one computer talk directly to another might seem straightforward enough in principle, but in practice there are two major **difficulties**.

(a) Each business wants to produce documents (and hold records on file) to its own **individual requirements** and structure. Thus a computer of X could not transmit data to a computer of Y because the records/data transmitted **would not be in a format or structure** to suit Y.

(b) Businesses may work to differing **time schedules**, especially when they are engaged in international trade. If a London company's computer wants to send a message to a computer in San Francisco, the San Francisco computer might not be switched on or otherwise able to receive the message.

7.26 Until recently different makes of computer could not easily 'talk' to each other. The problem of **compatibility** between different makes of computer was a serious one, and some form of interface between the computers had to be devised to enable data interchange to take place. This is less and less of a problem as businesses adopt common standards and set up sites on the **Internet.**

7.27 Joining an **EDI network** (there are several) is quite **expensive**, but many smaller companies are encouraged to do so by their **suppliers and/or customers**. Many of Marks and Spencer's suppliers have been converted to EDI.

Electronic Funds Transfer

7.28 Electronic Funds Transfer (EFT) describes a system whereby a computer user can use his computer system to **transfer funds**. For example it can make payments to a **supplier**, pay salaries into **employees'** bank accounts, or transfer funds from one bank account to another account by sending electronic data to his bank. Since businesses keep most of their cash in bank accounts, electronic funds transfer must involve the **banks** themselves.

SWIFT

7.29 A system for the electronic transfer of funds **internationally between banks** themselves is known as **SWIFT** (the Society for Worldwide Interbank Financial Telecommunications). If X in the USA wishes to make a payment to a company in, say, Germany, and if his USA bank and the German company's bank are members of the SWIFT network, the settlement between the banks themselves can be made through the SWIFT system.

CHAPS and BACS

7.30 Interbank settlements by the clearing banks **within the UK** are also made by electronic funds transfer, using the **CHAPS** system (Clearing House Automated Payments System).

7.31 Many large companies now pay the salaries of employees by providing computer data to their bank, using the **BACS** (Bankers' Automated Clearing Services) or BACSTEL service. It has been estimated that switching to BACS can save 90% on transaction charges.

Exam Tip

The examiner has emphasised the importance of information and communications technology. The Specimen Paper contained a question about its impact on the travel industry.

8 The Internet   12/02

8.1 The **Internet** is the technology that allows any computer with a telecommunications link to exchange information with any other suitably equipped computer.

8.2 Terms such as 'the net', 'the information superhighway', 'cyberspace', and the 'World Wide Web' are used fairly interchangeably.

Current uses of the Internet

8.3 The scope and potential of the Internet are still developing. Its uses already embrace the following:

(a)   **Dissemination of information**

(b)   Product/service development – through almost instantaneous **test marketing**

(c)   **Transaction processing**

(d)   **Relationship enhancement** – between various groups of stakeholders, but principally between consumers and product/service suppliers

(e)   **Recruitment** and job search – involving organisations worldwide

(f)   **Entertainment** – including music, humour, games and some less wholesome pursuits!

Growth of the Internet

8.4 It is estimated that 60% of households in the USA and 50% of households in the UK had Internet access by the end of 2002.

(a) Many households are now establishing multiple Internet access points eg Digital TV set, PCs, WAP phones.

(b) **Changes in the telecoms market** are likely to mean that Internet connection time will become cheaper.

(c) Digital television and WAP enabled mobile phones permit the Internet to be accessed without the necessity to use a personal computer.

(d) For many, the preferred Internet interface is not the PC but the **PDA (Personal Digital Assistant)**.

(e) **Internet kiosks** are becoming increasingly common in shopping centres and cafes.

8.5 A critical factor in the long-run expansion of the Internet is its use today by children, the adult consumers of tomorrow.

8.6 The Internet is not expanding at the same rate in every sphere of business. The rate of growth is influenced by:

(a) The degree to which the customer can be persuaded to believe that using the Internet will **deliver some added-value** - in terms of quickness, simplicity and price.

(b) Whether there are 'costs' which the **customer** has to bear – not exclusively 'costs' in the financial sense, but also such psychological 'costs' as the isolated on-line shopping experience.

(c) The **market segment** to which the individual belongs. The Internet is largely the preserve of younger, more affluent, more technologically competent individuals with above-average amounts of disposable income.

(d) The **frequency of supplier/customer contact** required.

(e) The availability of **incentives** which might stimulate Internet acceptance. For example, interest rates on bank accounts which are higher than those available through conventional banks (Egg), the absence of any charges (Freeserve), the creation of penalties for over-the-counter transactions (Abbey National), and the expectations of important customers (IBM's relationships with its suppliers).

Marketing at Work

In many areas, the Internet is still increasing in significance, although often at a slower rate than some optimists first envisaged.

Internet banking has proved relatively successful and now forms a significant niche in the banking sector. Both 'Internet only' and High Street banks have seen steady growth in the number of customers using web-based facilities to operate their accounts.

At the same time, many customers of traditional banks are not yet ready to abandon the channels they used in the past: even with Internet and telephone banking, many still visit their bank branches regularly.

Features of the Internet

8.7 There are several features of the Internet which differentiate it from what has gone before.

(a) **Changing models**

The Internet **challenges traditional business models** – because, for example, it enables product/service suppliers to interact directly with their customers, instead of using intermediaries (like retail shops, travel agents, insurance brokers, and conventional banks). Businesses are finding that they can cut out the middle man, with electronic banking, insurance, publishing and printing as primary examples.

(b) **Benefits for small companies**

Although the Internet is global in its operation, its benefits are not confined to large (or global) organisations. **Small companies** can move instantly into a global market place, either on their own initiative or as part of what is known as a 'consumer portal'. For example, Ede and Ravenscroft is a small outfitting and tailoring business in Oxford: it could easily promote itself within a much larger 'portal' called OxfordHighStreet.com, embracing a comprehensive mixture of other Oxford retailers.

(c) **Economies of information**

The Internet offers a **new economics of information** – because, with the Internet, information is free. Those with Internet access can view all the world's major newspapers and periodicals without charge.

(d) **Transaction costs**

The Internet reduces transaction costs and thus stimulates economic activity. According to one US calculation, a banking transaction via the Internet costs 1 cent, 27 cents at an ATM (automated teller machine) and 52 cents over the telephone. Infomediaries can enable significant savings to be enjoyed by small-scale or even single customers.

(e) **Speed**

The net supplies an almost incredible **level of speed** – virtually instant access to organisations, plus the capacity to complete purchasing transactions within seconds. This velocity, of course, is only truly impressive if it is accompanied by equal speed so far as the delivery of tangible goods is concerned.

(f) **New networks of communication**

Networks have sprung up between organisations and their customers (either individually or collectively), between customers themselves (through mutual support groups), and between organisations and their suppliers.

(g) **New business partnerships**

Small enterprises can gain access to customers on a scale which would have been viewed as impossible a few years ago. For example, a university can put its reading list on a website and students wishing to purchase any given book can click directly through to an online bookseller such as Amazon.com. The university gets a commission; the online bookseller gets increased business; the student gets a discount. Everyone benefits except the traditional bookshop.

(h) **Transparent prices**

Potential customers can readily compare prices not only from suppliers within any given country, but also from suppliers across the world.

(i) **Personal attention**

Even if personal attention is actually administered through impersonal, yet highly sophisticated IT systems and customer database manipulation.

(j) **Marketing segmentation**

Approaching such segments may be one of the few ways in which e-commerce entrepreneurs can create **competitive advantage**. As *Management Today* (March 2000) puts it:

'The starting point must be a neat niche, a funky few, a global tribe. You need to understand your particular tribe better than anyone else. The tribe is the basic unit of business... The good news is that there are lots of tribes out there - and some are enormous. It's just a question of identifying them, understanding them and meeting their needs better than anyone else.'

(k) **Flexibility**

The web can either be a **separate** or a **complementary** channel.

(l) **Presentation**

Presentation is **continuously improving** from single text and graphics to sophisticated multi-media sites.

(m) **Interactivity**

The level and power of **interactivity** is also increasing.

(n) **Pricing**

A new phenomenon is emerging called **dynamic pricing**. Companies can rapidly change their prices to reflect the current state of demand and supply.

8.8 These new trends are creating **pressure** for companies. The main threat facing companies is that **prices will be driven down by consumers' ability to shop around**.

Marketing at Work

The success of the Internet auctioneers e-Bay has highlighted how the Internet can provide additional mechanisms for doing business. Auctions can serve various purposes. They can establish a price for items that do not have a clear market price, such as antiques. They can be used to sell products that it would be difficult to sell through more traditional channels such as last minute deals on flights. They are also a mechanism for distributing products to a number of customers.

Websites

8.9 Most companies of any size now have a **website**. A site is a collection of web pages providing information in text and graphic form, any of which can be viewed simply by clicking the appropriate button, word or image on the screen.

BPP
PROFESSIONAL EDUCATION

Action Programme 3

What are the key elements of effective customer service through the web?

8.10 Surveys carried out by *Marketing Week* over the last couple of years have highlighted many common features, both good and bad, about brand websites. In general, unsurprisingly perhaps, technology brands such as IBM and Microsoft tended to have more appealing websites than fast-moving consumer goods (FMCG) and luxury goods brands.

8.11 The surveys found that the best websites generally score highly in the following areas:

- Detailed product information
- Information about how the brand could fulfil consumers' wants or needs
- Good use of sound and vision media
- Links to related sites and brands
- Tailoring of content to users' age and nationality
- Detailed information about local markets

8.12 A major drawback with a number of websites was that they were not personalised enough. For instance, distinctions made in Gillette's TV campaign between the targeting of women (highlighting product safety and attractiveness) and the targeting of men (highlighting hygiene) had not been reflected in its website; there were no separate sections for men and women.

8.13 Other significant shortcomings included:

- Navigation of sites being difficult
- Sites taking too much time to load (often because they contained too many images)
- Limited transaction capability
- Lack of focus on developing customer relationships
- Failure to offer free samples, or prizes for completing consumer surveys
- Inconsistency between offline and online offers
- Location at obscure addresses, making the brand difficult to find
- Lack of a website address on products or advertising
- Lack of links to other products
- Local subsites not being as advanced as the main site

Action Programme 4

Note details of three advertising campaigns that are currently going on, and visit the relevant websites.

(a) Do the websites link with, and reflect, the messages being given by the advertising campaign?

(b) Which of the above strengths and weaknesses do the sites possess?

(c) Are there any other major strengths and weaknesses that you can identify?

Marketing at Work

A CIM survey, published in December 2000, highlighted how different companies used their websites. The survey found that all companies surveyed with a turnover of over £50 million had websites, but only 56% of companies surveyed with a turnover of less than £1million had websites. In a two-year period, there had been an increase of 26% in the usage of sites for promoting new products and events, and 14% in online ordering and sales.

Less significant increases were reported in the use of websites for market research, providing support for existing customers, and increasing brand awareness. Between summer 1999 and 2000 average expenditure on websites had risen by over £15,000.

In particular the survey found that purchasing over the Internet in the business-to-business sector had risen from 8% to 27% between 1999 and 2000. In addition the proportion of companies using the Internet to monitor rivals' activities had increased over 12 months from just under ½ to about ¾.

Internal communication: intranets

8.14 The idea behind an **intranet** is that companies set up their own mini version of the Internet, using a combination of the company's own networked computers and Internet technology. Each employee has a browser and a server computer distributes corporate information on a wide variety of topics, and also offers access to the global Net.

8.15 Potential applications include daily company newspapers, induction material, online procedure and policy manuals, employee web pages where individuals post up details of their activities and progress, and internal databases of the corporate information store.

8.16 Most of the **cost** of an intranet is the staff time required to set up the system, which is often quite small. The **benefits** of intranets are:

(a) Money can be saved from the **elimination of storage, printing and distribution of documents** that can be made available to employees on-line.

(b) Documents on-line are **more widely used** than those that are kept on shelves, especially if the document is bulky (for instance company information handbooks, finance manuals and procedures manuals) and needs to be searched. This means that there are **improvements in productivity and efficiency**.

(c) It is much **easier to update** information in electronic form.

(d) Wider access to corporate information should open the way to **more flexible working** patterns. For instance if bulky reference materials are available on-line then there is little need to be in the office at all.

Commercial use of the Internet

Marketing

8.17 Besides its usefulness for tapping into worldwide information resources businesses are also using it to **provide information** about their own products and services. Customers are often reluctant to phone a company or ask to see a sales person to ask basic questions because they do not know who they should speak to and they are not quite sure what they want to know.

8.18 The Internet offers a **speedy and impersonal** way of getting to know the basics (or even the details) of the services that a company provides. For businesses it is **much cheaper** to provide the information in electronic form than it would be to employ staff to man the phones on an enquiry desk, and much **more effective** than sending out mailshots that people would either throw away or forget about when they needed the information.

8.19 Thus business use of the Internet is growing for any product or service about which **customers** are liable to engage in **information seeking**; in other words for most **intermittent**, relatively **high value purchases** such as washing machines, hi-fi and TVs, motor cars and the like.

8.20 As an Internet site can be accessed by any Internet surfer from any corner of the globe, **competitive retail prices** can be **sought**. Consumers should become far more cost-conscious and less inclined to support the domestic suppliers of the goods they seek if the price is not right. Provided the supply of merchandise is reliable, then the lowest price will win.

Marketing at Work

Peapod.com is an online supermarket and one of the more sophisticated recorders and users of customers' personal data and shopping behaviour. With over 100,000 customers in the USA, Peapod's website sells groceries that are then delivered to customer's homes. A list of previous purchases (including brand, pack size and quantity purchased) is kept on the site, so the customer can make minor changes from week to week, saving time and effort.

Peapod creates a database on each shopper. This includes their purchase history (what they bought), their online shopping patterns (how they bought it), questionnaires about their attitudes and opinions, and demographic data (which Peapod buys from third parties).

A shopper's profile is used by the company to determine which advertisement to show and which promotions/electronic coupons to offer. Demographically identical neighbours are thus treated differently based on what Peapod has learned about their preferences and behaviours over time.

Shoppers seem to like this high-tech relationship marketing, with 94% of all sales coming from repeat customers. Manufacturers like it too. The more detailed customer information enables them to target promotions at customers who have repeatedly bought another brand, thereby not giving away promotion dollars to loyal customers.

8.21 Knowledge of why people use the Internet will be essential to the marketer. Key groups are users who are using the Internet:

- To influence the technical development of the Internet
- To exchange ideas and publish knowledge
- For their own personal development, to improve their marketability
- To pursue their hobbies
- To help fulfil their own business objectives
- As an aid to their life outside work

Sales

8.22 Some people are very reluctant to supply their credit card details to a computer, although they will very gladly do so in a one-to-one transaction in a shop or over the telephone, and happily transcribe the details onto a bill that they are paying by post. Logical or not, customers need to be **reassured** about security before interactive purchasing increases at a faster rate.

8.23 Once people are used to this method of buying it is likely to become the **norm** for many transactions that are presently conducted by post, fax or phone.

Distribution

8.24 The Internet can be used to get certain products directly into people's homes. Anything that can be converted into **digital form** can simply be uploaded onto the seller's site and then **downloaded** onto the customer's PC at home. The Internet thus offers huge opportunities to producers of **text, graphics/video, and sound-based products**. Much computer software is now distributed in this way.

Marketing at Work

Airlines

The impact of the web is seen clearly in the transportation industry. Airlines now have a more effective way of bypassing intermediaries (ie travel agents) because they can give their customers immediate access to flight reservation systems. British Airways aims to sell at least half of its tickets online by the year 2003; one of the new low-cost airlines in the UK, EasyJet, has become the first airline to have over half of its bookings made online.

Travel agents

The web has also produced a new set of online travel agents who have lower costs because of their ability to operate without a High Street branch network. Their low-cost structure makes them a particularly good choice for selling low margin, cheap tickets for flights, package holidays, cruises and so forth. These low-cost travel agents have been joined, furthermore, by non-travel-agents who simply specialise in opportunistic purchasing (eg lastminute.com).

Tesco

In another arena, Tesco is already the world's largest Internet grocery business, but other companies are rapidly developing new initiatives. Waitrose@work allows people to order their groceries in the morning (typically through their employer's intranet communication system) and then have them delivered to the workplace in the afternoon: this approach achieves significant distribution economies of scale so far as Waitrose is concerned.

Financial services

The impact of the Internet is especially profound in the field of financial services. New intermediaries enable prospective customers to compare the interest rates and prices charged by different organisations for pensions, mortgages and other financial services. This means that the delivering companies are losing control of the marketing of their services, and there is a downward pressure on prices, especially for services which can legitimately be seen as mere commodities (eg house and contents insurance).

Virtual companies and virtual supply chains (VSC)

Key Concepts

A **virtual company** is a collection of separate companies, each with a specific expertise, who work together, sharing their expertise to compete for bigger contracts/projects than would be possible if they worked alone.

A traditional **supply chain** is made up of the physical entities linked together to facilitate the supply of goods and services to the final consumer.

A **Virtual Supply Chain (VSC)** is a supply chain that is enabled through e-business links (eg the web, extranets or EDI).

8.25 The **virtual company** concept has been around since the mid-1990s. Initially, companies attempted to work together using fax and phone links. The concept only really became a reality when technology such as **extranets** came into common usage. Companies are now able to work together and **exchange information on-line**. For example, engineers from five companies could design a product together on the Internet.

8.26 Many companies have become, or are becoming, more 'virtual'. They are developing into looser affiliations of companies, organised as a supply network.

8.27 Virtual Supply Chain networks have two types of organisation: producers and integrators.

(a) **Producers produce goods and services**. They have core competencies in production schedule execution. Producers must focus on **delivery to schedule** and **within cost**. The sales driver within these companies is on ensuring that their capacity is fully sold through their **networking** with co-ordinators. Producer are often servicing multiple chains, so managing and **avoiding capacity** and **commercial conflicts** becomes key.

(b) **Integrators manage the supply network** and effectively 'own' the end customer contact. The focus of the integrating firms is on **managing the end customer relationship**. Their core competence is in **integrating and controlling** the **response** of the company to customer requirements. This includes the difficult task of synchronising the responses and performance of multi-tiered networks, where the leverage of direct ownership is no longer available, and of often outsourced services such as warehousing and delivery.

8.28 Many of the most popular Internet companies are integrators in virtual company's eg Amazon.com and Lastminute.com. These organisations 'own' customer contact and manage customer relationships for a range of producers.

Problems with the Internet

8.29 To a large extent the Internet has grown organically **without any formal organisation**. There are specific communication rules, but it is **not owned** by any one body and there are no clear guidelines on how it should develop.

8.30 Cost is a major issue. Although the minimum hardware requirements can now be obtained very cheaply, for **effective** use a more powerful PC is needed.

8.31 Other significant issues include:

(a) **Weak infrastructure**

This includes slow modems in most domestic households. Clicking slowly through an electronic catalogue soon becomes tiresome, and the conventional, paper-printed version can suddenly seem very user-friendly.

(b) **Security fears**

More people are worried about security breaches over the Internet than about orthodox credit card fraud. Advances in electronic cash systems, including NatWest's Mondex card and plans to create 'E-money', 'Cybercash' and 'Digicash' may help.

(c) **Viruses**

Viruses are pieces of software which infect programs and data, possibly damaging them, and which replicate themselves. Virus scare stories are popular with many newspapers, and may mean that customers are cautious about taking up offers of free software, or opening Emails that they fear could contain viruses.

Marketing at Work

COMPUTER VIRUS TIMELINE

1981 Apple Viruses 1, 2, and 3 are some of the first viruses in the public domain. Found on the Apple II operating system, the viruses spread via pirated computer games.

1983 Fred Cohen, while working on his dissertation, formally defines a computer virus as 'a computer program that can affect other computer programs by modifying them in such a way as to include a (possibly evolved) copy of itself.'

1986 Two programmers replace the executable code in the boot sector of a floppy disk with their own code designed to infect each floppy accessed on any drive.

1988 One of the most common viruses, Jerusalem, is unleashed. Activated every Friday the 13th, the virus affects both .EXE and .COM files and deletes any programs run on that day.

1990 Symantec launches Norton AntiVirus, one of the first anti-virus programs developed by a large company.

1991 Tequila is the first polymorphic virus to cause significant damage. Polymorphic viruses make detection difficult for virus scanners by changing their appearance with each new infection.

1992 1300 viruses are in existence, an increase of 420% from December 1990. The Michelangelo scare predicts 5 million computers will crash, but only 5,000–10,000 actually do crash.

1994 The 'Good Times' e-mail hoax is widespread. The hoax warns of a malicious virus that will erase an entire hard drive by opening an email with the subject line 'Good Times'. The hoax, or a modified version, often resurfaces.

1999 The Melissa virus executes a macro in a document attached to an e-mail, which forwards the document to 50 addresses from the user's Outlook address book. The virus also infects other

Word documents and subsequently mails them out as attachments. Melissa spread faster than any other previous virus.

2000 In May The Love Bug worm shut down e-mail systems around the world. The 'Stages' virus, disguised as a joke email about the stages of life, spreads across the Internet. Unlike previous viruses, Stages is hidden in an attachment with a false '.txt' extension, making it easier to lure recipients into opening it.

2001 The Anna Kournikova virus which masquerades as a picture of tennis star Anna Kournikova, operates in a similar manner to Melissa and The Love Bug. It spreads by sending copies of itself to the entire address book in Microsoft Outlook. It is believed that this virus was created with a so-called virus creation kit, a program which can enable even a novice programmer to create these malicious programs. The Code Red worm attacked computer networks in July and August, affecting over 700,000 computers. Code Red took advantage of a vulnerability in Microsoft's Windows 2000 and Windows NT server software.

2002 Early in January LFM showed up as the first virus to infect Shockwave Flash (.SWF) files. It was named for the message it displays while it's infecting: 'Loading.Flash.Movie...'. In May the Javascript worm SQLSpider was released. It was unique in that it attacked installations running Microsoft SQL Server (and programs that use SQL Server technology).

(d) **Delivery problems**

However convenient it may be to order two cases of wine through a computer screen, they cannot be 'zapped' straight into the customer's cellar. Though they have been ordered electronically, they will arrive in a humdrum delivery van, and it may not be convenient to be at home to receive them. Moreover, the speed of ordering is seldom matched by the speed of delivery.

(e) **The Internet customer profile**

Customers are predominantly male. Only a fifth of Internet surfers are women, and just four per cent are children. Hence, retailers of trainers, jeans and beer are more likely to make sales than womenswear and cosmetics companies.

9 Technology and marketing

9.1 Technology affects marketing management in three principal ways:

- New ways of **producing** goods and services
- New ways of **distributing** goods and services
- New ways of **communicating** with target markets

Exam Tip

In the exam, you might be asked to comment on the significance to the marketer of specific technological developments, such as EDI or the Internet.

Marketing at Work

An example of technological failure, showing the importance of the wider organisational processes for the success of technology is provided by the *Taurus* project.

Taurus was a project, funded by various institutions in the City of London and managed by the Stock Exchange, to computerise certain aspects of share trading and registration. There was an existing computer system, Talisman, but for various reasons it was regarded as being no longer suitable.

However, the plans to develop a new computer system failed, at a cost to City institutions of about £500m and great damage to London's reputation as a financial centre. What went wrong? There was nothing inherently impossible about the task: automated settlement has been achieved in other financial centres in Europe.

(a) One reason was poor project management with inadequate control.

(b) The system was designed to replicate existing structures. Not to do so would have taken away business (and profits) from share registrar companies. The design was made unnecessarily complex in order to cater for all the vested interests. This, then, is an instance of the neutralisation of technology's possible benefits by wider social and organisational choices.

9.2 Evidence of new production possibilities brought about by new technology are all around us. For the marketer, completely new markets may be opened up (eg interactive CD-ROM players) while cost reductions may allow existing markets to expand very rapidly (eg mobile phones).

9.3 As we have seen there are many examples of the ways in which technology is opening up new communication possibilities.

(a) Cable and satellite television channels offer new **specialised programming** to highly targeted audiences, with the possibility of interactive television shopping, which in its most developed form allows customers to respond to advertisements through the television itself.

(b) IT is making **direct marketing** (by mail/phone) a very powerful communication medium.

(c) **Technology** itself can be used as a competitive weapon. Shared computerised airline booking systems can guide a customer who has to change planes to the preferred alternative.

9.4 IT can also be used to **facilitate** the **identification** of **customer needs**.

Action Programme 5

Marinoid Papers Ltd publish small pamphlets. Its journalists submit typed manuscript to a typesetter. The typesetter then prepares the story for printing. He selects metal letters which he assembles into a frame. The frame is inked, and the story is printed. The firm's technology is archaic. It had only one typeface, and its pamphlets look dull. Recently the managing director has purchased a desktop publishing and word processing system, with a great variety of typefaces and sizes and the chance to use graphics cheaply. What will happen to the journalist and typesetter as a result?

9.5 Technological developments in the macro environment can influence a firm's micro environment. Let us take the example of information technology in relation to the five competitive forces.

TECHNOLOGICAL DEVELOPMENTS AND THE FIVE COMPETITIVE FORCES	
New entrants *Barriers to entry*	IT can increase entry barriers if a lot of investment in new technology is needed or if shared systems lock customers and suppliers together. However, it may obviate the need to establish operations in different locations.
Bargaining power of suppliers	Power can be eroded if customers can easily compare supply terms. However power can be enhanced by sharing and electronic data interchange arrangements with customers.
Bargaining powers of customers	IT can raise switching costs, and can enable easier analysis of customer needs.
Existing and substitute products and services	IT is often the substitute product itself, but can also help in supplying knowledge more easily.
Competitive rivalry	IT can aid differentiation and focus, but can also lead to co-operation with rival businesses sharing the same databases.

Exam Tip

The examiner has identified the need for an understanding of the relationship between new technology and the natural environment, and also the broader significance of technical change.

Marketing at Work

Marketing Week in August 2000 described how the Internet has affected the book marketing scene. The biggest impact appears to have been on competitive pricing. Between May 1999 and August 2000, average selling prices in the book market fell by 3%. Internet sales grew sevenfold between May 1999 and August 2000. The growth is coming from the Internet taking sales from other sectors of the book market, in particular direct-to-consumer (mail order, book clubs and publishing direct) and independent/specialist bookshops.

Although the average number of books purchased each year increased between 1997 and 2000, evidence suggests that this is primarily due to increased buying by 'heavy buyers' – those buying 15 books or more a year. However the Internet appears to be well placed to take advantage of this market; the heavy buyer element accounts for 22% of Internet sales. Nevertheless there may be market problems caused by reliance on heavy buyers, since heavy buyers are very much influenced by price and have little loyalty.

In addition certain types of books (in particular computer and food and drink) account for a larger proportion of Internet sales than they do for overall sales. By contrast fiction only accounts for 16% of the net's sales value at present compared with 29% of the overall market.

In addition publishers' marketing activity is not just focused on Internet sales, but also stimulating an expansion in the percentage of the population buying books overall. This has been achieved by focusing on authors or books heavily featured in the media, for example Jamie Oliver's *Naked Chef.* The most notable success has been of course J K Rowling's *Harry Potter* series – during some weeks of 2000, 1 in 5 books sold was a Potter title.

Action Programme 6

Have a look at the websites of an online bookseller and a major publisher.

(a)   How do the websites draw the first-time searcher's attention to particular titles?

(b)   How easy is it for casual browsers to navigate the websites?

(c)   Are there special features of relevance to heavy buyers, or buyers that are regular customers of the site?

Chapter Roundup

- **Technology** includes apparatus, the techniques with which the apparatus is used, and the organisation of those techniques into social structures.

- Some commentators argue that technology can determine **work organisation**. The work of Trist would indicate however, that the psychological needs of those using technology are important factors in the successful adoption of technology.

- Technology is an important factor in **economic growth**. In theory, technology could be found to advance the **production possibility curve** to the right.

- In practice, **technological change** has been one of the most important motive factors in economic growth, but it is never the only factor.

- In organisations, technology can influence **organisation structures** by creating new jobs, requiring new skills. Technology can be a force for both **centralisation** and **decentralisation**.

- Technology requires new skills and creates new jobs. It also makes some jobs redundant. It can increase productivity.

- **New technology** might require new work practices, flexible manning, sub-contracting and so on.

- **Information technology** requires workers to have intellective skills (based on symbol manipulation) rather than action-centred skills (based on physical interaction with the production process).

- There have been major developments recently in **production, point of sale** and **office support systems**.

- Important developments in communications include **mobile communications, ISDN, CTI** and **E-mail**.

- The Internet can be used for **marketing, sales** and **distribution** purposes.

Quick Quiz

1 Technology consists of: ?

2 Apart from technological advances, what other conditions were needed in England for the Industrial Revolution to occur?

3

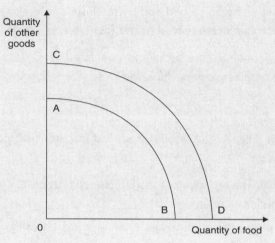

What is this, and what does it illustrate?

4 Give three effects of technology on total employment.

5 *Fill in the blank*

.... is a computer system which contains a base of knowledge which it can use to answer questions.

6 JIT planning stands for:

   A Job integrated technology planning
   B Just in time planning
   C Joint innovative techniques planning
   D Jocose impercipient theriac planning

7 Give four examples of features of an Executive Information System.

8 *Fill in the blank*

.... systems gather information about callers such as their telephone number and customer account number or demographic information.

Action Programme Review

1 There is often no right answer, but here are some ideas.

   (a) Will the foreign exchange earnings from Kwat justify the infrastructural investment at all? After all, the government will have to use the foreign exchange earnings to pay interest on loans. Option 3 might be the least risky here.

   (b) Does the country have an educational and technical infrastructure to support the technology? Road vehicles need spare parts and trained service personnel. Spare parts might be an additional drain on foreign exchange. Again Option 3 might be the least risky.

2   Here are some possible candidates, but you could have possibly thought of others.

(a)   Information technology requires programming skills. Although systems analysis has antecedents in operational research, programming and screen design are relatively new disciplines.

(b)   The replacement of the horse and cart by the train and motor car reduced the activities of blacksmiths and other horse-related trades (but created jobs in garages).

(c)   Most Western economies are becoming orientated towards the service sector. In the UK, there are now more employees employed in service industries than in manufacturing.

3   The following factors will be important.

(a)   Rapid response time. If the website is not fast, the transient potential shopper will simply click on to another.

(b)   Response quality. The website must be legible, with appropriate graphics and meaningful, relevant information supplied.

(c)   Navigability. It is important to create a website which caters for every conceivable customer interest and question. Headings and category-titles should be straightforward and meaningful, not obscure and ambiguous.

(d)   Download times. Again, these need to be rapid, given that many Internet shoppers regard themselves as cash-rich and time-poor.

(e)   Security/Trust. One of the biggest barriers is the fear that information they provide about themselves (such as credit card details) can be 'stolen' or used as the basis for fraud.

(f)   Fulfilment. Customers must believe that if they order goods and services, the items in question will arrive, and will do so within acceptable time limits.

(g)   Up-to-date. Just as window displays need to be constantly refreshed, so do websites require frequent repackaging and redesign.

(h)   Availability. Can the user reach the site 24 hours a day, seven days a week? Is the down-time minimal? Can the site always be accessed?

(i)   Site effectiveness and functionality. Is the web site intuitive and easy to use? Is the content written in a language which will be meaningful even to the first-time browser (ie the potential customer)?

4   –

5   The journalist can type in the copy directly to the system. A good journalist, however, is not necessarily a competent graphic designer. There is a real division of labour here. The typesetter might be made redundant, or might be retrained in graphic design to exploit the opportunities afforded by the new technology.

6   –

Answers to Quick Quiz

1   ■   Apparatus (tools, equipment)
    ■   Techniques (methods of using tools, work methods.
    ■   Organisation (social arrangement for productive ends)

2   ■   Single market
    ■   Efficient system of raising finance
    ■   workforce who preferred factory to agricultural labour

3   The production possibility curve illustrating how technology enables the economy to produce more goods and services than ever before.

4   ■   Requires new skills
    ■   Destroys old jobs
    ■   Increases productivity

5   Expert system

6   B   Just in time planning

7   ■   Provision of summary data
    ■   Ability to drill down to lower levels of information
    ■   Data manipulation facilities
    ■   User-friendly presentation of data

8   Computer Telephony Integration

Now try illustrative questions 21 and 22 at the end of the Study Text

BPP
PROFESSIONAL EDUCATION

Environmental challenges

14

Learning Outcome

☑   Assess the potential significance of current and future environmental challenges.

Syllabus Reference

☑   Assess the potential significance of environmental challenges to marketing in the future eg globalisation; single currency; information and communication technology; and environmental decline.

Key Concepts Introduced

- B2B
- B2C
- C2B
- C2C

- P2P
- M-commerce
- Monetary union
- Economic union

1 Setting the scene

1.1 In this chapter we consider challenges that are likely to have significant impacts on the environment in which marketing takes place in the future.

1.2 We start by summarising the principal types of change that might affect each element of the macro environment.

1.3 We then move on to consider certain recent and current developments in more detail. We shall first show that changes in working patterns, principally labour flexibility and the changing role of women in the marketplace are significant because of the changes in attitudes that they have meant. These changes affect the products bought and also the ways in which those products are promoted.

1.4 Other issues affect not only the products sold but also the ways in which resources are used. Environmental issues have led to changes in regulations and attitudes which must have an influence on the marketing process.

1.5 Lastly we discuss the influences on firms to widen their environments and specifically to take account of international concerns. One such pressure is the improvement in communications brought about by the use of the Internet. European Union developments, the single European market and currency are also of significance. Lastly we consider the degree to which these influences have led to globalisation of organisations, and the effect of globalisation on the way organisations are structured and on their approach

2 Changes in the macro environment

2.1 In this section we examine some main themes of change in the various elements of the macro environment.

Social change

2.2 Social change involves changes in the nature, attitudes and habits of society. Social changes are continually happening, and trends can be identified.

(a) **Rising standards of living**

These may result in wider ownership of consumer and luxury goods, which have implications for those industries.

(b) **Society's attitude to business**

In the European Union countries, increasing social obligations and responsibilities are being heaped on to companies, not least with respect to **environmental protection** and ethical conduct (towards customers, employees etc).

(c) **The workforce**

There has also been a decline in blue collar jobs and an increasing proportion of people employed hold clerical, supervisory or management jobs. Growth in productivity has led to an expansion in leisure time.

2.3 R Jones classified the social factors in a slightly different way, as follows.

(a) **Underlying factors**

These include UK population trends, education policy and the educational standards of the workforce, attitudes to acquiring skills.

(b) **People at work**

This means the labour market, trade unions and work attitudes. In these areas organisations are at the mercy of legislation and political pressures.

(c) **Individuals and society**

This category of social factors includes challenges to the existing social order, involvement by junior employees in decisions taken within their organisation, the social responsibility of employers to their employees, income and wealth distribution, and spending patterns.

2.4 Demographic change has implications for the following.

(a) **The demand for services and products**

In the UK, for example, we might expect the consequences of an ageing population to include greater demand for health care services.

(b) **The location of demand**

Again, in the UK, there appears to be a gradual population shift out of the inner cities towards suburbs and small towns.

(c) **Recruitment**

A decline in the number of young people entering the work force in the UK has encouraged companies to reconsider their attitudes to employing married women, who leave work to have children but who wish to return to employment later, and older personnel.

(d) **The wealth of the workforce**

The other consequences of an ageing population are that those in work will pay more in taxes to support the elderly and as the elderly need more care, people will need time off work to look after dependent relatives. Both these factors will affect the disposable income of people in work.

2.5 Although the impacts of cultural change may be indirect, they can nevertheless be very significant. They can affect not only demand, but also labour supply (increasing concern over work-life balance for example).

Economic change

The business cycle

2.6 As we saw in Chapter 10, an important indicator of economic activity is the **business cycle**.

(a) Some economists suggest that economic activity is always punctuated by periods of growth followed by decline, simply because of the nature of trade.

(b) Some industries prosper when others are declining. They are called **counter-cyclical** industries.

Economic trends: regional, national and international

2.7 Three levels of economic trend analysis need to be considered; regional trends, national trends and international trends. Many of these trends are often factors over which an organisation has no direct control, but which should be considered in the organisation's strategic plans.

2.8 A company's **local geographical environment** is important. It might be located in a growth area full of modern thriving industry, or it may be located in an area of urban decay. The economic future of the area will affect amongst other things wage rates, availability of labour, disposal income of local consumers, unemployment, the provision of roads and other services.

2.9 **'National' economic trends** are relevant to the individual characteristics of the firm's 'home' market and any overseas markets it trades in (exports, overseas production).

2.10 **World trends** might seem remote to the small or medium-sized business, but they can in fact have an important influence on the future of any company with plans to trade abroad, as importers or exporters.

Overseas competition

2.11 One of the key economic developments since 1945 has been the rapid growth of countries in Asia, free trade and freer movement of capital.

Changes in the national industry mix

2.12 Most advanced industrial economies have seen a shift from manufacturing to services such as retailing, education, health, tourism and communications. A large proportion of economic activity is taken up by services, such that the world economy is projected to be dominated by services by the early years of the next millennium.

2.13 Reasons for this shift are various.

(a) Increased **manufacturing productivity** means that the same level of output can be produced by fewer people. (This is similar to what happened in the last century to agriculture and food production.)

(b) The UK's **trade performance** suffered in the early 1980s, as many firms lost export markets because of the high value of sterling.

(c) **Developing countries** make some manufactured products more cheaply.

Marketing at Work

Cookson, the UK engineering and materials company, believes the expanding economies of Taiwan, India and China justify its plans to spend more than £100m on manufacturing in Asia (*Financial Times*, June 1998).

Despite economic problems affecting countries such as Japan and South Korea, Cookson aims to increase the proportion of its sales from Asia to about a third in five years' time.

It believes it has a big opportunity in using its metallurgical knowledge to increase the quality of steel made in China and at the same time utilise cheaper labour. Even though China is the worlds' biggest steelmaker, the sophistication is low by Western standards.

Political change

2.14 Given that organisations must operate within a political environment, it is political **change** that complicates the task of predicting future influences, and planning to meet them. **Political risk** is the risk to an investment or business arising from the political decisions taken by the government or as a result of the activities of its citizens.

2.15 Management ought to be aware of the following.

■ Whether political change could have a **significant impact** on their organisation
■ What **form** of **influence** the political change might have
■ What the **extent** of the **consequences** of any such change might be
■ What the **likelihood is** of the change taking place
■ How the organisation can **plan to cope** with the change, should it occur

2.16 **Political risk** is still relevant with regard to overseas investment, especially in large infrastructure projects overseas. History contains dismal tales of investment projects that went wrong, and were expropriated (nationalised) by the government. Gleason and Wells (Harvard *Business Review*, September-October 1995) suggest that the risk of nationalisation still exists, especially with infrastructure projects (eg-toll roads) in some countries.

■ Suspicion of foreign ownership is still rife, especially when prices are raised etc.

■ Opposition politicians can appeal to nationalism by claiming the government sold out to foreigners

■ Nationalising infrastructure owned by foreigners rarely deters other investors.

■ Governments might want to renegotiate a deal to get a better bargain.

2.17 In some countries, cultivation of the right political contacts (**guanxi** in China) is essential for decisions to be made in your favour. There is a fine line to be drawn between aggressive lobbying and corruption.

Action Programme 1

For a business of your choice, identify the most significant areas of political risk.

Natural environment

2.18 Environmental impacts may be direct:

■ Changes affecting costs or resource availability
■ Impact on consumer demand
■ Impact on power balances between competitors in a market

2.19 For example, environmental damage may place some competitors at a disadvantage because of additional operating costs to clean up the product or processes, or affect the availability of raw materials.

2.20 These may also be indirect aspects, for example, pressures from customers or staff as a consequence of concern over environmental matters.

Technological change

2.21 Technological change is rapid, and organisations must adapt themselves to it. Technological change can affect the activities of organisations as follows.

(a) **Type of products or services that are made and sold**

Consumer markets have seen the emergence of home computers, compact discs and satellite dishes for receiving satellite TV. Industrial markets have seen the emergence of custom-built microchips, robots and local area networks for office information systems. Technological changes can be relatively minor, such as the introduction of tennis and squash rackets with graphite frames, fluoride toothpaste and turbo-powered car engines.

(b) **Way in which products are made**

There is a continuing trend towards the use of modern labour-saving production equipment. The manufacturing environment is undergoing rapid changes with the growth of advanced manufacturing technology.

(c) **Way in which services are provided**

High-street banks encourage customers to use 'hole-in-the-wall' cash dispensers, and shops are now using computerised point of sale terminals at cash desks.

(d) **Way in which markets are identified**

Database systems make it much easier to analyse the market place.

(e) **Way in which employees are mobilised**

Computerisation encourages delayering of organisational hierarchies, but it also requires greater workforce skills. Technology frequently requires changes in working methods.

2.22 Organisations that operate in an environment where the pace of technological change is very fast must be flexible enough to adapt to change quickly and must plan for change and innovation, perhaps by spending heavily on research and development.

3 Changes in employment patterns

3.1 For the future, it is likely that Britain will see a number of changes in employment patterns.

(a) **Increasingly flexible workforce**

Workers no longer expects a job for life, and are prepared to work long or flexible hours rather than the traditional '9 – 5'.

(b) **Increased use** of **part-time labour**

Many individuals have multiple part-time jobs. Between 1984 and 1994, the number of part-timers in the UK increased from 4.9m to 6.3m, amounting to 25% of the labour force (20% in 1984). Five times as many women as men work part time.

Advantages of using part-time labour
Easier to match working hours to operational requirements
Easier to accommodate personal circumstances of key staff
Productivity of part-timers higher than of full-timers working for the same period
Absence levels of part-timers lower
Pool of trained employees available for possible switching to full-time work
Easier to recruit staff
Alternative to paying expensive overtime rates

(c) **Increase** in **temporary employment**

As costs have been cut, some organisations have employed temporary or contract staff to cover busy periods. Use of non-permanent staff means that employment matches activity, whilst costs are also saved in that non-permanent staff would not be paid for holidays or paid other benefits.

(d) **Homeworking**

More people are likely to **work from home** as telecommunications improve (see 3.2 below).

(e) **Self-employment**

More people are likely to be **self-employed**. A Labour Force Survey estimated that 3.1m were self-employed in Great Britain in 1996, 12.2% of all those in employment, compared with 11.3% in 1984. Ethnic minorities from Asia have higher than average rates of self-employment (*Social Trends*).

(f) **Knowledge workers**

An increased proportion of the workforce being **'knowledge workers'**, workers who use, process and produce knowledge. One aim of expanding higher and vocational education is to produce graduates able to cope with this new environment.

Homeworking and remote working

3.2 Advances in communications technology have, for some tasks, reduced the need for the actual presence of an individual in the office. This is particularly true of tasks involving computers. The worker can, for example, do keying-in tasks at home. The keyed-in data can be sent over a telecommunications link to head office. This approach is being adopted in publishing and journalism and there are other examples as well.

3.3 However, where tangible goods are involved in workers' activities, barriers to homeworking still remain, because of the costs of transporting the goods.

ADVANTAGES OF HOMEWORKING	
Organisation	**Individual**
Cost savings in space	Commuting time saved
Larger pool of labour	Work organised flexibly round domestic commitments
If use freelance homeworkers, no need to pay sick and holiday pay, or for periods when there is no work	Easier to concentrate on work at home?
PROBLEMS WITH HOMEWORKING	
Organisation	**Individual**
Difficult to monitor	If homeworkers are freelance, poor employment rights and career prospects
Team working is problematic	Isolation

Marketing responses

3.4 Marketers need to consider their responses to these changes, for example:

(a) **Mortgages** which **take account** of the short-term nature of prospective borrowers' employment contracts

(b) **Computers** which are **aimed** at combined leisure/business uses

(c) **Financial** services tailored to the needs of the **self-employed**

3.5 The worry for businesses is that whilst writers such as Handy identify the need for people to have a **'portfolio'** of skills, many people do not welcome the insecurity that current labour market trends imply.

3.6 They might be likely to defer expensive purchases such as cars or houses, owing to uncertainty about their ability to meet the long-term commitments.

3.7 This has been compounded by a perceived reduction in the safety net offered by the welfare state (eg the proposed reductions in state support towards paying unemployed people's mortgage interest). Of course, more than anything this offers an opportunity for financial services firms to offer insurance products tailored to this market.

4 Women at work

4.1 A longer-term change in the culture surrounding organisations in many countries is that related to female employment. *Social Trends* estimates that the number of women in the UK labour force has increased by one million since the 1980s.

4.2 This trend is related to:

- The growth in part-time jobs
- The rise in childbearing age
- Economic necessity, as unemployment has increased among the male population

BPP PROFESSIONAL EDUCATION

4.3 Only in recent decades has there been a widespread challenge to sex segregation in employment. The law has been changed in many countries to ensure that **non-discrimination**, in most cases, applies to all aspects of employment. Furthermore, the principle of equal pay for equal work and for equal value is enshrined in legislation.

4.4 That said, women still occupy fewer senior positions than men. There are a number of reasons for this.

(a) In some professions or jobs (eg accountancy) female participation is relatively recent, so that the **age profile** of the female participants means that women are predominantly young. This means they are less likely to have risen fast enough.

(b) **Part-time work**, in which female employment is concentrated rarely offers opportunities for promotion.

(c) There might still be **subtle discrimination** (a 'glass ceiling') at higher levels, and more obvious discrimination at lower levels.

(d) Women still generally take **more responsibility** for child rearing.

4.5 In addition to responding to legislative provisions, some employers have begun to address the underlying problems of equal opportunities, with measures such as the following.

(a) Putting **equal opportunities** higher on the agenda by appointing Equal Opportunities Managers (and even Directors) reporting directly to the Personnel Director

(b) **Flexible hours** or **part-time work**, 'term-time' or annual hours contracts (to allow for school holidays) to help women to combine a career with family responsibilities. Terms and conditions, however, must not be less favourable

(c) **Career-break** or **return-to-work schemes** for women

(d) **Fast-tracking school-leavers**, as well as graduates, and posting managerial vacancies internally, gives more opportunities for movement up the ladder to women currently at lower levels of the organisation

(e) Training for women-returners or women in management to help women to manage their career potential

(f) **Awareness training** for managers, to encourage them to think about equal opportunity policy

(g) The provision of **workplace nurseries** for working mothers would be a boon to many female workers; employers however appear reluctant to bear the cost

(h) **Positive action** to encourage job and training applications from minority groups

(i) **Alteration of premises** to accommodate wheelchair users

4.6 **Opportunity 2000**, a campaign led by Business in the Community, exists to promote the cause of working women in the UK. One of its sponsors, British Airways, announced that its goal would be that 32% of its employees at all levels should be women (to reflect the proportion of women in the workforce). Indications are that the campaign's success has been variable, with little progress on relative pay.

Marketing responses

4.7 The changing role of women is also reflected in attempts by marketers to target the growing number of women who have their own careers. Consider the following responses by marketers.

(a) Advertising is today **less likely** to **portray women** as **subservient housewives**, but instead as self-confident individuals.

(b) Women are purchasing more **traditionally male products**. For example, many car manufacturers target professional women with cars whose specification is likely to appeal to them.

(c) Products have emerged to make working **women's lives easier**, for example ready prepared meals.

4.8 However, there may have been less change in the distribution of sexual roles within the home, where women still do the bulk of childcare and home-making tasks. The marketer who wishes to target women as a market segment has therefore to reconcile the rather more complex employment and lifestyle patterns in the design of products/services and right marketing mix. As a general principle, products and services which will enable women to juggle the various demands made on them will be more successful than those which will not. Product designers also need to assess women's needs in product design.

Marketing at Work

The Women's Royal Voluntary Service, WRVS, has had to face a number of changes to the environment in which it operates. The core of the WRVS's work is wide-ranging, tackling social deprivation in communities and helping people deal with stress. However as Mark Lever, the charity's chief executive, has commented: 'It's a big frustration to me that when people think of the WRVS they think of middle-class ladies serving cups of tea.'

To alter perceptions, the charity is re-launching itself with a new logo and a media campaign emphasising the ways in which the WRVS helps vulnerable and isolated individuals.

Other significant changes are also being made. The charity has faced a falling volunteer base, resulting from a higher proportion of women with school-age or grown-up children having jobs. The WRVS has responded by providing flexible opportunities for volunteers to give as much time as they can, at evenings, weekends or sporadically, and also working with their employers to see if volunteering can be fitted around their jobs. The charity is also trying to recruit more volunteers from black or minority ethnic backgrounds, and is working with Mencap to recruit volunteers with learning disabilities.

The WRVS is also facing the challenge of obtaining income from new sources. At its peak central government funding amounted to £6.5 million, but government support has been dropping over the last few years and is expected to level out at £1 million in 2008. The charity is thus seeking to increase income from donations, appointing its first head of corporate fundraising and considering mailshots to individuals.

The WRVS is also trying to overhaul its hospital shops along commercial lines, and win service contracts with local authorities. It is however competing with the commercial sector and also its own suppliers in doing this. When competing, a major advantage the charity has is its volunteer base: 'My job is to promote the added value that our volunteers bring. I would not say that volunteers are better than the paid staff of our competitors, but their motivation is very different and they bring different qualities to the work.' Mark Lever commented.

Mark Lever believes that charities must face up to the challenge of responding to changes in society, even though it may mean internal upheaval. In the end necessary changes will produce benefits.

'Day in and day out we see people who are isolated and we really see the difference that we can make to their lives. This is why I want the WRVS to grow.'

The Times 23 February 2004

5 Environmental issues 12/02, 12/03

5.1 The marketing concept will undoubtedly be increasingly affected by environmental issues in the future. There is already a considerable impact on marketing policies. In 1990, 26% of all new products marketed in the USA were using a 'green' approach. In the past there has been a tendency to regard marketing, and business activities in general, as antithetical to the concept of 'green-ness', but now it is being recognised that the two are complementary, in many ways.

Marketing at Work

Genetically-modified crops are crops whose genetic structure has been modified to improve their quality or appearance. They are common in America, but their introduction is meeting resistance in the UK. Objections include the possibility of as yet unknown effects on the human body, and the potential effect on other plants or creatures in the area where the crops are grown. The anti-GM arguments have meant that GM foodstuffs have to be clearly labelled, and have acquired a poor reputation which makes them very difficult to market.

However one argument in favour of GM products is the possibility that developments may benefit agriculture in less developed countries. Marketing responses to GM foods may stress this aspect, and also the fact that extensive US testing has failed to find any significant problems.

Which environmental issues will impact upon businesses?

5.2 Among the environmental issues which are likely to be seen as relevant to businesses are the following.

(a) **Resource depletion**

This may influence business operation through impacts on the availability of raw materials through damage to soil, water, trees, plant-life, energy availability, mineral wealth, animal and marine species.

(b) **Genetic diversity**

This may not seem immediately important for business. However the development of many important new plants, animals, medicines and the new bio-technology which enables commercially valuable materials of all kinds to be synthesised, depends crucially on the availability of wild species from which resources of all kinds can be drawn. In the development of high-yielded and disease-resistant plants, for example, wild species are a critical resource.

Pollution

5.3 **Pollution concerns** are, of course, at the centre of most worries about the environment.

(a) **Water**

Businesses are finding themselves under more and more pressure to curtail the impacts of their activities on the **water table**, the **seas** and the **oceans**. Concern over the quality of drinking water, to which this has been linked, has generated a massive increase in the size of the bottled water market in the UK. In the late 1980s, growth rates were around 20% per annum.

(b) **Air**

The **quality of air** has been much discussed, owing to the effect of motor car exhaust, and the general impact of road vehicles - clearly this may well have a bearing upon distribution policies.

(c) **Land**

Concerns about the **pollution of land**, through landfill policies and the long-term damage wrought by industry upon the land it occupies, are all likely to require some policy changes over the next few years.

(d) **Noise**

Noise pollution is also likely to become more important, and this can have far reaching impacts on the operation of all manner of businesses.

Acid rain

5.4 Acid rain has been linked to **large scale damage to forests** throughout northern Europe and acidification of water supplies and of fish-bearing lakes and rivers. It has generated massive bills. The bills involved and the impacts on the natural environment and agricultural systems are so large that political pressures to constrain the effects of industrial production have increased enormously.

The ozone layer

5.5 Many are also worried about **ozone depletion**, caused by the CFC group of chemicals. Alternatives to CFCs are being developed to act as solvents in the electronics industry, and coolants in refrigerators. The use of CFCs for blowing polystyrene foam used as insulation by the building industry has been banned in some countries and is being phased out in many others. Even where products containing CFCs are legally available, consumers may refuse to buy them. This has speeded up the development of replacements.

Waste

5.6 Waste is causing just as much alarm, whether it is **nuclear waste** from power stations or industrial or **domestic waste** in landfill sites or water systems. There is **increased legislation** by governments to control waste disposal. New international agreements, arrived at by governments concerned, for example, about the effects of waste dumping on marine life and on beaches also lead to domestic legislation.

Climatic change

5.7 Whether excess carbon dioxide in the atmosphere has caused serious climatic change resulting in 'unnatural' weather is still open to debate. Potentially, the consequences could be profound, with average temperatures increasing and sea levels rising, with disastrous effects on agriculture and flooding of low lying areas.

5.8 If the climate did alter significantly, great changes would be necessary, including **new types of agricultural practices, different areas of habitation** and tourism, as well as **modification** to the **production processes** and **consumption patterns** which have been identified as contributory factors. Undoubtedly, laws would be enacted in a wide range of business and marketing related areas to enforce such restrictions as were thought appropriate.

Energy resources

5.9 Concerns about energy resources and about the environmental impacts of energy usage are related to the concern over climatic change. Some of the energy sources used at the moment are yielding far less of their potential than seems possible. Coal, for example, typically yields only 40% of its potential when burned to produce electricity.

5.10 **Energy saving programmes** are under way in most of the countries of the developed world, involving the development of **more efficient industrial equipment**, and projects such as **combined heat and power systems** serving neighbourhoods or industrial plants. **New energy efficient products** are also being developed. Legislation which would penalise the use of certain scarce or potentially wasteful energy sources, for instance a **carbon tax,** may well encourage the demand for energy efficient products.

Recycling

5.11 This practice is already widespread and the demand for products and packaging made from recycled materials, or from materials which lend themselves to recycling, is **increasing steadily**. Car manufacturers such as Mazda and Citroen are using plastic components to reduce vehicle weight and are recycling used components.

Animal welfare

5.12 In addition to concerns about the impact of production and consumption on the environment, there are also concerns about animal welfare. The **mistreatment of animals** in food production and concern about the inhumanity of certain kinds of animal husbandry techniques have produced a strong reaction among consumers. Increased vegetarianism has reduced the demand for meat in the UK, amongst other changes. There has also been an impact on the sales of cosmetics and other products in which animals are used in product testing.

5.13 Related to this, there have been a whole series of **food scares**, some of which have been related to the ways in which food is produced. Concerns about **food safety** and **dietary health** are closely linked to concerns about the use of chemicals and drugs in intensive husbandry and crop production, as well as the forms of feeding which have been employed. The scare over 'mad cow disease' has been linked to the use of recovered proteins from waste meat products in the production of animal feed.

Green pressures on business

5.14 As we saw earlier, pressure for better environmental performance is growing. Consumers are demanding better environmental performance from companies. Consumers are applying environmental criteria in many purchase considerations.

Marketing at Work

During 1995, Greenpeace activists boarded Shell's decommissioned oil rig, Brent Spar, in an attempt to force the company to reconsider the decision to sink the rig in mid-Atlantic rather than demolish and dispose of it on land. Shell's U-turn on the matter was prompted to a great extent by the beginnings of a consumer boycott of its products in Europe, particularly in Germany.

Deutsche Shell was caught out very badly, underestimating as it did the level of public feeling on the subject. It was forced to abandon a high-profile corporate environmental and community project advertising campaign which it had just launched. However, this case also demonstrated the importance of getting your information right. Greenpeace was forced to apologise eventually because it had substantially overestimated the amount of dangerous pollutants still contained within the Brent Spar rig. Shell's original plan is now accepted as being the most environmentally sound.

6 E-commerce   12/03

6.1 Communications and transport technology have shrunk the time it takes for people, messages and money to go from A to B. Communications include cultural products, such as films and books, and also the messages that marketers use to promote goods and services.

6.2 The technology behind communications systems has been around for some time, but it is now vastly more sophisticated; and the carrying capacity of the world's telecommunications networks far exceeds that of a few decades ago.

Marketing at Work

In September 1996 it was announced that Matrixx Marketing was to open a call centre in Salt Lake City, Utah, in order to take the overflow when the group's UK centre in Newcastle-upon-Tyne reaches capacity. This development will mean total immersion in British culture for the Matrixx staff in Utah, who have had to familiarise themselves with UK regional accents, pounds and pence, spelling differences, place names, and the British sense of humour.

Matrixx is just one example of the companies which now operate call centres – offices filled with telephones, computers and staff dedicated to answering calls from customers on behalf of client organisations. In addition, call centres may be used for telemarketing as well, ie outbound calls to prospective customers, plus calls about on-going transactions. One of the major players in the specific arena of telemarketing is the Mitre Group, which says, 'Entire businesses around the world are now being built exclusively on the telephone, with the sort of success that has prompted established players in the market to emulate them or face becoming a second-rate force'.

The Mitre Group provides call centre services to such clients as Microsoft, American Express and Sony.

The USA is the world leader in call centres. Some 50% of TV advertisements in the USA carry a telephone contact number, compared with only 19% of UK commercials. The US is also ahead in the use of free phone (0800) numbers to contact suppliers.

In the UK, only about two-thirds of calls initiated as a result of TV advertisements are answered, because the calls come in sharp flurries which overwhelm staff and clog telephone lines. Recruiting a call centre is much more economic than maintaining large numbers of staff against the occasional burst of activity.

It is expected that there will be rapid growth in the use of call centres over the next decade – though perhaps less so in Germany, where there is a high level of customer resistance to telephone shopping.

Electronic commerce and the Internet

6.3 The Internet allows businesses to reach potentially millions of **consumers** worldwide and extends trading time to seven days, around the clock. Electronic commerce worldwide is valued at US$12 billion, and is set to **reach US$350-500 billion by 2002**. The OECD forecasts global e-commerce to be worth $1 trillion by 2003-05.

6.4 Companies will need to develop new means of promoting their wares through the medium of the Internet, as opposed to shop displays or motionless graphics. Websites can provide **sound and movement** and allow **interactivity**, so that the user can, say, drill down to obtain further information or watch a video of the product in use, or get a virtual reality experience of the product or service.

6.5 For many companies this will involve a **rethink of current promotional activity**.

Possible strategies

6.6 There are four possible broad strategies that a company may adopt towards e-commerce.

(a) **Do not sell products through the Internet at all**

Reselling would also be prohibited. Provide only product information on the Internet. This may be an appropriate strategy where products are **large, complex and highly customised**, such as aircraft manufacturing.

(b) **Leave the Internet business to resellers**

The business would not sell directly through the Internet (ie do not compete with resellers). This can be appropriate, for instance, where manufacturers have already assigned exclusive territories to resellers.

(c) **Restrict Internet sales exclusively to itself**

The problem with this is that most large manufacturers do not have systems that are geared to dealing with sales to end users who place numerous, irregular small orders.

(d) **Open up Internet sales to everybody**

The market would decide who it prefers to buy from.

6.7 If the decision is made to enter into e-commerce a new e-business needs **support and long-term commitment from high-level management**. Ideally such a project should be sponsored by the chief executive or a board-level director.

Strategy	Comment
Outsource to your customers	What do we do for our customers that they would rather do for themselves and could probably do better? Examples: *www.cisco.com, www.dell.com.*
Cannibalise your own business	If there were an Amazon.com in our market, what would it be doing? Examples: *www.barnesandnoble.com, www.wsj.com.*
Host your competitors	How can we create a marketplace that includes our competitors, but that we own? Examples: *www.sabre.com, www.jewellery.com.*
Build one-to-one customer relationships	How can we make each customer feel that we built our organisation just for them? Examples: *www.My.yahoo.com, www.firefly.com, www.netgrocer.com.*
Make first contact	What is the first step our customers take in the chain of events that leads them to buy from us? How can we make contact with them? Example: *www.autobytel.com.*
Be a process integrator	What other things do customers need or do when they buy from us? Example: *www.autobytel.com.*
Catch rites of passage	What major life changes are customers going through when they come into contact with us? How can we help? Examples: *www.usnews.com, www.citibank.com.*
Create a community	What interests do our customers share? How can we create a place that people with those interests will keep coming back to? Example: *www.marshall.com.*
Create a niche portal	How can we make our site the portal our customers go to first? Example: *www.tesco.net.*
Pirate your value chain	How can we take over the roles of others in our value chain? Example: *www.dell.com.*
Re-intermediate on information value	How can we boost the value we add through information? Example: *www.marshall.com.*

Strategy	Comment
Go pure cyberspace	What if we made the digital world our first priority and the physical world second? Example: *www.egghead.com*.
Be a fast follower	What are our competitors doing that looks likely to be successful? How can we do the same thing faster? Example: *www.barnesandnoble.com*.
Think dream not transation	What dream do our customers start with that leads them to buy from us? How can we realise that dream? Example: *www.expedia.com*.
Beat the physical world	What can we do in the digital world that would be impossible or not feasible in the physical world? Example: *www.benjerry.com*.
Leverage the froth	What simple ideas would capture most media and public attention, even if short-lived? Examples: *www.travelocity.com*, *www.lastminute.com*.
Change the pricing model	Would our customers benefit from a different way of pricing, perhaps micro-payments or auctions? Example: *www.priceline.com*.
Convert atoms to bits	What physical world core competencies do we have that could be applied to the digital world? Example: *www.ups.com*.

Marketing at Work

Interactive digital TV offers similar e-commerce services to the Internet as part of its package of services. Contact can be made using a remote control, although the amount of information available is lower because of limited bandwidth. High start-up costs have restricted the number of suppliers, but in the UK there are several possibilities. Arguably many of the users that these cater for are people who do not have full Internet access.

The most popular service is Sky Digital's open service. A number of retailers place content on this site; they have to pay a fixed rent and a proportion of all sales revenue for the privilege. Initial indications suggested that many new customers have been attracted. HSBC registered 80,000 customers within 3 weeks of which 20,000 were new. Domino Pizza had 10,000 requests in the first 10 days.

Businesses who wish to explore this market have to decide whether to advertise interactively or seek a deeper involvement, offering new interactive services or e-commerce facilities for a limited number of products.

Constructing an effective strategy for e-commerce

Upgrade customer interaction	Creation of automated responses to frequently asked questions, setting fast response standards, using Email to communicate and ensuring website navigation is easy
Understand customer segments	Classifying each segment according to how likely it is to use e-commerce route, whether a personalised service relationship is desirable and what benefits customers need
Understand service processes	Understanding which processes can be automated and which transactions would consumers prefer to use the web for rather than say the phone
Define the role	Live interaction will be useful if cross-selling and conversion of enquiries into sales are possible, if trust is being built, or if customers prefer human contact
Decide technology	Deciding whether to run pilot programme first, or go for full integration straightaway
Deal with the tidal wave	Strategies for large initial response include having sufficient capacity for worse-case scenarios and using user-friendly technologies
Create incentives	Discounts to get consumers to switch to lowest cost channels, and disincentives for continuing to use existing channels
Decide on channel choices	Whether to offer a choice of channels (face-to-face, post, phone, Internet)
Exploit the Internet	Tailor-made sites for significant customers, proactive product/service offerings, mechanisms for turning browsers into buyers and creating communities of users
Implement	'Strategy is nothing until it degenerates into work.'

Important aspects of strategy implementation for e-commerce

6.8 The following aspects are very important.

(a) **Organisation and culture**

When organisations move into an electronic age, some people (and functions) **increase their corporate influence**, whilst others move into the shadows. The increasing use of technology is unsettling, especially for senior people (ironically, employees lower down the hierarchy are likely to be much more comfortable about technological innovation). The Internet promotes **freedom of information**, both upwards and downwards; this, for some managers, is equated with a loss of authority.

(b) **Systems and infrastructure**

Implementation of e-commerce often requires **integration of service systems**, particularly call centres, the web, and CRM processes. This in turn may require a company to **review its whole decision-making patterns** and make some difficult choices about existing 'legacy' procedures.

(c) **Training**

Effective e-commerce implementation requires both **staff and customers** to be **trained**. Dealing with electronic interaction demands different skills from those which are appropriate to staff who focus on voice communications. Dealing simultaneously with written and verbal interaction is likely to call for a new skill set.

(d) **Looking to the customers**

This is well summarised by Mike Harris, Chief Executive of Egg, explaining the need to **avoid rehearsed, scripted and bureaucratic approaches** which give the impression that technology is driving the interaction rather than the need to relate to people.

B2B, B2C, C2B, C2C, P2P

Key Concepts

There are various different types of commerce over the Internet.

B2B is business-to-business
B2C is business-to-consumer
C2B is consumer-to-business
C2C is consumer-to-consumer
P2P is peer-to-peer

6.9 B2C is just a name for traditional retailing activities of businesses to customers, carried out over the Internet.

6.10 B2B activities include:

- Sale and transfer of goods before they reach the end-user
- Supply chains and joint ventures
- Subcontracting
- Distribution and marketplaces
- Support services

6.11 According to the market research firm, Jupiter MMXI, the key factors for success in the B2B market are a high volume of transactions, backing from the industry leaders and real-world integration, linking online services with offline services such as telephone service and local customer support.

6.12 The B2B sector has seen major growth over the last few years.

(a) **Major companies** are setting themselves up as e-businesses. In November 1999, both Ford and General Motors announced that they were switching a major portion of their procurement and supply chain management to the web.

(b) IBM now requires **all its suppliers to quote and invoice electronically** – no paper documentation is permitted.

(c)   Many firms are using the Internet to exploit the **transparency of supplier prices**, and to maximise their purchasing benefits from the availability of world-wide sourcing. Robert Bosch, the German kitchen appliance manufacturer, **requires all its suppliers to have web-based catalogues** and prices.

(d)   Companies are also increasing their customer service through the web. Dell, the computer company, has created **extranets for its major business customers**, enabling them to receive personalised customer support, their own price lists, and some free value-added services.

Marketing at Work

One impact of B2B may be to reinforce the powers of very large organisations. The world's largest Internet company at one stage was apparently Covisint, an Internet autoparts supply exchange formed by GM, Ford and DaimlerChrysler.

6.13   The importance of C2B is growing. The key feature of C2B activity is that the consumer takes the initiative to contact the business, rather than the business contacting the customer.

6.14   The development of C2B has huge implications for how marketing is carried out. It moves companies away from deciding what they want to sell and persuading consumers by a vigorous marketing campaign, and towards focusing on what consumers want to purchase. Key priorities will be trying to reach more easily often disparate groups of consumers.

6.15   **C2C** is where the consumer sells to another consumer using the business as an intermediary. The eBay and Yahoo auctions are examples of C2C transactions.

6.16   **P2P** transactions are any transactions that transfer money from one individual to another. Systems are being developed that will handle money transfers without the need for clearance. This market has a lot of potential, as there is a great deal of demand for payments to be made by E-mail.

6.17   The best-known example of P2P is Napster, the company that allowed the exchange of music over the Internet and effectively bypassed the record companies.

M-commerce

Key Concept

M-commerce is mobile commerce.

6.18   M-commerce has developed out of wireless access to the Internet through consumers' hand-held devices. As a result consumers can now shop from anywhere, not just a set shopping or computer location. A survey by Accenture published in early 2001 found that one in ten mobile phone users and one in four personal digital assistant (PDA) users had used their devices to buy goods.

Marketing at Work

At the Palisade Shopping centre in New York, customers can opt to receive personalised messages from stores whilst they are in the shopping mall. PDAs are also proving a more popular means of obtaining product information by both customers and sales staff than the predecessor Interactive kiosk systems.

Systems have been developed that can help customers locate the products that they are after.

Disadvantages of e-commerce

6.19 E-commerce involves an unusual mix of people – security people, web technology people, designers, marketing people – and this can be very difficult to manage. The e-business needs supervision by expensive specialists.

6.20 At present, in spite of phenomenal growth the market is still fuzzy and undefined. Marketing, distribution, database development and customer services costs have proved very high for some companies.

Lack of trust

6.21 Above all, however, the problem with e-commerce is one of **trust**. In most cultures, consumers grant their trust to business parties that have a close **physical presence**: buildings, facilities and people to talk to. On the Internet these familiar elements are simply not there. The seller's reputation, the size of his business, and the level of customisation in product and service also engender trust.

6.22 Internet merchants need to elicit consumer trust when the **level of perceived risk in a transaction is high**. This is not always so (eg books) and research has found that consumers who have built up trust in an Internet merchant will ignore such concerns.

6.23 Internet merchants need to address issues such as fear of **invasion of privacy** and abuse of customer information (about their **credit cards**, for example) because they stop people even considering the Internet as a shopping medium.

6.24 Conventional thinking says that a company should pay no more to bring in a customer than the stream of profits that the customer will subsequently generate. Yet in the e-commerce context, investors have often rewarded companies for **customer acquisition** without asking any questions about how quickly those customers may disappear.

6.25 Similar turbulence is affecting the B2B world. Traditional manufacturing companies around the world, sensing the **potential benefits from automating transactions** with suppliers and customers, have rushed into e-commerce. Many have formed alliances to create their own on-line market place, especially in the automobile, aerospace and chemicals industries. By pooling their buying power, the organisations behind these alliances hope to have **more control** over their activities. This leaves the small, purely Internet-based commodity/component exchanges struggling to attract the volume of transactions needed to make them viable.

Marketing at Work

Flightbookers, a travel company, has very successfully developed its own e-business. It has a wide range of flights on offer, but the service has expanded to include car hire and hotels. The company is developing a pro-active package that will enable customers to assemble their own hire-hotel package. Another service is an aid to the last minute holiday booker, who states preferred destination and maximum amount prepared to pay; when something becomes available the company emails him.

Through advertising the company is seeking to develop its own brand values in order to ensure continued customer loyalty. The company is trying to exploit gaps but is aware that competitors will soon catch up: 'Every month in Internet time is worth a multiple in years.'

The Dotcom downturn

6.26 In March 2000 the US NASDAQ composite index, the flagship measure for the strength of the Dotcom sector, peaked at 5,068, having climbed from 2,000 in late 1998. By March 2001 it was back to 2,062. In Britain the Techmark 100 index fell to 2,308 during March 2001, having peaked at 5,743 during March 2000.

6.27 The list of Dotcom casualties during 2000 was a long one. It included Boo, Clickmango.com and eToys in Europe. Some areas where significant competition existed were badly hit, including pet products; Wetnose and Pets.com, which were significant players, both disappeared.

6.28 Efdex was the first significant B2B casualty. Other B2B pioneers such as VerticalNet and Ventro have attempted to reposition themselves as software vendors. *The Financial Times* commented: 'Far from allowing independent marketplaces to flourish and creating new trading opportunities, the Internet has been used most successfully by big business to reinforce existing procurement practices'.

6.29 Part of the problem was undoubtedly due to the unrealistic expectations that fed into stockmarket over-valuations.

Marketing at Work

The one-third share in Amazon.com that belonged to its founder, Jeff Bezos, fell in value by $10 billion during 2000. A report by Lehman Brothers in June 2000 suggested that the company could run out of money within a year. Commenting on this report, the *Economist* observed: 'For other dotcoms it was sobering. Amazon was, and is, the model e-tailer. Consumers love its vast selection and ease of use.... Many Internet companies have emulated at least some of Amazon's business practices, from its aggressive use of stock options to its deficit spending on a grand scale. If Amazon is broken, so will many other companies be.'

A further significant observation of the Lehman analysis was that Amazon 'was displaying the operational and cash flow characteristics of a normal retailer'. How come? Simply because, to guarantee rapid delivery, Amazon had to build and staff its own warehouses and fight to control its stock levels. This may however change over time with advances in the B2B sector. Logistics companies, trucking firms and other distributors may be able to provide the guarantees that Amazon needs, and hence Amazon may be able to spin its stock and distribution side off.

By February 2001 Amazon was forced to lay off over 1,000 employees and close two distribution facilities. The company's financial results have varied since. A surplus for the quarter ended 31 December was outweighed by much larger losses for the first two quarters of 2002.

However, the company moved into profit in late 2002, and 2003 turnover and profits were well above the growth levels forecast. This turnaround has been mainly due to cost-cutting and lower prices; attractive pricing appears to be as important in attracting customers as speed and convenience.

6.30 What are the prospects in the near future for Dotcom companies? The *Economist,* in June 2000, commented that Dotcom companies making losses might have to demonstrate to potential investors that they are getting closer to positive cash flows. Some companies have switched their emphasis from B2B to B2C. Others, for example About.com, have characteristics of several different types; the *Economist* suggested these be called B2C2B2B companies. The market will not invest in new sector companies per se but will consider 'how well a firm exploits the advantages of the Internet, how different it is from its rivals, whether it has secure patents...or how strong its brand name is.'

The Dotcom upswing?

6.31 In spite of the problems faced by the Dotcom sector in 2000 and 2001, some commentators remain confident that the Dotcom boom will return. In March 2002 the respected US economist W Brian Arthur suggested that the information technology revolution's best days still lay ahead.

6.32 Arthur drew parallels with the various sub-revolutions that occurred during the two centuries since the industrial revolution began. In particular he suggested the Dotcom revolution had parallels in timescale with the railway revolution in the UK; investment mania in 1845 being followed by a crash in 1847, but then by a steadier expansion with the result that the railway network increased to ten times its original size by 1915.

6.33 For Arthur's view to be correct, information technology must become so user friendly that people use it without thinking. The Internet has to be absorbed into people's day-to-day existence. This implies that the next stage will be consumer, rather than business-to-business driven.

6.34 There is evidence on Wall Street of interest in Internet names which have strong infrastructure in place and the financial wherewithal to ride out the downturn. Forrester Research, which follows technology trends, estimates that online businesses will more than triple to reach $7 trillion within five years.

Marketing at Work

Business and the Internet

We have seen that the Internet has the potential to turn business upside down and inside out, to fundamentally change the way companies operate, whether in high-tech or metal-bashing. This goes far beyond buying and selling over the Internet, or e-commerce, and deep into the processes and culture of an enterprise.

Some writers argue that companies can be either **'brick' or 'click'** businesses, but they can't be both: if they are a 'brick' operation – ie they have real premises, real shops, real factories and warehouses – then their culture will make it impossible for them fully to assimilate the drastic changes required in order to operate successfully in a 'click' environment. It is no accident, therefore, that companies like Prudential Assurance have initiated their Internet activities through stand-alone enterprises, using newly-recruited people situated in geographically-distinctive locations.

7 The Single European Market and EMU   12/03

7.1   The single European market is, in theory, supposed to allow for the free movement of labour, goods and services between the member states of the EU.

(a)   **Physical barriers** (eg customs inspection) on goods and service have been removed for most products. Companies have had to adjust to a new VAT regime as a consequence.

(b)   **Technical standards** (eg for quality and safety) should be harmonised.

(c)   **Governments should not discriminate** between EU companies in awarding public works contracts.

(d)   **Telecommunications** face **greater competition**.

(e)   **Financial services** can be provided in any country.

(f)   Measures are being taken to **rationalise transport services**.

(g)   There is **free movement of capital** within the community.

(h)   **Professional qualifications** awarded in one member state should be **recognised in the others**.

(i)   The EU is taking a co-ordinated stand on matters related to **consumer protection**.

7.2   Do not assume that there is already a 'level playing field'. There are many areas where harmonisation is a long way from being achieved. Here are some examples.

(a)   **Company taxation**

Tax rates, which can affect the viability of investment plans, vary from country to country within the EU.

(b)   **Indirect taxation (sales tax)**

Whilst there have been moves to harmonisation, there are still differences between rates imposed by member states.

BPP
PROFESSIONAL EDUCATION

(c) **Differences in prosperity**

There are considerable differences in prosperity between the wealthiest EU economy (Germany), and the poorest (eg Greece). The UK comes somewhere in the middle. This has meant grants are sometimes available to depressed regions, which might affect investment decisions and different marketing strategies are appropriate for different markets.

(d) **Differences in workforce skills**

Again, this can have a significant effect on investment decisions. The workforce in Germany is perhaps the most highly trained, but also the most highly paid, and so might be suitable for products of a high added value.

(e) **Infrastructure**

Some countries are better provided with road and rail than others. Where accessibility to a market is an important issue, infrastructure can mean significant variations in distribution costs.

7.3 The picture is further complicated by the forthcoming enlargement of the EU. Hungary, Poland, Slovenia, Estonia, Latvia, Lithuania, Malta, Cyprus and the Czech republic will be joining the EU in 2004, and Bulgaria and Romania are due to join in 2007.

7.4 This expansion will potentially open up marketing opportunities for businesses operating in new and existing member countries, with perhaps more benefits being derived by new members. The more alarmist elements of the press in certain countries have been highlighting the supposed 'flood of immigration', which they predict will occur when the new countries join and their labour forces have rights of movement within the EU.

Exam Tip

The impact of the EU enlargement was examined in December 2003, along with other international developments such as global summits. Make sure that you have a good general knowledge of major international political events and consider when you're reading about them how they will impact upon the marketing environment of businesses in your own country and abroad.

Action Programme 2

How do you think the existence of a single European currency (the euro) affects your company's administration?

Action Programme 3

Tommy's Toys Ltd manufactures model cars and trucks, which are normally battery driven. The firm has not gone into exporting very much because of the trouble caused by different product standards and requirements. What will be the consequences of the single European market for the company?

European Economic and Monetary Union

7.5 European Economic and Monetary Union (EMU) was a long-standing objective of the EU, reaffirmed in the Single European Act of 1985 and in the Maastricht Treaty of 1991.

Key Concepts

Monetary union can be defined as a single currency area, which would require a monetary policy for the area as a whole.

Economic union can be described as an unrestricted common market for trade, with some economic policy co-ordination between different regions in the union.

7.6 Although the whole package of measures included in European EMU is not paralleled anywhere else in the world, there have been many international monetary unions. There are three main aspects to European Monetary Union. Note that Denmark and the UK are not party to these arrangements.

(a) **Common currency**

A common currency is now used for normal everyday money transactions by everyone in the monetary union.

(b) **European central bank**

A European central bank has the role of issuing the common currency, conducting monetary policy on behalf of the central government authorities, acting as lender of last resort to all European banks and managing the exchange rate for the common currency.

(c) **Centralised monetary policy**

This applies across all the countries within the union. It involves the surrender of control over aspects of economic policy and therefore surrender of some political sovereignty by the government of each member state to the central government body of the union.

7.7 The conditions set for an EU country to participate in EMU were that it must meet certain economic convergence criteria, as follows.

(a) Consumer price **inflation** must, over the previous year, have been no more than 1.5 per cent higher than the average of the three best performing EU countries.

(b) **Long-term interest rates** must, over the previous year, have averaged no more than 2 per cent more than the average of three countries with the best consumer price inflation performance.

(c) A government's **deficit** should not exceed 5 per cent of GDP (gross domestic product) unless it has declined substantially or continuously or unless it is only temporarily above 3 per cent; additionally, the ratio of government debt to GDP should be no more than 60 per cent (unless it is approaching 60% at a satisfactory rate).

(d) The **currency** of the country should have remained within the normal bands of the ERM for a minimum of two years, without any devaluation.

7.8 EMU became a reality on 1 January 1999, when the **euro** became the official currency of participating countries. Although companies were able to use the euro in transactions from 1999, euro coins and banknotes only entered circulation from 1 January 2002. The UK retains the right to opt in or to opt out, depending on the government's decision at the time.

7.9 The Labour Government indicated that a referendum on entry was likely within two years of the 2001 general election, but no date had been fixed at the time of writing (Spring 2004).

7.10 Companies need to have in place a strategy for dealing with entry into the Euro that takes into account the following factors.

- Cost of conversion
- Transitional arrangements
- Effects on different products
- Competitor response including increased competition from other European countries
- Effects of movements in the Euro

Action Programme 4

How will European economic and monetary union (EMU), and a single European currency, affect the following UK businesses?

(a) A package holiday firm, mainly selling holidays to France and Germany.
(b) An exporter of power station generating equipment to developing countries in Asia.
(c) An importer of wine from Australia.

Do this exercise twice, firstly on the assumption that the UK participates in EMU, swapping sterling for the euro, and secondly on the assumption that it stays outside of EMU.

8 Globalisation

Marketing at Work

The experience of Levi-Strauss is one of the latest instances of the trend towards mass customisation, the process in which the economies of scale associated with mass production are combined with a 'personal' service which makes individual customers feel valued.

Customers at the Levi shops in London and Sheffield can try on prototypes from a stock of more than 300 pairs of jeans, and then fine-tune the measurements to provide a perfect fit.

The details are recorded on computer, together with the shopper's name and address; the finished product is shipped direct to the customer or back to the store for collection.

There is a price premium, but shoppers can re-order garments using a barcode sewn inside the jeans.

8.1　There are strong forces in the business environment drawing companies towards global marketing strategies, the most important of which are as follows.

(a)　**Demographic, cultural** and **economic convergence** among consumer markets and increasing homogeneity in the needs of industrial customers worldwide

(b)　**Increased need** for **investment** and research to ensure long-term competitiveness, longer lead times involved in bringing products to market and the growing return needed for this process

(c)　The **growing importance** of **economies of scale** (purchasing, manufacturing, distribution)

(d)　**Changes** in **regional economic cooperation** resulting in freer movement of goods and capital

(e)　The **impact** of **technology** on manufacturing, transportation and distribution

(f)　The **deregulation** of **national markets**, in areas such as air transport, financial services, telecommunications and power generation

Marketing at Work

Guinness has shown how companies can make significant profits in Africa despite high costs and infrastructure problems. Nigeria is the third largest market for Guinness in the world after Britain and Ireland. Guinness's success in Nigeria has been partly due to the success of an advertising campaign, featuring Michael Power, a James Bond like figure who appears in feature films financed by the company.

Guinness has also brewed various products with a taste, alcoholic strength and consistency tailored to Nigeria. The company has used local ingredients, principally sorghum, a common cereal in West Africa, which gives a drink a sweeter flavour. Other innovations include Malta Guinness, a non-alcoholic beer that appeals to a society in which born-again Christainity and strict interpretations of Islamic laws are significant factors.

Guinness has also benefited from perceived high barriers to entry. The company has negotiated downturns in the Nigerian beer market over the last twenty years. By already having a presence in the market, it has been best placed to take advantage of upswings as soon as they occur, by for example, buying and renovating run-down breweries.

Financial Times, 12 February 2004

Some differences between domestic and international marketing

8.2 Sound marketing principles are generally applicable universally. However, there are major environmental differences between home and overseas markets and therefore marketing principles need to be adapted accordingly. The major differences between domestic marketing and international marketing are given below.

Global or international marketing (IM)

8.3 Firms may be pushed into IM by domestic adversity or pulled into IM by attractive opportunities abroad. More specifically, some of the reasons firms enter into IM are the following.

(a) **Chance**

A company executive may recognise an opportunity while on a foreign trip or the firm may receive chance orders or requests for information from foreign potential customers.

(b) **Mature or declining home market**

IM may provide for sales growth since products are often in different stages of the product life cycle in different countries.

(c) **Intense competition in the domestic market**

Competition sometimes induces firms to seek markets overseas where rivalry is less keen. This was a major reason in Gillette's decision to begin marketing razor blades outside its US home markets.

(d) **Diversification**

Many companies enter into IM to **diversify** away from an over-dependence on a single domestic market.

(e) **Technology**

Technological factors may be such that a large volume is needed either to cover the high costs of plant, equipment, R&D and personnel or to exploit a large potential for economies of scale and/or experience. For these reasons firms in the aviation, ethical drugs, computer and automobile industries are often obliged to enter several countries.

(f) **Disposal of discontinued products**

IM can facilitate the **disposal of discontinued products** and seconds since these can be sold abroad without spoiling the home market.

(g) **Foreign opportunities**

Many firms are attracted into IM by **favourable opportunities** such as the development of lucrative Middle Eastern markets, marked depreciation in their domestic currency values, corporate tax benefits offered by particular countries and the lowering of import barriers abroad.

	Domestic	International
Cultural factors	National price Usually no language problems Relatively homogeneous market Rules of the game understood Similar purchasing habits	Diverse national prices Many language barriers Fragmented, diverse markets Rules diverse, changeable and unclear Diverse purchasing habits
Economic factors	Uniform financial climate Single currency Stable business environment	Variety of financial climates, ranging from very conservative to highly inflationary Currencies differing in stability and real value Multiple business environments, some unstable
Competitive factors	Data available, usually accurate and easy to collect. Competitors' products, prices, costs and plans usually known	Formidable data collection problems Many more competitors, but little information about their strategies
Legal factors	Relative freedom from government interference Political factors relatively unimportant	Involvement in national economic plans Government influence on business decisions Political factors often significant
Technological factors	Use of standard production and measurement systems	Training of foreign personnel to operate and maintain equipment Adaptation of parts and equipment Different measuring systems

8.4 Walsh gives a number of reasons for and against involvement in IM.

FOR AND AGAINST IM	
For	**Against**
Higher profits abroad	Profits affected by developments abroad
Increases in sales volumes allow reductions in unit costs	Need to adapt product/limit economies of scale
Extension of product life cycle	Better long-term strategy to develop new products
Disposal of excess production	May attract anti-dumping duties
Disposal of obsolescent goods	
Levelling out of seasonal fluctuations	
Diversification of risk	
Enhancement of prestige	

8.5 However, before getting involved in IM, the company must consider both strategic and tactical issues.

STRATEGIC CONSIDERATIONS

Fit with objectives | Fit with mission | Necessary resources available

TACTICAL ISSUES

Understanding customer needs | Dealing with foreign business culture | Foreign regulations | Management skills available

Which markets should the company enter?

8.6 In making this decision the firm must start by establishing its objectives. Here are some examples.

- What **proportion of total sales** will be overseas?

- What are the **longer-term objectives**?

- Will it enter one, a few, or many **markets**?

- What types of country should it enter (in terms of environmental factors, economic development, language used, cultural similarities and so on)? The major criteria for this decision should be as follows.

Market attractiveness — **WHICH COUNTRY?** — Competitive advantage

Risk — *to choose* — Size of entry barriers

8.7 Some products are extremely sensitive to the environmental differences, which bring about the need for adaptation; others are not at all sensitive to these differences, in which case standardisation is possible. A useful way of analysing products internationally is to place them on a continuum of environmental sensitivity. The greater the environmental sensitivity of a product, the greater the necessity for the company to understand the way in which its products interact with economic, socio-cultural and other environmental variables.

Environmentally sensitive
Adaptation necessary.
- Fashion clothes
- Convenience foods

Environmentally insensitive
Standardisation possible.
- Industrial and agricultural products
- World market products, eg denim jeans

Marketing at Work

Tan Wang Cheouw, a Singapore businessman, made his fortune trading electrical goods in Russia and Kazakhstan. In the mid 1990s he switched to selling coffee in the East European market, initially through his own MacCoffee instant brand, but subsequently diversifying into other hot drinks, cereals and candy. His company's profits rose by 33% in 2002.

Much of the company's success has been down to its advertising. This has included:

- Racy television commercials featuring an attractive model serving coffee to Ukraine's most popular boy band

- Advertising on trams, taxis, roadside banners and on the back of scooters

[handwritten in left margin: First set the objectives of the IM then choose the country]

- Sponsoring game shows, pop albums, soccer matches and sailing competitions

- Providing free cups of coffee to skiers.

Much of this advertising is carefully targeted to emphasise the unique qualities of the MacCoffee brand. This is important as in Russia there are at least 35 brands of coffee that, like MacCoffee, carry an eagle and an American flag. In addition it seems that the Russian market is much more brand conscious.

The advertising strategy is proving expensive; the price of television advertising has increased greatly over the last few years. However these costs also represent a barrier to entry, demonstrating the importance of being first in the market. Currently therefore Tan is seeking to expand into Middle Eastern countries, where there is at present little competition.

Far Eastern Economic Review, 15 May 2003

Exam Tip

You should look out for further developments in the areas we have discussed in this chapter, or any new areas which become important in the marketing environment.

Chapter Roundup

- Changes in **employment patterns** including increased labour flexibility and homeworking, may mean expensive purchases are deferred, and products developed which take account of changed financial circumstances or are of use to the homeworker.

- The enhanced role of women in many professions has meant increased markets for some traditionally 'male' or convenience products and changing portrayals of women in advertising.

- Ecological issues that may impact particularly over the next few years include resource depletion, genetic diversity and pollution problems. **Green marketing** may be one response to these concerns.

- The **Internet** offers several commercial advantages, but also has several limitations, which may limit the appeal of **online shopping** and **e-commerce.**

- The **Single European Market** and **European Monetary Union** will have major influences over the next few years.

- **Globalisation** has meant more businesses are considering **international marketing**.

Quick Quiz

1   Give three examples of homeworkers.

2   Give five examples of ways in which employers have addressed equal opportunities issues.

3   Which of the following are possible e-commerce strategies?

A   Do not sell products through the Internet at all
B   Leave the Internet business to resellers
C   Restrict Internet exclusively to itself
D   Open up Internet sale to everybody

4   B2B commerce is:

A   Business-to-business commerce
B   Branch-to-branch commerce
C   Back-to-back commerce
D   Barter-to-barter commerce

5   Economic unit is a single currency area, requiring a monetary policy for the area as a whole.

True   ☐

False   ☐

6   What are the three main aspects of European Monetary Union?

7   What is the main cultural difference that international marketers need to take into account?

8   Give four examples of forces in the business environment that are leading firms towards international marketing.

Action Programme Review

1   –

2   Here are some ideas - you probably have more.

■   Financial reporting - Euros not sterling
■   Confusion in salary structures and payscales as sterling payments are converted to Euros
■   Administrative matters relating to share capital
■   Conversion of trade debts into Euros

There are of course wider macro economic issues to consider, as the single currency will affect interest rates, comparative prices, and relationships with other currencies such as the dollar.

3   (a)   Tommy's Toys Ltd can expect more competition.

(b)   Tommy's Toys Ltd will find it easier to compete in Europe as there should be a convergence of product standards.

(The Single European Market is extremely significant for business. If you are based in the UK the Department of Trade and Industry can provide further information).

4   We can offer no definitive solution, but here are some points to consider.

(a)   For companies trading primarily **within** the EU, such as the package holiday firm, participation in EMU will mean a reduction in exchange rate volatility - businesses will be able to compete on the essentials of cost and productivity. An analogy is the USA - although there are many 'states' there is only one currency. Most of British trade is with EU countries.

(b) and (c)

Companies trading outside the EU would remain subject to exchange rate risk, based on the Euro rather than sterling. It all depends on how the European Central Bank manages the currency - if the Euro becomes a 'hard' currency, like the Deutschmark, then exports will cost more to overseas customers, but imports from overseas suppliers might be cheaper. Many internationally traded goods, such as oil or aircraft, are priced in US dollars anyhow, so the impact will be indirect.

Of course, if the UK stays out of EMU it will not be in a position to influence the monetary policies of countries which use the Euro, although these policies will undoubtedly affect the UK economy and British businesses.

Answers to Quick Quiz

1. - Traditional outworkers (home typists)
   - Itinerants (salesmen)
   - Personal services (hairdressing, music teaching)

2. Any five of:

   - Appointment of equal opportunities managers
   - Flexible hours
   - Career break/return to work schemes
   - Fast tracking women school leavers
   - Training in management
   - Awareness training
   - Workplace nurseries
   - Recruitment activities
   - Modification of premises for disabled users

3. All of them

4. A   Business to business commerce

5. False. The definition is of monetary union

6. - Common currency
   - European central bank
   - Centralised monetary policy

7. In society some groups will accept international products, but local product variations will be needed for other groups.

8. Any four of:

   - Demographic cultural and economic convergence
   - Increased need for investment
   - Growing importance of economies of scale
   - Changes in regional economic co-operation
   - Impact of technology
   - Deregulation of national markets

Now try illustrative questions 23, 24 and 25 at the end of the Study Text

Part D

Environmental information systems

The marketing information system

15

Learning Outcomes

☑ Recognise the importance of information in marketing, planning and decision making

☑ Outline the uses of marketing research

☑ Appreciate the variety of information sources available inside and outside the organisation

☑ Evaluate the quality and cost-effectiveness of information obtained

☑ Explain the process for collecting information about the marketing environment from relevant primary and secondary sources

☑ Compare and contrast various techniques for collecting information about the marketing environment

☑ Appreciate the variety of ways in which information can be presented for business use

BPP
PROFESSIONAL EDUCATION

Syllabus References

☑   Explain why information is important to organisations

☑   Explain the concept of a marketing information system and its key role in effective marketing decision-making

☑   Explain the importance of marketing research and the information benefits it can provide

☑   Identify key sources of internal and external information

☑   Utilise, interpret and present secondary and primary data in identifying environment trends and estimating current demand

☑   Explain the importance of new systems and the continuing impact of new technologies

Key Concepts Introduced

■   Marketing research   ■   Qualitative research

■   Quantitative research   ■   Marketing intelligence system

1   Setting the scene

1.1   Part D of this Study Text deals with the systematic gathering of information for marketing. This chapter introduces the idea that information is vital for decision making, and gives an overview of the types of information that can be obtained through marketing research. It also discusses the various sources of information.

1.2   Information technology plays a key role in information management, and we finish off the chapter by looking at databases and marketing information systems.

Exam Tip

The essential point to remember is the role that information plays in all marketing activity and decision-making. You may be tempted to take this for granted, but it is the core underlying theme of this syllabus. You may for example be asked about the information sources and research methods that would be used to produce specific data.

2 The importance of information

2.1 In a sense, an organisation is a **system of information flows**.

The organisation as an information system

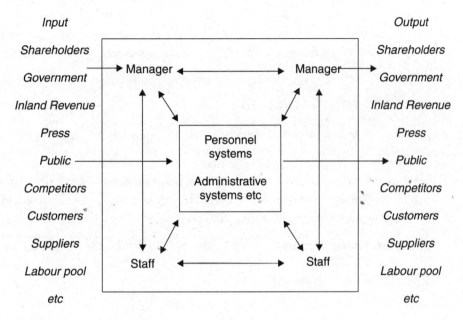

2.2 All human **action and decision-making** is based on information: about the environment, the needs or wants of the individual, the likely outcomes of the action or decision and so on.

Marketing at Work

Procter & Gamble have devised a Statement of Business Principles, setting out 10 guiding principles for all their activity. The top three are as follows:

Plan all action in advance. Always forecast business in relation to expenditure, always check that the business is reaching according to forecast, and always be ready to adjust plans as necessary.

Base all actions on facts. One fact is worth many judgements. Strive always to find the factual truth as a subject before acting. This applies to all fields of business: product, packaging, advertising, promotions and expenditure.

Always know the objective of your actions. Know what advertising, individual promotions and sales plans are intended to do and judge their success by whether they achieve objectives.

Information and the marketing orientation

2.3 Peter Drucker wrote that: 'Marketing is the whole business seen from the point of view of its final result, that is from the **customer's** point of view'. A marketing orientation to business suggests that the purpose of business activity is to find out what people want, and to give it to them: to **make what you can sell**, not sell what you can make.

2.4 'Finding out what people want' is one key area of marketing research. You might think: 'Why does that require research? Marketers are people too: why can't we use our own experience, instincts and knowledge to make marketing decisions?'

2.5 Jim MacNamara *(Marketing and Promotion Handbook)* advises: 'Remember a key truism used in public relations: Your target audience does not think the way you do. If they did, you wouldn't need to influence them... It is vital in marketing communication and promotion to not only know whom or what your target audiences are, but to know as much as you can about them.'

How much information?

2.6 Having said that information is necessary for all decision making, some points must be recognised.

(a) Most decisions are based on **incomplete information**. All possible information is not available. Beyond a certain point, the gathering of more information would not be worth the extra time and cost of obtaining and analysing it.

(b) **Too much information** makes decision making harder rather than easier.

Action Programme 1

Make a poster of the three Procter & Gamble business principles listed earlier.

3 Marketing research   12/03

Key Concept

Marketing research is 'the systematic gathering, recording and analysing of data about problems relating to the marketing of goods and services' (American Marketing Association).

3.1 Marketing research is used by organisations for a number or purposes.

- Identify **changes** in the existing market price
- Build up a **bank of information**
- Improve **market awareness**, to inform negotiations with suppliers
- Help in making plans for the future and mentoring the success of current plans
- Solve *ad hoc* problems

3.2 Marketing decisions are made under conditions of uncertainty and risk. Marketing research aims to **reduce the risk** by providing information about the variables involved in the decision, and the possible outcomes of particular decisions and actions.

3.3 A wide variety of information may be relevant to marketing decisions.

TYPES OF RESEARCH	
Market	■ Analysis of the market potential for existing products ■ Forecasting likely demand for new products ■ Sales forecasting for all products ■ Study of market trends ■ Study of the characteristics of the market ■ Analysis of market shares ■ Consumer attitudes ■ Influences on supply ■ Product usage
Product	■ Customer acceptance of proposed new products ■ Comparative studies between competitive products ■ Studies into packaging and design ■ Forecasting new uses for existing products ■ Test marketing ■ Research into the development of a product line (range)
Price	■ Analysis of elasticities of demand ■ Analysis of costs and contribution or profit margins ■ The effect of changes in credit policy on demand ■ Customer perceptions of price (and quality)
Promotion	■ Motivation research for advertising and sales promotion effectiveness ■ Analysing the effectiveness of advertising on sales demand ■ Analysing the effectiveness of individual aspects of advertising such as copy and media used ■ Establishing sales territories ■ Analysing the effectiveness of salesmen ■ Analysing the effectiveness of other sales promotion methods
Distribution	■ The location and design of distribution centres ■ The analysis of packaging for transportation and shelving ■ Dealer supply requirements ■ Dealer advertising requirements ■ The cost of different methods of transportation and warehousing

Exam Tip

In the exam you may be asked to state what further information (not given in the case study) you would need in order to make a particular decision. Be aware of what sorts of information are helpful for different decisions you make, or see made, regularly: this is the first step to an efficient information search plan.

Primary and secondary research

3.4 One way of classifying research approaches is by the nature of the sources of data they use. We saw earlier in this Study Text that data can be classified as primary or secondary.

Quantitative and qualitative research

3.5 Another way of classifying research is according to the type of data gathered.

> ### Key Concepts
>
> **Quantitative research** gathers statistically valid, numerically measurable data.
>
> **Qualitative research** focuses on values, attitudes, opinions, beliefs and motivations.
>
> (a) Quantitative research answers questions such as: How many? What percentage? How often? How many times? How much? Where? This is essentially *demographic*, statistical information, telling the marketer who buys what, and where, in what quantities and at what price.
>
> (b) While quantitative data may show that 75% of men aged 18-35 drive a car, *qualitative* data might reveal how they go about choosing a car, how they feel about their car, what would make them change cars and so on. This is essentially *psychographic* information.

3.6 Quantitative data is usually gathered by survey, and qualitative data by personal interviews and discussion groups. Both types of data may be gathered from primary and/or secondary sources.

> ### Action Programme 2
>
> Give examples of qualitative and/or quantitative data that might be gathered in the following circumstances.
>
> (a) The sales of a product appeared to be declining in a particular region
> (b) You wanted to know whether customers would support night-time opening
> (c) You were about to schedule TV advertising

Research objectives

3.7 Yet another means of classification is by **research objective**. There are three main kinds of research objective: exploratory, descriptive and causal.

(a) **Exploratory research**

This aims to **originate ideas and hypotheses**, rather than to test or measure existing ones. It is a **preliminary phase** before **designing research** to solve specific problems, and may make use of various sources of data.

(b) **Descriptive research**

This measures and estimates the **frequencies** with which things occur, and the degree to which **variables are correlated**.

(c) **Causal research**

This seeks to establish **cause-and-effect relations** between variables so as to explain and/or predict events. It often involves **experimental research**. So, for example, an organisation may trial a particular campaign with and without a certain feature (say, a response incentive) to isolate the difference made by that feature.

Limitations of marketing research

3.8 However, marketing research does not give all the answers. Some experts openly doubt the value of marketing research, citing examples of successful companies who never engage in it, and of struggling companies who have invested a great deal in it. Sometimes it is undoubtedly a waste of time - why?

(a) The design of the research took no account of the **specific decisions** that needed to be made.

(b) The research was **badly designed** and/or badly carried out.

(c) The results were **inconclusive**, so that the wrong decision was made, or the right decision was made but failed to convince the people who had to carry it out.

(d) The results were **ignored**, misinterpreted, misunderstood or misused.

(e) The research was well designed and the results were logically aimed at solving the problem but the necessary action was either **rejected** or unjustifiably deferred because it was untenable to key decision-takers. For example, the recommendation to withdraw from a particular customer communications strategy or campaign may be unacceptable to a marketing director who regards it as his creative innovation.

3.9 Marketing research makes use of a lot of data which is the result of asking people 'What do you think?', 'What would you do?', 'Would you buy?', even if the questions are not phrased quite so baldly. Are the answers received the 'right' ones? Not necessarily.

(a) Because questions tend to be **hypothetical**, respondents may be irresponsible and give an impulse response which they would reappraise and change given more time (hence the usefulness of postal questionnaires compared to on the spot interviews).

(b) Many people are **inherently conservative** when giving their opinion (especially about spending money), but may in fact be impulsive or innovative in practice.

(c) Conversely, **vanity** may make some people respond as innovators in a survey, on the basis of self-delusion, but in practice they may be very conservative when it comes to buying or using new-technology media.

(d) The **nature** of the interview or the **personality** of the interviewer may incline the respondent to give the answer he thinks the researcher wants to hear, rather than a genuine one. (People may understate the extent of their TV watching, or select the more respectable of the magazines they consume, for example.)

(e) **Insufficient information** and the artificiality of the context may result in misleading answers. (People may fail to recall a particular ad or direct mail package, for example, if it is inadequately described.)

3.10 The results of marketing research must always be seen as only one input in to the decision-making process.

> (Marketing research) ... helps to reduce the risks in business decisions, but will not make the decision. (Raymond Kent, *Marketing Research in Action*)

4 Sources of information   6/03, 12/03

4.1 As we saw above, **primary** sources of information are the most desirable, whatever the source: customers, consumers, supply chain partners or other businesses.

4.2 Here, we will look at **secondary** sources of information.

- **Existing data** generated and held by the organisation
- **Published information**, both general and industry specific
- Bought-in **market research reports**
- The Internet
- General **environmental scanning**

Internal data records

4.3 Information gathered in the course of operations and transactions may be relevant to marketing planning and control.

4.4 Such information often goes back several years, so that comparisons can be made and trends extrapolated.

Published information

4.5 We have seen that the **government** is a major source of economic, industrial and demographic information and data can also be obtained from sources such as specialist providers, professional institutions and research agencies.

4.6 While some government sources are general and others trade-, market- or profession-specific, bear in mind that general information may be applicable to your target market: keep an open mind for relevant data. Department of Transport budgets, for example, may be on the need-to-know list for car manufacturers.

Action Programme 3

Does your organisation, or individual department, have a library or libraries of published materials such as books, reference works, trade journals or newspapers? What titles are regularly stocked? How often is the information updated? How is the information categorised or indexed?

Bought-in reports

4.7 Much of the above published material is in the public domain. It is accessible and inexpensive to gather, but may need considerable analysis and processing in order to produce sufficiently targeted information for a specific organisation's needs. On the other hand, tailor-made information is only available by commissioning or undertaking primary research, which is a costly exercise.

4.8 A middle course may be to buy in reports prepared externally, whether as primary research for another organisation which is then syndicated, or as a commercial service to industry data users.

4.9 As we have seen there are a great many commercial sources of secondary data, and a number of guides to these sources are available.

4.10 There are commonly used sources of data on particular industries and markets such as Economist Intelligence Unit and Euronote publications.

Audits

4.11 Various audits generate published reports which can be bought by marketers.

Consumer panels or home audit panels

4.12 **Consumer panels** consist of a representative sample of consumers who have agreed to have their attitudes and buying habits monitored over a period of time. There are established panels for the purchase of groceries, consumer durables, cars, baby products and many others.

4.13 **Consumer panels** generate a vast amount of data which need to be sorted if they are to be digestible.

(a) Standard trend analysis shows how the market and its major brands have fared since the last analysis, grossed up to reflect the population.

(b) Special analyses depend on industrial preferences.

SPECIAL ANALYSES

Source of purchase · Frequency of purchase · Demographic · Tracking of individuals

Trade and retail audits

4.14 **Trade audits** are carried out among panels of wholesalers and retailers, and the term 'retail audits' refers to panels of retailers only. A research firm sends auditors to selected outlets at regular intervals to count stock and deliveries, thus enabling an estimate of throughput to be made. Sometimes it is possible to do a universal audit of all retail outlets. EPOS makes the process both easier and more universal.

4.15 The audits provide details of the following.

(a) **Retail sales**

For selected products and brands, sales by different type of retail outlet, market shares and brand shares.

(b) **Retail stocks**

Stocks of products and brands (enabling a firm subscribing to the audit to compare stocks of its own goods with those of competitors).

(c) **Selling prices**

The prices charged in retail outlets, including information about discounts.

 Marketing at Work

In the 1980s, Coca-Cola decided to change its flavour to compete with Pepsi. Market research, taster tests and so forth elicited favourable responses to the change, and so the new formulation was introduced. A small group of consumers vociferously opposed the change; and this opposition spread suddenly and rapidly like an epidemic, forcing Coca-Cola to re-introduce the old formula.

It was hard to detect the reasons for this, but if some consumers perceived Coke to symbolise 'American values', then changing the formula appeared to be an assault on them.

Consumers, who had initially favoured the product, turned against it, for reasons that could not be predicted by market researchers.

4.16 This case exemplifies three issues.

- The **limitations of planning** and organisational information gathering

- The unexpected **random behaviour** of the environment

- The way in which small causes (a few disaffected Coke-drinkers) can generate major consequences by feedback

The Internet

4.17 We have seen that the Internet can be a fast, efficient way to search for and access secondary data world-wide.

(a) Governments, educational institutions, libraries, commercial organisations and agencies have **home pages** on the **World Wide Web** which contain information and include links to other sites where information can be found. Well-designed sites typically have their own indexes and menus, as well as marked hypertext links that allow the browser to jump to related areas and topics.

(b) **Search engines** (such as Yahoo, Lycos, and Excite) maintain large databases of web pages, and can be used to locate relevant sites by word search.

(c) **Internet indexes** are another way of locating information on a particular subject: Yahoo is currently the biggest and most popular index available.

(d)   Gopher and WAIS (Wide Area Information Service) are also tools for searching through indexed materials and finding articles based on what they contain.

(e)   **Newsgroups** and mailing lists (for e-mail on selected topics of Internet) act as a kind of bulletin board service, where people post messages and articles on various topics.

4.18   It can be difficult conducting an efficient data search unless you know what you are doing. However, the Internet is friendly enough for you to be able to **browse** in areas of interest and follow links. As you discover relevant sources of information, you can add them to your favourites list to create a shortcut for regular reference.

General environmental scanning

4.19   Environmental scanning is simply the process of keeping your 'radar' switched on to what is going on in your market place. **Market intelligence** can be gleaned in many ways.

- Any newspaper, magazine, trade or academic journal
- Conferences, exhibitions, trade shows
- Personal contacts in the trade
- Personal experience and observation of the market

5   Evaluating and presenting information

5.1   All data collected should be **evaluated** using the following criteria.

(a)   Is the data **relevant** to the purpose for which it was collected?

(b)   Is it **up-to-date**?

(c)   Is it **reliable and accurate**?

(d)   Is the source of the data **credible** and objective, or unbiased? Look for the following.

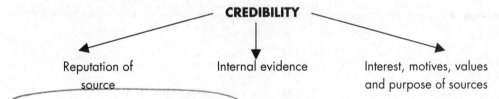

CREDIBILITY

Reputation of source   Internal evidence   Interest, motives, values and purpose of sources

(e)   Is the data subject to **confirmation**, or comparison with data from other sources? Are you prepared to risk basing decisions on uncorroborated data?

(f)   Is the data based on a large and representative statistical sample of the relevant population?

(g)   Has the data been gathered in a way that makes it **meaningful and reliable**? Has the same question been put to all respondents? Were all terms consistently defined? Did researchers lead or suggest 'right' answers? Were the respondents influenced by the researcher, or each other, or the desire to be nice?

(h)   Has the data collection and analysis been worthwhile? Has it fulfilled its purposes at a **reasonable cost** in money, time and effort?

Analysis and presentation of research findings

5.2 Quantitative research quite often presents raw data: lists or tables of numbers, or ticks in boxes. This data must be analysed in order to identify key features, trends, probabilities and averages.

5.3 Qualitative research also presents raw data in the form of records of words in narrative form. This data must be analysed in order to summarise, interpret, categorise and measure the frequency of responses, for presentation in quantitative or statistical form.

5.4 The **management information**, or **decision-support** information, resulting from data analysis must be formatted for **presentation** to the target user.

- Printed tables
- Charts
- Graphs
- Narrative reports
- Oral presentation with visual aids
- Interpretation and recommendations

6 Marketing databases

6.1 As well as using external databases, many organisations have developed their own databases. A marketing database can provide an organisation with much information about its customers and target groups. **Every purchase a customer makes has two functions**.

- Provision of **sales revenue**
- Provision of **information** as to future market opportunities

COMPREHENSIVE CUSTOMER DATABASE	
Contact	■ Names and addresses ■ Contact (telephone, fax, e-mail)
Professional	■ Company ■ Job title ■ Responsibilities
Personal	■ Age ■ Family details ■ Interests ■ Publications read
Transactions	■ Products/services ordered ■ How often ■ How much spent
Call/contact history	■ Sales/after-sales calls made ■ Complaints/queries ■ Meetings at shows/exhibitions
Credit payment history	■ Credit rating ■ Amounts outstanding ■ Aged debts
Credit transaction details	■ Items on order ■ Dates ■ Prices ■ Delivery arrangements

COMPREHENSIVE CUSTOMER DATABASE	
Special account details	■ Membership number ■ Loyalty or incentive points ■ Discounts awarded

6.2 The sources of information in a customer database and the uses to which this can be put are outlined in the diagram below.

(a) Customer service can indicate particular concerns of customers. For example, in a DIY store, if customers have to ask service staff where items are stored, the volume of complaints might indicate **poor signage** and **labelling**.

(b) Complaints also indicate **deficiencies in the product** or the fact that customer expectations have been poorly communicated.

(c) **Geodemographic information** relates to the **characteristics of people living** in different areas. Even simple post-code information can contain a lot of data about the customer.

(d) Other customer information can be gleaned by orders and enquiries that they place.

6.3 Information technology has been critical in the development of internal databases. It has created **new marketing techniques** and **new marketing channels**. **Database marketing** allows vast amounts of customer data to be stored cheaply and to be used to produce more accurate mailshots as well as other marketing tactics. This is important if a firm is able to gain an advantage over competitors by accessing and applying technologies that a competitor is unable to develop.

7 Information and communication technology and marketing information systems 12/03

7.1 Many marketing decisions are taken on a **continuous basis.** For example, decisions are taken at least annually on various aspects of the marketing mix, such as sales, advertising and sales promotion. Management need information to take such decisions. A continuous source of information is also required for control purposes. A **marketing information system (MkIS)** meets these needs. A diagrammatic representation of an MkIS is shown at the end of section 7.

Key Concept

A **marketing intelligence system** is a set of procedures and sources used by managers to obtain everyday information about pertinent developments in the marketing environment.

7.2 The MkIS comprises all computer and non-computer systems which can help the marketer. As a result an MkIS is often built up from several different systems which may not be directly related to marketing, and will contain

(a) The **internal reports (and accounts) database** which provides: results data, measures of current performance and sales, costs and stock information. An improvement in the timeliness, availability and distribution of reports improves the internal report system.

(b) The **marketing intelligence system** provides happenings data (what competitors are doing) and information on developments in the environment. It also scans and disseminates a wide range of intelligence.

7.3 Data collected needs to produce **coherent information**.

(a) The system must allow for the easy and effective **storage and retrieval** of data.

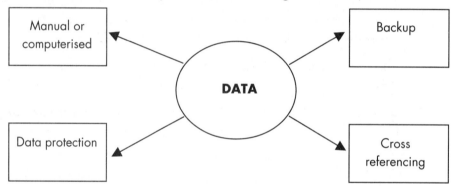

(b) Irrelevant data must be eliminated.

(c) **Dissemination of information** considerations include who should receive information and how to distribute information regularly (through newsletters).

7.4 Cost and organisational implications of MkIS

(a) **Training** of existing and new staff will be necessary.

(b) Staff with **specialist skills** might have to be recruited and so job descriptions and specifications might need to change.

(c) Organisational considerations might include the **reallocation of duties**.

7.5 Design of MkIS

(a) Users should **understand** the systems and be in a position to evaluate and control them.

(b) The system must be regularly **reviewed** and feedback improved.

(c) The true meaning of the information provided must be clarified.

(d) The MkIS must be **flexible**.

(e) A system is only as effective as designers and users make it.

The features of an effective MkIS

7.6 As an example of an MkIS in action, let us visualise a company which has identified **quality service** as a strategic priority. To meet this goal, the MkIS must do the following.

(a) Provide managers with **real time** information on how customers and staff **perceive the service** being given, on the assumption that **what is not measured can't be managed**.

(b) Measure quality of both service and customer care so as to provide evidence that they do matter, the implication being that **what is seen to be measured gets done**.

(c) Monitor how (if at all) the **customer base is changing**.

(d) Perhaps provide a basis on which bonus payments can be determined, on the grounds that **what gets paid for gets done even better**.

7.7 Data and information about customer service may be gathered in many ways but overall **systems design criteria** are important.

(a) **Management's access to the information must be easy and direct**, ideally via PC or networked terminal.

(b) **The cost of data/information gathering should be minimal**.

(c) **Data gathering should be low intensity**. In other words, it should not cause excessive inconvenience to respondents or other information sources. Preferably the data will be gathered without customers being aware of it.

(d) Data gathering should be regular and continuous since a small amount of data gathered regularly can build a considerable database. Regular data gathering produces more reliable results because it reduces the likelihood of sample bias of one kind or another.

Components of a computerised MkIS

7.8 A typical computerised MkIS could be described as having four components.

(a) A **data bank** will store raw marketing data, such as data about historical sales and data from market research findings.

(b) A **statistical bank** will store programs for carrying out computations for sales forecasts, making advertising spending projections, calculating sales force productivity and so on.

(c) A **model bank** will store marketing models for planning and analysis.

(d) A **display unit** (VDU screen and keyboard) will allow the marketing manager to communicate with an MkIS. Alternatively, marketing reports can be printed out in hard copy form.

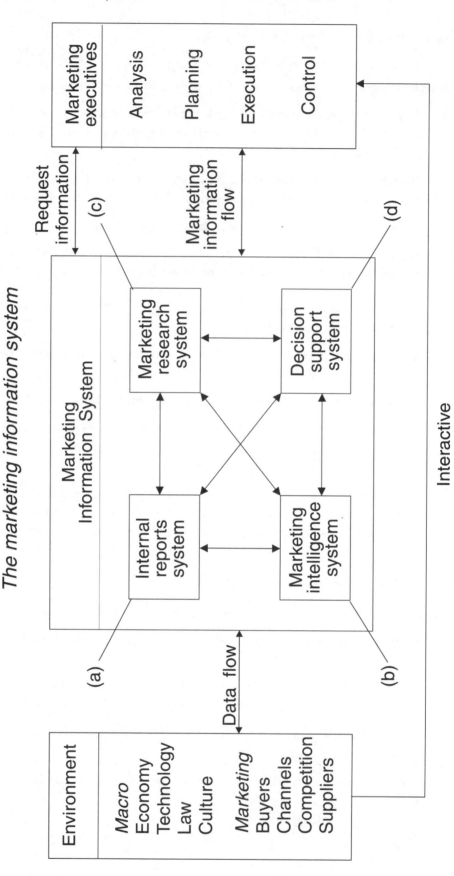

The marketing information system

Chapter Roundup

- **Information** (measurement, facts and data, analysis) is required for rational decision making, particularly for marketing, which requires a detailed, realistic understanding of the customer's needs and wants, the marketing mix and the marketing environment.

- Decisions must be made with **partial information**, to avoid analysis paralysis, and must sometimes allow for non-rational influences, particularly when innovation is required.

- **Marketing research** can operate across the extended marketing mix and the marketing environment.

- Data may be **qualitative** (psychographic) and/or **quantitative** (statistical, demographic) and derived from primary and/or secondary sources.

- Secondary sources of information include:

  - internal data records
  - published information
  - bought-in reports
  - the Internet and intranets
  - general environmental scanning

  All these sources are available internationally.

- Data must be evaluated for:

  - relevance
  - up-to-dateness
  - accuracy
  - the credibility and objectivity of the source
  - corroboration/confirmation
  - correct methodology in sampling and data collection
  - cost-effectiveness

- Data must be analysed and presented as information, accessible and relevant to the needs of the intended user.

- Information communications technology has had a major impact upon the development of data bases and marketing intelligence systems.

Quick Quiz

1   Define marketing research.

2   Descriptive research measures and estimates the frequency with which things occur, and the degree to which variables are correlated.

True ☐

False ☐

3   What is the difference between quantitative and qualitative research?

4   Fill in the blank.

....................consist of a representative sample of consumers who have agreed to have their attitude and buying habits monitored over a period of time.

5   Give four examples of ways that data can be presented to users.

6   What two functions do purchases by customers have?

7   Define a marketing intelligence system.

8   Which of the following types of research would not be relevant to marketing decisions?

A   Product
B   Promotion
C   Delivery
D   Distribution

Action Programme Review

1   If you think this is a frivolous exercise, consider that:

■   These three principles are the key to all the marketing activities discussed in this Study Text, and a useful checklist for effective action

■   The presentation of information is an important marketing skill in itself

2   (a)   Quantitative data on sales volume comparing region-on-region and year-on-year to establish amount (units, value, %) and rate of decline. Qualitative data on why consumers are less happy with the product.

(b)   Quantitative data on volume of sales in comparable times/markets during night hours, percentage support among sample groups. Qualitative data about people's attitudes to night shopping, possible fears (related to area?).

(c)   Quantitative data on audience figures at scheduled times, demographics of audience, cost of advertising. Qualitative data on audience response to the ad.

3   This is important information for any workplace research you may have to do – not least, for assessment of your skills in this area of the syllabus!

Answers to Quick Quiz

1   The systematic gathering, recording and analysing of data about problems relating to the marketing of goods and services.

2   True.

3   Quantitative research gathers numerically measurable data, qualitative research focuses on values, attitudes, options, beliefs and motivations.

4   Consumer panels.

5   Any four of:

- Printed tables
- Charts
- Graphs
- Narrative reports
- Oral presentations
- Interpretation and recommendations

6
- Provisions of sales revenue
- Provision of information on future market opportunities

7   A set of procedures and sources used by managers to obtain everyday information about pertinent developments in the marketing environment.

8   C   Delivery

Now try illustrative questions 26 and 27 at the end of the Study Text

Information systems and change

16

Chapter Topic List
1   Setting the scene
2   Scenarios and forecasting
3   Marketing audits
4   Using SWOT analysis
5   Impact analysis
6   The product life cycle

Learning Outcomes

☑   Appreciate the approaches available to cope with environmental change

☑   Undertake an environmental audit for an organisation and assess the probable impact of significant opportunities and threats

Syllabus Reference

☑   Explain the techniques available for forecasting future demand and coping with the challenges of environmental change

Key Concepts Introduced

- Scenario building
- Marketing audit
- SWOT analysis
- Impact analysis
- Product life cycle

1 Setting the scene

1.1 We end the main body of this Study Text by considering how organisations can use the information available to forecast future demand and changes.

1.2 We firstly consider scenario building and forecasting. **Scenarios** take account of a variety of future factors, and essentially are designed to provide a guide on what might influence business developments. **Forecasts** by contrast are designed to come up with a quantified answer which is generally meant to indicate a particular course of action.

1.3 We then consider how an organisation might go about auditing its environment, objectives and activities in order to improve its own performance.

1.4 In section 4 of the chapter we discuss analysing an organisation and its environment in terms of its own **strengths** and **weaknesses**, and the **threats** and **opportunities** it faces.

1.5 In section 5 we briefly consider **impact analysis**, how major changes might affect an industry, an organisation and an organisation's strategy.

1.6 A useful technique that can be applied to individual products is **product life cycle analysis**, discussed in section 6. This technique attempts to recognise stages in a product's sales history, and how these can be related to the management of the product.

2 Scenarios and forecasting   Specimen paper, 6/03

Scenarios

2.1 Michael Porter tries to analyse how firms choose **competitive strategy** when faced with future uncertainties. Porter believes that all firms face uncertainty, but 'uncertainty is not often addressed very well in competitive strategy'. A problem with forecasting is that many managers underestimate the probability of rapid or discontinuous change.

Scenario building

Key Concept

Scenario building is the process of identifying alternative futures, ie constructing a number of distinct possible futures permitting deductions to be made about future developments of markets, products and technology.

2.2 Scenarios are used in several situations.

(a) **Contingency plans**

These can cope with the arrival of threats or opportunities which, although they may arise at any time, are of indeterminable probability. For example, a chemicals company may develop a scenario of a major spillage at one of its plants and then set up emergency routines to cope with it. They cannot assess how likely the spillage is to occur in actual practice.

(b) **As a prediction technique**

Step 1. A series of alternative pictures of a future operating environment is developed which are consistent with current trends and consistent within themselves.

Step 2. The impact of each different scenario upon the business is assessed and specific strengths and weaknesses highlighted.

Step 3. Contingency plans are drawn up to implement in the event of a given scenario coming true, or to implement now to give protection against the scenario.

Industry scenarios

2.3 Porter believes that the most appropriate use for scenario analysis is if it is restricted to an industry. An **industry scenario** is an internally consistent view of an industry's future structure. It is not a forecast, but a possibility. A set of industry scenarios is selected to reflect a range of possible futures. The **entire range**, not the most likely 'future', is used to design a competitive strategy. The process is as follows.

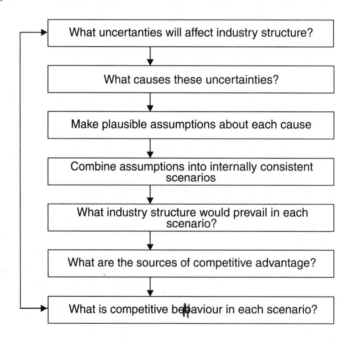

2.4 This is not a simple process in practice, despite appearances.

(a) **Identification of uncertainties**

Identifying **uncertainties** in the industry's future is hard, as those uncertainties may be caused by the prospect of discontinuous change. Uncertainties hardest to anticipate are those originating outside the industry (eg microelectronics).

(b) **Independent uncertainties**

Independent uncertainties do not derive from other uncertainties in the scenario. Scenarios should only be constructed on the basis of independent uncertainties. For example, an industry might be vulnerable to both global warming and a change of government. These uncertainties are independent of each other.

(c) **Causes**

[handwritten: as now the price of petrol is high an uncertainty would be the use of public transport and the price of petrol would be the source]

Identifying the **causal factors** is necessary to determine the source of uncertainties. For example, if an uncertainty is motor transport usage (and hence, say, the demand for tyres) a causal factor might be the price of petrol.

(d) **Interrelation of elements**

A scenario depends on a **logical view** as to how the various elements of the industry structure inter-relate.

2.5 Scenarios based on normal managerial assumptions are useful. Assumptions should be consistent with each other.

2.6 An analysis of the scenario involves:

Step 1. Determining the future industry structure

Step 2. Developing the implications of the scenario for industry attractiveness

Step 3. Identifying implications for competitive advantage

2.7 The future industry structures identified in each scenario will have an impact on the competition in different ways. Some scenarios will highlight the probability of **price competition** and **downward pressure on prices**. Some competitors will be better than others to cope with price competition.

2.8 How can scenarios be used to formulate competitive strategy? In other words, what are the implications of each scenario?

■ A strategy built in response to only **one** scenario is risky, whereas one supposed to cope with them all might be expensive, and might result in contradictory measures.

■ Approaches to choosing scenarios as a basis for decisions about competitive strategy are as follows.

SELECTING WHICH SCENARIOS SHOULD BE BASIS OF STRATEGY	
Assume the most probable	This puts a lot of faith in scenario building process; if less probable scenario occurs, consequences may be serious
Hope for the best	Strategy is based on scenario most attractive to the firm; likely to involve wishful thinking
Hedge	Choose strategy that produces satisfactory, though not optimal results
Play wait and see	Follow others' strategies. Prudent, but sacrifices first move advantages
Influence the future	Influence demand for related products and other variables that could mean favoured scenario is more likely to occur

Macro scenarios

2.9 **Macro scenarios** use macro economic or political factors, creating alternative views of the future environment (eg global economic growth, political changes, interest rates). Macro scenarios developed because the activities of oil and resource companies (which are global and at one time were heavily influenced by political factors) needed techniques to deal with such uncertainties.

Marketing at Work

Shell Corporation is a famous user of scenarios. Among short-term scenarios to be used as the basis of immediate contingency plans are:

(a) Nuclear destruction of the Gulf states

(b) Major tanker spillage

It is with these in mind that Shell has developed oil reserves in the USA and North Sea and has a spillage containment task force on perpetual standby.

Forecasting

2.10 Examples of forecasting techniques, where the past is a relatively good guide to the future and where movement in the environmental variables is slow, are as follows.

(a) **Moving averages**

This technique removes fluctuations by averaging the results of a fixed number of periods, to eliminate seasonal variations.

(b) **Time series analysis**

In this case, data for a number of months/years are obtained, and compared. The aim of time series analysis is to identify seasonal and other cyclical fluctuations and the long-term underlying trends.

An example of the use of this approach is the UK's monthly unemployment statistics which show a **headline figure** and the **underlying trend**.

(c) **Regression analysis**

This is a quantitative technique to check any underlying correlations between two variables (eg sales of ice cream and the weather). One of these variables (eg ice-cream sales) is dependent on the other (eg the weather).

(d) **Exponential smoothing**

By this method, a new forecast for the next period's results is obtained by the following formula.

New forecast = old forecast + $\propto$ (most recent observation – old forecast)

where $\propto$ is the smoothing factor or smoothing constant. $\propto$ will be in the range 0 to 1, but its actual value is chosen subjectively depending on which value would have been most suitable in the past.

[handwritten margin note: refers to former condition / earlier behaviour — more]

(e) **Econometrics**

This discipline is the study of economic variables and their inter-relationships, using computer models. Short-term or medium-term econometric models might be used for forecasting. This method of forecasting depends on the firm's ability to identify key 'indicators' of change, in advance of the change actually occurring and the ability to predict the span of time between a change in the indicator and a change in market demand.

(f) **Technological forecasting**

Forecasting technological changes is problematic. Discontinuous change is hard to predict, and some technological developments are hard to predict.

2.11 Quite often the data available will be scarce. In this situation a variety of judgemental, or qualities forecasting methods can be used.

Expert opinion

2.12 These techniques involve the selection of key knowledgeable people or industry players who are interviewed and asked to assign probabilities to possible future outcomes. The experts might include people such as dealers, distributors, suppliers, marketing consultants and trade associations.

Delphi method

Specimen paper, 12/03

2.13 The Delphi method is the most refined version of expert opinion; it can be used if there is little historical data on which to base a forecast or if results are unstable and/or uncertain. A **group of experts** are asked individually to provide their views on what will happen in the future.

(a) To begin with, each expert gives an **independent opinion**.

(b) The opinions of each expert are collated. Extreme views are discarded, and a draft **consensus** view is formulated.

(c) The draft consensus is circulated to the experts for their **further comments**, and depending on how they respond, the consensus might be amended.

(d) The process will continue until a forecast for the future has been prepared which has the acceptance of all or most of the panel of experts.

(e) When there is some uncertainty among the experts, **probability weightings** might be given to different possible future scenarios or events.

Executive judgement

2.14 This method of forecasting is based on the **intuition** of one or more executives. The approach is very unscientific but it has the advantages of being quick and inexpensive and it can work well if demand for the product is relatively stable and the executive in question has years of appropriate experience. Intuition is swayed heavily by recent experience, however, and so the forecast may be overly **optimistic** or **pessimistic**.

Marketing research

2.15 Marketing research methods include opinion surveys, analyses of market data, and questionnaires designed to gauge the reaction of the market to a product, a price and so on (all qualitative forecasting techniques). Marketing research is often very accurate in the short term but longer-term forecasts based on surveys may not be accurate because people's attitudes and opinions change.

Historical analogy

2.16 When past data is not available, data on **similar products** can be analysed to establish the life cycle and expected sales of a new product. Obviously care is needed in using analogies which relate to different products in different time periods but such techniques can be useful in forming a broad impression for the medium to long term.

Cross-impact analysis

2.17 **Key trends** are identified as those having high importance or high probability of occurring. The question is then asked 'If event A occurs, what will the impact be upon other trends?' The results are used to build sets of domino chains with one event triggering other events. In other words, cross-impacts are taken into account.

Multiple futures

2.18 Researchers build pictures of **alternative futures**, each one of which is internally consistent and has a certain probability of occurring. The major purpose of building alternative futures in this way is to stimulate management into thinking about and planning for **contingencies**.

Decision/hazard forecasting

2.19 Researchers identify **major events** taking place in the environment which could impact upon the organisation. Each event is rated for its convergence with several major trends taking place in society and for its appeal to major publics in society. The higher the event's convergence and appeal, the higher the probability of it taking place. The critical events identified in this way are then researched further.

The problems of forecasting

2.20 Human society is inherently complex; the world economy arises out of the interactions and activities of six billion individuals. It is hard enough to predict the weather. Meteorologists have to employ the most sophisticated computer systems to develop a viable simulation of the world's climate systems. It is not surprising that forecasts for human social and economic activity are always tentative and shaky. Often, the longer the time span, the greater the uncertainty in forecasting.

2.21 There are a number of problems involved in forecasting technological and social trends. Some of these problems arise from a misapplication of forecasting techniques; others arise from inherent uncertainties in the forecasting process. We discuss some of them below.

2.22 The danger of regression analysis is that the relationship between two variables may only hold in a **certain range of values**. Take the example of temperature and ice cream. You would expect ice cream consumption to rise as the temperature becomes hotter, but:

(a)   There is a maximum number of ice creams an individual can consume in a day, no matter how hot it is.

(b)   If you continue raising the temperature, people will not be able to buy any ice creams at all, as they will have died from the heat.

(c)   There may be other factors determining ice cream consumption (eg the availability of substitute products such as cold drinks).

2.23 Another possible problem with forecasting is that forecasters may **underestimate the impact** of certain factors on forecast variables. A good example is provided by **traffic projections** for the UK. It is well known that London's orbital motorway, the M25, was designed to take far fewer cars a day than currently use it; hence the constant traffic jams, and the controversial plans for widening it. Why might the forecasts have been so wrong?

(a)   **Effect of many colours**

Planners may have underestimated the extent to which increased **economic growth** would lead to increased car ownership and usage.

(b)   **Local traffic**

Planners may have underestimated the extent to which the M25 would be used for purely **local or short distance traffic**. It is used as a conduit between various areas in London's periphery, as well as a means for longer distance traffic to avoid going through London.

(c)   **Feedback**

Critics of the government's road building schemes assert that the model is flawed in a more serious respect, in that it fails to take account of **feedback**. In other words, they say that building roads to avoid congestion is self-defeating, as roads generate more traffic: businesses relocate; people use their cars when they would otherwise have gone by train; more and longer journeys are made possible. This congestion leads to more road building which leads to more traffic usage which leads to more congestion: a sort of vicious spiral.

2.24 The underlying message therefore is that the models on which forecasts are based **over-simplify** the behaviour which they are supposed to represent.

Forecasting and chaos theory

2.25 This brings us on to a further problem, which identifies the limitations of trend analysis. This is the concept of non-linearity, evident in **chaos theory**.

> Due to the instability of the marketing world, some action will have a dramatic effect well outside the limits of its 'objective' power, while other major initiatives will go largely unnoticed. We have all heard the announcements of major technological breakthroughs (remember, for instance, the rotating cylinder engine used by NSU, once hailed as a major innovation?) with no reasonable short- or medium-term commercial results. On the other hand, there are many examples of a minor adjustment to a specific product creating great success, or a chance meeting setting off a chain of events leading to major commercial effects.'
>
> Torsten Nilson (Chaos Marketing, 1995)

BPP PROFESSIONAL EDUCATION

Marketing at Work

An example of a successful minor change is the chance encounter between Lord Cohen, then head of Tesco, and a young salesman, Ian McLaurin, in the bar of a Hertfordshire hotel in the 1970s. As a result of this meeting, Cohen recruited McLaurin for a trial six months.

Eventually McLaurin became a director of Tesco and was instrumental in the abandonment of Green Shield trading stamps, to say nothing of the transformation of Tesco from a down-market retailer into a giant which has overtaken Sainsbury in terms of both sales and profitability.

2.26 The implications of chaos theory are as follows.

(a)   Certain outcomes are very sensitive to **initial conditions**. This is difficult to demonstrate simply, except to say that a series of major events (say, World War I) may have a very small and seemingly insignificant beginning (the death of a single man in Serbia).

(b)   **Very complex phenomena** can be produced by the **interaction of simple factors**, but it is not always possible to predict at any one time how these phenomena will interact.

2.27 Chaos theory is being applied to a number of different disciplines, including stock market prices, and annual population patterns. It is better at interpreting past data than predicting the future.

Problems of macro forecasting

2.28 Given the difficulties of forecasting relatively discrete and simple matters such as ice cream consumption or traffic flows, it is surely much harder to forecast, over any period of time, wider social trends, that is the development of the macro environment. The reasons are similar, however.

- A **trend** might be **extrapolated beyond** the **range** where it is appropriate.

- Forecasters **underestimate** the **complexity** of the system they are modelling.

- Very minor events can have **serious long-term consequences**. Nobody at IBM predicted that the personal computer would eventually threaten the mainframe business.

- Some modellers may assume that a **possible** outcome of a system is a **certain** outcome.

- **Action taken** as a result of a forecast can **increase** the **likelihood** of an event happening. During the Cold War, both sides assumed the **other** was belligerent, and that any conflict would result in the worst possible outcome, and they planned for it accordingly.

- Forecasters may be **politically motivated** or wish to promote certain causes.

Scenarios and forecasts compared

2.29 The table below summarises the main differences between scenarios and forecasts.

	Scenarios	Forecasts
Nature	Possibility	Prediction
Consists of	List of qualitative factors	Quantified most likely outcome based on certain assumptions
Limitations	Individual scenarios are not a complete view of all that might happen	Assumptions made may be incorrect/too strong & may take insufficient notice of uncertainties
Use in decision-making	Information to help decision between various courses of action	Indicator of likely success of particular course of action

2.30 Scenarios are meant to help management decision-making but judgement in interpreting the scenarios will still be required. Forecasts by contrast are generally designed to indicate what the decision should be.

3 Marketing audits   Specimen paper

Key Concept

'A **marketing audit** is a **comprehensive, systematic, independent and periodic** examination of a company's - or business unit's - marketing environment, objectives, strategies and activities with a view of determining problem areas and opportunities and recommending a plan of action to improve the company's marketing performance.'

(Kotler, Gregor and Rodgers, 1977)

3.1 A marketing audit does not exist in the compulsory formal sense that an external financial audit does. For proper strategic control, however, a marketing audit should have the following features.

(a) It should be conducted **regularly**, for example once a year.

(b) It should take a **comprehensive** look at every aspect of every market and ingredient in the marketing mix. It should not be restricted to areas of apparent ineffectiveness (for example, an unprofitable product, a troublesome distribution channel, low efficiency on direct selling).

(c) It should be carried out according to a set of predetermined, specified procedures, that is it should be **systematic**.

The audit procedure

3.2 A marketing environment audit should consider the following areas.

Micro environment	
Suppliers	The availability of resources, selling policies
Distribution	The main distribution channels and their efficiency levels and potential for growth
Markets	Developments in major markets, market growth, and changes in turnover and profits. Performance of different market segments.
Customers	Customer views on price, product quality and service given by organisation and its competitors. Decision processes of different types of customer.
Competitors	Objectives and strategies, market share, and strengths and weaknesses. Developments in future competition (see also Chapter 7, section 6).
Stakeholders/ publics	The groups that are of particular importance, and how they have been dealt with
Political/legal	Impact of new laws. Other developments in central and local government affecting laws and regulations in key areas, for example advertising, competition and price control.
Micro environment	
Economic	Impact of current economic trends, particularly affecting factors influencing demand, and organisation's response.
Social/cultural	Impact of current demographic changes and action taken in response to these. Current public attitudes towards business/industry. Changes in values and lifestyle of consumers.
Technology	Current changes in technology, and whether or not organisation is at forefront of technological changes. Impact of changes, including decreases in production costs or development of substitute goods.

3.3 A marketing environment audit should be linked in with other aspects of a marketing audit.

(a) **Marketing strategy audit**

What are the organisation's **marketing objectives** and how do they relate to overall objectives? Are they reasonable?

Are enough (or too many) **resources** being committed to marketing to enable the objectives to be achieved? is the division of costs between products, areas etc satisfactory?

(b) **Marketing systems**

What are the procedures for formulating marketing plans and management control of these plans? Are they satisfactory?

(c) **Marketing organisation audit**

Does the organisation have the structural capability to implement the plan?

(d) **Marketing functions**

A review of the effectiveness of each element of the mix (eg advertising and sales promotion activities) should be carried out.

REVIEW

Sales and price levels	**Products**	**Distribution system**
Supply and demand	Each product	New channels
Customer attitude	Product mix	New delivery arrangements
Price reductions		

(e) **Marketing productivity**

How profitable and cost effective is the marketing programme?

4 Using SWOT analysis   Specimen paper

4.1 One of the most useful tools for sorting and analysing information is a SWOT analysis.

Key Concept

SWOT stands for **strengths, weaknesses, opportunities** and **threats**.

4.2 SWOT analysis is a management tool which can be used in a wide variety of situations. **Its value is as a technique to help you sort information** and it does not, in itself, provide ready made answers.

(a) **Strengths and weaknesses**

Strengths and weaknesses analysis involves looking at the particular strengths and weaknesses of the organisation itself and its product/service range.

(b) **Opportunities and threats**

An analysis of **opportunities and threats** is concerned with profit-making opportunities in the business environment, and with identifiable threats, for example falling demand, new competition, government legislation etc.

4.3 This simple technique provides a method of organising information in identifying possible strategic direction. The basic principle is that an organisation or its environment can be described in terms of features, each described as either a strength, weakness, opportunity or threat.

Action Programme 1

Explain to someone who does not work in commerce what strengths, weaknesses, opportunities and threats are.

4.4 This information is presented as a matrix of strengths, weaknesses, opportunities and threats. Effective SWOT analysis does not simply require a categorisation of information, but also requires some **evaluation** of the **relative importance** of the various factors.

(a) **Significance to customers**

The most important features are those **perceived as significant by consumers**. Listing corporate features that internal personnel regard as strengths or weaknesses is of little relevance if they are not perceived as such by the business's consumers.

(b) **Independence of factors**

Threats and opportunities are conditions presented by the external environment and they should be **independent** of the business.

(c) **Production possibilities**

The organisation has also to take into account its **production possibilities**, its ability to exploit the opportunities indicated by the analysis, and the likely **returns** and the **risks** (such as the impact of competition) involved in the possible courses of action. Sophisticated analysis uses measures such as expected value.

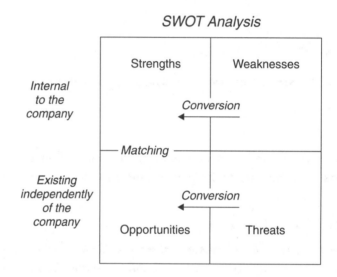

SWOT Analysis

4.5 SWOT analysis is often presented using a cruciform chart, as in the diagram above. This involves a tabular listing of the significant strengths, weaknesses, opportunities and threats to present the conclusions of the analysis. In the example below, the development of a single, simple potential strategy from the analysis is illustrated.

Strengths	Weaknesses
£10 million of capital available Production expertise and appropriate marketing skills	Heavy reliance on a small number of customers Limited product range, with no new products and expected market decline Small marketing organisation
Threats Major competitor has already entered the new market	**Opportunities** Government tax incentives for new investment Growing demand in a new market, although customers so far relatively small in number

4.6 Here, the company appears to face the danger of losing its existing markets and must diversify its products and markets. The new market opportunity exists to be exploited. Since the number of customers is currently few, the relatively small size of the existing marketing force would not be an immediate hindrance. A strategic plan could be developed to buy new equipment and to use existing production and marketing to enter the new market, with a view to rapid expansion.

4.7 In this example, a strategy emerges readily from our simplified cruciform chart. Reality is, of course, likely to be much less clear-cut. In practice, a combination of individual strategies and a complete analysis and evaluation of all the alternatives would be required.

Analysis of an organisation's internal capabilities

4.8 **Strengths** and **weaknesses analysis** is internal to the company and is intended to shape its approach to the external world. For instance, the identification of shortcomings in skills or resources could lead to a planned acquisition programme or staff recruitment and training. First, the strengths and weaknesses analysis involves looking at the findings of the position audit.

4.9 The appraisal should give particular attention to the following.

(a) **A study of past accounts and the use of ratios**

By looking at **trends**, or by comparing ratios (if possible) with those of other firms in a similar industry, analysts can identify strengths and weaknesses in major areas of the business. This is a key area of strengths and weaknesses analysis, and here, financial data and techniques of assessment provide hard data for decision making.

(b) **Product position and product-market mix**

(c) **Cash and financial structure**

If a company intends to expand or diversify, it will need cash or sufficient financial standing in order to acquire subsidiaries or for investing in new capacity.

(d) **Cost structure**

If a company operates with high fixed costs and relatively low variable costs, it might be in a relatively weak position with regards to production capacity. High volumes of production and sale might be required to break even. In contrast, a company with low fixed costs might be more flexible and adaptable so that it should be able to operate at a lower breakeven point.

(e) **Managerial ability**

While objective data should be used, the danger is that management may well overestimate their own ability or be unable to form a useful evaluation.

4.10 Typically, the analysis would use information from the following areas of company activity.

Marketing	Success rate of new product launches
	Advertising: evaluating advertising strategies and individual campaigns
	Market shares and sizes: is the organisation in a strong or weak position?
	Portfolio of business units: new, growth, mature and declining markets
	Sales force organisation and performance
	Service quality
	Customer care strategies: nature of markets targeted
Products	Sales by market, area, product groups, outlets etc
	Margins and contributions to profits from individual products
	Product quality
	Product portfolio: age and structure of markets
	Price elasticity of demand for products

Distribution	Delivery service standards - lead times for competitors and products
	Warehouse delivery fleet capacity
	Geographical availability of products
Research and development (R&D)	R & D projects in relation to marketing plans
	Expenditure on R & D relative to available assets
	Evaluation of R & D in new products/variations on existing products
	Appropriateness of R & D workload/schedules to competitor activity
Finance	Availability of short-term and long-term funds, cash flow
	Contribution of each product to cash flow
	Returns on investment from individual products
	Accounting ratios to identify areas of strength or weakness in performance
Plant and equipment and other facilities. Production	Age, value, production capacity and suitability of plant and equipment
	Valuation of all assets
Management and staff	Age profile, skills and attitudes
	State of industrial relations, morale and labour turnover
	Training and recruitment facilities
	Manpower utilisation
	Management team strengths and weaknesses
Business management: organisation	Organisation structure in relation to the organisation's needs
	Appropriateness of management style and philosophy
	Communication and information systems
Raw material and finished goods stocks	The sources and security of supply
	Number and description of items
	Turnover periods
	Storage capacity
	Obsolescence and deterioration
	Pilfering, wastage

4.11 When the analysis has been carried out, the following type of report might be produced.

Strengths

(a) Marketing, products and markets
   (i) Products A, B and C are market leaders
   (ii) Product D, new product launch, high profit potential
   (iii) Good brand images
   (iv) Good relations with suppliers and dealers
   (v) Good packaging and advertising appeal

(b) Production
   (i) New factory in North West, fully operational for next year
   (ii) Thorough quality inspection standards

(c) Finance
   (i) £0.5 million cash available from internal resources
   (ii) Further £2.0 million overdraft facility, so far unused

(d)   Management and staff

    (i)   High skills in marketing areas of packaging, sales promotion, advertising and sales generally

    (ii)   Good labour relations, except at one plant which has low productivity

Weaknesses

(a)   Marketing

    (i)   Products X, Y and Z contribute no profit

    (ii)   Products P, Q and R are declining and will lose profitability in three years

    (iii)   Sales of product D are dependent upon a high level of sales of complementary products (for example, razor blades and razors)

    (iv)   No new products, except for D, have been successfully launched in the last two years

(b)   Research and development

    (i)   No major new products have been derived from R & D for two years. Becoming too dependent on acquisition for additions to product range

    (ii)   Little control over R & D budget

(c)   Production

    (i)   Plant at most factories has an average age of 8.7 years

    (ii)   New developments could threaten ability to compete

    (iii)   High level of spoiled goods on lines 3, 7, 9 at one location

    (iv)   Low productivity on all lines at one plant

(d)   Management and staff

    (i)   Poor labour relations at plant with low productivity

    (ii)   Senior executives approaching retirement with no clearly recognisable successor

    (iii)   Success of the organisation too dependent on senior executive charisma

Analysis of an organisation's marketing environment

4.12 The internal appraisal highlights areas within the company which are strong and which might therefore be exploited more fully, and weaknesses where some 'defensive' planning might be required to protect the company from poor results. Following the position audit and the environmental analysis, external appraisal aims to identify profit-making **opportunities** which can be exploited using the company's strengths. Analysis would also anticipate environmental **threats** (a declining economy, competitors' actions, government legislation, industrial unrest etc) against which the company must protect itself.

4.13 This is the opportunities and threats part of SWOT analysis.

4.14 Threats involve the following issues.

■   **Threats** to the **company** or its **business environment**

BPP)))
PROFESSIONAL EDUCATION

- **Competitors' position** in relation to these threats
- The company's **capacity to resist threats**, corrective action, contingency strategies

4.15 The environment in which opportunities and threats may arise can be divided into two elements. **Macroenvironmental factors**, which cannot be controlled in the short term, are the factors we have discussed in previous chapters.

Action Programme 2

Can you think of examples of political, economic, social and technological factors which might offer opportunities or be a source of threats?

Competitors

4.16 **Competitor activity**, which is the main microenvironmental factor, is also vitally important. Michael Porter suggests that analysis of competitors should involve the following.

4.17 Future competitors' strategies must be anticipated. It is especially important to identify competitors' weaknesses in export markets, or where foreign competitors might penetrate home markets.

Exam Tip

The Specimen Paper gave an indication of the level of detail you may face in questions on this area, asking about the threats and pressures posed to the travel industry by technological change and competitive uncertainty.

ENVIRONMENT ANALYSIS REPORT

Opportunities

(a) Political

    (i) Deregulation of the distribution market in the UK has allowed competitors to enter the marketplace, previously the domain of the state-owned monopoly supplier. This increases our range of potential customers in the UK and makes us less dependent on exports.

    (ii) Removal of EU trade barriers has increased the size of the marketplace.

    (iii) Expansion into Eastern Europe will enable access into new markets.

(b) Economic

    (i) Relatively weak state of sterling is helping exports.

    (ii) UK economy coming out of recession, so customer confidence ('feel-good factor') improving.

(c) Social

    (i) We have an excellent 'green' image already and can capitalise on this. Our reliance on US markets has contributed to our being well ahead in this area.

    (ii) We are well thought of as a 'local' employer through our attention to social responsibility issues.

(d) Technological issues

    (i) Our new marketing database will allow good targeting of customers, especially as new companies set up following deregulation.

    (ii) UK/US standards are being adopted in Asian markets, so we can compete there with existing products.

(e) Competition

    (i) Our reputation as a key supplier of the former state-owned monopoly gives us a head start against new start-up competitors.

Threats

(a) Political

    (i) Lack of agreement on standardisation across Europe means that French/German derived standard may be adopted in preference to ours (UK/US agreed).

    (ii) 'Black market' in certain Eastern European states needs to be overcome in some way, given our ethical stance.

    (iii) Uncertainty in run up to UK general election will affect the development of the sector in the UK.

(b) Economic

    (i) Any strengthening of sterling resulting from improvement of UK economic position will make exports less attractive on price alone.

    (ii) Increased competition from suppliers based on Pacific Rim makes it difficult for us to compete there and in the US on price.

(c) Social

    (i) Increased focus on health and safety from EU is increasing cost of compliance and related overheads.

    (ii) Cost of maintaining 'green image', important in UK and US, will damage our potential in Eastern Europe where some competitors (and customers) are unconcerned with such issues.

(d) Technological

    (i) Our main competitors control their distribution process more fully than we do in this area, as they have invested in new computer systems.

(e) Competition

    (i) The two competitors to the former state-owned monopoly which were awarded licences first have merged, thereby pooling their R&D resource. There are suggestions that they will develop or buy their own manufacturing operation rather than buy from companies like us.

Action Programme 3

For an organisation of your choice, identify from its annual accounts, press coverage and relevant websites the main opportunities and threats that it has faced over the last few years. Consider also whether the information suggests that the opportunities and threats are likely to change in the near future.

5 Impact analysis   12/03

Key Concept

Impact analysis is used to analyse the effect upon a business of developments in its environment.

5.1 There are various types of impact analysis.

Competitor analysis

5.2 This represents a comparison of the impact of **various environmental factors** on a range of competitors within a market. Factors to be considered may span the broad range of macroeconomic influences covered in Part C of this book. The analysis aims to assess whether the broad impact in terms of **sales**, **profits** or **market position** will be **positive** or **negative** and the **relative strength** of the impact on each competitor.

Business impact analysis

5.3 This represents an analysis of the effect of a range of environmental factors on the **major types of sales**, the **selling price** and **costs of a single business**. These environmental factors may include developments in substitutes, changes in the age composition of the population and the consequences of the increased use of information technology.

Trend impact analysis

5.4 This aims to assess the impact up-to-date and the likely future impact of individual environmental factors such as changes in the prices of complementary goods.

Cross analysis

5.5 This involves the assessment of the effect of a change in one variable on other variables.

Refocusing

5.6 One aim of impact analysis is to cause managers to ask whether, when responding to environmental factors, they should aim to change fundamentally the way business is done or whether they should make more limited changes in operations or approaches to marketing.

Marketing at Work

The death of the book?

For many years, people have speculated that IT would lead to the death of print media. For example, Encyclopaedia Britannica announced in 1998 that it was going to put its entire output on CD-ROM and no longer publish the huge multi-volumed encyclopaedia for which it is known.

Yet companies such as Dorling Kindersley produce both books and CD-ROMs. They encourage self-testing and enable the user to drill down to greater levels of detail if an answer is wrong. CD-ROMs cannot easily be used on public transport and, for many leaning activities, the sequential approach of a text is better.

BPP's i-Learn and i-Pass CD-ROMs for accountancy students are published as additional products, not as substitutes for Study Texts.

6 The product life cycle

6.1 Many firms make a number of different products or services. Each product or service has its own financial, marketing and risk characteristics. The combination of products or services influences the attractiveness and profitability of the firm. The profitability and sales of a product can be expected to change over time.

Key Concept

The **product life cycle** recognises distinct stages in a product's sales history.

Marketing at Work

GlaxoSmithKline has for many years produced **Zantac** an anti-ulcer drug. Patents expire after a defined period.

The company had been anticipating this development for a while and has invested in new drugs to provide income when returns from Zantac fall.

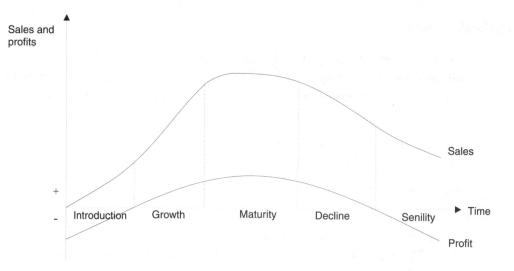

6.2 Introduction

(a) A new product takes time to find **acceptance** by would-be purchasers and there is a slow growth in sales. Unit costs are high because of low output and expensive sales promotion.

(b) There may be **early teething troubles** with production technology.

(c) The product for the time being is a **loss-maker**.

6.3 Growth

(a) If the new product gains market acceptance, **sales will eventually rise more sharply** and the product will start to make profits.

(b) **Competitors** are attracted. As sales and production rise, unit costs fall.

6.4 Maturity

The rate of sales growth slows down and the product reaches a period of maturity which is probably the longest period of a successful product's life. Most products on the market will be at the mature stage of their life. Profits are good.

6.5 Decline and senility

Some products reach a stage of decline which may be slow or fast. Eventually, sales will begin to decline so that there is over-capacity of production in the industry. Severe competition occurs, profits fall and some producers leave the market. The remaining producers seek means of prolonging the product life by modifying it and searching for new market segments. Many producers are reluctant to leave the market, although some inevitably do because of falling profits.

6.6 Senility

Senility occurs when sales are so low that losses are made on the product.

The relevance of the product life cycle to marketing planning

6.7 In reviewing outputs, planners should take the following actions.

(a)   **Review existing products**

They should undertake a **regular review** of existing products, as a part of marketing management responsibilities.

(b)   **Obtain information**

Information should be obtained about the likely future of each product including analysis of past trends, the history of other products, market research and an analysis of competitors. The future of each product should be estimated in terms of both sales revenue and profits.

(c)   **Discuss estimates**

Estimates of future life and profitability should be discussed with any experts available to give advice, for example research and development staff about product life, management accountants about costs and marketing staff about prices and demand.

6.8   Once the assessments have been made, decisions must be taken about what to do with each product. The choices are:

(a)   **Continue** selling the product, with no foreseeable intention of stopping production

(b)   **Initiate action to prolong a product's life**, perhaps by advertising more, by trying to cut costs or raise prices, by improving distribution, or packaging or sales promotion

(c)   **Plan to stop producing** the product and either to replace it with new ones in the same line or to diversify into new product-market areas

Difficulties of the product life cycle concept

6.9   (a)   **Recognition**

How can managers recognise where a product stands in its life cycle?

(b)   **Not always true**

The traditional S-shaped curve of a product life cycle does not always occur in practice. Some products have no maturity phase, and go straight from growth to decline. Some never decline if they are marketed competitively (eg certain brands of breakfast cereals). Research has indicated that the model is most likely to be relevant for products of mass consumer demand.

(c)   **Changeable**

Strategic decisions can change or extend a product's life cycle.

(d)   **Competition varies in different industries**

The financial markets are an example of markets where there is a tendency for competitors to copy the leader very quickly, so that competition has built up well **ahead** of demand.

Chapter Roundup

- There are various **forecasting techniques** organisations can use. **Scenario building**, looking at an internally consistent view of the future, is a particularly useful technique and can be viewed at the **industry** and **macro** levels.

- **Marketing audits** should be conducted at least once a year, and should review thoroughly an organisation's micro and macro environments.

- **SWOT analysis**, analysing strengths and weaknesses, opportunities and threats, enables an organisation to analyse its **internal capabilities** and **marketing environment**.

- **Impact analysis** means analysing the effect of a significant change on the industry, the industry's competitive forces and a firm's competitive strategy.

- Business should be aware of what stage of the **product life cycle** its products have reached, and plan to improve its existing products or develop new ones as appropriate.

Quick Quiz

1 *Fill in the blank*

    .... is the process of identifying alternative futures which indicate future developments of markets, products and technology.

2 Give the main steps involved in industry scenario building by completing the boxes.

3 Which of the following is likely to be the least satisfactory method of choosing scenarios as a basis for strategy decisions?

    A   Influence the future
    B   Hope for the best
    C   Hedge
    D   Play wait and see

4   The Delphi method involves the collation of views of experts to obtain a consensus.

     True   ☐

     False   ☐

5   Give four examples of problems with macro forecasting.

6   *Fill in the blanks*

     A marketing audit is a

     ■   ....

     ■   ....

     ■   ....

     ■   ....

     examination of a company's marketing environment.

7   What is the difference between strengths and weaknesses on the one hand, and opportunities and threats on the other hand?

8   Which of the following is not a stage in the product life cycle?

     A   Introduction
     B   Growth
     C   Consolidation
     D   Maturity
     E   Decline
     F   Senility

Action Programme Review

1   (a)   A **strength** may be a particular skill or distinctive competence which the organisation possesses and which will aid it in achieving its stated objectives. Examples may include experience in specific types of markets or specific skills possessed by employees, or factors such as a firm's reputation for quality or customer service.

     (b)   A **weakness** is simply any aspect of the company which may hinder the achievement of specific objectives. This may be, for example, limited experience of certain markets/technologies, or the extent of financial resources available.

     (c)   An **opportunity** is simply any feature of the external environment which creates conditions which are advantageous to the firm in relation to a particular objective or set of objectives.

     (d)   A **threat** is any environmental development which will present problems and may hinder the achievement of organisational objectives. An opportunity to some firms may constitute a threat to others.

2   Opportunities and threats may arise in the following areas.

     (a)   **Political**: legislation involving, for example, pollution control or a ban on certain products would be a **threat** to various industries, but also an **opportunity** for selling, eg lead-free petrol and suitable cars. Taxation incentives, rent-free factory buildings, or investment grants might be available for exploitation. Government policy may be to increase expenditure on housing, defence, schools and hospitals or roads and transport and this gives **opportunities** to private companies and the relevant government organisations alike. Political upheaval might damage market and investment prospects, especially overseas.

(b) **Economic**: unemployment, the level of wages and salaries, the expected total market behaviour for products, total customer demand, the growth and decline of industries and suppliers, general investment levels etc. At an international level, world production and the volume of international trade, demand, recessions, import controls, exchange rates.

(c) **Social**: social attitudes will have a significant effect on customer demand and employee attitudes. Social issues such as environmental pollution, women's roles, and the need to solve social problems offer **opportunities** for new products and services. Demographic change and population structure will provide continuing product **opportunities**. There are recognised opportunities for growth in the personal pensions market. Unemployment will strongly affect the total spending power of consumers. This has been a chronic and long-term **threat** in certain parts of the UK.

(d) **Technology**: new products appearing, or cheaper means of production or distribution will clearly have profound implications in these types of analysis.

3   –

Answers to Quick Quiz

1   Scenario building

2

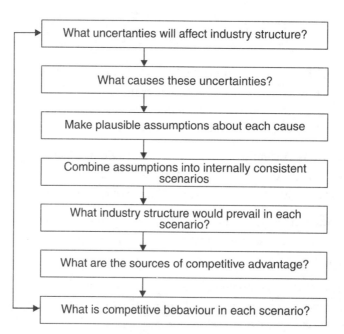

3   B is least satisfactory. It is the most subjective of the four methods, relating more to what the firm would like to happen, rather than what will happen.

4   True

5   Any four of:

■   Extrapolation of a trend beyond its appropriate range
■   Over-simplification of the system modelled
■   Minor events having long-term consequences
■   Assumption that a possible event is a certain one
■   Forecasts being self-fulfilling if action is taken
■   Bias of forecasters

6   ■   Comprehensive
     ■   Systematic
     ■   Independent
     ■   Periodic

7   Strengths and weaknesses refer to the organisation itself, opportunities and threats refer to the situation in the external environment.

8   C   Consolidation

Now try illustrative questions 28, 29 and 30 at the end of the Study Text

Question bank

1 Organisations (20 marks)   *32 mins*

(a) Using a representative example, prepare a slide presentation explaining the strengths and weaknesses of one of the following forms of organisation:

(i) A voluntary sector organisation
(ii) A private sector organisation   **(10 marks)**

(b) Explain the potential marketing advantages possessed by a small business compared to a public limited company.   **(10 marks)**

2 Types of organisation (20 marks)   *32 mins*

Write brief notes on the advantages and disadvantages of the following.

(a) Partnerships   **(10 marks)**
(b) Limited companies   **(10 marks)**

3 Marketing (20 marks)   *32 mins*

(a) Give a brief definition of marketing.   **(4 marks)**

(b) Explain the distinction between the marketing concept, the product-orientation concept and the sales-orientation concept.   **(16 marks)**

4 Mission statements (20 marks)   *32 mins*

The managing director of TDM plc has recently returned from a conference entitled 'Strategic planning in the 21ˢᵗ century. Whilst at the conference, she attended a session on Corporate Mission Statements. She found the session very interesting but it was rather short. She now has some questions for you.

'What does corporate mission mean?'

'Where does our mission come from and what areas of corporate life should it cover?'

'Even if we were to develop one of these mission statements, what benefits would the company get from it?'

You are required to prepare a memorandum which answers the managing director's questions.

5 Challenges and change (20 marks)   *32 mins*

You are to give a presentation to a group of marketing managers on the topic: 'challenges and change in the marketing environment'.

Prepare notes for this presentation, paying particular regard to:

(a) The nature of change in the marketing environment
(b) An overview of four or five major challenges
(c) An outline of the specific marketing challenges posed by two of them

BPP
PROFESSIONAL EDUCATION

6 Sectors (20 marks)

32 mins

(a) Compare the main characteristics and objectives of public sector, private sector and voluntary sector organisations. **(10 marks)**

(b) In reference to the private sector, examine, using examples:

  (i) The drivers for change in that sector

  (ii) The role of the marketer in the change process **(10 marks)**

7 Turbulence (20 marks)

32 mins

The marketing environment is often characterised by turbulence and uncertainty.

(a) Explain the term **environmental turbulence** in this context. **(4 marks)**

(b) Identify, with justification, **four** potential sources of turbulence in an industry of your own choice. **(12 marks)**

(c) What are the problems of using past trends to predict future behaviour?

(4 marks)

8 Systems (20 marks)

32 mins

(a) Explain what is meant by an open system. **(6 marks)**

(b) In the context of a business of your choice, define its micro environment and explain what distinguishes this from its wider environment. **(14 marks)**

9 Stakeholders (20 marks)

32 mins

(a) Define the terms internal, connected and external stakeholders. **(6 marks)**

(b) Discuss how stakeholder analysis can affect organisational behaviour. **(14 marks)**

10 Pressure groups (20 marks)

32 mins

You have been asked to give a talk covering the means by which consumer or environmental groups may seek to influence business decisions and the role which marketers can play in accommodating the genuine concerns of such groups.

Prepare slides to accompany your talk summarising the main points that you will cover.

11 Learning environment (40 marks)

64 mins

The importance of a learning environment

If organisations are to survive, achieve profit and grow, their rate of learning has to be equal to, or greater than, the rate of change in their environment.

This requirement is straightforward to state, simple to agree with, but often difficult to effectively implement. Those who have recognised the importance of being 'continuous learning' organisations include Microsoft, Intel and GlaxoSmithKline.

Continuous learning requires systems to scan and monitor the external environment and then respond positively to the changes which are occurring. Benchmarking and competitor analysis should be undertaken to provide comparison with internal indices of achievement in key result areas, such as market standing and innovation.

The key of encouraging continuous learning is to encourage employees to behave as if they were not part of a traditional organisational hierarchy. The customer does not experience the organisation as a chain of command but as a one-to-one relationship with an individual employee. The quality, or otherwise, of this experience may largely determine whether the customer becomes a repeat buyer.

Customers have 'moments of truth' with all organisations. This may be when they call customer service for advice, or are met at reception or most critically when they complain. Customers will talk about the bad experiences to over a dozen others, so reinforcing the negative perceptions. Boards of Directors have no direct control over these 'moments of truth', of which there may be many each working day, and they should not seek to control day-to-day operations in an effort to do so.

Directors should be taking active steps to learn from their customers and focus on the effectiveness of their 'customer facing staff'. The former must be identified together with their needs, wants and perceptions of what constitutes value-for-money relative to the offerings of competitors. The latter either create or destroy the reputation of the business, irrespective of its mission, its social responsibilities, its promotional budget and its values.

(Drawn from ideas in *'The Fish Rots from its Head'*, Bob Garratt, Harper Collins, 1997)

(a) Select two of the following terms used in the article. Explain the meaning of each and briefly indicate their significance to the marketer.

(i) Social responsibility
(ii) Competitor analysis
(iii) Key result areas
(iv) Board of Directors **(2 × 5 marks each)**

(b) The article stresses the need for 'continuous learning' at a rate which exceeds the rate of change in the environment.

(i) Prioritise the main types of environmental change you would recommend an organisation monitors in an industry or country of your choice. **(10 marks)**

(ii) Giving examples, suggest sources and methods to help predict the environmental changes taking place. **(10 marks)**

(c) How would you organise and control day-to-day marketing operations to ensure that 'customer facing staff' produces positive rather than negative moments of truth for key stakeholders? **(10 marks)**

12 Five forces (20 marks) 32 mins

You have been asked to provide a summary report to your product managers on the subject of Michael Porter's five force structural analysis.

(a)   Explain to them the relationship between the five forces and long-run profitability in the market concerned. **(14 marks)**

(b)   Recommend *one* strategy that could help maintain profitability in the face of these five forces. **(6 marks)**

13 Environmental influences (20 marks)   *32 mins*

Various areas of the environment are said to influence policies of both business and non-business organisations. One classification identifies these environmental influences as being political/legal, economic, social/cultural and technological. Describe how they influence the policy-making of organisations.

14 Demography (20 marks)   *32 mins*

'If demography has its way, Asian and other developing economies should continue growing for decades to come.'   *(Economist 13/9/97)*

(a)   Prepare a brief for a group of international marketers on the long-term importance of demography to the future growth of any economy. **(10 marks)**

(b)   Outline other key factors that determine a country's real rate of economic growth. **(10 marks)**

15 Family life cycle (20 marks)   *32 mins*

(a)   What do you understand by the following terms?

   (i)   Lifestyle
   (ii)   Reference groups
   (iii)   Family life cycle **(6 marks)**

(b)   Comment on how lifestyle may vary over *three* stages of the family life cycle. **(9 marks)**

(c)   Suggest *two* useful information sources to consult on this aspect of the environment. Comment on the content of *one* of these sources. **(5 marks)**

16 Business cycles (20 marks)   *32 mins*

(a)   With the aid of a diagram explain the concept of the business cycle. **(10 marks)**

(b)   Draw up a table which shows the main features of each phase of the business cycle. **(10 marks)**

17 Worldwide policies (20 marks)   *32 mins*

Economic policies around the world are converging on four basic realities:

(a)   Emphasis on market mechanisms rather than the state
(b)   Provision of a stable economic framework
(c)   More outward looking trade
(d)   Encouraging partnerships and stakeholder involvement

Draw on your knowledge of the marketing environment syllabus to discuss the nature and significance of **two** of the above realities to marketers.

18 Economics and legislation (20 marks)   *32 mins*

You are to prepare a presentation for departmental colleagues in your organisation (or an organisation of your choice) relating to one of the following areas:

(a)   The economic environment   – objectives, policy, performance and future prospects
(b)   The legislative environment   – key developments affecting consumers and competition

19 Legal terms (20 marks)   *32 mins*

Distinguish the meaning of the following pairs of legal terms and briefly state their importance to the marketer.

(a)   Standards and statutes   **(10 marks)**
(b)   Product liability and trade descriptions   **(10 marks)**

20 Levels of awareness (20 marks)   *32 mins*

What effects are increasing levels of environmental awareness likely to have on the marketing activities of a food manufacturer?

21 Advances (20 marks)   *32 mins*

(a)   Identify two recent advances in technology and discuss the benefits they have brought to the consumer.   **(10 marks)**

(b)   How have recent developments in technology helped companies improve their marketing operations?   **(10 marks)**

22 Impact (20 marks)   *32 mins*

(a)   What is the significance of technical change to the marketer?   **(8 marks)**

(b)   Comment on the impact of technical change on the natural environment and suggest what direction marketing activity must take if future growth is to become sustainable.

                                                                                              (12 marks)

23 Globalisation (20 marks)   *32 mins*

What is meant by globalisation in:

(a)   Products?   **(4 marks)**
(b)   Organisation structure?   **(8 marks)**
(c)   Markets?   **(8 marks)**

24 Elements (20 marks)   *32 mins*

Discuss the impact of the following environmental elements on the marketing operations of a large retailer.

(a)   Changing lifestyles of women
(b)   Population begins to age rapidly

25 Working at home (20 marks)   *32 mins*

'There are virtually no technical barriers, no legal barriers and no cost barriers to having people working at home – the only barriers are human ones.'   *(Financial Times Report)*

Your Marketing Director has read the above quotation and wishes you to prepare a briefing paper for a working party that has been set up to consider the issue. This brief should address the following:

(a)   The meaning of the statement
(b)   How the human barriers may be overcome
(c)   Any marketing opportunities arising
(d)   The implications of also shopping from home

26 Benefits of technology (20 marks)   *32 mins*

You are advising the Board of a hotel and leisure organisation and you have responsibility for computer-based technology in the organisation. The Board wants to ensure that its information systems provide the best possible service for customers and that information which is generated enhances decision making in the organisation.

You are required to prepare a report on the benefits of information communication technology in this type of organisation.

27 Information sources (20 marks)   *32 mins*

You have been appointed to the newly created co-ordinating role of 'Marketing Information Officer' in a medium-sized organisation.

Produce a report with the following headings, illustrating how you would fulfil this role.

1   How to classify different information sources
2   The key features of an effective information system
3   Examples of sources used in the micro and macro environments
4   Two representative examples of the uses of such information
5   A short appendix on any ethical issues arising for the organisation

28 Opportunities and abilities (20 marks)   *32 mins*

(a)   Discuss what is meant by the term marketing opportunities.   **(12 marks)**

(b)   Discuss the internal factors that an organisation should consider when deciding whether or not to pursue a marketing opportunity.   **(8 marks)**

29 Forecasters (20 marks) *32 mins*

Your government has approached an independent group of economic forecasters to undertake a SWOT analysis of the national economy.

Prepare a short series of relevant slides to support the forthcoming presentation of this analysis.

30 Major bank *32 mins*

As a marketing manager you are given responsibility for improving customer service levels in your branch of a major bank which is a provider of financial services to the public at large. In this context your manager has emphasised the importance of having good information systems.

Required

Prepare notes for a presentation to staff on the following points.

(a)   The elements of a good marketing information system in this context   **(8 marks)**

(b)   The importance of good information systems in providing customer service   **(12 marks)**

Answer bank

1 Organisations

(a) The strengths and weaknesses of voluntary sector organisations will be illustrated here with reference to employment training schemes.

(i) **Voluntary sector organisation**

Strengths

- There are **no shareholders** who would expect a short-term return on their investment.

- There is less chance of **conflict** between social goals and profit goals.

- Voluntary organisations may be **trusted** more by users than a comparable private sector organisation, for whom users may be suspicious of the company's profit motives.

- There may be greater **dedication** from staff who share the voluntary organisation's vision.

- 'Staff' may be prepared to give their services for **free**.

Weaknesses

- The **absence** of a **profit motive** may lead to **unfocused** management whose results are difficult to monitor.

- There may be a reluctance to act in a **business-like way**, thereby resulting in poor services to users.

- Users may **not** expect to **pay** for services provided, but overhead costs must still be covered.

- Voluntary workers may be **less committed** to their job as they will not lose pay for poor performance.

(ii) **Private sector organisation**

Strengths

- Profit objectives give a **focus** for management and can be easily monitored.

- The need to earn profits focuses management's attention on **value creation**. Without satisfied users of its service, the company will not survive against competition.

- Private companies have been effective at **improving customer service** in many sectors and this could be brought to bear on the employment training sector.

- The discipline of an **employment contract** can maximise the performance of employees.

Weaknesses

- **Costs** may be **higher** as shareholders require an adequate return.

- There may be **conflict** between the **objectives** of **shareholders** and the objectives of **users**.

- **Social considerations** are less likely to be taken into account by a private company.

- Many users may **mistrust** the **service** being provided by a private sector company.

- People are **less likely** to **volunteer** their services for a private company, compared to a voluntary sector organisation.

(b)   Small businesses have many potential marketing advantages over public limited companies. The following are particularly important advantages.

(i)   **Overheads** costs may be **lower** as a result of having no headquarters staff overheads, among other costs. These cost savings can be passed on to customers, giving a big advantage in price sensitive markets. This effect is noticeable in the market for small building work.

(ii)   Because there is **less bureaucracy** in a small company, it can **respond more quickly** to changes in the marketing environment. It can therefore exploit market niches before their larger competitors move in.

(iii)   The relative lack of bureaucracy can also facilitate the **development** of **innovative products**, for which a larger company may have not had the courage to pursue.

(iv)   Small business owners are generally **closer** to their **customers** and may have better knowledge of the marketing environment than decision makers in large organisations whose knowledge comes through lengthy research processes.

(v)   Small businesses can often claim to offer a **personal service** where each customer is known by name. In some markets this can be a big advantage.

2   Types of organisation

(a)   **The partnership**

A partnership exists when two or more people **carry on business together**, owning the business property jointly and sharing the profits in an agreed ratio (without the business being incorporated as a company). Each partner puts in capital, and usually also his own efforts into the business, and a partnership may employ a number of other individuals. The **advantages** of a partnership are as follows.

(i)   Individuals can **combine** their **skills** which might be the same or complementary and efforts in a joint enterprise.

(ii)   Partners can **combine** their **capital** and so provide more finance for the business than each partner could do individually as a sole trader.

The **disadvantages** of a partnership are as follows.

(i)   The success of the business depends on the partners being able to **work together** in agreement and with complete trust in each other.

(ii)   **Important decisions**, needing agreement by all the partners, might be **slow** to reach.

(iii)   Unless the partnership is an LLP (Limited Liability Partnership), partners are **personally liable** for the debts of the business to an unlimited extent, which can make being a partner as risky as being a sole trader.

(iv)   **Effective planning** and **control** of the partnership often depend on **good organisation**.

(b)   **Limited companies**

Companies are organisations incorporated under the Companies Acts. They have a **separate legal identity** from the persons who own it (shareholders) and with limited companies, the liability of shareholders for the debts of the business is limited to their investment in the share capital. Companies may be **private** or **public**. Many private companies are managed by their proprietors (owner-directors).

The advantages of the company as a business organisation are as follows.

(i)   The shareholders have **limited liability**, and so their risk is less than for sole traders or partners.

(ii)   The **ownership and management** of companies can **alter frequently** without the company itself necessarily being affected.

    (1)   Shareholders can sell their shares, and new shareholders can acquire shares.

    (2)   Management can be changed.

(iii) Companies can **raise finance** by **issuing new shares**. Public companies have access to investment capital through the Stock Market.

(iv)   To grow into a large business, an organisation must have **adequate sources of finance** and it is usually only the company or state-owned enterprise that has access to suitable sources.

The disadvantages of the company as a business organisation are as follows.

(i)   The company is subject to the **regulations** of the Companies Act 1989 (public companies are also subject to the rules of the Stock Exchange).

(ii)   Shareholders and managers (and other employees) might have **differing objectives**.

(iii) Management (the board of directors) is only **periodically accountable** to the owners.

(iv)   The performance of the business is subject to **public scrutiny**, since the accounts of companies must be filed (albeit in the case of small companies in a modified form).

3   Marketing

(a)   '**Marketing** is the **management process** which identifies, anticipates and supplies **customer requirements** efficiently and profitably.' It covers not only selling activities, advertising and sales promotions, but also product design, production, production control, quality control, after-sales service and credit for customers. More succinctly, marketing can be seen as creating the environment in which selling will take place.

(b)   (i)   The marketing concept may be defined as a **management orientation** where customer needs are considered of paramount importance. Since technology, markets, the economy, social attitudes, fashions, and the law are all constantly changing, customer needs are likely to change too. The marketing concept assumes that changing needs must be identified, and products or services adapted and developed to satisfy them.

(ii) A **product-orientated firm** is one that believes that if it can make a good quality product at a reasonable price, then customers will inevitably buy it with a minimum of marketing effort. The firm will probably concentrate on product developments and improvements, and production efficiencies to cut costs.

If there is a **lack of competition** in the market, or a shortage of goods to meet a basic demand, then product orientation should be successful. However, if there is competition and over-supply of a product, demand must be stimulated, and a product-orientated firm will resort to the 'hard-sell' or 'product push' to 'convince' the customer.

(iii) A **sales-orientated firm** is one that believes that in order to achieve cost efficiencies through large volumes of output, it must invest heavily in sales promotion. This implies that potential customers are by nature sales-resistant and have to be persuaded to buy, so that the task of the firm is to develop a strong sales department, with well-trained salespersons. The popular image of a used car salesman or a door-to-door salesman would suggest that sales orientation is unlikely to achieve any long-term satisfaction of customer needs.

Assessment

An implication of the marketing concept is that an organisation's management should continually be asking **'What business** are we in?'

(i) With the **product concept** and **selling concept**, an organisation produces a good or service, and then expects to sell it. The nature of the organisation's business is determined by what it has chosen to produce, and there will be a reluctance to change over to producing something different.

(ii) With the **marketing concept**, an organisation commits itself to supplying what customers need. As those needs change, so too must the goods or services which are produced. An example is the Hollywood film industry's reassessment of what business it was in, from 'movies' to entertainment, so that it started to operate TV and video companies, working with TV, instead of competing with it.

The marketing concept should be applied by management because it is the most practical philosophy for achieving any organisation's objective. By applying the marketing concept to product design, for example, the company might hope to make more attractive products, and achieve sales growth.

4 Mission statements

To: Managing Director
From: Anne Accountant
Date: 29 February 20X1

Subject: Mission Statements
Contents: Introduction
Mission statement and strategic planning
Originating a mission statement
The scope of mission statements
The benefits of mission statements

Introduction

A **mission** can be defined as a business's basic function in society. It is often visionary, open-ended and has no time limit for achievement. It is possible however to reach a more expanded definition of mission to include four elements.

(a) **Purpose**. Why does the company exist, or why do its managers and employees feel it exists?

    (i) To create wealth for shareholders, who take priority over all other stakeholders

    (ii) To satisfy the needs of all stakeholders (including employees, society at large, for example)

    (iii) To reach some higher goal and objective ('the advancement of society' and so forth)

(b) **Strategy**. This provides the commercial logic for the company, and so defines

    (i) The business the company is in

    (ii) The competence and competitive advantages by which it hopes to prosper

(c) **Policies and standards of behaviour**. Policies and strategy need to be converted into everyday performance. For example, a service industry that wished to be the best in its market must aim for standards of service, in all its operations, which are at least as good as those found in its competitors. In service businesses, this includes simple matters such as politeness to customers, speed at which phone calls are answered, and so forth.

(d) **Values**. These relate to the organisation's culture, and are the basic, perhaps unstated beliefs of the people who work in the organisation. For example, a firm's moral principles might mean not taking on an assignment if it believes the client will not benefit, even though this means lost revenue. An example of this can be found in the standards of professional ethics required of accountants.

A **mission statement** is a document embodying some of the matters noted above. A mission statement might be a short sentence, or a whole page. It is intentionally unquantified and vague, and is sometimes seen as a statement of the guiding priorities that govern a firm's behaviour. Mission statements are rarely changed, as otherwise they have less force, and become mere slogans.

(a) **Purpose**

    (i) The firm's purpose might be described in terms of **more than** just **self interest**. A pharmaceutical company might define its corporate mission as 'the well-being of humanity'.

    (ii) The firm's **responsibility** to its **stakeholders** should be set out.

(b) **Strategy**

    (i) The statement should identify the **type of business** the firm is engaged in.

    (ii) The statement should perhaps **identify the strategy** for competitive advantage the firm intends to pursue.

(c) **Values**

    (i) The statement should **identify values** that link with the firm's purpose.

    (ii) The values should **reinforce** the **corporate strategy**.

(d) **Behaviour standards**

    (i) Defined standards of behaviour can serve as **benchmarks** of performance.

    (ii) Individual employees should be able to **apply** these standards to their own behaviour.

(e) **Character**

    (i) The statement should **reflect** the organisation's actual behaviour and culture, or at least its aspirations for improved behaviour and culture.

    (ii) The statement should be **easy to read**.

Objectives, on the other hand, are the embodiment of a mission statement in a commercial context. They specify the meaning of a mission in a particular period, market, or situation.

Originating a mission statement

A mission statement **originates** at the **highest levels** of the organisation. It is possible that, given a mission statement is meant to inspire as well as direct, a process of consultation with employees should take place to determine what the mission statement should be, or to assess what would be laughed out of court. A company which declared its commitment to customer service in a mission statement, but whose practices for years had been quite the opposite, would have problems in persuading employees to take it seriously. The fact that the employees were consulted about the current ethos in a formal procedure would make the mission statement more effective. The mission statement would be introduced as part of an attempt to change the culture of the organisation.

The scope of mission statements

All areas of corporate life can be covered by a mission statement. This is because it is broadly based, and as a statement of an organisation's values and objectives, it should affect everyone in the organisation. That means its scope is wide-ranging. If it did not affect everybody in each department, from managing director to clerk, then its power would be lessened, and its purpose poorly satisfied.

For example, if a company's mission highlights the provision of **good quality products and services**, then this does not only include the way in which products are made and services delivered, but the way in which commercial relationships are conducted. Given that a successful business requires, in the long term, good commercial relationships, 'quality' applies to these as well.

The benefits of mission statements

The benefits of mission statement are that they:

(a) **Describe** what the **company** is about

(b) Provide a **guiding philosophy** where there are doubts about the direction a company should take, or a decision an individual manager or employee should make

(c) **Display** the **area** in which the company is operating

(d) **Enable** the **communication** of a common culture throughout the whole organisation

(e) **Stimulate debate** as to how the mission can be implemented

5 Challenges and change

> **Tutorial note**. Remember that you have been asked to make a presentation. This answer is based on car manufacturers.

(a) **Challenges and change in the marketing environment of car manufacturers**

    (i)   The car market is not stable. It is constantly changing.

    (ii)   The more successful car makers are those that have successfully responded to change in their marketing environment.

(b) **Main sources of change**

    (i)   **Customer preferences**. There has been change in the features and benefits that buyers seek from a car. In most Western countries, an emphasis on speed and performance has been replaced by an emphasis on **safety and economy**.

    (ii)   **Change in composition of buyers**. In most Western countries, there has been change in the make-up of new car buyers. In particular, **more women** are now buying new cars in their own right. There has also been an increase in the numbers of affluent young people buying new cars.

    (iii) **Change in social attitudes**. Cars are increasingly being seen as an **anti-social** element with increasing levels of congestion and air pollution.

    (iv) **Changes in government policy**. Partly in response to the above, cars have attracted increasing attention from politicians, with threats of **increased taxation** and reduced freedom to use cars as motorists would desire. The government's decision as to whether or not to join the Euro is also important.

    (v)   **Changes in channels of distribution**. The number of **independent distributors** of cars in the UK is **decreasing**, giving more power to the newer larger dealer organisations. At the same time, new forms of online competition have emerged to challenge established dealers' position in the market.

(c) **Outline of two of the most important challenges facing car manufacturers in the UK**

    (i)   **The development of the euro zone**. In 1999, most countries of the EU became part of a common currency zone, with the UK remaining outside. One aim of the development of the euro has been to **harmonise prices of goods** throughout the EU. The presumption is that if goods are priced in all countries in the same currency, variations between different countries will become more transparent and will eventually be reduced.

          The development of transparent euro pricing poses a significant challenge for manufacturers who sell cars in the UK. Car prices in the UK are currently significantly higher than in most other EU countries, according to a number of sources. Transparency of prices would logically lead to **erosion** of the **margins** that car manufacturers are able to earn in the UK.

          An immediate challenge to car manufacturers comes from importers who specialise in sourcing new cars from low price EU markets and passing some of the cost saving on to buyers in the UK. This undermines established car dealers and also undermines the brand position of a company.

(ii) **Threats to the UK system of tied car dealers**. In the UK, car dealers are generally tied to a manufacturer by an agreement which many would regard as quite restrictive. The car manufacturer can insist on independent dealers' showrooms being equipped to a certain specification. It can also insist that **no competing brands** are **stocked**, either of new cars or of replacement parts. Approved dealers may have to agree not to sell on new cars for distribution through non-approved dealers. This system has suited car manufactures well because it has allowed them considerable control over their product from the point that it leaves their factory to the point of purchase.

The challenge to car manufacturers comes from a review of the system of tied dealerships which will be initiated by the European Commission. The present system is allowed under a temporary dispensation. The challenge for car manufacturers is to show that the system continues to offer benefits to the public. These include comprehensive after-sales service, stocking a wide range of spare parts and higher levels of safety as recalls of defective cars can be made more easily.

If the dispensation is not extended, car manufacturers must face the challenge of not being able to restrict their cars to sale by approved dealers only. This would mean that any dealer could sell any other manufacturer's cars. It might also mean that supermarkets and other non-motor retailers would become more active in the sale of new cars.

6 Sectors

> **Examiner's comments**. This question was not as popular as might have been expected given that there were 10 relatively easy marks on offer for section (a). With marks available for both characteristics and objectives, it should have been a relatively easy task to produce three for each type of organisation.

(a) **Public sector**

Characteristics. It is difficult to define public sector organisations as a whole because they embrace quasi-public sector organisations (eg non-departmental public bodies). Main characteristic is ownership by government; often bureaucratically run; high level of accountability.

Objectives. Typically set performance objectives (eg number of operations performed by a hospital), subject to a budgetary constraint, profit objectives less common.

Private sector

Characteristics. Wide range of business units, from sole trader to public limited company. Based on owners holding equity in the business and taking risks. Limited companies have separate legal identity from owner of the business.

Objectives. Essentially motivated by profits, although growth objectives may also exist (possibly as a means towards achieving profit objective). There are also informal objectives held by managers.

Voluntary sector

Characteristics. A diverse range of organisations, many covered by the provisions of the Charities Act. Some organisations comprise groups of amateurs joining together for a cause. Others, eg Oxfam, are professionally managed. This group is funded largely by donations and some trading activities and government grants.

Objectives. Their main objective is to advance the cause which is the reason for their being. Profit objectives not important, except for some trading activities. Managers of larger voluntary sector organisations may develop their own informal objectives.

(b)   (i)   **Drivers for change in the private sector**

These are the main drivers for change in its broadest sense.

- **Political** – new legislation, eg on employment rights, requires companies to change their practices.

- **Economic** – periods of recession and prosperity drive a need for retrenchment and new product development.

- **Social** – changing social habits and demographics render some existing products less useful, while requiring new innovatory products (eg more ready prepared meals for busy households).

- **Technological** – new technologies can make established products redundant (eg typewriters). New technology, eg the internet – can become a norm in a sector, requiring all companies to change their working practices if they are to remain competitive.

(ii)   **Role of the marketer in the change process**

These are the main roles:

- To collect information about environmental change and to analyse and disseminate this information through a marketing information system

- To facilitate internal change (eg working with HRM departments in training front-line staff to use new on-line services)

- To communicate change to customers so that they feel reassured and not alienated by new product, new distribution methods etc

7 Turbulence

Examiner's comments. It was important to have a grasp of the turbulence concept in order to successfully answer section (b). Potential sources of turbulence were often confused with longer term change, thereby inviting all manner of non-turbulence inducing sources to be suggested.

(a)   **Environmental turbulence** refers to a state where the environment is changing, often in an unpredictable way. The implication of turbulence is that the key defining characteristics of the environment (eg household incomes, technology, social trends) will be different next year compared to what they are today. The presence of turbulence makes forecasting difficult.

(b)   **Four potential sources of turbulence in the UK car industry**

(i)   **Change in legislation governing relationships with dealers**. In the UK, car manufacturers have benefited from a 'block exemption' which allows them to restrict the activities of their franchised dealers. With the end of this exemption, new forms of distribution are likely to emerge. There is a possibility of retailers such as Tesco entering the market to sell cars, potentially causing turbulence.

(ii) **High value of sterling**. This has created problems for UK manufacturers of cars as it makes their cars more expensive in overseas markets. Further turbulence is provided by the fact that a strong exchange rate makes imported cars cheaper.

(iii) **Recycling requirements**. An EU directive requires car manufacturers to take responsibility for disposal of their cars at the end of their life. This may create uncertainty in the costs involved, especially for smaller car manufacturers.

(iv) **Change in taxation on cars**. In 2002, new rules for taxing company cars came into force. This created turbulence by changing the pattern of demand for new cars. Fuel-inefficient cars suffered while sales of small, cleaner cars increased.

(c) **Past trends and future behaviour**

In some environments characterised by stability, past performance can be a very good guide to future behaviour. However, the number of industry sectors where this is true has shrunk. Increasing turbulence in environments implies that the environment tomorrow will be quite different to the environment as it exists today. It follows that past performance based on previous environmental conditions may have little bearing on performance under a new set of environmental conditions.

8 Systems

> **Tutorial note**. As is so often the case, the examiner found that candidates departed from the question as asked. Always make sure that you address the exact requirements of the question. Not to do so simply wastes time and loses marks.
>
> **Examiner's comments**. In (a), weaker candidates were often confused as to whether the micro environment was internal or external to the organisation. Average candidates tended to discuss the relevant stakeholders of the micro environment and the main elements of the macro environment but either did not focus on distinguishing between them or overlooked the need to set the answer within the context of a business (a major weakness). Excellent candidates provided a relevant and interesting application to an organisation they knew well.

(a) A system can be defined as a series of **interdependent components**, where change in one component has an effect – direct or indirect – on other components. For example, a central heating system is one where a change in one element – temperature – activates a thermostat, which in turn activates a boiler until the system reaches its desired operating temperature. An **open system** is one where it is not possible to define all the elements of the system. The marketing environment is such a system, in which many indirect factors, eg changes in technology, consumers' attitudes and overseas competition, can affect the marketing activities of a company within this system.

The following report is prepared with specific reference to the car manufacturer Rover.

(b) **Defining the micro environment**

An environment for any system can be defined as anything which is **external** to that system and therefore not a functioning part of it. Various levels of an organisation's environment can be defined in terms of their **proximity** to the system itself. The **micro environment** of Rover can broadly be defined as comprising all those individuals and organisations whose activities can **directly impinge** on the company itself. By contrast, Rover's **macro environment** comprises **general forces** and pressures which may not affect the company immediately and directly, but may eventually do so.

The micro and macro environments can be contrasted with reference to the **competitive environment**. Other competitors and customers directly impinge on a company and therefore form part of its micro environment. By contrast, proposed new fair trading legislation does not directly affect a company, but it can ultimately affect the relationships between a company and its customers. It therefore forms part of a company's macro environment.

The micro environment of Rover includes the following elements.

(i)   Customers, both current and potential
(ii)   Suppliers, both current and potential
(iii)   Pressure groups
(iv)   Regulatory agencies
(v)   Intermediaries (eg car dealers)

9   Stakeholders

(a)   All organisations have stakeholders: these are individuals and groups who are **affected** by or **affect** the **performance** of the organisation in which they have an interest. Typically they would include employees, managers, customers, suppliers, creditors, shareholders (if appropriate), pressure groups and society at large. The table below provides a useful method of classifying the different stakeholder groups.

Internal stakeholders	Connected stakeholders	External stakeholders
■ Employees	■ Customers	■ Pressure groups
■ Management	■ Suppliers	■ Government
	■ Creditors	■ The community
	■ Shareholders	

Internal stakeholders are individuals **directly connected** with the organisation, since they are its employees. Their aims, objectives and activities are likely to have a major impact on how the organisation operates.

Connected stakeholders are individuals who have a **direct connection** with the **organisation's performance** whether as financial backers, customers, part-owners, suppliers or distributors and so on. Their position both affects and is affected by the decision taken by the internal stakeholders.

External stakeholders are generally groups, such as central and local authorities, pressure groups, professional associations and society at large, which operate largely at **arm's length** from the organisation but still often have a stake in its performance (for example, if it pollutes the atmosphere).

(b)   **Variety of stakeholder interests**

Stakeholder analysis provides a useful approach to understanding organisational behaviour since it focuses attention not only on the **different individuals** and groups that interact with the organisation, but also on the **variety of interests** which these individuals and groups may pursue and which may have a direct bearing on the firm's performance.

Employees, for example, tend to be principally concerned with issues such as wage levels, working conditions, job security and personal development, whereas owners (eg shareholders) are more likely to stress the importance of a satisfactory return on their investment, the need for efficient management and management accountability. While at

BPP
PROFESSIONAL EDUCATION

times the objectives of these two groups may be relatively consistent, at other times they are likely to conflict, and this will present an organisation's management with the dilemma of how to balance the conflicting interests.

The resolution of this problem is likely to be reflected in management decisions and would normally be conditioned by a variety of factors, including the relative bargaining strength of the parties involved and the structure of the relationships between them.

Stakeholder influence on management

Stakeholder influence on management - and hence on organisational decisions and behaviour - can operate at a variety of levels. At the **strategic level**, for instance, the firm's mission and objectives, and the strategies to achieve these, are likely to be constrained primarily by the **interest** of its **owners** (eg shareholders), as interpreted by the individuals chosen to manage its affairs (eg directors). But is also likely that the other stakeholders, most notably customers and creditors, will exercise an important influence.

Similarly, at both the **planning** and **operational levels**, a complex pattern of stakeholder influence is likely to be experienced, ranging from general requirements to operate within a particular legislative framework laid down by the government (eg on health and safety at work) to more specific influences emanating from customers requiring products of a particular quality in a particular place at a specific time.

Other factors

The attractiveness of the stakeholder approach to organisational analysis should not be allowed to mask the wide range of other factors which can help to explain organisational behaviour. In particular it is important to recognise the influence of a firm's **external environment** on the attitudes and activities of its managers. Factors as diverse as a change of government, technological development, economic recession and demographic change can all be influential in explaining why organisations behaved in particular ways at specific times. These factors are not necessarily linked to the activities of specific stakeholders. In short, the stakeholder approach can only provide a partial guide to understanding behaviour and should be used as one tool amongst many by the organisational analyst.

10 Pressure groups

Slide 1

Definition of pressure groups

Groupings of people who join together to try to:

(a)   Influence activities and decisions of individuals, organisations or governments
(b)   Represent interests of their members

Slide 2

Types of pressure groups

(a)   Interest or protective groups, protecting interests of particular sections

Examples - trade unions, professional bodies

(b)   Cause or issue groups promoting particular issues

Examples - environmental protection, animal rights or penal reform

Slide 3

Techniques used by pressure groups

(a) Direct lobbying of management to achieve or prevent particular course of action
(b) Pressuring government, eg to achieve changes in legislation
(c) Media campaigns to raise public awareness and gain support
(d) Direct appeals to public to get them to pressurise businesses
(e) Commissioning research to strengthen case for or against particular cause

Slide 4

Possible reactions of businesses

(a) Polite dismissal
(b) Negotiation and consultation
(c) Accommodation of the pressure group's point of view

Slide 5

Role of marketing in accomodating pressure group

(a) Publicising their response both directly and via the media
(b) Communicating their decision both internally and externally
(c) Promoting benefits of their decision especially via advertising or public relations
(d) Instigating changes in product design and/or packaging
(e) Developing enhanced public image

Slide 6

Conclusion

Pressure group's activity may change buyer behaviour

∴ Short-term costs of responding < Long-term benefits

11 Learning environment

(a) (i) **Social responsibility**

Commercial organisations survive and succeed by making satisfactory levels of profits for their shareholders. Customers are crucial to bringing in revenue to a company, and hence allowing it to create profits. But in seeking revenue from customers, a company may find itself undertaking actions which are harmful to society in general. Its actions may meet with approval from customers in the short term (expressed by their willingness to buy) but be harmful to them in the longer term (eg cigarettes). **Social responsibility** is about marketers recognising the consequences of those of their activities that go beyond the immediate effects on their revenue generating customers.

Significance to the marketer

The first challenge for the marketer is to **recognise** the possible **harmful consequences** of their actions on society (eg increased pollution, safety issues, implications for social exclusion). Marketers must realise that if socially irresponsible action is not kept in check, **regulators** may limit or ban the offending marketing actions, making it difficult for them to serve their target customers. It must also be realised that many profitable customers may **refuse** to

buy from companies that are perceived to be acting in an anti-social way. For example, some customers of Shell boycotted the company following its attempt to dump the Brent Spar oil platform at sea.

(ii) **Competitor analysis**

It is too easy for marketers to look inwardly at their organisations and become product-focused. Marketing-led organisations **focus** on their **customers** by gaining a **thorough understanding** of their **needs** and **buying behaviour**. An essential part of this involves **identifying** and **understanding** the **competitors** that enter a potential customer's choice set. A customer judges competitors on the basis of the organisation's **image**; the **features** of the products they offer; their ease of **availability**; **value for money** and the extent to which they satisfy their needs. Products may at first sight seem quite different to anything that a company offers, but in fact they could be competing to satisfy a similar level of basic need.

Significance to the marketer

Marketers must **identify** who their **main competitors** are, including potential new competitors, who may be able to satisfy customers' needs just as well as itself (eg supermarkets have become competitors for many banks' services). After identifying who the competitors are, a company should undertake a **comparative analysis** (or benchmarking) of its own products against the competitors. Various criteria should be used to assess the attractiveness of product of competitors in the eyes of potential buyers.

(iii) **Key result areas**

The key results for most commercial organisations is to earn a sufficiently **high level of profits** for its shareholders. However, profitability represents the cumulative effects of many marketing related activities and it is useful for managers to have guidance on **targets** and **actual performance** in each of these areas. Some key result areas will be financially based and feed directly through to profitability (eg sales levels, margin, acquisition cost per customer). However, there are many more indicators which do not have any immediate relationship to financial accounting, but may be crucial in maintaining a competitive and profitable position in the market place. These typically include customer **satisfaction levels**, **complaint levels** and comparative ratings by consumer panels.

Significance to the marketer

The marketer must gain a thorough **understanding** of the factors that lead to long-term **profitability**, even though these may not have an immediate financial impact. Routine measurement must be undertaken, both internally and in comparison to **competitors' performance** in these areas (eg Are competitors achieving higher levels of customer satisfaction?).

(iv) **Board of Directors**

Directors are appointed by shareholders to act as the **governing body** of a limited company. The Companies Acts have given company directors a number of rights and responsibilities that essentially require that they act within the law for the best interests of shareholders. One director would normally be appointed as Managing Director with additional rights and responsibilities. The Board of

Directors is the ultimate source of authority within a company, although many decisions of a day-to-day nature may be delegated to a Chief Executive Officer, or other employees of the company. Major issues would normally require approval of the Board of Directors.

Significance to the marketer

Marketers must recognise the **authority** vested in the Board of Directors on behalf of shareholders. The board has responsibility for all functions within a company, although one member of the board may be given specific responsibility for marketing. Nevertheless, the Board of Directors would expect to be involved in major proposals from the marketing department which could significantly affect the nature of the company and its ability to comply with Companies Acts legislation.

(b) (i) This section is answered with respect to the UK car market. The following type of environmental change are listed in their order of priority for a company such as Rover.

    (1) **Competitor analysis**. The company should understand the effects of new low-cost car manufacturers competing for Rover's traditional markets. Many Far Eastern brands, such as Lexus, have now grown in status to challenge Rover's traditional high standing.

    (2) **Technological developments**. Rover should remain abreast of new technologies and seek to incorporate them ahead of its main competitors (eg additional safety equipment).

    (3) **Buyer's preferences**. The attributes sought in a new car change over time (eg there is now more emphasis on safety and less on speed). Rover should ensure that it monitors and responds to these changes.

    (4) **European Monetary Union**. The single European currency may bring pressure to harmonise prices within Europe.

    (5) **Government regulation**. Rover should understand and try and anticipate the UK and EU governments' attitudes towards potentially anti-competitive practices, such as discriminatory pricing and tied dealership networks.

    (6) **The economic environment**. Car buying is closely related to the economic cycle and Rover should monitor and respond to changes in the level of economic activity. As the economy recovers, it should ensure that it has sufficient stocks of new cars.

It should be noted that the above priorities may change from time to time. For example, monitoring the attitudes of regulatory agencies has become a major issue but was of less significance (although still important) in earlier years.

(ii) The following sources of information and methods of environmental analysis relate to the most important types of environmental change facing the Rover car company in the UK car market.

    (1) **Competitor analysis**. Monthly reports are produced by the Society of Motor Manufacturers and Traders which show the market share of each manufacturer within the UK market. This will give an indication of current and recent trends, but needs to be supplemented with other sources of intelligence about what is likely to happen in the future. Regular scanning of the **car trade press** may give some indication of likely future competitor activities.

(2) **Technological developments**. The most useful source of information about technological change may come through scanning the trade press, for cars and related engineering sectors. Attending **major car shows** will give some indication of recent developments. An examination of futuristic 'concept cars' may give clues to future developments.

(3) **Buyers' preferences**. There are now many sources of information about buyers' preferences. 'Off-the-shelf' sources such as **Mintel** may contain information specific to car buying. Rover can supplement this with its own specially commissioned research among car buyers, and by scanning consumer magazines such as 'Which?'.

(4) **European Monetary Union**. The company should **monitor** the quality **business press** to gain an understanding of the impact of the euro within the existing euro area. This can be supplemented with information for the company's own contacts and sales agents throughout Europe.

(5) **Government regulation**. Following the quality press will give some indication of the general direction of government thinking. For more precise feedback, Rover could employ **lobbyists** to enter into a two-way dialogue with key government influences.

(6) **The economic environment**. ONS statistics available on-line will give an indication of changes in the pattern of consumers' expenditure. More detailed information relevant to specific sectors is provided by organisations such as GfK, who also measure consumer confidence, an important indicator of **future** economic conditions.

(c) Evert Gummerson described all employees of an organisation as **'part-time marketers'**. This recognises the fact that no matter how hard a marketing department tries to undertake marketing activities, it is often front-line operations staff who can thwart their plans.

These are some commonly used methods by which companies organise and control their day-to-day marketing operations to ensure favourable reactions from customers to the action of 'customer facing staff'.

(i) **Mission statement**. Make quite sure that all employees share a vision that is realistic and achievable.

(ii) **Recruitment**. Ensure that criteria used to recruit staff relate to customers' preferences rather than being a matter of administrative convenience. For example, an ability to smile may be more important than formal qualifications.

(iii) **Training**. Make sure staff have the necessary training for them to be able to perform their job well. Inadequate training soon becomes apparent in the eyes of customers. For example, restaurant waiting staff who are asked to deputise in a hotel reception without having had training in reception procedures may be unable to deliver an acceptable level of customer service.

(iv) **Monitoring and feedback**. Staff should be regularly monitored, not in a confrontational 'snooping' manner, but as part of a process of continual improvement. Results should be shared with employees. Good performance should be rewarded. Poor performance should be discussed with employees and, where necessary, appropriate training undertaken.

(v) **Customer expectations**. Finally, it should be noted that employees may be seen by customers to be failing because customers' expectations are too high. If a company is not able to provide training and resources for front-line staff to deliver a high quality of service, they should not raise expectations in advertising.

12 Five forces

> **Tutorial note**. You are asked for a 'summary' in this question. This obviously means it should not be too long. Specifically, try to deal concisely with as many points as you feel it necessary to make. You want the product managers to get as much information as possible from the report without having to spend all day reading it. Note that part (b) only asks for one strategy.
>
> **Examiner's comments**. Very few candidates were able to put the five forces model into the context of the question, ie long-run profitability. The marks available in part (b) were going for stating the chosen strategy and then demonstrating how the strategy was a defence against each of these forces. Too many candidates chose instead to describe the strategy itself.

(a) Michael Porter identified a five forces model which affects the intensity of competition within an industry. Their relationship to long-term profitability in the market concerned is discussed below.

   (i) **The power of suppliers**

   The power of suppliers is likely to be high where **input materials** are **scarce**, and/or there is **collusion** between suppliers to restrict supplies of a vital input. During the mid-1990s there was a world shortage of computer chips which led to the profits of computer manufacturers being closely dependent upon their ability to obtain this vital component of their product. Some companies are totally dependent upon one supplier, for example British train operating companies must rely on Railtrack for the provision of track facilities. In this case the impact on a firm's profitability is limited by **regulatory control** of the supplier. Even in the absence of regulatory controls, the impact of suppliers on long-term profitability is likely to be moderated by the emergence of **substitute products** and/or **suppliers**.

   (ii) **The power of buyers**

   Buyers can exercise considerable power over suppliers in markets where **buyers** are **large** in size and **small** in number relative to suppliers. The loss of sales to such key buyers can severely harm the long-term profitability of a supplier. In the UK grocery sector, it has been noted that four retail chains now control about three quarters of all grocery sales. It follows that a manufacturer of grocery products must normally ensure that their products are stocked by the big four retailers, if they are to have any chance of building sales volumes. Manufacturers have frequently accused retailers of having a 'take it or leave it' attitude to suppliers, where they will only buy on terms which give minimal profits to the supplier.

   (iii) **The threat of new entrants**

   Markets are frequently transformed by the emergence of **new competitors** who challenge existing business practices. They may come from within the business sector, but are based in overseas markets and bring their expertise and **economies of scale** to challenge the existing companies (eg Aldi and Netto moving into the UK retail grocery sector). At other times, companies from a different industry sector can challenge existing companies with **lower costs** and a **more customer-friendly product** (eg retailers moving into banking in the UK during the late 1990s). In both cases, the threat to existing companies' profitability is likely to be more short-term than long-term. Over time, existing companies can respond to a challenge through cost cutting and/or product modification.

(iv) **The threat of substitute products**

The long-term profitability of many industries has been challenged by **substitute products**, eg typewriter manufacturers were challenged by the appearance of computers. Unless a company embraces the new technology which underlies the substitute product, the effects on long-term profitability could be catastrophic.

(v) **Intensity of rivalry**

Profitability is affected by the level of **competitive activity** between companies operating in a market. In some markets (eg estate agents in some towns) there may be a tacit acceptance of each other's position. At other times, much more aggressive competition through price cutting and promotion can be good for customers, but reduce the long-term profitability of all firms involved.

(b) A strategy of **differentiation** could help to maintain profitability in the face of these five forces, for the following reasons.

(i) A **differentiated product** gives a company a relatively unique product, possibly allowing it a price premium.

(ii) Customers may show great levels of **loyalty**, even when new competitors emerge.

(iii) If the product is aimed at small **niche markets**, it may be a less attractive target for new market entrants who seek the biggest market possible.

(iv) Through **differentiation**, a company can incorporate **new developments** in technology and stay one step ahead of its competitors.

To be effective, a differentiation strategy must be based on a **continuous assessment** of a firm's **strengths** and **weaknesses** relative to its **opportunities** and **threats**. **Changing customer tastes** must be monitored and **new products developed** where a company has a competitive opportunity. Only by continually adapting its differentiated product will a company achieve long-term profitability.

13 Environmental influences

Tutorial note. The acronym PEST (political-legal, economic, social-cultural, technological) is an alternative to SLEPT. If our solution below looks rather longer than you could achieve in the exam, don't worry: we've given you a wide range of examples, from which your own may be drawn.

(a) **Political/legal factors**

(i) Political factors can take the form of **direct legislation or controls**. An example is the Broadcasting Act which put up for auction the franchise for independent television companies. Other political activities are regulation and control (the desire by politicians to be seen to be 'doing something').

(ii) Other political factors include:

(1) Wars
(2) Alliances between states (eg 'tied' aid)
(3) Political parties' ideological preferences (eg in favour of privatisation)

(iii)   The government can aid business by providing a more stable operating environment and by direct financial assistance. Examples of such assistance include the following.

   (1)   Setting or targeting appropriate interest and exchange rates

   (2)   Providing education and training relevant to business either directly through the state educational institutions or via grants to firms and local technical and educational councils

   (3)   Protection of intellectual and physical property through making the laws (eg patents, theft) and enforcing them

   (4)   Economic planning of key industrial areas, for example information technology

   (5)   Acting as a customer to the private sector, for example when purchasing from the aerospace and defence industries

   (6)   Giving incentives for capacity expansion, for example capital allowances and investment grants

   (7)   Giving support to emerging business, for example the Business Expansion Scheme

   (8)   Creating entry barriers by restricting the activities of foreign businesses in the country, or by imposing import tariffs

Conversely, the government can act as an **impediment** to business. Governments may be the source of instability and lead to costs, in addition to tax, being incurred on organisations. There is an argument that the commercial logic which drives competitors and markets can be learned by an adaptive organisation and hence allowed for. The government can be less easily anticipated. Examples of the government acting as an impediment to business include the following.

   (1)   **Creation of legal regulations** which are costly to comply with

   (2)   **Distortion of markets** by the use of indirect taxation and discretionary production licenses

   (3)   **Uncertainty and volatility** in financial markets occur when governments change their policies in response to political pressure

   (4)   **Imposition of restrictions** such as monopolies and mergers controls and equal opportunities legislation may limit business activities

   (5)   **Putting short-term political advantages** before long-term national benefit

   (6)   **Acting solely** on behalf of sectional interests

(b)   **Economic factors**

This factor manifests itself through markets, customers, investors, suppliers, labour, competition, price levels and, indirectly, legislation and government policy.

(i)   **Markets** are **continually changing**. Old markets can decline and new ones emerge. An organisation sells its produce to markets, therefore changes must influence the organisation's decisions about what products to sell and where to sell them.

(ii) The availability of capital and investors willing to put money into an organisation will **influence** the **spending decisions** of the organisation. An organisation will not raise money to invest if the profits from the investment are insufficient to pay sufficient interest or dividends on the money raised.

(iii) The **supply and cost of raw materials** or energy can influence an organisation. If raw materials are in scarce supply, it might be necessary to switch to a substitute material. If the raw material is a commodity with large fluctuations in price, it might be prudent to buy forward to remove uncertainties in a future buying price. High energy costs might persuade an organisation to close down factories.

(iv) The **availability of labour**, its skills and cost, are an aspect of the economic environment. An organisation may site its operations in areas where labour is either cheap or well-paid, skilled and productive.

(v) An organisation with **competitors** must always be aware of their activities, so as not to be out-manoeuvred in the market.

(vi) **Government legislation and policy** are clearly influential. Fiscal policies will determine rates of taxation and government grants, as well as government spending as a customer. Monetary policies will affect the cost of borrowing. Membership of the EU has influenced the choice of markets for many British companies, because of lower tariffs.

(vii) **Inflation** inevitably influences an organisation's decisions with respect to buying, rewarding labour and investors, setting prices and so on.

(c) **Social/cultural factors**

(i) **Health and safety of products** and their impact. The last twenty years have seen increased pressure against cigarette smoking in Europe and the United States. In consequence of this tobacco companies have been forced to diversify either away from tobacco into packaging and insurance or to find different markets for tobacco products.

(ii) **Careful handling** of the product. The nuclear industry has to handle waste carefully. The chemical industry has to avoid the risk of leakages.

(iii) **Pollution** of the environment. This can be audible, visual or toxic. Airlines must control noise of operations and fly aircraft that comply with noise levels, Oil refineries must be screened for view and emissions from chimneys and waste outlets controlled.

(iv) **Trade relations**.

(v) **Treatment of employees**.

(vi) **Avoidance of sharp practice**. Companies must behave acceptably towards customers, creditors and employees.

(vii) **Fashion changes**. In the West there is a new strong lobby against the use of sealskins, and other animal skins for fashion garments.

(viii) The **needs** and **expectations of customers** in relation to the organisation's products will influence the organisation. Customers may expect an organisation to offer cheap price goods or alternatively quality goods for a high price (for example Rolls Royce); they might expect certain standards of service from a nationalised industry. Organisations should try to fulfil their customers' expectations.

(d) **Technological factors**

    (i) New technology might affect **methods of production** (the development of robots), storage (containerisation), sales and distribution (some years ago, the development of supertankers).

    (ii) **Computerisation** has transformed information systems in organisations, the nature of office working, and the techniques available for management decision making.

    (iii) New technologies may **alter** an organisation's **requirements for staff** (numbers, education and skills). Already in Britain, the long-term decline in manual working seems apparent.

    (iv) **New types of product** become available for selling to customers. Consumer products which have emerged in recent years are home computers, video recorders and digital watches.

    (v) Technology also affects the **availability and price of energy**.

    (vi) Various researchers (such as Woodward) have suggested that an **organisation's structure** is determined by the technology it uses.

    (vii) Researchers at the Tavistock Institute (for example Trist) suggested that the behaviour of employees at work is influenced by their **technological surroundings**.

14 Demography

Examiner's comments. The key word in part (a) was 'importance'. Many candidates produced a list, rather than an outline of factors.

(a) **Briefing for ABC Ltd export department: The importance of demography to economic growth**

Demography is the study of populations in terms of their size and characteristics. Among the topics of interest to demographers are the age structure of a country, the geographic distribution of its population, the balance between males and females and the likely future size of the population and its characteristics.

A number of reasons can be identified why demographic factors can affect the future growth of an economy.

    (i) Firstly, on the demand side, demographic change influences the **size of the market** that is available within a country. For example, demographers can predict changes in the proportions of the population that are dependent and those who have their own income. A country with a high proportion of elderly or young people is less likely to have a workforce which will generate consumer spending. The high proportion of young people in many less developed countries is one reason why these countries have less wealth: dependent children and adults consume wealth rather than create it.

    (ii) Secondly, demographic trends have **supply side implications**. Countries grow by having a pool of highly trained and motivated labour to create wealth. The high levels of dependency referred to above also have the effect of reducing the number of people available to work.

Other factors that need to be taken into account in studying the link between demographics and economic growth include the following.

(i)   The **ethnicity** of the population: many countries are notable for how different ethnic groups contribute to economic growth, for example it has often been commented that the Chinese community in Indonesia has been an important vehicle for economic growth in that country.

(ii)   **Household structure**: different types of household structures can encourage or inhibit members from gaining educational qualifications and being free to gain employment outside the family unit.

(iii) **Regional distribution** of the population: there is evidence that countries with widely dispersed populations are in a weaker position to create wealth than countries with major metropolitan areas.

(b)   In addition to demographic factors described above, the following factors contribute to real economic growth (that is, growth in the underlying value of a country's output, after allowing for inflation):

(i)   **Government regulation of the economy**. There is argument about what role government should have in stimulating economic growth, with some free market theorists arguing for a 'hands off' approach as the best means of stimulating growth through competition. However, governments are essential to **protect investors** against practices which could impede growth, for example governments protect patents and the rights of inward investors. Many governments have contributed to growth by supporting key industry sectors with start-up grants.

(ii)   An adequate technological and business **infrastructure**. There is evidence that businesses have a number of infrastructure prerequisites if they are to survive and grow. These include efficient road and rail communications; telecommunications; an effective banking system and a well developed distribution system.

(iii) **Education**. Many studies have shown the impact of education on long-term growth. For countries to gain competitive advantage in new and growing markets, rather than being stuck with declining industries, they need to train people for **tomorrow's skills**. This has been seen to good effect in the 'tiger economies' of the Far East which based much of their growth in the 1990s on a workforce which had developed skills in electronics. The same is also true of Ireland.

(iv)   **Availability of natural resources**. Countries have grown by exploiting their natural resources, which may be minerals (eg gold mining in South Africa); agricultural based (eg New Zealand) or sights and climate (eg Switzerland and the Canary Islands).

(v)   **Entrepreneurship**. To secure growth, it is not sufficient to have in place all of the above. Entrepreneurs are necessary to bring together the resources and to create value in the eyes of customers. The success of many far eastern countries has been attributed to the presence of an entrepreneurial culture, which may be absent in many Eastern European countries.

15 Family life cycle

Tutorial note. The danger in part (a) is that you may be tempted to write too much – there are only two marks available for each explanation. Part (b) asks for illustration of three stages of the family life cycle. You will do yourself no favours by showing how lifestyle varies over its entirety. It will waste time and tell the examiner that you are happy to ignore his instructions. Part (c) is a little more challenging – make sure you understand what 'sources' are.

Examiner's comments. This was a popular question which attracted a lot of weak answers, although some high marks were achieved. Answers to part (a) showed good understanding, but part (b) was characterised by a lack of focus on *lifestyle* – candidates needed to write about attitudes, activities and opinions but very often did not. There remains a lack of knowledge of information sources despite numerous questions on it in the past.

(a)   (i)   **Lifestyle** refers to the overall **pattern** of **behaviour** and attitudes held by an individual. This can be quite independent of such factors as income and occupation which have traditionally been used to categorise buyers.

There are many ways of classifying individuals' lifestyles, for example 'healthy', 'conformist', 'ostentatious' and 'adventurous'. They can be difficult to measure but stereotypical pictures of these people can help in targeting.

(ii)   **Reference groups** are those individuals and groups referred to when going through the buying decision process. The **values** of the reference group influence an individual's evaluation of choices available. Reference groups can be direct/primary (eg the influence of colleagues at work or college) or they can be secondary and indirect (eg the influence which a pop star or football player can have on a purchase decision).

(iii)   **Family life cycle** describes the stages that families go through in terms of the impact on expenditure. From single adult to married couple with no children; then with children; followed by no children again and finally a solitary survivor. The total disposable income of a family is likely to differ significantly between stages, as are product preferences. Of course, not all families go through this idealised cycle (for example divorce and remarriage can alter the traditional pattern).

(b)   Variation in lifestyle between:

(i)   Single adulthood
(ii)   Young married couple with no children
(iii)   Married couple with dependent children

(i)   **Single adulthood**

For many people, this is a period of **high disposable income**, because although income may represent the low point of a career ladder, there are typically few financial commitments. With no family responsibilities, this group is able to indulge itself in activities of hedonistic value, for example attending pop concerts or eating out frequently. An individual may still be trying to establish their identity and may purchase aspirational branded products for this purpose. With no family responsibilities, lifestyle may be dominated by preoccupation with the needs of today rather than planning for the future.

(ii)   **Young married couple with no children**

This again is a relatively prosperous period with two incomes and no costs associated with dependent children. Such individuals can often afford to indulge themselves with **luxury purchases**, such as overseas holidays and fashionable

409

clothing. However, this group is more likely to have established its identity, and purchases for the purpose of enhancing an image may begin to decline. On the other hand, they may become more **future oriented**, for example by taking out mortgages and savings schemes.

(iii) **Married couple with dependent children**

At this stage, an individual's disposable income may fall as children **consume resources**. As well as money, children will consume resources of time. Less time and money will be available for pursuing other lifestyle activities. Caring for children, for example attending school functions and buying clothes for the children lead to a lifestyle which is less hedonistic and self-centred.

It should be noted that all three stages described above are stereotypical and that circumstances and resources can influence the transition from one stage to the next.

(c) **Social trends** is an annual publication of the UK Office for National Statistics. It brings together information from a number of sources (eg registers of births, marriages and deaths; Department of Health statistics) to present a snapshot of the lifestyles of the UK population. The following contents are particularly useful for understanding lifestyles.

(i) The allocation of household financial budgets

(ii) The amount of time that members of households spend taking part in various activities

(iii) The composition of households

(iv) Per capita consumption of a range of goods and services

(v) Educational qualifications obtained

(vi) Timing and rate of marriage

16 Business cycles

(a) Levels of business activity vary over time. On some occasions businesses may face **boom** conditions with rapidly rising demand for the goods and services they produce. At other times the reverse may be the case, with demand falling and businesses experiencing difficult trading conditions. Such variations in demand and therefore output often occur in a **cyclical** fashion with growth in national output (ie national income) followed by a slow-down in growth which ultimately turns to a fall in national income before a recovery occurs once again. This cyclical pattern of economic activity is known as the **business cycle** or **trade cycle** and can be illustrated as in the diagram below.

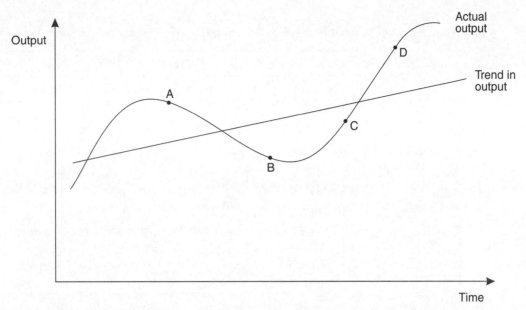

Figure 1: The business cycle

The diagram indicates that the typical business cycle has four main phases, known as **recession**, **depression**, **recovery** and **boom**. At point A, the economy is entering the **recession** phase, characterised by falling levels of demand, declining business confidence, a disinclination to invest in new projects, a reduction in stock levels and ultimately the shedding of labour (ie rising unemployment) and the closure of some firms.

Where no stimulus to demand exists, economic activity may decline even further culminating in a **depression** within the economy (point B) with its associated problems of high unemployment, low business confidence and low levels of consumer demand.

When depression occurs it may be relatively short-lived or could last for some time before confidence returns to the economy and demand starts to rise. At point C the economy enters the **recovery** phase with rising levels of output and income and (subsequently) increased employment. As businesses become more confident about future prospects, investment tends to increase and businesses are able to achieve high levels of profits as sales and prices recover.

A continuation in these trends can push the economy into the **boom** phase (D) with its high levels of spending, output, investment, business confidence and business profits, together with a tendency towards rising price levels (ie inflation) as consumption tends to outstrip the economy's capacity to meet the demand. Ultimately, the boom phase may give way to a recession and the cycle begins once again at higher levels of average output.

(b) A summary of the main features of the business cycle is shown in the table below.

Key variables	Cyclical phase			
	Recession	Depression	Recovery	Boom
Demand	Falling	Very low	Rising	Rising fast
Unemployment	Rising	High	Eventually falling	Falling
Investment	Falling	Very low	Recovering	High
Business confidence in future	Declining	Very low	Starting to recover	High
Profitability	Falling	Very low	Rising	High
Prices	Stabilising	Stable or falling	Stable or rising slowly	Rising
Capacity	Over-capacity starting to occur	Significant over-capacity	Rising use of idle capacity	Output capacity reached

The essential point to remember is that the different variables are inter-related. For example, falling levels of demand depress business confidence and cause a reduced level of investment, a reduction in the labour force and subsequently a decline in profitability which if unstoppable can move the economy into a depression. By the same token a recovery in demand tends to feed positively into business confidence, investment, profitability, employment and so on, and can culminate in boom conditions before the economy goes into the next phase of the cycle. It should also be noted that despite periodic slumps and booms, the long-term trend in output tends to be consistently upward (see Figure 1), indicating that national income (or output) normally rises over time in the long run. Accordingly, while successive falls in national income may mark the onset of a recession at a particular point in time, these levels of national income may still be higher than those measured in some recent previous periods, including periods characterised as booms.

17 Worldwide policies

Examiner's comments. Most candidates chose (d) and one other. Candidates needed to show clearly that they were discussing nature and significance. In (a) candidates often had trouble defining market mechanisms, and discussing why a shift away from central planning was important. In (b) most answers discussed the importance and significance of sustainable growth. (c) provided opportunities to discuss globalisation and the World Trade Organisation which were not generally taken. Poorer answers to (d) consisted of all candidates knew about partnerships and stakeholders rather than their nature and significance, and some answers discussed legal partnerships rather than organisation-stakeholders collaborations.

Impact of recent economic policies on marketers

(a) **Emphasis on market mechanisms rather than the state**

This can be seen in many countries through such actions as:

(i) Deregulation of previously regulated markets

(ii) Privatisation of state owned organisations

(iii) Creation of many 'arms' length' agencies of government

(iv) Encouragement of individuals to rely on their own means, rather than those of the state (eg in respect of pensions)

There have been worldwide trends during the 1990s and the current decade, although the pace of change has varied between countries. In the former Soviet Union, the pace of change has been much more dramatic than in the USA which has traditionally had a large private sector.

The changes represent **opportunities** and **challenges** for marketers. Companies which previously enjoyed protected markets have had to learn new disciplines of marketing, turning their attention away from production planning to meeting customers' needs.

Many private sector organisations have profited from shifts away from government domination of the company. Many public utility services, for example, are now provided by **profit seeking private organisations** which must understand and practice marketing.

Many new positions for marketers have been created within government organisations, as these are increasingly being set customer focused performance targets.

(b) **Provision of a stable economic framework**

The international economy, and the economies of individual countries have a habit of going through cycles of **prosperity** and **recession**. Growth which is too rapid may bring about inflation and high interest rates which eventually trigger a recession, which in turn will be self correcting. There have been many 'boom and bust' cycles in the past, but now it is suggested by some that we have mastered the art of national and economic management to avoid a repeat of this cycle. There is some evidence for this, for example the slowdown in the Asian economies during the late 1990s did not lead to the global recession which many people had expected to be a consequence. However, despite this, economic cycles continue to exist at national level, even though their impact may not be as severe as in the past.

A **stable economic framework** is of great significance to the marketer as it reduces the riskiness inherent in marketing planning. In industries where production lead times are great, the risk of a company having insufficient or excessive supply because of an inaccurate forecast about the marketing environment is reduced. Rather than spending a lot of time developing short-term opportunities, a stable economic environment allows a marketer to **plan long-term** and to develop products which will deliver **long-term value** to customers.

(c) **More outward looking trade**

The average share of nations' GDP which enters international trade increased during the 1990s. This came about as a result of the World Trade Organisation's efforts to **reduce international trade barriers** and countries' desires to exploit the benefits of comparative cost advantage. It has been recognised that countries with a relatively open trade policy are likely to be the most successful in terms of GDP per head.

There have been differences between countries in the rate at which they have become more outward looking on trade. Some countries, such as Singapore and Hong Kong have a long tradition of **open borders** and have therefore not had to look outwardly much more than they did previously. On the other hand, countries such as China have remained relatively inward looking.

More outward looking trade presents challenges and opportunities for marketers. The challenges is to **think globally**. With the rapid development of worldwide communications, especially the Internet, it is becoming easier for overseas suppliers to

attack a firm's traditional **domestic market**. This improvement in communication also allows marketers to go on the offensive in overseas markets, which with the reduction in tariff barriers have become more attractive.

(d) **Encouraging partnerships and stakeholder involvement**

The 1990s has seen a trend towards co-operation rather than confrontation in business relationships. This is manifested in such ways as **efficient, co-operatively managed supply chains**, **joint problem solving** between **buyer** and **seller**, and greater **consultation** with **interested stakeholder groups**, such as employees, consumer groups and local communities. There have been many examples of where two co-operating companies have collectively achieved more than each of them would if they acted alone.

Some commentators have noted, however, that many partnerships are entered into quite opportunistically and many fail after a short time. Where partnerships become firmly rooted, they can also lead to allegations of **anti-competitive practices** by regulatory bodies.

For the marketer, consideration must be given to ways in which it can enter partnerships in order to gain a competitive advantage in its market place. In the airline sector, most airlines would lose some of their competitive advantage if they did not belong to a global partnership (eg the Star Alliance). On the other hand, many companies have succeeded in niche markets without the possible complications of global partnerships (eg many 'low-cost' airlines have succeeded without membership of a global alliance).

18 Economics and legislation

Examiner's comments. This was by far the least popular question on the paper and was not generally very well done. Most of the material presented tended to be unspecific and highly superficial. It was also acceptable to provide the national economic or legal context rather than that of the UK.

Tutorial note. This answer has been prepared in the context of the internet portal Yahoo!

(a) **The economic environment**

The economic environment of Yahoo! comprises the micro- and macro-economic environments.

The **micro-economic environment** comprises the **customers, competitors, suppliers, intermediaries and government regulators** that the company encounters in its day-to-day activities. In this environment, the objective of the company is to be a successful competitor which makes an adequate return for its shareholders by delivering good value services to its customer.

The company's policy has been to develop a **sustainable competitive advantage**. It aims to achieve this through **product development**, a **reputation for reliability** and by **promoting these benefits** to consumers. The company has grown to a point where it can benefit from **economies of scale** relative to its competitors.

Performance to date has been below the initially high expectation of the company. The company grew rapidly on the back of the 'dot.com' boom of the late 1990s, and the general economic prosperity of that period. In this economic environment, the company succeeded in capturing large numbers of users, and, more importantly, large numbers of advertisers who pay to place banner adverts on the company's websites. When the dot.com bubble burst in 2000, the company was badly affected. Many investors lost confidence in the sector. Many of the company's advertisers either went out of business, or cut back the amount of spending on advertising with Yahoo! The fall of many dot.com companies also coincided with the slowdown in the global economy, resulting in less expenditure by consumers and businesses. Directly and indirectly this has had an effect on Yahoo!

In the longer term, Yahoo! has established a service which is superior in many ways to its competitors, many of whom have gone out of business. The economic environment of Yahoo! should improve when the **global economy recovers** and it finds itself facing fewer competitors.

(b) **The legislative environment**

Yahoo! finds itself operating in a very uncertain legal environment. In principle, an Internet Service Provider such as Yahoo! is **subject to** the **laws** of the countries that it operates in. To this extent, the legal environment impacts on it in a number of important ways.

(i) The company's dealings with its customers, intermediaries and employees are governed by the **law of contract**. Increasingly, statutory intervention has affected the company's relationships with these groups (eg the Consumer Protection Act and Unfair Contract Terms Act affects the company's dealings with private customers).

(ii) The company uses the law to **protect its trade mark** against imitation services.

(iii) The company must **comply with the UK Data Protection Act 1998**, just like any other business which records personal data about customers.

However, there are also many issues in the company's legal environment which do not apply to conventional companies, and which pose threats and opportunities for the company. Some of these are listed below.

(i) It is **not** always **immediately clear** where a contract is made using the Internet, and therefore which country's judicial system should apply.

(ii) The **law of libel** is very unclear. Some countries' legal systems have held an Internet Service Provider to be liable to libellous messages that they carried, regardless of whether they were responsible for designing the content of the message.

(iii) Issues are continuing to emerge about the **legality of holding personal information**, for example through the use of 'cookies'. Again, the question of which country's legal jurisdiction applies is raised.

(iv) There is increasing concern about the **potential anti-competitive effects** of large **multi-media organisations** which can restrict the availability of films and other resources which are considered to be an essential part of a nation's culture.

(v) The EU is currently (2001) implementing its proposal for an **'electronic signature'** which will provide a legally binding signature in place of a written signature which is currently required for some forms of documentation (eg house purchase).

19 Legal terms

> **Tutorial note**. You are asked to answer *two* of the sections of the question. Answers for all four are provided here.
>
> **Examiner's comments**. Few attempted this question despite the generous choice and the straightforward nature of the points required. The importance to the marketer was less well treated than the meaning of the terms particularly in reference to statutes and red tape.

(a) **Standards and statutes**

Standards act as guidelines by which goods and services companies operate. To achieve significance, the meaning of a standard must be widely known, so that buyers and sellers can refer to the standard as a common basis for negotiation. Sometimes, buyers may insist on purchases meeting a specified standard. Also, governments can insist that products sold in a particular market meet a specified standard. The standard itself could have been developed by a government agency or an independent agency. The British Standards Institute (BSI) is a widely used source of product standards.

Statutes, by contrast, become mandatory on all people affected. While a firm may have some discretion in deciding whether to adopt a standard, it may be compelled by statute, for example, in the use of ingredients for its food markets.

For the marketer, statutes constrain marketing decisions. Because they normally apply to all companies in a market, they cannot be used to gain competitive advantages. However, failing to meet statutory requirements can lead to prosecution of a firm and adverse publicity surrounding it. Firms often adopt standards voluntarily to gain a competitive advantage. For example, many buyers of some products are willing to pay premium prices for goods which meet BSI standards.

(b) **Product liability and trade descriptions**

Product liability refers to a company's **responsibility** to all users and others who come into contact with its products. The company is said to owe a **duty of care** to avoid injury. For example, a toy company which sells a dangerous toy owes a duty of care not only to people who buy its toys, but also to anybody who eventually uses them.

Trade description refers to the manner in which traders describe goods offered for sale. In the UK, legislation makes it an offence for a company to give inaccurate descriptions of its products, for example in relation to performance, price or quality.

For marketers, product liability requires new products to be comprehensively tested for the uses described by the company. If a product is not deemed to be safe to use in all situations, the company must make this quite clear in its publicity material.

The cost of failing in this respect can be heavy fines and compensation claims, as well as long-term harm to its image.

20 Levels of awareness

Increasing levels of environmental awareness are manifested in many ways. Environmental concerns receive increasing coverage in the media and an organisation that is revealed as pursuing environmentally harmful policies may suffer from a poor public image. **Pressure groups** may be formed to campaign against bad practices, often lobbying government for a change in legislation. Finally, the increasing awareness of individual consumers lead some segments of buyers to switch their purchases from an organisation that they see as bad to one that they see as good.

The effects of increasing levels of environmental awareness on a food manufacturer can be examined by looking at how they affect the main areas of marketing activity. These are listed below.

Market research

As a first step, the company should set up a research programme to understand better the environmental expectation of food purchasers. In particular, it should identify the following points.

(a) What **specific 'green' factors** do buyers look for when choosing a particular type of food? For example, how important is the fact that carrots have been grown without the use of insecticides?

(b) To what extent are the **environmental credentials** of the food supplier, as opposed to the credentials of the product, important in influencing consumer choice?

(c) What **segments of the population** are particularly conscious of environmental concerns and motivated to make purchases on this basis?

(d) What are the company's **competitors** doing to try and satisfy environmental concerns?

Product development

(a) Following thorough market research, product development should try and develop foods which **satisfy consumers' identified needs** (for example, developing cheeses which are free of artificial preservatives).

(b) It is important that products are **tested** to ensure that they provide a comparable level of performance in line with consumers' expectation. Although consumers may prefer environmentally friendly foods, they may be unhappy about accepting products that perform significantly worse (eg many buyers may not tolerate a preservative-free cheese which goes mouldy very quickly).

(c) There can be **publicity advantages** to firms who are first to develop new environmentally sensitive products. There may also be cost savings.

Pricing

Research should have established what, if any, **price premium** customers are willing to pay for an environmentally friendly product.

Promotion

(a) Promotion for the environmentally sensitive food must be carried out **sensitively** and avoid allegations that the company is merely 'cashing in' and exploiting environmental concerns.

(b) As well as promoting specific products, a company will find it important to **promote its image** as a caring company that is concerned for the environment.

Distribution

(a) A company that has sold its food through large volume supermarket chains may find these are unable or unwilling to handle products that have been reformulated in an environmentally friendly manner. Short shelf lives and variable product quality may be incompatible with the operations and quality standards of a major supermarket chain. A food manufacturer may therefore have to consider using **alternative, more specialised retailers**.

(b)   Research should have shown where the segment of environmentally aware customers is most likely to shop. If they do not typically patronise its traditional outlets, it may have to seek **new outlets**. For example, many buyers of organic foods prefer to buy their food from specialised small retailers rather than supermarkets.

21 Advances

(a)   **Home banking** is a recent technological advance which allows bank customers to **communicate** with the bank's computer network **online** via a screen (for example, a home computer linked to a television monitor) or by telephone. This has brought a number of benefits to consumers.

The service is relatively flexible, allowing various facilities such as statement requests, balance and transaction enquiries and automated bill payments. New services, such as foreign currency orders, may be added. Obviously, cash withdrawals still generally need to be dealt with at branches or at automated teller machines (ATMs).

As home banking is generally based on computer programmed procedures, reliability is high compared with banking transactions involving bank staff members. Furthermore, the convenience of 24-hour operations, the time saved by not having to visit bank branches so often and reductions in the number of banking transactions which need to be dealt with by post are all benefits to the home banking user.

Consumer choice is preserved in that there remains the choice of carrying out transactions at bank branches as usual. Cost savings made through reductions in numbers of branch-based transactions should feed through to consumers in lower account charges.

Electronic facsimile transmission is another advance which has brought various benefits to consumers. The main users of fax machines are still businesses, but it is likely that the number of private individuals with fax machines will increase in the future, helped by the fact that it is not necessary to install a dedicated telephone line for the machine.

Consumers' choice of methods of transmitting messages is widened by the availability of fax machines in cases where the receiver of the message also has a fax machine. Where the sender or recipient has no machine, it would be possible to use a fax bureau although there is then a loss of convenience.

Fax machines allow printed messages to be transmitted at the speed of a telephone call. The cost compares favourably with the alternative of letter post if the message is relatively short. The speed is of particular advantage for messages to be sent overseas.

The main disadvantage for the consumer compared with letter post is the loss of quality resulting from the digital scanning of the document to be sent by facsimile. The loss in quality will be much lower where the message can be down-loaded directly from a computer file.

(b)   Marketing involves the **identification, anticipation** and **supply** of customer requirements efficiently and profitably. Each of these elements of marketing has been aided by developments in technology in recent years.

Market research seeks to **identify customer requirements**. The production of market forecasts and sales forecasts has been made easier by computerisation of data collection and analysis methods. The computer spreadsheet (eg Excel) provides a very flexible tool for producing such forecasts.

Efficiency of communication with customers and potential customers through direct marketing methods has been greatly enhanced by telecommunications and word processor technology. More potential customers now have telephones and mailshots can be tailored to meet the anticipated requirements of particular customers.

The **efficient anticipation** and **supply of customer requirements** is aided by a number of developments. An example is the linking of sales terminals with inventory systems such as that used in Argos retail outlets, where terminals record the level of unsatisfied demand by counting the number of orders for goods which are out of stock. Computerised integration of sales processing and inventory systems enables sales analyses to be produced more accurately and more quickly for marketers' use, as well as improving financial control. Automation of warehouses is appropriate for some products, and this improves inventory control greatly.

In conclusion, although recent technological advances have been extremely rapid, there is undoubtedly some way to go in the process of harnessing these advances in a wider number of businesses to the benefit of marketing.

22 Impact

> **Tutorial note**. Note that part (b) deserves significantly more of your time than part (a), given the allocation of marks between the two.
>
> **Examiner's comments**. This was a reasonably popular question which required a grasp of the broader significance of technical change to the marketer as well as the interrelationship between new technology and the natural environment. Weaker candidates did not take a sufficiently broad view of the first part of the question but were content to view it in relation to the product alone. In the second part a number of candidates clearly had no idea what the natural environment was or chose to ignore it in preference to a general discussion of the direction of marketing.

(a) Technical change affects the marketing of different products to differing extents. For example, technological change has had a relatively limited impact on the marketing of funeral services, but has had a dramatic effect on the marketing of telecommunications-related services.

Technical change is of significance to firms in the following ways.

(i) Technology allows **new products** to be **developed** and made available to the public. The market for cellular telephones is a product of technological innovation.

(ii) New methods of producing existing products can allow **costs** to be **reduced** and **new market opportunities opened up**. For example, aviation technology has reduced airlines' costs, thereby opening up new markets for long-haul travel.

(iii) **New promotional opportunities** are presented by technological developments. **Satellite television** and the **Internet** are examples of new media which are now available for firms to promote their products with.

(iv) Closely related to new promotional opportunities are **new distribution opportunities**. Powerful **databases** and **inventory tracking** systems have allowed companies to handle distribution more efficiently, and in many cases to be able to deal directly with customers rather than acting through intermediaries.

(v) Customers' **expectations of quality** are constantly **increasing** and new technology allows firms to provide goods and services which are of a higher and consistent standard of quality.

(b) Firm's marketing decisions can affect the natural environment in a number of ways.

(i) The **falling costs** of producing many goods has resulted in **increased demand** for them. For example, the cost of producing cars has fallen in real terms, on account of improvements in manufacturing efficiency. This has resulted in more cars being produced, thereby consuming **more natural resources**, such as iron and aluminium. Against this, technical change has also allowed products to be made with fewer natural resource requirements. In this way, cars are designed to be just as rigid as previously, but use less steel. Increasingly, technology is allowing components of cars to be recycled, or made of renewable materials.

(ii) During **consumption** of a product, further natural resources are consumed. For example, during the use of a dishwashing machine, electricity is used and waste chemicals discharged into water courses. Again, technical change has been a double-edged sword. While it has allowed for new products to be made available to the market (and thereby pose a threat to the natural environment), change has also allowed products to be much more friendly towards the environment. So dishwashers now consume less water and electricity than previously.

(iii) Once consumers have finished with a product, there is usually some **residual waste** (eg packaging materials, scrap cars, waste detergents). Disposal of this waste can pose a threat to the natural environment, for example through pollution of water courses. Technical change has on the one hand created problems for the natural environment (by stimulating sales of product in the first place). But it is also allowing **new solutions** for waste disposal. New techniques are being developed to **recycle** used products in a cost-effective way (for example, waste glass and metals are increasingly recycled).

(iv) **Distribution decisions** affect the natural environment. While a consistent and reliable supply chain may involve having a small number of suppliers and centralised warehouses, the implications of this can include greatly increased traffic movements and consequent pollution. Technology has again partly offset some of these problems, for example through the use of more fuel-efficient lorries.

In practice, it can be very difficult to assess the impact of technical change on the natural environment, because many innovations have both benefits and disadvantages. For example, the introduction of cars which use unleaded fuel may reduce the harmful effects of lead in the environment, but increase the problems of benzene which has been linked with cancer.

Growth for the nation as a whole, as well as for individual firms, may be unsustainable if natural resources become exhausted, and only obtainable at a very high price. In this context, marketers can take a number of steps to bring about sustainable growth for their company, as follows.

(i) By **developing products** which use **sustainable resources**, a company will not be faced with suddenly escalating input costs. In many cases the development of an environmentally friendly version of a product will not adversely affect its technical performance or costs, thereby not endangering its market performance. (For example, aerosols not containing CFCs perform comparably to those containing harmful CFCs).

(ii)   Where **product performance** is **reduced**, firms should seek to **promote** the **benefits** of using a product made from sustainable resources. Many segments of markets may be happy to sacrifice performance in return for knowing that their purchases are not harming the natural environment.

(iii)   Firms should **anticipate proposed legislation** to protect the environment and be ready to adopt new measures and gain a lead on competitors who only change to new product designs when forced to by legislation.

(iv)   Where market growth appears to be unsustainable, firms can develop **alternative products** which are more sustainable. For example, the growth of private cars in cities may be unsustainable, so some car manufacturers have invested in urban public transport systems.

(v)   The public at large is becoming increasingly critical of firms who do not pay due consideration to the natural environment. By adopting a more environmentally friendly approach to the way it does business, a firm can develop a more favourable image and avoid, in the extreme, consumer boycotts.

23 Globalisation

(a)   A **global product** is one that is sold throughout the world. It is a standard product although it might be marketed in different ways in each country. Examples include:

(i)   Oil

(ii)   Foreign exchange

(iii)   Aeroplane engines

(iv)   Certain brands of soft drinks (eg Coca Cola)

(b)   **Organisation structure**

Global or boundary-less corporations have come into being for the following reasons.

(i)   Companies now produce and sell in a **wide variety of countries**.

(ii)   To serve these various markets, a company can **invest** in **more than one country**.

(iii)   Companies make decisions primarily with regard to their **global ambitions**, and do not take their legal nationality into account.

There is thus an increasing number of stateless corporations, whose activities transcend national boundaries, and whose personnel come from any country. However, it is debatable how global many of these organisations are.

(i)   Most multinationals, other than those based in small nations, have **less than half** of their **employees** abroad.

(ii)   Ownership and control of multinationals remain **restricted**. This is partly because of the way in which capital markets are structured.

(iii)   **Top management** is rarely as multinational as the firm's activities.

(iv)   **National residence and status** is important for **tax reasons**. Boundary-less corporations are not recognised as such by lawyers or tax officials.

(v)   The bulk of a multinational's **research and development** is generally done in the home country, where strategic decisions are made.

BPP)))
PROFESSIONAL EDUCATION

(vi)   Where capital is limited, 'global' companies stick to the **home market** rather than developing overseas ones.

(vii)   Finally, **profits** from a global company must be **remitted** somewhere. Firms like Reuters are quoted on a number of stock exchanges worldwide, but they are exceptional.

(c)   **Global markets**. It is sometimes asserted that the 'free world as a whole can be viewed as a global market'. In other words, goods can be made and sold anywhere in the world, and competition can exist between firms from any country. The growth of trade and the movement towards trade liberalisation should encourage this view.

However, the existence of global markets should not be taken for granted in terms of all products and services, or indeed in all territories.

(i)   Some services are still subject to **managed trade** (eg some countries prohibit firms from other countries from selling insurance) and there are some services which by their very nature can never be exported (eg haircuts, visits to stately homes) from the home territory, although they can be provided to visitors.

(ii)   There is unlikely ever to be a global market for **labour**, given the disparity in skills between different countries, and restrictions on immigration. Companies can best respond by relocating, but this is not always a viable commercial option.

The global market for some items is much more extensive than for others. The market for oil is truly global. Oil is produced in many countries and consumed everywhere.

24 Elements

> **Tutorial note**. To get good marks for this question, you must set out the impacts of the factors as they specifically affect a large retailer.
>
> **Examiner's comments**. The overall standard was good, with solid appreciation of the relevant trends and their likely impacts. A number of candidates overlooked the large retailer context and discussed the impacts on marketers, in general reducing their potential marks, however most achieved good focus on the question.

(a)   (i)   **Impact of changing lifestyles of women on the marketing operations of a large retailer**

There is an increasing level of employment among women, especially full-time employment among career-oriented women.

Likely impact on a large retailer

Women are increasingly financially rich, but 'time-poor'. Retail formats are therefore increasingly emphasising convenience in the services they offer and the products they sell. In the grocery retail sector, this is manifested in extensive ranges of prepared foods and the resurgence of 'convenience' stores in town centres and at petrol stations. Home delivery and home shopping offers new opportunities.

(ii)   **Delayed marriage**

Women are tending to delay marriage and to spend less time out of the labour market bringing up children.

Likely impact on a large retailer

Women are now increasingly buying goods and services which were previously considered a male preserve. As an example, the proportion of BMW cars sold to women has increased. Career women may represent important new or growing segments for many companies. The desire of many career women to return to work soon after childbirth can lead to opportunities for retailers offering child care related facilities, for example a crèche attached to a store.

(iii) **Changing role of women in the family**

As a result of the above changes, women's traditional subservient role at home has been challenged.

Likely impact on a large retailer

Change in family structures leads to changes in decision making for a wide range of goods and services. Purchases such as furniture, overseas holidays and groceries are increasingly likely to be based on a joint decision. Women are increasingly likely to have their role as buyer of groceries replaced by a man. For retailers, promotion, services offered and product ranges must reflect the preferences of all members of the decision making unit.

(iv) **Higher educational achievements of women**

More women are participating or have participated in higher education.

Likely impact on a large retailer

Retailing has traditionally relied on a pool of unskilled and poorly paid female labour. With rising expectations and abilities, their pool may dwindle, so retailers must consider operating systems which require fewer but better paid staff.

(b) **Impact of an ageing population on the marketing operations of a large retailer**

The ageing of the population in many Western countries is manifested in many ways.

(i) An increase in the proportion of the population **aged 65** and above
(ii) A particularly great increase in the number of **'very old'** people (aged 80+)
(iii) A **fall** in the **proportion** of the population which is aged 16 and under

Impacts on a large retailer

(i) **Product ranges** offered must reflect the changing structure of the population. A fashion retailer, for example, should devote more space to meeting the needs of the elderly, rather than the young population which is growing at a slower rate.

(ii) **Store design** should reflect the needs of the elderly, for example clear labelling for those who may be visually impaired. Elderly segments tend to prefer traditional values rather than fashionability for its own sake.

(iii) Elderly segments may prefer an emphasis on **personal service** provided by more mature employees, and home delivery services.

(iv) An increasing proportion of elderly people are retiring with **private pensions** which allow them to lead a comfortable lifestyle. Price may become less important than quality of service received.

(v) Retailers must avoid lumping all elderly people into one segment (and indeed, all people of any age group). The elderly includes **sub-groups** which are diverse in their income, mobility and attitudes and each should be targeted with appropriate product offers.

(vi)   The falling relative number of children in the population, and the reduction in family size which this implies, will lead to parents demanding **higher quality goods** and **services** for their children, as rising real household incomes are distributed among fewer children.

(vii)   Finally, the ageing of the population has implications for the **recruitment** of staff by retailers. The large pool of young people who are prepared to accept poorly paid jobs will diminish. Retailers should exploit the opportunities provided by the large elderly segment which many employers have found to offer a reliable, loyal and flexible source of labour.

25 Working at home

> **Examiner's comments**. This question tended to be better answered by UK candidates; weaker answers from candidates in developing countries reflected the fact that homeworking is not common. Answers to (b) tended to be too focused on control and financial incentives. Answers to (c) were weaker with too much focus on opportunities for the individual rather than the organisation; suggestions often tended to be accounting and cost-based. Many answers to (d) were too general and failed to focus on marketing implications. The briefing aspect of this question was also often not considered.

(a)   The technology to enable home working has been developed considerably during the past two decades. **Telecommunications technology** has allowed information to be passed quickly and cheaply between workers regardless of their location. The likely future trend is for the cost of information transmission to fall and the reliability and capacity to increase. However, it should be noted that this statement applies primarily to workers whose main work processes revolve around knowledge management. Where tangible goods are involved in workers' activities, **barriers** to home working may still **remain**. The cost of transporting goods has, if anything, been increasing. The opportunities for outsourcing manufacturing production, for example, have not been as great as for the outsourcing of knowledge management. Even in the case of knowledge workers, problems in monitoring home workers' performance and developing motivation remain.

(b)   Human barriers to home working focus on the potential difficulty of motivating teams of workers and supervising individual workers' performance. However technology has the potential to overcome some of these problems. Where tasks are straightforward and repetitive, workers can be monitored with simple **performance measures**. For a telephone operator working at home, the time taken to answer an incoming call can be routinely measured. A sample of calls can be recorded and the worker assessed for the quality of their interaction with a customer. **Mystery customers** may phone up employees and test the quality of service provided.

In the case of non-routine work, for example editing of technical manuals, performance can best be measured by the tangible **results** produced. In these circumstances it may be more appropriate to pay workers by results rather than per hour. However, this may not appear attractive to many people who see the certainty of a regular pay cheque.

The problem of **team working** remains a problem. There have been numerous attempts to create virtual communities using video conferencing facilities. However doubt remains about whether the quality of group interaction which emerges from this is of the same standard as face-to-face interaction.

(c)   There are numerous marketing opportunities arising from an emphasis on home working. Where a company faces a highly variable pattern of demand, it may use a large pool of home workers as a standby resource to be brought on line at times of peak demand. This would be less expensive than retaining staff in a central office and would allow a higher quality of response to customers.

Staff who work at home may be **less stressed** than those who have to spend a long time commuting and make arrangements for child minders etc. This may be reflected in a higher standard of service received by customers.

Home working may **reduce** a company's **costs**, thereby allowing it to pass on lower prices to customers.

(d)   Home workers who use information technology to work from home may also be expected to **use** the **same technology** to **shop** from home. They will probably be more familiar and confident with the technology than the general population. Because they are at home more than their office-based colleagues, they will have less problems accepting deliveries from Internet-based shopping companies. However, there is the opposite argument that home workers will seek variety in their lives and will be more likely than most to get out of their home. Shopping in High Street shops represents such variety.

26 Benefits of technology

REPORT

To: The Board
From: Anne Adviser
Date: 7 December 20X0
Subject: The benefits of information communication technology

Introduction

The organisation now uses computers and communications technology to manage almost all of its activities. For example:

(a)   Bookings for rooms or leisure activities can be made by customers over the telephone or at any of our hotels from any other hotel.

(b)   Catering supplies are managed using a constantly updated central stock control system and electronic data interchange with our suppliers.

However, it is in the **retrieval of information** and **manipulation** of it for use that computers have had their most profound impact. Various types of application are commonly cited in support of this, notably decision support systems, executive information systems and expert systems. I shall take the first two as examples.

(a)   **Decision support systems**

The term 'decision support system' (DSS) is usually taken to mean computer systems which are designed to produce information in such a way as to help managers to make better decisions. It is now often associated with information **at the touch of a button** at a manager's personal computer or workstation. DSS can describe a range of systems, from fairly simple information models based on spreadsheets to expert systems.

A decision support system **integrates** many of the functions supplied by information systems so that managers may use them more easily and on a wider range of both structured and unstructured problems. Examples of the types of decisions which they might support include a decision on whether to lease or buy company cars; an examination of options as to capital structuring and consequences of alternatives; and decisions on the introduction of a share option scheme.

(b) **Executive information systems**

An EIS is likely to have the following features.

(i) **Provision** of **summary-level data**, captured from the organisation's main systems (which might involve integrating the executive's desk top micro with the organisation's mainframe)

(ii) A facility which allows the executive to **drill-down** from higher levels of information to lower)

(iii) **Data manipulation facilities** (for example, comparison with budget or prior year data, trend analysis)

(iv) **Graphics**, for user-friendly presentation of data

(v) A **template system**. This will mean that the same type of data (eg sales figures) is presented in the same format, irrespective of changes in the volume of information required.

At the heart of an executive information system is a **corporate model**, which holds key information about the organisation. A **database** is used to store the underlying data and the corporate model holds such information as organisational structure including performance indicators such as ratios, and reporting cycles as appropriate. This model provides the interface between the database and the executive, who as a result does not have to define how information should be displayed. The corporate model contains rules as to how the information should be presented and aggregated. The model can be amended if required.

(c) **Customer/client service**

Future developments in customer or client service are likely to take advantage of the link between telecommunications and computers (the so-called **information superhighway**) and set up direct interactive links between customers at home and service providers. **Multimedia** applications offer enormous opportunities in marketing applications where we want to show off our wares.

At present, however, the most important computer application in this area is one that has been mentioned already, the **database**.

The database concept is based on considering what data can be provided and then suiting that to the needs of particular applications, rather than beginning with the needs of particular applications.

Thus, for example, a bill for an overnight stay at one of our hotels provides not just a figure to post to the accounting system but a huge amount of useful information for marketing purposes: what services customers buy, with what frequency, where they live (how far they are willing to travel to make use of our facilities), what credit card they use, and so on.

If the bill is entered into (or is accessible by) a database this provides a comprehensive file of data for a number of different users. Each user will have access to the same data for their own processing applications, and at the same time if required. This removes the need for duplicating data on different files and it means, for example, that customer information will always be up-to-date and as full as possible.

Thus, because they allow previously disparate information to be linked up, databases allow customers' needs to be monitored far more closely than ever before and so served and satisfied far more precisely than ever before.

The information has always been there. Computers have made it available and useable.

27 Information sources

Plan for Managing Information within the company

These are my proposals for how information should be managed within the company. My report identifies five key areas.

1   **Classification of information resources**

    The company collects information from a number of sources. The main sources are

    ■   **Routinely collected internal sources**, eg analysis of sales invoices, customer comments and complaints

    ■   Marketing intelligence gathered through our **monitoring** of the **local press**, trade press and sales personnel's reports

    ■   **One-off market research exercises** undertaken by ourselves

    ■   Ongoing **customer satisfaction surveys** handled by an external research agency

2   **Key features of an effective information system**

    An effective information system must have the following characteristics.

    ■   **Speed**. We must be able to collect, analyse and disseminate information before it becomes out-of-date and irrelevant.

    ■   **Reliability**. We must be able to trust that the results are subject only to a reasonable amount of variation and sampling error.

    ■   **Cost effectiveness**. We must balance the need for reliable, up-to-date information with the need to keep our data collection costs down.

3   **Examples/sources used in the micro and macro environment**

    Micro environment

    ■   Internally collected sales data
    ■   Industry association routine monitoring studies
    ■   Consultants' reports on our industry sector
    ■   Competitors' briefings and annual reports

    Macro environment

    ■   HM Treasury statistics on retail price inflation, growth in GDP and government expenditure

    ■   Consultants' and industry association reports on the broader economic outlook for our industry

    ■   Solicitors' briefing notes on how new legislation may affect our industry

■ *Financial Times* for country and industry – specific reports

4 **Example of uses of this information**

Sales data

We routinely record information about our sales, but currently do not analyse it sufficiently. In future we should conduct **greater analysis** to **spot trends**, which we can then act upon. We should analyse trends in terms of:

■ Types of customer
■ Types of product
■ Geographical location of customer
■ Time of year

GDP data

We should establish more clearly a link between **changes in GDP** and **changes in our volume of sales**. We can try to establish this link by analysing historical data. In future, we can study government forecasts of GDP and adapt our output accordingly.

5 **Ethical issues**

We must **maintain integrity** in our **use of data** and ensure that it is not used for purposes other than those which the information provider intended. We must abide by the Data Protection Act 1998. In cases where ethical issues do arise, we should establish a small committee (including possibly an impartial external member) to adjudicate on such issues.

28 Opportunities and abilities

(a) **Marketing opportunities**

A marketing opportunity exists whenever there is a **gap between demand and supply**. When there is an unfulfilled demand, an opportunity exists for an enterprising marketer to fulfil this by supplying suitable goods and services at the right time, at the right place and at the right price. For example, in the UK a demand may exist for beer outside normal pub opening hours, especially during hot weather. A pub which opens earlier can make a profit by fulfilling this demand, ie exploiting this marketing opportunity.

The tightening of the drink/drive laws in Europe led to an increase in demand for low alcohol beers and lagers which provided a marketing opportunity for those brewers who were able to identify and close this gap between demand and supply.

In hot weather demand increases and thereby provides a marketing opportunity for increased sales of cold drinks and ice-cream.

Marketers need to recognise that demand changes over time, due to changes in the so-called **environmental factors** (Political, Economic, Sociological, Technological) and competition. Increased concern over health in the western world has provided marketing opportunities for all sorts of diets, sporting equipment and health clubs, as well as for books on how to keep healthy and a great variety of lotions and potions.

Equally, demand for existing goods and services will normally diminish over time due to technological advances and/or changes in fashion. To stay in business therefore, a company needs to modify its goods and services or provide new goods and services in order to meet changing customer wants and needs.

Alternatively a company may identify new markets for existing goods and services, for example a demand for British bread in Paris and a demand for British stores such as Marks and Spencer and Sainsbury in France.

Awareness of opportunities

Companies need to be continuously on the **lookout for marketing opportunities** if they wish to grow. Marketing growth opportunities have been classified by Ansoff as falling under four general categories:

(i)   Market penetration: Existing products for existing markets (more of the same)

(ii) Market development: Existing products for new markets

(iii) Product development: New products for existing markets

(iv) Diversification: New products for new markets

Would-be marketers and firms wishing to stay in business must be capable of both **recognising and exploiting marketing opportunities**, ideally **before competitors** do so. They must also be capable of **analysing these opportunities** so as to quantify demand and to determine an appropriate marketing mix. These requisites imply an adequate and continuous supply of marketing information ideally formalised in a MkIS (Marketing Information System).

In summary, a marketing opportunity exists whenever circumstances allow an organisation to take advantage of demand from a particular group of people or indeed from other organisations.

(b)   Having identified a marketing opportunity an organisation has to decide whether it is capable of **exploiting** it. In making this decision the organisation has to assess its resources both currently and in the future. Clearly an organisation is constrained by its resources and will normally have set overall objectives in light of these. An organisation's internal capabilities can conveniently be categorised using the normal business functions framework, as follows.

(i)   **Financial capabilities**

Clearly there are limits to what an organisation can afford. An organisation's financial capability might be defined as its cash reserves, working capital and its capability to borrow money to invest.

(ii) **Production capabilities**

An organisation is constrained in the types of goods or services it can supply by the limitations of its plant, machinery and the skills of its operatives.

(iii) **Marketing capabilities**

A company's marketing capability is limited by its **marketing mix**, namely its **products, prices, promotion and place** (distribution outlets). Within the promotion element, an organisation may only have a certain number of salespeople, with limited product knowledge, limited selling skills and limited contacts. Marketing managers' expertise may not be particularly broad. For these sorts of reasons an organisation operating in industrial markets, if faced with an opportunity to move into consumer markets, may decide that it does not possess the right marketing capabilities to achieve this.

(iv) **Personnel capabilities**

An organisation employs a limited number of staff, each of whom has limited expertise and skills. It may not be able to expand its staff quickly enough (or be able to train existing staff into acquiring new skills) to take advantage of a short-term marketing opportunity such as a sudden rise in demand for heating equipment during a particularly cold spell in the weather.

The above examples show that it is extremely important that a company **analyses its internal capabilities**. Failure to recognise the constraints imposed by limitations in these capabilities could lead to the grasping of a wrong marketing opportunity with catastrophic results.

29 Forecasters

> **Tutorial note**. A series of four slides can be used, covering S, W, O and T respectively.
>
> **Examiner's comments**. A wide quality range arose in answer to this question. Those receiving excellent marks provided slide format as requested and supplied a series of focused summary bullet points.

SWOT analysis of the national economy

Strengths (internal features)	Weaknesses (internal features)
Stable political system	Declining industrial base
Sophisticated economic and financial system	Underinvestment in education and training
Good communications network	Underinvestment in technology and infrastructure
Increasingly flexible labour market	Relative underinvestment in research and development
Relatively stable multi-cultural society	Skills shortages in some sectors
Stable legal system	Burden imposed on public finances of growing dependant population
Membership of supranational and inter-national politico-economic organisations (eg WTO, EU)	Productivity levels in some industries
Highly developed marketing infrastructure	Tendency for price inflation

Opportunities (external features)	Threats (external features)
Development of markets with enlargement of European Union	Overdependence on imported manufactures
Growth potential in Eastern Europe	Threat from low-wage producers (especially Far East manufacturers)
Attraction of further inward investment to UK	Exchange rate instability
Increased opportunities in global infor-mation technology and communications	Political and economic uncertainty over question of single European currency
Increased tourism opportunities	Costs of implementing internationally agreed environmental standards
Market development in Southern Africa	Danger of increased protectionism in retaliation to common external tariff

30 Major bank

> **Tutorial note**. Our suggested answer to this question is structured around the idea of slides showing ideas/principles which would be shown to staff, and presenter's notes linked to each slide.
>
> **Examiner's comments**. This question was well answered on the whole. Poorer answers failed to give any sort of context.

(a) Slide 1 | *The Marketing Information System (MkIS)*

Note. This presentation will explain what is meant by an MkIS and how it is made up.

Slide 2 | *Definition*

An **MkIS** is used to collect, analyse, disseminate and store data relevant to the needs of the organisation. It is part of the Management Information System (MIS) of the organisation.

Slide 3 | *MkIS Kotler model*

The marketing information system

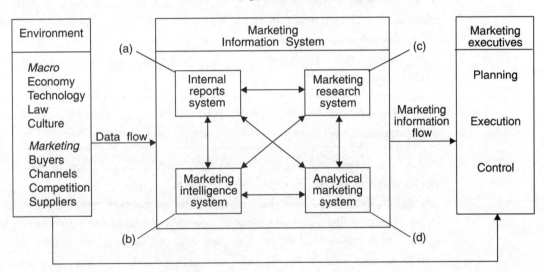

Notes. The system is based on a flow of information. Data comes in from the external environment (macro and micro) and information feeds out to management to assist planning, implementation and control. This constant flow of information is vital to support marketing decisions taken on a continuous basis. For example, an upturn in economic activity may boost consumer confidence leading to an increase in the demand for mortgages. The four constituent parts of the MkIS will be considered in more detail.

Slide 4 | *Internal reports system*

Notes. The **internal reports system** provides the following.

(i)   Results data
(ii) Measures of performance
(iii) Sales, cost and stock information

Slide 5 | Marketing intelligence system

Notes. A marketing intelligence system allows the systematic collection of **qualitative and quantitative research**.

(i) It provides up-to-the-minute event data
(ii) It provides information on developments in the environment
(iii) It scans and disseminates a wide range of intelligence

Slide 6 | Marketing research system

Notes. Such a system studies **marketing problems, opportunities and effectiveness**

Slide 7 | Analytical marketing system

Notes. There are various types of **analytical marketing systems**, all of which use models to explain, predict and improve the marketing process.

Slide 8 | Management information

Notes. The flow of information from the MkIS will assist managers with **planning and control**. It will help them to make the right decisions given the prevailing influences within the wider environment. The bank will therefore be better able to provide the financial services the public want, in a form that they need. This of course leads to higher levels of customer service.

(b) Slide 9 | An effective internal report system is vital in providing customer service

Notes. The system will provide results data and show accurate measures of **current performance levels** (number of complaints, frequency of complaints, categories of complaint). These can then be compared to target and any corrective action taken. Information on sales levels will allow comparisons to be made against competitors. Is our market share falling? Information on the stock of leaflets and brochures should avoid stock-outs. Standard customer data should be held, including contact details, bank services used etc to build a comprehensive customer record database. To allow any necessary corrective action to be taken speedily, all reports need to be produced on time and made available to the staff/managers who need them.

Slide 10 | An effective market intelligence system is vital in providing customer service

Notes. The system will provide **information on competitor activity**. This will enable the bank to keep up with its competitors and will ensure that it counters any new financial initiatives they may take. The performance of the bank should be benchmarked against that of its competitors. The system will gather intelligence on new developments and changes within the financial markets generally. This will include intelligence data on customer service trends, not only in banking but also in related sectors, such as insurance. It will scan and disseminate information from the wider environment which might impact on the business and will facilitate intelligence feedback from internal sales staff about customer service problems, types of enquiry etc.

Slide 11	An effective marketing research system is vital in providing customer service

Notes. Marketing research takes three basic forms:

(i) **Internal**

    (1) Company records (including centralised data)

    (2) Employee knowledge

(ii) **External (published)**

    (1) Government statistics

    (2) Financial sector magazines, journals and newspapers

    (3) Published reports, conference and seminar papers

    (4) Books covering financial services

(iii) **Primary research**

    (1) Own survey

    (2) Commissioned via MR agency

Information from any of these sources can be used to improve the quality and quantity of marketing of offerings and can lead to an improvement in customer service levels. Surveys can be used to gauge existing customer satisfaction levels and whether levels are improving. Recurrent problems can be identified and it is possible to establish whether complaints tend to come from the same people or from a cross-section of the public. Questionnaires could be used to establish which financial services people actually need and to provide information on how offerings are perceived. Focus groups can provide information on the public's perception of the bank.

A good marketing system uses **models** to explain, predict and improve processes. They can be extremely useful in markets such as financial services where there are a large number of inter-dependent variables. Their role in anticipating and predicting outcomes can have a positive bearing on future levels of customer satisfaction.

Slide 13	Organisational implications

Notes. For the MKIS to be effective, some **organisational changes** may be required.

(i) Additional training

(ii) Recruitment of staff with specialist skills

(iii) More streamlined structures

If handled properly, the resulting increase in efficiency should result in improved customer service.

Slide 14 | Summary |

Notes. A good MkIS will allow target levels of customer service to be achieved by providing timely, relevant and accurate data to assist the bank in anticipating and satisfying customer needs.

Specimen paper

The Chartered
Institute of Marketing

Certificate in Marketing

Marketing Environment

5.23: **Marketing Environment**

Time:

Date:

3 Hours Duration

This examination is in two sections.

PART A – Is compulsory and worth 40% of total marks.

PART B – Has **SIX** questions; select **THREE**. Each answer will be worth 20% of the total marks.

DO NOT repeat the question in your answer, but show clearly the number of the question attempted on the appropriate pages of the answer book.

Rough workings should be included in the answer book and ruled through after use.

© The Chartered Institute of Marketing

BPP
PROFESSIONAL EDUCATION

Certificate
in Marketing

5.23:   Marketing Environment – Specimen Paper

PART A

An Overview of the Marketing Environment

Marketing has become a fundamental business philosophy applied within increasingly competitive markets. In fact it is being adopted by large sections of the **private**, **public** and **voluntary sectors** alike. In each, it is the needs of the customer that provides the springboard for marketing activity. Marketers in all types of organisation must identify or anticipate these needs and then develop products or services that will satisfy them through an exchange process.

The organisation itself may constrain the extent to which it can effectively satisfy the identified needs. Most private businesses, for example, are limited by the need to earn a satisfactory level of profit for their **shareholders** and if prospective sales or returns from an activity fall short of this requirement they are unlikely to be continued. However, it may also be argued that the more effectively a business satisfies customer needs, the more likely it will achieve a **competitive edge** over rivals and realise its financial objectives.

Public sector organisations pursue social objectives, but are also likely to be resource constrained and will need to account the interests of various interested groups in achieving value for money.

Marketing management is in essence concerned with mobilising the resources of the organisation so that they successfully meet the changing needs of the internal and external stakeholders on whom they depend. It is not just the customer who is the focus of attention but often a range of interested groups who all may make a critical contribution to the organisation.

The sum total of these changing needs, pressures, constraints, threats and opportunities are commonly referred to as the organisation's marketing environment. Much of this environment is beyond the direct control of the marketer but marketing activities may influence significant elements in the micro environment.

A key to a true marketing orientation is the ability to adapt to changes in the organisation's marketing environment. Where opportunities or threats cannot be easily influenced, they can be monitored, forecast and assessed for their implications. Such knowledge can provide a powerful edge for the more proactive organisation.

Adapted from The Business and Marketing Environment by Palmer and Hartley. McGraw-Hill, 3rd Edition

PART A

Question 1.

a. Define **two** of the following terms highlighted in the article and provide a **bullet point summary** of their significance for the marketer:

    i)   Voluntary sector.

    ii)   Competitive edge.

    iii)   Shareholders.

(10 marks)

b. Given the suggestion in the article that the private business is limited by the need to earn a satisfactory profit, brief your Marketing Manager on the nature and significance of objectives pursued in the private sector as compared with those pursued in the public sector.

(12 marks)

c. The case states that much of the marketing environment is beyond the direct control of the marketer. Provide a summary of the merits and the means of understanding the changes taking place in this environment.

(10 marks)

d. Identify **four** critical stakeholder groups of The Chartered Institute of Marketing and state one critical contribution made by each to its effectiveness.

(8 marks)
(40 marks in total)

PART B – Answer THREE Questions Only

Question 2.

a. Why is it important for a firm to monitor its industry environment?

(8 marks)

b. Identify the means or sources available to monitor its industry and competitors.

(8 marks)

c. List **four** good reasons for not colluding with competitors.

(4 marks)
(20 marks in total)

Question 3.

Write a memorandum to your immediate manager outlining **three** social or lifestyle trends that have led, over the last two decades, to significant changes in your society. Include an appendix outlining the marketing implications of these changes for either a public or private sector organisation of your own choice.

(20 marks)

Question 4.

a. List **four** government economic objectives and their equivalent economic indicators.

(4 marks)

b. State the current numerical value of the indicators you have identified in a country of your choice.

(4 marks)

c. Select **one** government economic objective and discuss what policies would be used to help achieve it and any marketing implications that might arise from its implementation.

(12 marks)
(20 marks in total)

Question 5.

The Marketing Director is concerned at the apparent unreliability of quantitative forecasts concerning the likely state of the economy in the first decade of the new century.

Your Manager has delegated you the task of preparing a report to explain and evaluate the following alternative techniques:

a.   Environmental audit.

b.   Delphi technique.

c.   Scenarios.

(20 marks)

Question 6.

The travel and tourism industry appears to be entering into a new age of technological change and competitive uncertainty.

a.   Outline threats and pressures currently facing the industry within its marketing environment.

(12 marks)

b.   Provide a summary of the potential marketing opportunities for the industry arising out of information communication technologies, such as, digital television and the Internet.

(8 marks)
(20 marks in total)

Question 7.

Prepare a series of slides highlighting, with appropriate examples, the significance to marketers of **three** of the following aspects of environmental information systems:

i)   Information.

ii)   Marketing research.

iii)   Secondary data.

iv)   Marketing information system.

(20 marks)

Answers to Specimen paper

1 (a) (i) **Voluntary sector**

The voluntary sector comprises organisations that do not operate for profit, but to satisfy a social objective of some sort. They often provide goods and services to users without charge, and often rely on volunteers to provide labour inputs. However, voluntary sector organisations often charge for services and pay staff.

Significance for the marketer

- Voluntary sector organisations can have high levels of loyalty from the public

- Users/consumers may favourably evaluate the services of a voluntary sector organisation

- Nevertheless, voluntary sector organisations are increasingly having to compete with other types of organisations for funding

(ii) **Competitive edge**

An organisation is said to have a competitive edge where it has a distinct advantage (in the eyes of customers) compared to other organisations providing similar goods and services.

Significance for the marketer

- Must identify the nature of a competitive edge and exploit it

- A competitive edge can be eroded very quickly by competitors – marketers must continuously explore new ways of maintaining a competitive edge

- Must understand emerging competencies of competitors

- A competitive edge must be relevant to the needs of customers

(iii) **Shareholders**

Shareholders own a share of the equity capital of a company. This entitles them to a share of the profits of the company and a share of the voting to decide policy of the company, (although the Articles of Association may limit voting rights). Shareholders also share the risk of a company, although this risk is often limited to the value of their paid-up shares.

Significance for the marketer

- Marketing plans need the broad approval of shareholders if they are going to be capable of implementation

- Communication activity is often aimed at sharesholders

- Shareholders are often targeted as customers for the company's products

(b) These are the main areas in which objectives pursued by the private sector are likely to be different compared with those pursued by the public sector.

- *More diverse objectives*

  Private sector organisations are essentially driven by profit and sales objectives. Public sector organisations must additionally set social objectives and performance objectives (eg a hospital is likely to specify the number of each type of operation to be carried out).

■ *Qualitative v quantitative objectives*

Public sector organisations are more likely than private sector organisations to set qualitative service objectives, although this distinction is often blurred between the two sectors.

■ *Transparency of objectives*

Private sector organisations often like to keep many of their objectives secret, in order to confuse competitors. Public sector organisations are accountable to a much wider range of stakeholders and therefore objectives need to be more transparent for all to see.

■ *Time period of objectives*

A range of objectives are set by organisations, from short to long-term. It is often said that public sector objectives are influenced by the political election cycle.

(c)   The main merit of understanding the marketing environment which is beyond the direct control of the marketer lies in the ability it gives the marketer to anticipate change. With such an understanding of the environment and how it is continually existing, an organisation can be prepared to adapt to environmental change rapidly.

These are some of the means by which an organisation can understand the changes taking place in its environment:

■ Gathering, analysing and disseminating environmental intelligence in order to create a 'learning organisation'. Intelligence can be gathered through such sources as trade journals, conferences, sales personnel feedback etc. This approach is only as good as the vigour with which information is analysed and disseminated.

■ Retain specialist consultants who are specialist in a particular aspect of the environment eg technology, social trends. The company must be able to incorporate such advice within an organisational knowledge base.

■ A marketing information system can provide early warning signals of change in the environment, for example through long-term changes in the sales level of particular products. Collecting information in this way (as in the previous two ways) can be expensive and a balance has to be struck between the value of the information and the cost of obtaining it.

(d)   **Four stakeholder groups of the CIM**

1.   *Members*

The CIM exists to serve members. The continuing financial and moral support of members is critical to the organisation's continuing success and relevance.

2.   *Customers*

CIM provides services (eg training courses) to non-members. The revenue generated by these activities can be critical to avoid deficits on overhead costs occurring.

3.   *Education establishments*

Many colleges provide tuition to satisfy the examination and the Professional Development requirements of CIM. Without the support of these establishments the educational mission of CIM will be greatly weakened.

4.   *Suppliers*

Like most organisations, CIM buys in supplies from a number of sources. Withdrawal of services of key speakers at conferences organised by CIM may be seen as critical.

2

(a) **Reasons why it is important for a firm to monitor its environment**

A number of areas of concern can be identified:

■   Need to monitor trends in customer preferences. By spotting emerging trends, the firm can switch its resources to products with a growing demand, and away from those which are going out of fashion.

■   Need to monitor competitors. New sources of competition can emerge to threaten the firm, both from within the industry sector and from beyond.

■   Need to monitor supplier activities. New competitive sources of supply may emerge (eg from lower cost Far Eastern products). Suppliers may develop new technologies which the firm can incorporate into its own production methods.

■   Need to monitor government attitudes to the sector. Policy statements may lead to new legislation which affects the industry. The firm can seek to amend new legislation where this is harmful to the industry. Where legislation is actually passed, the firm can prepare for its implementation ahead of its competitors.

(b) **Means and sources of information**

Sales personnel. These are close to industry trends and the firm should arrange and collect, analyse and disseminate intelligence gathered by sales personnel.

Industry Associations. Most industry sectors have a trade association which disseminates intelligence through newsletters and seminars.

Retained consultants. The firm may pay a consultant to keep a watching brief over developments in the industry sector. A consultant may be able to do this more effectively and efficiently than relying solely on the firm's own personnel.

Media cuttings. The media (newspaper, TV, radio, Internet) can be regularly trawled for emerging trends. A firm may engage a specialist agency to do this.

Analysis of the firm's own data. Routine analysis of sales figures, disaggregated by product type and market segment may give a clue about emerging trends within the industry.

(c) **Reasons for not colluding with competitors**

■   The firm may face a fine from a regulatory agency if it is found to be in breach of legislation prohibiting anti-competitive behaviour.

■   An investigation may itself waste valuable management time, so it is advisable to avoid suspicion of collusion.

■   Collusion with other companies implies restricting some aspect of a company's marketing plan. It may in the long term be more profitable for the company to pursue its marketing plan single-mindedly.

■   Collusion can be unstable where one of the colludes gains a cost advantage over the others.

3 Three social changes/lifestyle which have had effects on society

1.   A growing number of individuals are becoming money-rich, but time-poor. This has affected society's attitudes in a number of ways, for example with respect to childcare, the value of family life and the desire for immediate gratification.

2.   As individuals become financially more secure, their motivation to buy products typically changes from a need for necessities to a desire for the unusual and challenging. Society now places greater merit on goods and services which are purchased for their aesthetic, rather than purely utilitarian value.

3.   There has been increasing concern by many groups within society on the benefits from healthy living. Society no longer regards as abnormal those individuals who prefer not to smoke/drink alcohol/regularly exercise.

Marketing implications for a grocery retailer

Businesses have responded to the changes identified above in a number of ways.

1.   The growing number of money-rich, time-poor households presents new opportunities for businesses to provide convenient solutions to this group at a premium price. Many of the major UK retailers have identified this opportunity and developed home delivery services. Somerfield stores was an early retailer to develop a home delivery service which delivers customers' shopping to their home or place of work. Subsequently, many retailers have further developed this service proposition, most notably by allowing shoppers to do their shopping using the Internet from the convenience of their home or office.

     Additionally, grocery retailers have responded by developing new products which are attractive to busy people, such as gourmet ready-prepared meals.

2.   The move from satisfying basic needs to more esoteric higher level needs has implications for the product ranges offered by grocery retailers. Many have responded by offering more exotic ranges of fruit and vegetables. In addition, many retailers have offered menu advice and themed food areas to make it easier for customers to put together the ingredients for authentic foreign cuisine.

3.   Consumers' increasing interest in healthy lifestyles has been reflected in a range of products which offer health benefits. Many grocery retailers have developed their own label ranges of 'low-fat' products. Further developments have occurred with low cholesterol and low salt products. Many retailers stock low alcohol wines as an alternative to traditional wines.

     Many grocery retailers have sought to capitalise on growing interest in healthy living by linking themselves with health promotion organisations, an this has resulted in in-store promotions and jointly produced information pamphlets.

4 (a) Four government objectives/economic objectives.

1.   Maintain a stable level of prices with the economy. The economic indicator for this is the level of inflation, in the UK most commonly measured using the Retail Prices Index (RPI).

2.   Maintain a stable exchange rate. The indicator for this is the value of the nation's currency in terms of other foreign currencies.

3. Maintain economic growth. This is indicated by the rate at which Gross Domestic Product (GDP) is expanding or contracting.

4. Maintain a low level of unemployment. This is typically indicated by the number of people currently out of work and/or claiming unemployment, expressed as a percentage of the total working population.

(b) **Numerical value of indicators for the UK, first half of 2003**

1. **Stable prices**. The annual level of inflation, measured by the Retail Prices Index (RPI) during the year to June 2003 was 2.9%.

2. **Exchange rates**. During the first half of 2003, the value of sterling was in the range 1.6-1.7 US dollars and about 1.38-1.55 Euros.

3. **Economic growth**. Forecast economic growth for 2003 was 2.0% to 2.5%.

4. **Employment**. During this period, the total number of people unemployed, based on the ILO definition from the Labour Force Survey, was 1,474,000 in May/June 2003, representing 5.0% of the workforce.

(c) **Government policies to maintain a stable exchange rate**

The following steps are typically taken by governments to maintain stability in a nation's currency.

■ Adjust interest rates – a higher interest rate will attract 'hot' money and thereby increase the value of the currency. Lowering interest rates will have the opposite effect. Implications for marketing: The use of interest rates is quite a blunt tool. Higher rates may have the effect of reducing consumers' discretionary expenditure, and hence their ability to purchase a company's products. Higher interest rates may also affect a company's costs where it has borrowed heavily.

■ Reduce government expenditure and hence the need for government to borrow money. Implications for marketing: This will have a general deflationary effect and may lower the general level of consumer demand in the economy. Also, many companies supplying to government (eg road builders) may be directly affected by cutbacks in government expenditure.

■ Reduce inflationary pressures within the economy, for example by increasing personal taxation where excessive spending by consumers is causing inflationary pressures. Implications for marketing: As noted above, this might reduce consumers' expenditure.

■ Encourage exports and inward investment, while trying to provide substitutes for imports. Implications for marketing: Firms may capitalise on export assistance schemes.

■ Sometimes, governments have taken direct action to control prices, and hence maintain a stable currency. These actions include limits on wage rises and the need to seek prior approval for price rises. Implications for marketing: These actions can have serious implications for marketers, and may make it difficult to adjust prices in accordance with market demands.

5 Evaluation of alternative forecasting techniques

(a) *Environmental audit*

This is a comprehensive, systematic, independent and periodic examination of a company's marketing environment, objectives, strategies and activities. It is undertaken with a view to determining problem areas and opportunities and recommending a plan of action to improve the company's marketing performance.

The environmental audit is not itself a framework for decisions. It is essentially a set of procedures by which an organisation explicitly asks questions, about the internal and external environments in which marketing operates, as well as the performance of the marketing functions themselves (such as the firm's distribution and proving effectiveness). It is usually undertaken by an independent and objective external organisation or individual.

To be effective, an environmental audit requires the availability of good quality, timely information. A self-audit could be undertaken, but at the risk of a loss of objectivity. The process of undertaking an environmental audit can be costly and time consuming so a company must ensure that it makes effective use of this technique.

(b) *Delphi technique*

This technique involves a number of experts, usually from outside the organisation, who (preferably) do not know each other and who do not meet or confer while the process is in play. A number of pictures, or scenarios of the future are drawn up by the company. These are then posted out to the experts. Comments are returned and the scenario(s) modified according to the comments received. The process is run through a number of times and the scenario being amended on each occasion. Eventually a consensus of the most likely scenario is arrived at.

It is often considered that this technique is more accurate than relying on any one individual, because it involves the collected wisdom of a number of experts who have not been influenced by dominant personalities. Nevertheless, the effectiveness of the result is dependent on the quality of the individuals who participate. It can become a slow and cumbersome process.

(c) *Scenarios*

Scenario building is an attempt to paint a picture of the future. It may be possible to build a small number of alternative scenarios based on differing assumptions. This qualitative approach is a means of handling environmental issues that are hard to quantify because they are less structured, more uncertain and may involve very complex relationships.

Scenario building among senior management will help individuals to confirm or moderate their views. A new perspective may be taken on forthcoming events. A wider perspective may be taken by individuals who may become more sensitive to the environment and the impact it can have on business. A more cohesive view may be adopted by senior management which may help strategy formulation and planning.

The scenarios may be built up over a number of meetings which may be either totally unstructured or semi-structured, with each meeting focusing on different aspects of the environment. The approach may be used at different levels of management in a large organisation; a multinational company may build scenarios at the global, regional and country level.

Scenario building is a useful technique for visualising possible future marketing environment, and has been used by the UK Government's Foresight Programme, which attempts to bring together experts from industry, academia, and government in an attempt to identify and evaluate trends in technological developments. However, it must be remembered that scenario building in itself will not make decisions about which actions a company should take.

6 (a) Threats and pressures currently facing the travel and tourism industry

- Threats of terrorism. Following the events of September 2001, many potential customers have been deterred from travelling. While there was some recovery in demand following the events, many people remain concerned about the effects of further unexpected terrorist activities. Terrorism also has the effect of increasing travel companies' costs (eg through higher insurance premiums), thereby reducing their profitability.

- Declining natural resources. Travel and tourism continues to harm the natural environment, for example, through the use of fossil fuels and the over-development of tourism destinations. It is a challenge for the industry to try and deter governments from imposing more restrictions on the operation of travel related services.

- Alternatives to travel. It must be remembered that for most leisure travel and tourism services, consumers may often quite happily substitute a non-travel related service. Following the events of September 2001, many consumers deferred their holidays and instead spend money on new items for their home.

- Virtual tourism. Furthermore, information technology is allowing many aspects of tourism services to be experienced without leaving home. Video-conferencing has the potential to reduce the need for business meetings. Within the personal leisure sector, virtual tours of a destination may reduce the desire to actually visit the destination.

- New forms of competitors emerging. The Internet has enabled new forms of virtual competitors to appear. Many intermediaries have emerged to challenge traditional travel agencies.

(b) Potential marketing opportunities for the travel and tourism industry arising out of information technologies

These are the main ways in which information technology will offer opportunities for the industry.

- Information technology can allow new types of services to be offered to consumers – self-select package holidays, for example.

- New technology can allow existing services to be produced more cheaply, thereby widening their market through being able to charge lower prices. In this way, more efficient web-based booking systems have allowed new markets for air travel to develop.

- Technological developments have allowed new methods of distributing tourism services. New intermediaries such as Expedia.com have emerged and increasing levels of Internet access at home has led to many more consumers booking online.

■ New opportunities for companies to communicate with their target customers have emerged, with many travel companies using computer databases to target potential customers and to maintain a dialogue with established customers. This has been achieved through database-driven direct mail, telemarketing and increasingly, Internet-based marketing.

7 Significance to marketers of environmental information

(i) *Information*

Information is the link between an organisation and its operating environment. It comprises quantitative and qualitative data about phenomena which have an impact on the organisation. To be useful, information must be collected, analysed and disseminated with an appropriate level of speed and accuracy. What is appropriate depends upon the task in hand. Information requirements in a fast-moving market such as computer hardware are likely to be quite different to information required to assess demand for a new underground railway.

We need to distinguish between the terms 'knowledge' and 'information'. Even though in some senses they may be used interchangeably, many writers have suggested that the two concepts are quite distinct. In fact, knowledge is a much more all-encompassing term which incorporates the concept of beliefs that are based on information ... Information only becomes knowledge in the hands of someone who knows what to do with it.

(ii) *Marketing research*

Large organisations operating in complex environments need to adopt a structured approach to their information collection activities. Marketing research is one aspect of these collection activities. Data collected should be as up-to-date and relevant to a problem as time and cost constraints allow.

The stages of the marketing research process can be described in a simple, linear format. A model exists for this process, which begins with the definition of the research problem and ends with the presentation of the findings. This process follows the basic pattern of enquiry that is adopted for other forms of scientific or academic research.

The trigger for marketing research can usually be related to a gap in the market information which is currently available to a firm. For example, a company may have comprehensive information on the current market for its products, but lacks information on new market opportunities for which its product range could be adapted.

Very often, marketing research activity fails because the 'problem' to be researched has been inadequately thought through and expressed as a research brief. For example, a company may be facing declining sales of a product and commission research to investigate customers' liking of the product's features relative to competitors' products. However, the real problem may be to understand the macroeconomic environment which may explain why sales of that category of product are declining.

(iii) *Secondary data*

Data sources are traditionally divided into two categories according to the methods by which they were collected. Secondary research is often referred to as desk research. Its distinguishing feature is that it is second-hand to the user, as it was collected previously for some other purpose. Data could be second-hand because it has already been collected internally by the organisation, although for a different primary purpose. Alternatively, the information could be acquired second-hand from external sources.

Most organisations would approach a research exercise by examining the available sources of secondary data.

Internal information, on products, costs, sales etc may be accessed through an organisation's Marketing Information System. Where such a system does not exist formally, the information may still be available in relevant departmental records, though it would probably need to be re-worked into a format that market researchers can use.

Secondary research can be a useful starting point for a research exercise. If somebody else has collected data or published a report in a closely related area, it is often much cheaper to buy that report rather than starting to collect data afresh. Reports by organisations such as the Economist Intelligence Unit (ECU) may at first sight seem to be very expensive, but set against the cost of undertaking the research from scratch, their cost begins to look relatively good value. Secondary research can be carried out internally by a company's own employees, although some specialist knowledge is required in knowing which sources of information are likely to be useful. Undertaking unnecessary primary research when similar information is available through secondary sources is an expensive and time-consuming exercise.

(iv)   *Marketing information system*

Many analyses of organisations' information collection and dissemination activities take a systems perspective. The collection of marketing information can be seen as one sub-system of a much larger management information system.

A marketing information system has been defined by Kotler as a system that '.... Consists of people, equipment and procedures to gather, sort, analyse, evaluate and distribute needed, timely and accurate information to marketing decision-makers'.

A marketing information system can conceptually be seen as comprising four principal components, although in practice, they are operationally inter-related.

- Internal data, particularly important in respect of operational and control functions.

- Marketing research is that part of the system concerned with the structured collection of marketing information.

- Marketing intelligence comprises the procedures and sources used by marketing management to obtain pertinent information about developments in their marketing environment.

- Marketing decision support systems comprise a set of models that allow forecasts to be made.

List of key concepts and Index

See overleaf for information on other
BPP products and how to order

CIM Order

To BPP Professional Education, Aldine Place, London W12 8AA

Tel: 020 8740 2211. Fax: 020 8740 1184
email: publishing@bpp.com
online: www.bpp.com

Mr/Mrs/Ms (Full name) _____

Daytime delivery address _____

Postcode _____

Daytime Tel _____

Date of exam (month/year) _____

	2004 Texts	2004 Kits	Passcards
PROFESSIONAL CERTIFICATE IN MARKETING			
1 Marketing Fundamentals	£19.95 ☐	£9.95 ☐	£6.95 ☐
2 Marketing Environment	£19.95 ☐	£9.95 ☐	£6.95 ☐
3 Customer Communications	£19.95 ☐	£9.95 ☐	£6.95 ☐
4 Marketing in Practice	£19.95 ☐	£9.95 ☐	£6.95 ☐
PROFESSIONAL DIPLOMA IN MARKETING			
5 Marketing Research and Information	£19.95 ☐	£9.95 ☐	£6.95 ☐
6 Marketing Planning	£19.95 ☐	£9.95 ☐	£6.95 ☐
7 Marketing Communications	£19.95 ☐	£9.95 ☐	£6.95 ☐
8 Marketing Management in Practice	£19.95 ☐	£9.95 ☐	£6.95 ☐
PROFESSIONAL POST-GRADUATE DIPLOMA IN MARKETING			
9 Analysis and Evaluation	£20.95 ☐	£9.95 ☐	£6.95 ☐
10 Strategic Marketing Decisions	£20.95 ☐	£9.95 ☐	£6.95 ☐
11 Managing Marketing Performance:	£20.95 ☐	£9.95 ☐	£6.95 ☐
12 Strategic Marketing in Practice	£26.95 ☐	N/A	N/A
	SUBTOTAL		£ ☐

POSTAGE & PACKING

Study Texts and Kits

	First	Each extra	Online
UK	£5.00	£2.00	£2.00 £ ☐
Europe**	£6.00	£4.00	£4.00 £ ☐
Rest of world	£20.00	£10.00	£10.00 £ ☐

Passcards

	First	Each extra	Online
UK	£2.00	£1.00	£1.00 £ ☐
Europe**	£3.00	£2.00	£2.00 £ ☐
Rest of world	£8.00	£8.00	£8.00 £ ☐

Reduced postage rates apply if you **order online** at www.bpp.com

Grand Total (Cheques to *BPP Professional Education*) I enclose
a cheque for (incl. Postage) £ ☐

Or charge to Access/Visa/Switch

Card Number ☐☐☐☐☐☐☐☐☐☐☐☐☐☐☐☐

Expiry date _____ Start Date _____

Issue Number (Switch Only) _____

Signature _____

We aim to deliver to all UK addresses inside 5 working days. A signature will be required. Orders to all EU addresses should be delivered within 6 working days.

All other orders to overseas addresses should be delivered within 8 working days.

** Europe includes the Republic of Ireland and the Channel Islands.

REVIEW FORM & FREE PRIZE DRAW

All original review forms from the entire BPP range, completed with genuine comments, will be entered into one of two draws on 31 January 2005 and 30 July 2005. The names on the first four forms picked out on each occasion will be sent a cheque for £50.

Name: _____   Address: _____

_____

_____

How have you used this Text?
(Tick one box only)

☐ Self study (book only)

☐ On a course: college_____

☐ With BPP Home Study package

☐ Other _____

Why did you decide to purchase this Text?
(Tick one box only)

☐ Have used companion Kit

☐ Have used BPP Texts in the past

☐ Recommendation by friend/colleague

☐ Recommendation by a lecturer at college

☐ Saw advertising in journals

☐ Saw website

☐ Other _____

During the past six months do you recall seeing/receiving any of the following?
(Tick as many boxes as are relevant)

☐ Our advertisement in *Marketing Success*

☐ Our advertisement in *Marketing Business*

☐ Our brochure with a letter through the post

☐ Our brochure with *Marketing Business*

☐ Saw website

Which (if any) aspects of our advertising do you find useful?
(Tick as many boxes as are relevant)

☐ Prices and publication dates of new editions

☐ Information on product content

☐ Facility to order books off-the-page

☐ None of the above

Have you used the companion Practice & Revision Kit for this subject?   ☐ Yes   ☐ No

Your ratings, comments and suggestions would be appreciated on the following areas.

	Very useful	Useful	Not useful
Introductory section (How to use this text, study checklist, etc)	☐	☐	☐
Setting the Scene	☐	☐	☐
Syllabus coverage	☐	☐	☐
Action Programmes and Marketing at Work examples	☐	☐	☐
Chapter roundups	☐	☐	☐
Quick quizzes	☐	☐	☐
Illustrative questions	☐	☐	☐
Content of suggested answers	☐	☐	☐
Index	☐	☐	☐
Structure and presentation			

	Excellent	Good	Adequate	Poor
Overall opinion of this Text	☐	☐	☐	☐

Do you intend to continue using BPP Study Texts/Kits/Passcards?   ☐ Yes   ☐ No

Please note any further comments and suggestions/errors on the reverse of this page.

Please return to: Glenn Haldane, BPP Professional Education, FREEPOST, London, W12 8BR

REVIEW FORM & FREE PRIZE DRAW (continued)

Please note any further comments and suggestions/errors below.

FREE PRIZE DRAW RULES

1 Closing date for 31 January 2005 draw is 31 December 2004. Closing date for 31 July 2005 draw is 30 June 2005.

2 Restricted to entries with UK and Eire addresses only. BPP employees, their families and business associates are excluded.

3 No purchase necessary. Entry forms are available upon request from BPP Professional Education. No more than one entry per title, per person. Draw restricted to persons aged 16 and over.

4 Winners will be notified by post and receive their cheques not later than 6 weeks after the relevant draw date. List of winners will be supplied on request.

5 The decision of the promoter in all matters is final and binding. No correspondence will be entered into.